Toronto
Architecture

A City Guide

Second Edition

D1234075

Patricia McHugh

Photographs by Susan McHugh/Maps by Tom Sam

M&S

McClelland & Stewart Inc.
The Canadian Publishers
481 University Avenue
Toronto, Ontario
M5G 2E9

Canadian Cataloguing in Publication Data

McHugh, Patricia
    Toronto architecture: a city guide

2nd ed.
Bibliography: p. 276
Includes index.
ISBN 0-7710-5520-X

1. Historic buildings – Ontario – Toronto -
Guide-books. 2. Architecture – Ontario – Toronto -
Guide-books. 3. Buildings – Ontario – Toronto -
Guide-books. I. McHugh, Susan. II. Title.

FC3097.7.M24 1989   971.3'541   C89-093223-9
F1059.5.T688A25   1989

Printed and bound in Canada

Inclusion of a building in the guide does not imply access.

Contents

Contents cont'd

Preface to the Guide

The oldest building in Toronto is a 1794 cabin built by John Scadding, aide to the city's founder, John Graves Simcoe. The newest is any one of dozens completed just yesterday. In the intervening span of some 200 years, only two substantial examinations of Toronto's architecture have been essayed: Eric Arthur's 1964 *Toronto, No Mean City*; and William Dendy's 1978 *Lost Toronto*. The latter concerns itself with buildings that have been lost to us. Arthur too considered many long-gone buildings and other examples have been demolished even since he wrote; he ended his survey with 1900.

Yet Toronto, as it stands, is possessed of a rich variety of architecture. There are buildings of all types, styles, materials, and quality here, from elegant Georgian manors to theatrical Post-Modern offices. And amazingly, they embroider our streets side by side, in an easy grace that suggests for Toronto a very special urban fabric. My book, then, is an initial attempt to detail this city's architectural look.

Organized in the form of walking tours, the book is intended primarily as a field guide. Buildings are described just as a resident or visitor might see them along the street, including not only the well-known and singular stars but also a sampling of more modest structures in between. I wanted to make possible a comprehensive picture of the cityscape by encouraging direct observation of the buildings that go to make it up. This goal dictated 20 in-depth, walkable tours focused on the whole of the downtown core, rather than a cross-metro skimming.

Each walk is autonomous, but tours within any one of the ten cohesive geographic areas into which I have divided the guide connect with one another and could be combined (average walk time is about 1½ hours). Short introductions to each of the ten areas provide historical, social, and architectural overviews that should help to inform the individual entries. Of these, there are 750: houses, churches, apartment buildings, offices, factories, warehouses, and commercial blocks.

The commentary under the entries treats of architectural history—of styles, building materials, methods of construction, and sites. Admonitions that architecture is about "space" notwithstanding, emphasis in the guide has necessarily been on outward features, as most of the listed buildings are private and not open to the public. I have also offered aesthetic judgements, based on what I consider to be a building's expression of principles of proportion and craftsmanship, as well as observations about a building's appropriateness and usefulness. Arguments about whether architecture is craft or fine art abound, but neither view can deny its utilitarian function. Evaluation of building aesthetics and function may then come together in a consideration of social concerns. Because social life inhabits and influences architecture just as architecture inspires and limits the life of the citizen, buildings truly do represent what life was, is, and even what it may become.

Although the book is first a field guide, designed to provide those who live, work, or visit in the city with some readily available information about the buildings they see, I hope it will also prove valuable to scholars. The data (primary sources and methodology are outlined under Sources of Information) have been three years in the gathering. The 750 buildings examined offer a clear picture of certain stylistic trends and periods. Far from being behind Britain and the United States, in some respects Toronto has been much further in the advance than was heretofore thought. On the other hand, the data reveal that some styles and methods lingered here for an inordinately long time. And two modes specific to Toronto have emerged—what I call Toronto Bay-n-Gable and The Annex House (outlined in the Description of Styles).

I have come to admire this city that allows me to live within walking distance not only of the city hall and university, but also of Bloor Street; and with a municipal park as my front garden! Once I came not only to pass but also to *see* them, I found in Toronto's buildings a fertile source of information and delight. It is the possibility of this pleasure which my book seeks foremost to convey.

Patricia McHugh
Toronto, 1985

Preface to the Second Edition

One thing that producing a guidebook teaches is never to expect to write *fini* on the look of a place. Healthy cities are always in the process of becoming, the vital signs of their appearance ever in flux. During the four years since the first edition of *Toronto Architecture: A City Guide*, this city has indeed changed, both for better and for worse.

Some buildings detailed in the first edition are now stamped "Demolished." Torontonians must mourn such losses as the richly sculptural Williams Building on Yonge Street and the historic O'Brien house on College Street.

Still, more buildings have been conserved than lost. Not a few previously described as "wonderful but mouldering" have been rehabilitated and can now simply be called wonderful. These include residences all across town as well as larger edifices—the Opera Centre on Front Street and Ontario Heritage House on Adelaide, for example.

Of course, not all renovations are well done or adequately conceived, and these lapses have been noted too. Inappropriate window glazing is a widespread disease, for example—one pane where there once were six, or six where style dictates one, a change that seems minor until one observes how it deforms the characteristic style of a building.

Falling between conservation and demolition, the odd spectre of one-wall preservation has arisen recently, whereby only the face of the old is saved for attachment to the body of the new. While many seem intrigued by this façadism—dramatic surgery in which one wall is cut out, splinted for a time, and then re-attached—my own view is that such tokenism does little to preserve any sense of the past or inspire faith in the future. It is virtual demolition. This second edition describes a number of instances of the phenomenon where none existed before.

By far the worst change to the look of the city in the last four years is the tremendous surge of building in the downtown core (12 million square feet of new office space—equivalent to eight Commerce Courts—approved 1986–88). Contrary to Toronto's 1976 Central Area Plan lauded in the first edition, downtown suffers now from gigantic scale, congested streets and sidewalks, and disappearance of open space, as well as loss of older, smaller buildings, all of which threaten Toronto's fundamental strengths as a varied and visually attractive city.

As for these big new buildings themselves, Toronto may soon have the best second-rate architecture in the world! Certainly the most exciting recent buildings are not these moribund towers, but relatively small structures such as the School of Hospitality on Adelaide Street East by Carruthers Shaw & Partners, and Metropolitan Place by Brisbin Brook Beynon. Distinguished in themselves, these buildings also respect their streetscapes and do much to enliven the city.

Sectors of Toronto that do seem to remain unchanged are the near-suburbs. When offered the opportunity to expand the guide, I thought at first to chronicle the harbour front, but since that area is so far from "done," I chose instead to add two walks in Toronto's most ballyhooed near-suburb—Rosedale. It may come as surprise to many, but Rosedale is virtually a development of the early 20th century, and therefore a good model for understanding many Toronto neighbourhoods, most of which were begun in that era.

Some changes in the book are the result of new research, notably my own into the 1910s, '20s, and '30s periods, and that of others into the buildings of the 1950s and 1960s. For further fresh data and insights, my thanks—again—to those agencies mentioned in Sources of Information, and especially to the many architects, descendants, and householders who have written me since publication of the first edition. The number of buildings introduced in this second edition is 150, bringing the total now to 900.

PMcH
1989

The Look of Toronto

There are a variety of forces that go to make the look of a city, but essentially they are these: the spirit of the age; the *raison d'être* of the place; the character of the populace; and the nature of available resources—that is, site, climate, materials, and technology. Although the thrust of these influences may change over time, new tendencies generally build on foundations already in place. Nowhere has this been more true than in Toronto.

The Georgian Town

Toronto was settled by the British in 1793. It was the end of the Georgian period, that elitist age of elegance, order, and refinement. The young military town—the site was chosen for its good harbour and remoteness from the American border—at first had resource and reason only for order. A geometric gridiron of ten square blocks was laid out by the military surveyors facing the bay at the eastern end of the harbour, centred on today's King and Sherbourne Streets. The gridiron had been employed at least as far back as Roman times in the design of "instant" towns, and it continued to make good sense for a society whose buildings were based on the right-angle cube. The first structures that lined those unpaved streets of "Muddy York" were unassuming detached wooden dwellings, responsive to little more than the fundamental task of architecture, that of shelter.

As governing capital of the new colonial province of Upper Canada, however, Toronto was to be more than a simple military outpost. The cadre of "gentlemen" civil servants brought in to run the province introduced Georgian elegance and refinement as soon as they could, and quickly commenced to put up a number of impressive churches and public structures intended to contain and articulate that which the community most valued, a symbolic representation that is the second important task of architecture. By 1834, the year Toronto was granted incorporated city status by the province, lordly classical pediments of a two-storey brick courthouse and similar-looking jail were self-confidently pronouncing order and civility for the little settlement of 9,000, while a Renaissance stone St. James' Church pontificated God's assuring presence.

The houses they built following the temporary settling-in period were derived from the Georgian homeland as well, although the colonial situation and harsher climate rendered Toronto's dwellings more simple and solid-seeming. Some of them, such as The Grange, were quite grand, however. This formal-looking brick manor was built in response to the provincial governor's "park lot" scheme. The governor had hoped to encourage establishment of a colonial aristocracy for his outpost of Empire, and to that end awarded 30 senior officials 100 acres each on which to create expansive estates ringing the little town. Set out in narrow 1/8-mile strips running north from Queen Street (originally called Lot Street) to Bloor Street (originally First Concession Line), the park lots further extended the town's grid pattern and today account for Toronto's many long north/south thoroughfares.

Fine residences also rose on Adelaide Street East and Front Street West (then the water's edge), although there was really no residential district *per se*. The town proper was small and compact, circumscribed by the area a person could comfortably walk. Houses stood singly or in rows with buildings for banks, hotels, and shops; indeed, the latter were often combined as houses. Because of their proximity and mixed-use character, these well-mannered colonial structures employed a similar architectural look and scale. Toronto's settlers had most assuredly brought English order, clarity, and reasonableness to the Canadian wild.

The Victorian City

Following the War of 1812 and mercantile fortunes made on profiteering, Toronto began to think that its true *raison d'être* was not solely fixed and dignified government, but also enterprising, crass commerce. Supporting this interest were the good harbour, and after 1850, St. Lawrence canals and railway lines. Between 1834 and 1854 Toronto's population almost quadrupled to over 30,000, and the city prospered as a major trade centre, second only to Montreal in British North America.

Toronto's self-made merchants and bankers perfectly represented the industrious and earnest spirit of the Victorian Age into which they were moving: hard-working, ambitious, outwardly complacent yet in restive search of symbols that would lend them legitimacy and authority. They built rich monuments to capitalism in an eclectic variety of styles, hoping to capture not beauty of form so much as efficacy of allusion: Gothic manor houses, Italianate villas, Romanesque abbeys, Queen Anne cottages. Many of these picturesque extravaganzas still stand, parading Victorian vigour on streets such as Jarvis, St. George, and Queen's Park. (The advent of horse-drawn omnibuses and, in 1861, the street railway made it possible for citizens to live in an area separate from their place of work, marking the beginning of residential and business segregation.)

A memory of the Victorian city also exists in the flamboyant warehouses and factories on Front Street East, one of which (no. 139–145) originally processed and shipped the thousands of pigs that gave the name "Hogtown" to Toronto in this era. Other manifestations are the stout high-steepled churches that punctuate so many downtown corners, endowed by the captains of commerce as yet another affirmation of their respectability, rootedness, and ties to the British homeland. "Hogtown" was also known as "Toronto the Good." These Victorian structures were almost invariably built of brick.

The first bylaw to its new charter passed by the incorporated City of Toronto in 1834 dealt with the prevention of fire, and bylaws regulating fire hazards—and therefore building materials—dominated the cautious lawmakers concerns for at least the next 75 years. (Toronto, nevertheless, has suffered two Great Fires, one in 1849 and another in 1904.) Brick was legislated for wide areas of the city, and Toronto's claypits were able to provide both red and yellow varieties. The latter variety was termed "white" in the 19th century, and originally was thought of as a substitute for stone, a material not readily available here (limestone came from Ohio; granite from Quebec). The extensive use of both red and yellow brick for a single building became a favourite design device, a device consistent with the city's seeming predilection for simple, flat surfaces to give the appearance of solidity.

It is interesting in this regard that row housing such as that inhabited by the wealthy in London, New York, and Montreal, was almost unknown here. Even the middle class eschewed the row housing that gave definition to 19th century streets in most cities of this size. Instead, Victorian Toronto built double houses—single buildings comprised of two "semi-detached" dwellings, one beside the other separated by a common party wall. Set about 20 feet back from the street with a patch of garden in front, these symmetrical double houses, their roof lines broken by picturesque barge-boarded gables, imparted a softened, almost suburban look to the city. Yet they were not anti-urban. Built so close together as to resemble a row, these two- and three-storey semi-detached dwellings encouraged a sense of community by providing a harmonious human scale for the street. At the same time, they offered an inviting, gentle passage between public and private space—from sidewalk through small garden to front door. Toronto's most palpable heritage from the Victorian city is surely this complex sense of accommodation—the reconciliation of individual and community, home and street, suburban and urban.

The Edwardian Metropolis

In the last decades of the 19th century, Toronto's sensibilities began to enlarge to encompass a new ideal of the city as not only the place from which government regulated and commerce provided, but also as the receptacle and nurturer of the highest forms of culture and society. In this view, Toronto seemed one with many cities in the United States in their effort to make in the New World centres of civilization that would be as expansive, as rich, as great, as those of the Old. It was a period of prosperity and optimism across North America, and confidence of vision gave rise to physical expansion of the rapidly industrializing cities through annexation of surrounding communities; exaltation of the centre through construction there of grand and imposing public buildings; and finally, noble plans to make of the whole a beautiful, healthful, inspiring place—a metropolis, or "mother city."

Toronto had already annexed the Village of Yorkville in 1883. In 1884 it added Brockton and Riverdale, and in 1889 Seaton Village and Parkdale. In 1900, with a population of almost 200,000, Toronto ranked as one of North America's major centres. By 1912 it had taken over nine more outlying municipalities and doubled its population. What made annexation feasible were new trolley networks crisscrossing the metropolis and transporting populace between jobs, homes, and downtown core.

At the downtown centre, Toronto set about architecturally highlighting its perceived role as a political, transportation, and cultural leader of Canada. A cavalcade of impressive civic monuments began to rise, touching public pride as no others had before and awakening Toronto's sense of progress, possibility, and world place. These included the Provincial Parliament Building (1892), the [Old] City Hall (1899), Royal Ontario Museum (1914), Art Gallery of Toronto [Ontario] (1918), and Union Station (1920).

Toronto's original metropolitan vision was very European in that it did not include skyscrapers. Toronto City Council debated a long time before assenting to Toronto's first in 1905, the 15-storey Traders Bank designed by New York architects Carrère & Hastings. There were arguments about sanitation, safety, and traffic, as well as aesthetics—many Torontonians thought the tall buildings "unsightly." Paris at the time had a limit of six storeys and London too spurned the new architectural giants. But in New York City by 1913 there were 175 structures of 15 storeys or more (the Woolworth Building had over 50), and Toronto ultimately embraced the New World and elected not to limit height. Having made the decision, the metropolis set about building The Tallest Building in the British Empire. That title graced four Toronto buildings, then a Montreal entry, before finally coming to a 33-year rest in 1929 upon Toronto's 34-storey Canadian Bank of Commerce.

Of all Toronto's idealistic City Beautiful schemes, which had parkways radiating in all directions from an ennobled city core, only the wide Beaux-Arts expanse of University Avenue was implemented before the Depression intervened. As a result there was no massive replacement of the Victorian city here as happened in some North American cities. Toronto's pre-eminent bequest from this era, however, is undoubtedly the understanding gained at that time of the role architecture and planning can play in the quality of daily life, and most particularly the influence of the citizenry in shaping that role. That Torontonians today, through independent citizens' groups as well as the municipal process, enjoy a good measure of control over what happens to their urban environment is a direct legacy of the metropolitan ideal.

The Modern Cosmopolis

In the United States, the pattern of urban development following World War II was determined by the automobile, expressway, and developer-suburb which offered every man the possibility of a home of his own through federally assisted loans and mortgages. Satellite shopping centres grew up to serve the new suburban communities, drawing off energy from the downtown, which, with an ever-poorer population, began to decay.

Toronto too built instant suburbs—Don Mills was an award-winning model of its kind. But older near-suburbs—the fragile North American middle city—remained healthy thanks to waves of immigrants who had begun to arrive here, bringing new life to the low-scale Victorian residential streets. If the one- or two-family house on its own lot has now emerged as the preferred North American form—domestic symbol of personal achievement and independence for immigrant and native alike—it was a precept that Toronto, with its urban/suburban double houses, knew all along.

The newcomers brought much more to Toronto than urban well-being, however. The tremendous growth in human resource, and its multi-cultural character, has made of Toronto, finally, a cosmopolis—a world city of close to 3 million people whose diversity and difference have come together to create a place of urbane vigour and grace. This manifests itself in the cosmopolis's variety of neighbourhoods, each with its own colours, signs, and adaptations of built form—Portuguese glazed-tile icons superintending Victorian brick houses on Bellevue Avenue for example. That its neighbourhoods do not dominate and conquer one another, and yet are not chaotic either, means that Toronto's distinct communities act to accommodate and enhance the whole; this is surely urbanity in the best sense.

Toronto's innermost core has remained vital as well. True, Toronto did succumb in the late 1950s and early '60s to the urban-renewal mania (Regent Park, St. James Town), before Reform politics and citizens groups spearheaded a move to more generous solutions in the form of rehabilitation and sympathetic infill.

A similar story unfolded in the downtown business district. Toronto was the largest, most powerful city in Canada by the 1960s, and money flowed into the cosmopolis, feeding the financial, commercial, and communications industries that thrived here as well as the mighty office towers to house them. Old buildings were levelled, the skyline rose dramatically, and Toronto was about to become indistinguishable from International Style high-rise cities around the world. The cautionary call that came from the newly elected Reform city council resulted in Toronto's 1976 Central Area Plan. The envy of many municipalities, this visionary program served to discourage mass redevelopment while encouraging generally smaller as well as mixed-use buildings with a high residential component; put a priority on continuity of streetscape and especially *streetline*; and, finally, fostered integration of the urban fabric through historic building preservation combined with complementary new building construction.

The issues raised by the 1976 Central Area Plan also served to alert Torontonians to the rich diversity of their particular urban landscape, a landscape that juxtaposes Georgian formality, Victorian vigour, Edwardian grandeur, and modern technology and pluralism.

Through all its eras Toronto has in one way or another demonstrated a concern for order, reason, accommodation, discipline, restraint. These concerns have at times led to its being called boring, bland, utterly dull, "flat city." Yet the physical attributes that give rise to those epithets—neatness, simplicity, repetition, low scale, for instance—are among the very characteristics that some urban theorists now believe make a city less confusing and threatening, more graspable and emotionally satisfying—in short, "a livable city." There are other criteria that go to make a city inviting. Toronto is far-sighted in its efforts to enhance the sensuous, adding warm brick pavement here, bold coloured banners there, street trees and open green spaces for surprise and solitude, as well as other small details that help orient what already abides here.

The look of Toronto, and how compelling that look is to be in the future, will rest most decisively, however, upon the ways in which Toronto's patterns of diversity are nourished in the years to come. The look of Toronto will be determined by how the European and American influences, the immigrant and native experiences, the old and new styles, the high and low buildings, the brick walls and green spaces are stimulated to interact, and in interacting, to provide for the citizenry a vibrant public environment. For a great city is one where differences not only *exist*, but where differences *create* lively encounter and open discourse. It is only through such discourse that Toronto can genuinely acquire a sense of itself as a good and fruitful place to be.

Description of Styles

O ne of the most efficient ways to describe a building is to attach a stylistic label to it—a word or two that may denote not only physical properties but also historical period, geographical source, building method, even cultural determinant. It is probably because stylistic labels in architecture do conjure up so much that they are far from precise and universal. Terms vary from epoch to epoch ("Gothic" was once "modern"), and from writer to writer (one scribe's "Second Empire" is another's "French Renaissance"). Styles with the same name vary from place to place as well. A Queen Anne house in Toronto is not identical to one in New York, nor does a New York example mimic its London counterpart.

One way to sort out changes in architecture is to think of the various styles in cycles that alternate between classical and picturesque. One or a series of symmetrical, orderly classical styles is countered by one or a series of asymmetric, dynamic picturesque styles, in turn succeeded by a reactive wave of classical styles, and so on. (An intermediate classical *and* picturesque style such as Italianate may intervene, and of course there is always overlap.) Following are the names of styles as used in this guide and a few notes on the what, where, and why of them. Definitions apply specifically to Toronto buildings, as do relevant dates. And remember, some buildings are so idiosyncratic and eclectic as to defy classification by style. They're often the most interesting of all.

Georgian: 1800–1875
The Georgian style derived from an Anglo-Dutch simplification of Italian Renaissance and Baroque architecture. Especially influential were the buildings and writings of 16th-century Northern Italian architect Andrea Palladio. It was named for the first four King Georges, whose reigns— 1714 to 1830—coincided with the style's major period of popularity in England. Toronto was settled by the British near the end of the Georgian period and this small-scale classicism was the young colony's first real architectural expression.

The Georgian style was used for both two-storey detached houses and two-, three-, and four-storey row houses and shops. It was also adapted for public buildings, churches, factories, and warehouses. Toronto's Georgian buildings followed British example but were simpler and plainer. They are characterized by a rectangular box-like shape with a symmetrical façade organized horizontally and centred on a formal entrance bay (except in side-hall plans). Cladding is wood, roughcast, or red or yellow brick (called white brick at the time). Roofs are either hipped or end gable, with plain or dentilled cornices, large tall chimneys, and often dormer windows. Doorcases may be elaborate with toplights and sidelights. Raised basements, columned porticoes, and centre pediments are typical Palladian-evolved features. Windows are generally straight-topped of sliding-sash type with from six to 12 panes of glass in each sash. Sills and lintels are of wood or stone, or there may be relieving arches of radial brick set flush with the wall. Decorative brick quoins may appear at corners of brick houses.

Toronto continued to build in Georgian style long after it had passed out of fashion in the homeland. In later versions, however, picturesque features were appended to the classical Georgian, notably cladding of yellow brick with red brick accents, or red with yellow; windows with a gently rounded curve at the top and fewer panes; and perhaps a decorative brick corbel table enriching the cornice.

Neo-Classicism or Classical Revival (Greek and Roman): 1825–1860

There are no buildings remaining in Toronto that can properly be called Roman Revival. As for Greek Revival, although it was considered symbolically apt for the new American nation where it dominated residential architecture in the 1830s and '40s, it gained little following among the citizenry of Toronto. Only a few Greek Revival houses are known. Its chaste, formal look did appeal, however, to Toronto's city fathers, who considered it appropriate—just as they had in Regency England—for important commercial and civic buildings. Greek Revival buildings are characterized by a symmetrical and boxy shape, sometimes with Greek columns and entablature; smooth stone or yellow-brick cladding (to approximate the colour of stone); and low-pitched or flat roofs. Windows and doors are straight-topped and lintelled. Greek-inspired decorative motifs include floral anthemia and the Greek fret.

Gothic Revival and High Victorian Gothic: 1845–1890

The Gothic Revival style first appeared in England in the late 1700s, part of the same nostalgic impulse that prompted the Middle Ages settings of Sir Walter Scott's chivalric novels. The style's appeal then blossomed with the Victorians, who saw it as a way to recapture both medieval romance and a sense of national and ecclesiological "appropriateness."

Still in thrall to British tradition and example, Toronto was quick to embrace the picturesque style. English prototypes were closely followed for Gothic Revival churches. In fact, actual prescriptions sent out by the Anglicans' Camden (later Ecclesiological) Society in Cambridge were used. Three forms were revived: squat, high-steepled **Early English**, with masonry cladding and pointed single-light windows; complicated **Decorated** or **Middle Pointed**, featuring windows of curvilinear tracery; and attenuated **Perpendicular**, marked by slender spires, elongated pinnacles, and crenellations.

For later High Victorian Gothic churches, Toronto architects used the general shapes and pointed arches of Gothic Revival but added a variety of cladding materials for a rich polychrome effect. These were also inspired by English models, which in turn had been influenced by John Ruskin's writings on the application of colour in architecture.

Sources for Gothic Revival residential architecture came more directly from the United States, where the style was promoted for single detached houses through builders' guides, notably those of Alexander Jackson Davis and Andrew Jackson Downing. Toronto's Gothic Revival houses are typically symmetrical 1½-storey cottages with centre gable or asymmetric two-storey L-shaped structures. Cladding may be roughcast or red or yellow brick. Roofs are steeply pitched and multiple-gabled with curvilinear bargeboard trim. Windows are tall and slender, either straight-topped or pointed-arched, sometimes protected by decorative drip-moulds.

Later High Victorian Gothic houses featured two colours of brick, usually red with yellow for decoration; fatter, heavier ornament, especially bargeboards; and corbel tables running under the eaves as well as other decorative brick patterns and panels.

Italianate: 1845–1885

What has come to be called "Italianate" style actually was conceived first in England as a revival of dignified early Renaissance forms to heroically illumine gentlemen's club buildings. The style was broadly adopted in the United States for detached houses, but upon transatlantic translation became freer and less classically self-contained. American pattern books illustrated vague, romantically expansive Italian country villas by the score. Americans liked the flexible style because an Italianate house could be made to look as picturesque as a Gothic one without Gothic's burden of "Englishness." Toronto had no such aversion to seeming English, however, and Italianate houses here are spiked with not a little Gothic Revival dash.

Italianate houses may be symmetrical or asymmetric. They sometimes feature a tall, off-centre tower and often a long veranda. Cladding is usually yellow brick. Roofs are flat or low-pitched with extended eaves, generally set with ornate brackets. Windows are round-headed with projecting window heads or flush relieving arches. In the period, wooden detailing was most often painted a creamy white or very dark green.

Toronto Bay-n-Gable: 1875–1890

The facility with which local builders achieved a graceful marriage of Italianate and Gothic Revival modes is abundantly visible in Toronto's Bay-n-Gables, a distinctive form of double and row house that appeared all across the city in the fourth quarter of the 19th century. Characterized by polygonal end bays atop of which spring pointy gables edged in decorative bargeboards, these pleasing rhythmic compositions are virtually Toronto's architectural trademark. The oldest known example standing is the Struthers/Ross house in Yorkville designed by Grant & Dick in 1875 [17/19b]. It may have been the inspiration for the army of speculatively built Bay-n-Gables that followed.

Typically, Bay-n-Gable houses are of soft orangey-red brick with yellow-brick accents. Earlier examples tend to have Italianate round-headed windows, angled bays, and steep gables. Those dating from the late 1880s show more Queen Anne influence, with rectangular bays, straight-topped windows, and lower pitched gables.

Renaissance Revival: 1845–1890

A more ambitious, full-blown Renaissance Revival (French and English as well as Italian) than that sprinkled on Italianate houses was embraced by mercantilist Toronto for commercial blocks, warehouses, and factories. In this, it was following the example of the United States and its mid-century cast-iron architecture. Though whole cast-iron façades never enjoyed much favour in Toronto, iron was common for interior supporting columns as well as for selected exterior ornamentation. The Renaissance Revival style also appealed to Victorians as a way to project both classical tradition and a fashionable look for civic and bank structures. It was not rigidly proscribed and allowed builders and architects a relatively free hand.

Two modes are seen. Conservative Renaissance Revival buildings are symmetrical and boxy, without columns. They are clad in smooth-looking brick or stone. Roofs are low-pitched or flat. Windows are straight-topped with cornice, segmental-, and/or triangular-pedimented window heads. The more flamboyant examples are also symmetrical and rectangular, but they are usually taller than they are wide. Cladding may be stone, but is more often brick. Roofs are flat with ornate cornices. Windows are round-headed in a variety of arch forms, with bold window heads. Decorative details, classically inspired and frequently rendered in cast iron, are rich and profuse.

Second Empire: 1866–1890

Prominent during the contemporaneous reign of Emperor Napoleon III (1852–1870), this was not a revival style *per se*, although the French were certainly drawing on Baroque and Renaissance tradition. The Second Empire style came to Canada from France via the United States and to a lesser extent via England. It was first used here in 1866 by Toronto architect Henry Langley for Government House [demolished] and then dominated major public architecture during the 1870s and domestic architecture through the 1880s. It then fell from favour as quickly as it had risen. For that key period, however, the impressive and ornamental style perfectly captured the air of entrepreneurial ambition that characterized Toronto in the years following Confederation.

Second Empire buildings typically take the shape of symmetrical square blocks that are richly decorated for a highly sculptural profile. Cladding is usually yellow brick with red brick decorative touches, less often red with yellow. Roofs are always of the mansard type—straight, convex, or concave—pierced by dormer windows. Doors and windows are round-headed and often paired, with moulded window heads. Decorative details may include brackets at eaves, quoins, and belt courses. The brick was sometimes painted for protection, usually in a colour to match its natural hue.

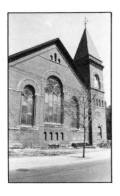

Romanesque Revival: 1870–1910

The descriptive label "Romanesque" refers to the reintroduction of classical Roman architecture after the Dark Ages had all but extinguished it, especially the Roman arch as it appeared in the massive-walled abbeys that rose across Europe in the 10th and 11th centuries. The Victorians revived the form, calling it the "round-arched style." Architects here occasionally used Romanesque Revival for churches (especially Presbyterian), but like Britain and unlike the United States, Toronto preferred Gothic. Romanesque Revival structures may be symmetrical or asymmetric, the latter sometimes with towers of differing heights. Cladding is smooth-looking brick or stone. Windows and all openings are round-arched. Decoration may include arcaded corbel tables, buttresses, and parapeted towers.

Richardsonian Romanesque: 1886–1900

Henry Hobson Richardson, considered one of America's greatest architects, created a version of the Romanesque so distinctive and personal that buildings inspired by his designs have come to be called Richardsonian Romanesque. The style was first used in Toronto for the Parliament Building begun in 1886 to designs by Buffalo architect Richard A. Waite. This was followed in the next decade by all manner of fine buildings in the weighty and massive-looking style, notably by Toronto architects David Dick, E. J. Lennox, David Roberts, and William Storm.

Richardsonian Romanesque buildings have a chunky shape, either symmetrical or asymmetric, often with a tower. Cladding is rock-faced ashlar, sometimes with red brick. Roofs are high with broad planes. The characteristic wide, round arches occur over entry porches and sometimes windows. Otherwise the deep-set windows are straight-topped with a single pane of glass in each sash and perhaps a transom. Decorative elements include stubby stone columns and the stone or terracotta foliate ornamentation called Byzantine leafwork.

Queen Anne: 1880–1915

This revival style was initiated by Richard Norman Shaw and fellow British architects who set about re-creating the mix of Italian classicism (symmetry, pilasters) and Dutch picturesqueness (red brick, curly gables) that had marked English dwellings of the mid-17th century (for Shaw to call them Queen Anne, who ruled 1702–14, was really inaccurate). In North America, the style's popularity spread rapidly after the British erected two widely publicized Queen Anne buildings at the 1876 Centennial Exposition in Philadelphia. Queen Anne houses are typically single detached. Shaw's white-trimmed Queen Anne buildings often appeared serenely classical, but on this continent an exuberant manipulation of space and detail weighted the style toward a more decided picturesqueness. Utilizing an abundance of towers, turrets, gables, dormers, and bay windows, their form is self-consciously asymmetric. Cladding is complicated, combining stone; hard, dark red brick; terracotta tile; and wood. Roofs are high, hipped or gabled, with high chimneys. Windows are generally single-pane sash; transoms and round-arched toplights are common. Decoration includes wooden spindlework, terracotta panels, and stained glass.

After about 1895, Queen Anne houses "filled out" and became boxier-looking, with classical columns replacing turned posts and Palladian windows and dentil mouldings common. This adaptation (like Shaw's early version) is sometimes labelled **Free Classic**.

The Annex House: 1888–1899
For the Lewis Lukes house of 1888–90 [19/6], E. J. Lennox combined the rock-faced ashlar and solid appearance of Richardsonian Romanesque with the asymmetry and picturesque detail of Queen Anne. The result was a hybrid form that was soon copied for single and double houses throughout Toronto's Annex area and elsewhere in the city.

Second Classical Revival: 1890–1930
Repeating the time-honoured seesaw of traditional/picturesque styles, architects returned to classical forms at the turn of the century, especially for public commercial buildings such as railway stations, hotels, and banks. Of the various approaches, the most prominent in Toronto were the massive and austere **Neo-Classical Revival**, with buildings parading Greek orders and lintelled windows and doors; the dramatic as well as ornamental **Edwardian Baroque**, emphasizing plastic, sculptural qualities; and the **Second Renaissance Revival**, a reworking of the logical, serene motifs and forms of the Renaissance, most notably to articulate the tripartite division of Toronto's early skyscrapers into "base, shaft, and capital." All three versions are sometimes, loosely, termed "Beaux-Arts" (see Glossary).

Late Gothic Revival or Neo-Gothic: 1895–1935
In the early 20th century, a period of rapid and confusing change, Gothic was marshalled as a style of reassuring "pastness," especially efficacious for its aura of moral and social order. Late Gothic Revival was most often used for churches and school and university buildings, the latter sometimes called **Collegiate Gothic**. This style is plainer, less self-consciously picturesque, and more substantial-looking than Gothic Revival or High Victorian Gothic.

Georgian Revival or Neo-Georgian: 1895–1940
The classical tradition reasserted itself in residential architecture in this period with Georgian Revival, a replay of Toronto's first attachment to a style of comforting domesticity. Georgian Revival houses are similar to original Georgian, but they are generally larger and almost always of red brick picked out with light-coloured wood or stone details. The style was also popular for clubhouses and small apartment houses.

English Cottage Style, Jacobethan, or Neo-Tudor: 1895–1940

The label Neo-Tudor identifies sundry picturesque reincarnations of English 16th-century cottages and manor houses. As in that post-medieval century, the first decades of the 20th saw feverish housebuilding with whole suburbs appearing almost overnight. Neo-Tudor structures were appreciated for their relative simplicity with just enough picturesque detail to suggest a "period house." The most noteworthy examples were the early **English Cottage Style** houses of Arts and Crafts architects C.F.A. Voysey and Edwin Lutyens, whose free, modern rendering of Tudoresque vernacular forms was much copied in North America (in Toronto especially by Eden Smith, who is said to have done some 2,500 such houses). Later designs often lacked the earlier originality, and, bandaged in yards of expensive but false half-timbering, have been dubbed "Stockbroker Tudor." Another tag, **Jacobethan**, is applied to large, formal structures such as school buildings, notably those that sport Jacobean curved parapeted gables. Obviously diverse, Neo-Tudor buildings share a blocky but asymmetric shape, usually dominated by one or more bold front-facing cross gables. Cladding may be stucco, brick, stone, or a combination thereof. Roofs are prominent and steeply pitched, usually side-gabled, with elaborate chimneys. Windows are typically mullioned and transomed casement type, frequently arranged in strings of three or more.

Commercial Style: 1895–1930

This term is used to describe the first tall buildings—five storeys or higher—whose flat roofs and orderly, sleekly framed, and many-windowed façades frankly represented their commercial purpose as well as skeletal construction. Conceptualized as a plain two-way grid, these "skycages" were celebrated for their "rationality" and "honesty." Applied ornament is usually minimal but may take the form of classical, Gothic, Romanesque, Sullivanesque, and/or Art Deco decorative touches. The style was first and most fully developed in Chicago. In Toronto, Commercial Style was more than competently explored in the Spadina Avenue loft buildings of the 1910s and '20s.

Art Deco, Art Moderne, or Style Moderne: 1925–1955

This style was appropriated for both multi-storey skyscrapers and low-slung two-storey commercial buildings and residences. Art Deco high-rises can be identified by their massive, relatively smooth cubist forms, often with roofline setbacks; vertically emphasized fenestration; colourfulness; and flattened geometric, abstract, often exotic and fantastic ornament. Low Art Moderne structures are more likely to feature rounded curves and horizontally streamlined fenestration. Toronto's Moderne influence came via the United States, especially New York City where the Art Deco skyscraper was born. Though primarily associated with the 1920s and '30s, in Toronto Moderne rounded corners and setbacks continued to appear on new buildings after World War II, and one large enterprise, the Bank of Nova Scotia, was constructed in 1949–51 using Moderne plans first drawn up in 1929 [6/27a].

International Style: 1947–1975

As formulated in Europe during the 1920s by such masters of the Modern Movement as Le Corbusier, Walter Gropius, and Ludwig Mies van der Rohe, the International Style—as it later came to be called—was meant to herald a new machine aesthetic appropriate to a new industrial age. The founders' program of purism is seen in regular, repeated parts; precise, technically perfect use of materials; and absence of ornament. Their credo, "form follows function," dictated the horizontal emphasis of tall buildings to indicate layers of office or apartment floors, one atop another, and the breakup of houses into asymmetric arrangements of "floating" white stucco boxes to signal separate distinct rooms. High-rise boxes are sheathed in curtain walls of prefabricated parts, the façades ranging from rhythmic three-dimensional concrete waffles to planar all-glass skins. Toronto's International Style masterpiece, the Toronto-Dominion Centre [6/29], dates to 1964 when critics were already beginning to denigrate this once-venerated form as the "boring box."

Neo-Expressionism: 1950–

This term is applied to individual, sculptural buildings whose sweeping curves and surprising juxtapositions of form are meant to confront the more common rectangularity of the built environment. Because the style is inherently exhibitionist, most Neo-Expressionist buildings are well known: New City Hall [7/12], O'Keefe Centre [1/17], Roy Thomson Hall [3/5], the apartment houses of Uno Prii [20/5].

Brutalism: 1960–

Brutalism is an asymmetric style that emphasizes a rowdy, rough-and-ready attitude, especially in its use of exposed raw concrete. In Toronto, the style has often been chosen to dress educational and cultural institutions such as the St. Lawrence Centre for the Arts [1/16].

Late-Modernism: 1975–

Buildings that take as their departure point the modern International Style are collected under the heading Late-Modern. Two antithetical trends are discernible: the "boring box" made less boring by giving it an idiosyncratic shape so that it becomes a singular landmark in the streetscape; or the "boring box" made blatantly more so by the overarching use of reflective glass so that—its façade now little more than a mirror of other, surrounding buildings—it virtually "disappears" from the streetscape. Interestingly, these trends are often combined in schizoid Late-Modern edifices that adopt both faceless mirrorplate surfaces and aggressive profiles.

Post-Modernism: 1977–

Promoted as a movement to reintroduce many of the traditional elements that revolutionary modernists had zealously cast aside, Post-Modern buildings are often symmetrical and formal looking, with forms and applied ornament abstracted from past architectural styles to create symbolic, historic, and cultural allusions. In addition, the introduction of new colourful materials and surprising, often playful juxtapositions has earned Post-Modern buildings a reputation for the unique and ironic.

Area I

Walk 1: Old Town
Walk 2: Front Street East

Area I

This is where the city began. The Indian "place [of] trees [and] water," Toronto, had already served sporadically in the mid 18th century as a French fort and trading post before John Graves Simcoe arrived in 1793 to establish a colonial capital for Britain's new province of Upper Canada on this spot. Simcoe was an army man, commander of a light infantry regiment called the Queen's Rangers, when he was named governor of the province. The little village that his surveyors laid out in precise military fashion and re-christened York was the ten-block rectangle bounded by present-day George, Berkeley, Adelaide, and Front Streets (then the water's edge). Aside from a military garrison built about a mile west of the town proper, substantial construction was slow to begin. There were relatively few skilled labourers, and the governor's inexperienced "gentlemen" officials were in no hurry to settle in—actually most of them wished the capital could be located elsewhere than "Muddy York." By 1810, York's 600 or so inhabitants could claim only one brick house—that of trader Laurent Quetton St. George on King Street—and 107 others of wood. The Anglicans had a clapboard church on King Street and the farmers an open square for a market on New Street (now Jarvis). The legislature met in the town's only other brick building, a one-storey, two-winged structure at the foot of Parliament Street (now Berkeley). There were six stores, a distillery, brewery, and small wooden jail.

The War of 1812 changed all this. With increased commissariat buying as well as shortages followed by inflated prices, shopkeepers were in a position to make small fortunes, and many of them did. A growing middle class of tradesmen began to infuse new energy into the lackadaisical civil-servant society, and the frontier settlement expanded quickly. By the time of incorporation as a city in 1834 (and reversion to the name Toronto), the place could boast a classically inspired brick courthouse and similar-looking jail, a large market building with city hall chambers above, a new stone St. James' Church for the Anglicans plus two others for the Methodists and Presbyterians, and a fire hall and school—all situated in the blocks between Jarvis and Toronto Streets in what had come to be called Old Town. Although the best residential area had shifted from here about a half-mile west to New Town [*AREA II*], Adelaide Street East could show off many large and impressive Georgian houses. And on King Street, shops of expensive brick were going up alongside those of wood. Most of the taverns were located around the market. The slums were east and north of St. James Church (Toronto had experienced a great influx of poor immigrants from depression-torn Britain after the Napoleonic Wars). The red light district was on Lombard Street.

Many of Old Town's early structures disappeared in the Great Fire of 1849, which raged over the blocks around King, Adelaide, Church, Jarvis, and George Streets, and time has taken toll of the others. Only three Old Town buildings from the pre-1834 period are known to remain: the 1827 Bank of Upper Canada at Adelaide and George Streets [1/7]; the 1834 residence and office of Postmaster J.S. Howard, a few doors east [1/7]; and the brick mansion of Judge William Campbell, c. 1822, which had stood at the top of Frederick Street at Adelaide [moved to University Avenue in 1972; see 3/2]. There may be other buildings, but neglect and remodelling have so hidden them that their visual impact is negligible.

It is from the next era then, the era associated with the optimism and prosperity of the 1850s, that Toronto's architectural legacy really begins. In this period the classically endowed Toronto City Hall [1/1] and St. Lawrence Hall [1/2] went up along Jarvis Street. (Incorporation had seen the creation of five saintly-designated political wards, of which this area was St. Lawrence.) A mighty new St. James' Church [1/8] was begun across the way at Church Street, and the imposing Magistrates Court [1/24] and Seventh Post Office [1/23a] found agreeable ground a little to the west. Once an eclectic jumble of buildings, the area was gaining genuine dignity and focus as the centre of municipal government. But even more, Toronto had become a city of shops, with retail establishments stretching one after another along King Street, now the main thoroughfare. These first commercial rows were invariably Georgian in style and scale, with two, three, or four floors of residential flats and/or offices rising above the shops, four flights being the maximum up which tenants could be expected to walk.

As their trade expanded, merchants found themselves more and more involved in matters of finance and transportation. Because extended credit was necessary for business, the merchants fostered the development of banks; and then railroads and shipping to bring in their goods, which came from Montreal, Britain, and the United States. Not satisfied with retail sales alone, they became wholesalers as well, selling to country shop-keepers in the provincial hinterlands. It was as the commercial heart of the province that Toronto was to grow and flourish. Warehouses were needed, and these dutiful Georgian and lusty Victorian structures rose in great numbers along Wellington Street and especially Front Street (no longer at the water's edge after 1856 when Esplanade Street was born from landfill into the lake, but still close to shipping and railway depots).

The actual manufacturing of goods was less impor-tant in Toronto's early business scenario. The first industries were few and far between, scattered along the shores of the Don River and Lake Ontario. Like Gooderham and Worts Distillery [2/9], they initially produced little more than was needed for local

iew of King Street East
a lithograph of 1834
owing brick courthouse
id jail and a stone St.
imes' Church.

consumption. Later, manufacturing firms built factories near the harbour and railways, especially to the east along Front Street. As warehousing and manufacturing moved in, residents moved out. One exception was the working-class Irish who had settled in the eastern reaches around Little Trinity [2/12a] and St. Paul's Church [2/24]; this section of Toronto continues to function as a vital residential neighbourhood. But most of the district deteriorated. When a new city hall was finished on Queen Street West in 1899 [7/11], other government and business concerns started trekking westward too, to Bay Street [AREA IV] and University Avenue [AREA V]. The fine stores vanished from King Street to reappear marching up Yonge [AREA III], before finally settling along Bloor Street [AREA IX]. Development of the city in the late 19th/early 20th centuries virtually left this part of Toronto behind, and many historic buildings were lost to neglect. Even more devastating were the zealous schemes of the 1960s which levelled great patches of the area for parking lots in the name of "urban renewal."

N ow this is changing. With completion of the first phase of the city-sponsored St. Lawrence Neighbourhood project [2/1], which in turn has spawned private residential development, the heart of the area is again becoming a mix of dwellings, hotels, shops, and offices. It is not a jumble, however. New buildings are being thoughtfully orchestrated with parks and spruced-up 19th-century survivors—the view of St. James' Cathedral through the twin Market Square Condominium buildings [1/11] is a grand urban vista. If anything, there is sometimes a feeling that it is too carefully planned, slightly stagey with pseudo-Victorian lights dotting the streets. But as the area becomes more and more utilized—more active, more mellow—these "theme park" concerns are fading. The glory of Toronto is that it always has the grace to be itself.

Walk 1: Old Town

1 South St. Lawrence Market incorporating the second Toronto City Hall, 91 Front St. E., Henry Bowyer Lane, 1844–45; remodelled, J. Wilson Siddall, 1904.

A giant yet tidy structure, this red-brick behemoth neatly ingests its predecessor—the city hall of 1845—leaving part of that building's stone and yellow-brick outline and portals to form the only real decoration here. The city hall, a large pedimented three-storey affair, had done quintuple duty: arcaded market hall on the ground floor, shops and offices in the wings, council chamber on the second floor, police station in the basement.

All served well enough until the 1890s when city fathers moved to a more architecturally up-to-date and fashionably located edifice [7/11]. Rather than abandon this old civil servant, it was decided to make of it a large unified food hall, the South St. Lawrence Market. The cupolaed pediment and wings were all but eliminated and sweeping new arched walls built to boldly envelop the remaining shell. In need of refurbishing by the 1970s, this remarkable adaptation was given yet another lease on life when the former council chamber was imaginatively renovated to serve as a civic art gallery, and the elegantly classical rear façade of the original 1840s city hall uncovered to create an historical set for the modern-day market.

2 St. Lawrence Hall, 151 King St. E., William Thomas, 1850–51.

St. Lawrence Hall is Toronto's Victorian classicism at its very best. What is so memorable here is not just the exquisite carved stone and cast iron—perhaps the finest in the city—but the way in which the whole composition projects both delicacy *and* power. Thomas was one of a handful of accomplished British architects who came to Toronto in this period, bringing with him the ability to design in a multiplicity of appropriately evocative styles. The energy that flows through this, Thomas's municipal gem, made it the supreme representation of the booming town's new civic pride. With majestic Corinthian-columned front and domed cupola, St. Lawrence Hall stands out grandly from its neighbours; yet, built right up to the sidewalk in line with shopfronts along King Street, it joins the streetscape too.

Like the city hall, St. Lawrence Hall housed a variety of services: municipal offices, shops, public market, and most notably, a sumptuous 100-foot-long Great Hall for public gatherings. Boasting an elaborate plaster ceiling, gleaming crystal chandeliers, and an abundance of gilt decoration, this third-floor assembly room hosted the city's most gala social, political, and cultural events for almost 75 years. Then, with the rest of the area, St.

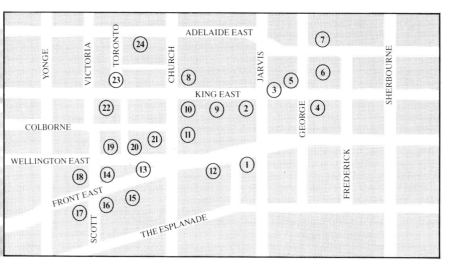

2 *St. Lawrence Hall, c. 1860*

Lawrence Hall was sadly neglected in this century. It was not until Canada's 100th birthday in 1967—and due to no little agitation by architect/historian Eric Arthur—that the building was finally recognized and then restored as Toronto's official Centennial project. Today, with a new market hall behind and Market Street transformed into a pedestrian mall, St. Lawrence Hall shines anew as a distinguished symbol of the city's 19th-century past.

The rows of shops on the blocks proceeding from King Street East and Jarvis are among Toronto's most enduring, providing a nostalgic glimpse of the 19th-century commercial setting of St. Lawrence Hall and her sister civic structures.

3a 150–154 King St. E. (three-unit commercial block), 1850; rehabilitated, Clarke Darling Downey, 1988.

Nicely restored example of the quietly formal Georgian style which marked Toronto's architectural beginnings. Built as shops with residential flats and offices above, such buildings occasionally rose to five storeys, though even the four seen here were unusual for low-scale Toronto. This row replaced an earlier one of 1833 which had burned in the Great Fire of 1849. New safety bylaws enacted at that time dictated construction of the brick party walls rising above the roof. Yellow brick was employed to suggest the look of stone; very popular in the 1850s and '60s, the idea probably came from St. Lawrence Hall [1/2].

3b 167–185 King St. E. (one-, two-, and four-unit commercial blocks), 1834–43.

Though constructed at different times, the buildings in this block are similar, displaying considerate Georgian sensibility for the *streetscape entire*. The style follows the pattern seen across the street at no. 150–154 [1/3a], but with more expensive stone lintels and sills. The attention-getting mansard roofs at nos. 173 and 185 were added in 1880 when the Second Empire style was all the rage and neighbourly good manners didn't seem so important. The same goal undoubtedly prompted the other, less felicitous alterations as well. This is the oldest *line* of buildings standing in Toronto.

4 Originally Little York Hotel, 187 King St. E., Langley Langley & Burke, 1879–80.

Sculpturally rich Second Empire, with high mansard, elaborate dormers, and rhythmic fenestration to make the Little York profitably inviting. The hotel's name harks back to the town's early 1800s appellation when it was sometimes referred to as *little* York to differentiate it from *New* York.

5 Originally Sovereign Bank, 172 King St. E., George W. Gouinlock, 1907.

In the early 1900s, architects returned to classical forms after the Victorian romance with picturesqueness had palled. The Classical Revival style especially appealed to image-conscious bankers, who seemed to be erecting Greek temples and Florentine *palazzi* on every down-

7b *Bank of Upper Canada, De La Salle Institute, Fourth Post Office*

:own street corner. Here, for example, is a
neat Renaissance Revival palace with crisp
Ionic pilasters, triangular-pedimented window heads, and some nifty keystones.

**5 George Brown College/originally Christie,
Brown & Co., 200 King St. E. thru to 235
Adelaide St. E. (warehouses and factories),
1874-1914; remodelled, Alan E. Moody,
1977.**

This picturesque architectural assortment,
which once housed a venerable Toronto
maker of biscuits, is now the St. James
campus of George Brown College. Rehabilitation at its contextual best.

**a George Brown School of Hospitality, 300
Adelaide St. E., Carruthers Shaw & Partners,
986-87.**

And a very hospitable building it is
too—one of the best in recent years to
translate the theoreticians' "critical region-
lism" into progressive architecture that
breathes place and time, past and present.
Its abiding domestic character is seen not
east in the deep sheltering entry, compan-
onable fenestration, and sociable garden.

**7b Originally Bank of Upper Canada, 252
Adelaide St. E., probably William W. Baldwin or John Ewart, 1825-27.**

**Originally De La Salle Institute, 258 Ad-
laide St. E., Henry Langley, 1871-72.**

**Originally J. S. Howard house and Fourth
Post Office, 264 Adelaide St. E., 1833-34.**

Solid and costly looking, Toronto's first
bank building surely impressed the small
pioneer society it served. Founded in

1822, the bank initially had quarters in a
nearby house. It was a measure of the
burgeoning wealth of the little town, the
capability of its architect, and the influence of the bank's shareholders—mostly
members of the ruling oligarchy—that
this classically inspired spectacle could
have been so quickly achieved. Imagine
this finely cut limestone structure standing
on the edge of the frontier town, a town
composed of little more than muddy
streets and wooden houses.

With a virtual monopoly in the province, the Bank of Upper Canada prospered, throwing up country branches as
well as enhancing these premises with a
new brick wing and Doric porch. Expansion led to over-extension, however, and
in 1866 the bank failed. The building was
purchased by the Christian Brothers for
use as a Roman Catholic boys' school.

In 1871, the Brothers constructed a
yellow-brick school building to the east of
the bank to designs by Henry Langley in
the mansard-roof Second Empire style.
Then in 1874, they acquired the three-
storey red-brick Georgian house at 264
Adelaide. More space and streetscape
concerns dictated the addition of mansards to the bank and to the house at this
time as well. No architect is known for
the house; it was built for the town's
postmaster, who conducted business
through the door on the left.

The school quitted the site in 1916.
Years of desultory use followed before
this intriguing trio of buildings was
acquired by a local history buff, lawyer
Sheldon J. Godfrey, and substantially
restored for modern use.

8 *Cathedral Church of St. James, 1923*

8 Cathedral Church of St. James, 106 King St. E., Cumberland & Ridout, 1849–53; additions, Langley Langley & Burke, 1874.

Sober English Gothic and utterly dignified, St. James' perfectly proclaimed its ties with the British homeland and with its conservative, elitist bishop, John Strachan, who for a time practically ran the province. The fourth St. James' on the site, construction began after the Great Fire of 1849 destroyed its predecessor. The design by transplanted British architect Frederic Cumberland tried to follow dogma of the day in drawing on English prototypes with a porch/aisled nave/chancel plan that was studiously expressed on the exterior. The idea was to assert architectural correctness—and thereby religious superiority—for all to see. But the chancel ended up being shorter than the theorists would have it, and the tower, spire, porches, and finials were not added for "all to see" until 20 years later. At 306 feet, the tower and spire are the tallest in Canada, second tallest in North America after New York's St. Patrick's.

The monochromatic exterior—the stone dressings stand out hardly at all from the yellow brick—and the blunt aspect of the Gothic forms combine to make St. James' very stolid and serious looking. The interior is more dramatic, with an elaborate hammerbeam ceiling, marbled apsidal chancel (where Bishop Strachan is buried), impressive Queen Anne organ cases, and a stained glass window (to the Hon. William Jarvis) by Tiffany & Co. of New York, c. 1900.

9 Formerly Army & Navy Clothing Store, 133–135 King St. E. (two-unit commercial block), Langley & Burke, 1887–88.

This is one of Toronto's most alluring buildings, juxtaposing the decorative virtuosity of brick and terracotta with surprising and dramatic proportions. The two-storey-high double windows—great arches of multi-paned, metal-framed glass springing from a heavy metal beam—had probably never been seen in the city before this, and for sheer visual invention and excitement, not since. The drama is even more pronounced today with new glazing stretching clear across the ground-storey front. A valuable gem.

9 *133-135 King St. E.*   **10a** *107-111 King St. E.*

10a 107-111 and 125 King St. E. (commercial blocks), 1841; no. 109 remodelled, c. 1885.

These four shops remained standing after the Great Fire of 1849 and so predate some of those on King Street east of St. Lawrence Hall, but they differ little in style. The elegance of the Georgian design—handsomely revived at nos. 111 and 125—depends on the careful proportions and unerring placement of the windows in the façade. Joseph Rogers, a furrier and hatter, presided at no. 109 for over 30 years.

10b Toronto Sculpture Garden, 115 King St. E., opened 1981.

First there were Georgian row shops on this site; then the illustrious 1893 cast-iron emporium, Oak Hall; starting in 1938, a "parking yard;" and now a city park devoted to changing displays of outdoor sculpture. The empty plot does nothing for the continuity of the streetscape, but there is no denying the theatrical vistas the gap opens up.

11 Market Square Condominiums, 80 Front St. E. and 35 Church St., Jerome Markson, 1982.
Gooderham Court Condominiums, 34 Church St., Edward I. Richmond, 1981.

Up-to-date but compatible additions to this historic area, Market Square was built adjacent to the site of the early town's first market square. Gooderham Court Condominiums had similar good intentions but to less stylish effect.

The warehouses along the south side of Front Street East form one of the most compelling streetscapes in Toronto. Virile, flamboyant, yet inherently solid, these three- and four-storey buildings perfectly represented the prosperity and self-confidence of the 19th-century mercantile city. They were put up in a period when there was much commercial activity, and they included space for offices and show-rooms as well as storage. Although interiors were generally unadorned, exteriors drew on several styles for architectural embellishment, including Georgian, Second Empire, and Renaissance Revival. The latter especially, with its vision of a vigorous Venetian commerce—not to mention its profusion of windows—greatly appealed to the practical merchants. The buildings were covered in flashy red and yellow brick or august stone, with a few in newly useful cast iron.

12a Originally Edward Leadlay Co., 87 Front St. E. (warehouse), 1865; additions, including mansard, 1871.

A fine warehouse with Georgian proportions plus a Second Empire mansard roof. Leadlay was a dealer in "Wools, Hides, Skins & Tallow," which paid for a grandly picturesque house in the west end [15/15].

12a, b, c *Front Street East*   **13** *Gooderham Building mural*

12b 81–83 and 85 Front St. E. (warehouses), 1861.

A dignified Renaissance Revival look for three warehouses with square-loading bays (now windows) as the central focus. The confusing mansard was added to no. 85 later. Early tenants were wholesale druggists and leather and wool dealers.

12c Originally Alexander M. Smith Co., 77–79 Front St. E. (warehouse), 1861.

Tiers of windows organized between piers, a common design device, here given an extra fillip by the lunettes that cap the composition. Early occupants handled wool, tobacco, and grain.

12d 67–69 Front St. E. (warehouse), 1877; restored, 1987.

The meticulous restoration of this ornate Renaissance Revival building received a Toronto Historical Board award of merit.

12e 71 Front St. E. (offices), Moriyama & Teshima, 1981.

One of the city's most gracious infill buildings.

13 Gooderham Building, 49 Wellington St. E., David Roberts, 1891–92.

Toronto's very own "flatiron" building, predating its larger, more famous New York cousin by ten years. The triangular shape was dictated by the awkward site where Wellington and Front Streets intersect (the first street followed the city's grid pattern, the second the line of the

waterfront). Built by a scion of the influential distillery family as headquarters for his financial empire, this theatrical endeavour owes its eye-catching appeal to more than just shape. With a richly textured façade and kingly chateauesque towered roof that still dominates this busy corner, the building stands as apt symbol of the Gooderham family's powerful position in the community. Roberts also designed a number of the distillery buildings [2/9] and many prominent Gooderham residences about town [11/22b, 12/21a, 19/30].

The punning *trompe l'oeil* artwork on the rear of the Gooderham Building entitled "Flatiron Mural," created by Derek Besant in 1980, is becoming a famous Toronto landmark in its own right. Actually, the windows depicted are not those of the Gooderham Building at all; they are copies from the Perkins warehouse across the street at 41–43 Front Street East [1/15b].

14 Berczy Park, Front to Wellington St., Scott to Church St., opened 1975.

At one time lined with handsome warehouses similar to those on the south side of Front Street, this wedge-shaped block was ignominiously cleared in the 1960s for a car park. The area's latter-day rehabilitation has called for *real* parks, and so the asphalt flat is now felicitously grassed and hillocked.

The park was named for William Berczy, an entrepreneurial portrait painter and architect who brought 64 German families to settle in Upper Canada in 1794 on the promise of 64,000 acres of free

15a, b, c *Front Street East*

and. The government reneged on the grant, but Berczy's son Charles went on to become postmaster of Toronto and the first president of Consumers' Gas Company. Two of the colony's more intriguing pioneers, they deserve better than the sentimental bronze sculpture at the Scott Street entrance dedicated to them.

15a Originally Dixon Building, 45–49 Front St. E. (three-unit warehouse), possibly Walter R. Strickland, 1872–73.
Toronto's only remaining building with a totally cast-iron façade and a tribute to architectural illusion. This building really does look as if it were constructed of painted wood and stone, but the whole front—except for windows—consists of units of cast iron fabricated at the Toronto foundry of W. Hamilton & Son. (Cast-iron aficionados will be able to tell by the crisp, hard-edged quality of the detail; the rest of us might look for telltale signs of rust!) The landlord was real estate speculator B. Homer Dixon [see also 15/2]. His first tenants were, west to east: John Smith & Co.; Copp, Clark & Co.; and the Canada Vinegrowers' Association.

15b Originally F. & G. Perkins Co./formerly Perkins, Ince & Co., 41–43 Front St. E. (two-unit warehouse), Macdougall & Darling, 1874–75.
An exuberant Victorian warehouse redolent of Venetian *palazzi* with its variety of arched windows and red and yellow brick standing in for the colourfulness of Renaissance marble. The Perkinses were wholesale grocers.

15c Beardmore Building/originally T. Griffith Co., 35–39 Front St. E. (three-unit warehouse), David Roberts, 1872–73.
Yet another flamboyant façade to enhance mundane warehousing. Griffith was a wholesale grocer; Beardmore a manufacturer of leather goods and owner of one of Toronto's most notable houses [14/11].

16 St. Lawrence Centre for the Arts, 27 Front St. E., Adamson Associates, 1967–70; interior remodelled, Thom Partnership, 1982.
Architectural Brutalism, with musty-coloured, right-out-of-the-mould concrete slabs weightily pronouncing a message of 1960s avant-garde vigour. A more refined exchange carries on today in the newly remodelled, more intimate interior.

17 O'Keefe Centre for the Performing Arts, 1 Front St. E., Earle C. Morgan with Page & Steele, 1956–60.
Renewed appreciation of buildings of the 1950s make this finely detailed Neo-Expressionist extravaganza with its swooping cantilevered canopy look better and better, though the 3,200-seat house is still too big for proper performances.

18 A.E. LePage Building, 33 Yonge St. thru to Scott St., Webb Zerafa Menkes Housden, 1982.
One of the best things about this real estate giant's new glass edifice is the way it has been symmetrically composed and sited as an unobtrusive screen behind the picturesque Gooderham Building [1/13], thus preserving Toronto's favourite picture-postcard of itself.

19 *Wellington Square*

22 *King Edward Hotel*

19 Wellington Square and The Wellington, 26 and 30 Wellington St. E. (office and condominium buildings), Edward I. Richmond, 1982.

Two refined black glass towers edged in grey granite and linked by an unusually hospitable plaza, with a handsome colonnade of square pillars that both carries the street line and "encloses" the space. The elegant and prominent fountain sculpture by Andrew Posa for once proves a meaningful adjunct to the architectural conception.

20 Originally Hutchison Building, 36–42 Wellington St. E. (four-unit commercial block), 1854–55.

A genteel Greek Revival quartet of shops parading an unusual band of half-windows at the attic storey (at no. 42, the windows became full-size when the roof was raised). In 1855, shop tenants included a saloonkeeper and a dry goods merchant. The landlord was John Hutchison, soon to become Toronto's 13th mayor, after which the depression of 1857 forced him to leave the province. Better times followed, however, and Boyd and Arthurs, prominent wholesale grocers, next assumed all four premises.

21a Originally Milburn Co., 47–55 Colborne St. (five-unit warehouse and commercial block), E. J. Lennox, 1887–89.

Lush Richardsonian Romanesque by Toronto's master practitioner. Cast-iron columns alternating with those of masonry at the ground storey made possible large expanses of glass for the shopfronts. Owner Milburn was a wholesaler of patent medicines and occupied two shops; other tenants purveyed beer supplies and wine and liquor. A heady brew here, architectural and otherwise.

21b Originally McRae Co., 41–45 Colborne St. (three-unit warehouse and commercial block), 1888–89.

The same rich red brick and deep-set windows as next door, but here smooth light-coloured stone is the decorative contrast. Such crisp icing on a Romanesque cake makes for a very unusual morsel, indeed.

22 King Edward Hotel, 37 King St. E., Henry Ives Cobb with E. J. Lennox, 1901–02; eighteen-storey addition, Esenwien & Johnson, 1920.

Fashionable Edwardian classicism to herald a new monarchy and a new era of metropolitanism for Toronto (the design was by one of America's leading architects). The King Eddie reigned supreme as the city's de luxe establishment hostelry for almost 60 years before the steady decline of the neighbourhood finally overtook it. Today, thanks to the area's renaissance, the *faux marbre* columns intrigue again in the lobby and the celebrated plasterwork captivates anew in the restaurant.

23 *Toronto Street, c. 1878*

23b *17 Toronto St.*

Toronto Street was once among the city's most beautiful, a block-long tout ensemble of gracious three- and four-storey office buildings. "Progress" has replaced most of the early structures and the elegant streetscape is gone forever, but isolated buildings do remain to suggest what the 19th-century city had to offer.

23a Argus Corporation/originally Seventh Post Office/formerly Department of Customs/formerly Bank of Canada, 10 Toronto St., Cumberland & Ridout, 1851–53.

In the 1850s this was lauded as a "plain but commanding" building, and it's still true. Dignified with a chaste four-columned Ionic portico recessed between side piers, the one-time post office confidently projects harmony and order in the best tradition of the Greek Revival. The grace of the design extended to a Doric-columned screen and counter in the interior, prominent royal arms of England at the roofline, and curved rear corners accommodating a carriageway that originally circled the building. Mail delivery was not general then and most people had to come to the post office to get their mail. But it was open seven days a week, daily 8 a.m. to 7 p.m.; Sundays 9-10 and 4-5!

23b Counsel Trust/originally Consumers' Gas Company of Toronto Chambers, 17 Toronto St., Grant & Dick, 1876; additions, David B. Dick, 1882, 1899.

Pedimented doorway, polished red granite columns, fluted Corinthian pilasters, scalloped lunettes, veluoted keystones, modil-lioned cornice, bosses and friezes, string courses and garlands—this is Toronto's flamboyant Renaissance Revival palace *par excellence*. That David Dick was one of Toronto's best late 19th-century architects can well be seen with this masterful conception, especially in its careful recent restoration.

23c Originally Trust & Loan Co., 25 Toronto St. (office building), Henry Macdougall, 1870–71.

Toronto's Victorian version of a dignified 16th-century Florentine *palazzo*, the reticent strain of Renaissance Revival that seldom garners the attention it deserves. This is truly one of the city's most refined buildings, though it does need its cornice and parapet, removed some years ago for fear they would fall on someone's head.

24 Originally York County Magistrates Court, 57 Adelaide St. E., Cumberland & Ridout, 1851–53.

Drawing on the same repertoire as for his Seventh Post Office [1/23a], Cumberland has here made the Greek Revival not only commanding but downright awesome. The weighty square Doric columns still dominate this block, much as they must have done in the 1850s when the building boasted two long brick side wings. It is hoped that the gentler-scale Georgian rear façade will one day overlook a new Courthouse Square, thoughtfully returning the site to its original role.

Walk 2: Front Street East

1 St. Lawrence Neighbourhood, Canadian National railway tracks to Front St., Yonge to Parliament St. (housing complex), Irving Grossman, Klein & Sears, Vaclav Kuchar & Associates, Boris A. Lebedinsky, Jerome Markson, Matsui Baer Vanstone Freeman, Robinson & Heinrichs, J. E. Sievenpiper, Sillaste & Nakashima, Thom Partnership, 1977–82.

Toronto's mass housing project to end all mass housing projects, and so far a good one. The grid of the surrounding area has been woven in to the mile-long development, making the neighbourhood part of a continuum of the city's life and streets. The scale is human, with none of the buildings rising higher than a manageable eight storeys. Satisfying proportions, warm brick tones, and architectural niceties such as rhythmic bays and arches keep up with Victorian neighbours. The buildings encompass medium-rise apartment blocks and low-rise row houses, with different architects having produced a variety of compatible designs. And finally, there is an economic and social mix here, co-op owners and subsidized renters. All seem to be attracted by the inclusion of schools and playgrounds, the participatory spirit that runs the place, and the pride engendered by being part of a felicitous new endeavour.

2 Originally W. Davies & Co./formerly Toronto Safeworks, 139–145 Front St. E. (factory), 1866–67; rebuilt after fire, William W. Blair, 1883; additions, 1890, 1907.

Typical Toronto Victorian factory, with yellow-brick relieving arches and piers standing out as both structural members and simple decoration against red-brick walls. In 1867, this corner was the William Davies pork packing plant. The premises were taken over by J. & J. Taylor Toronto Safeworks in 1871, which was responsible for the buildings we see today, including the 20th-century all-red-brick extension. Safes were big business in the 19th century: fireproof, burglarproof, and lovely pieces of iron to decorate the office.

3 Young People's Theatre/originally Toronto Street Railway Co. stables/formerly Toronto Street Railway Co. electric power house, 165 Front St. E., 1887–88; remodelled, Zeidler Partnership, 1976–77.

This handsomely rehabilitated building, boldly reminiscent of a medieval fortress, is what remains of a much larger complex designed to house the nucleus of municipal transport, the horse-drawn streetcar. (The horses were stabled on the first two floors; the hayloft was on the third.)

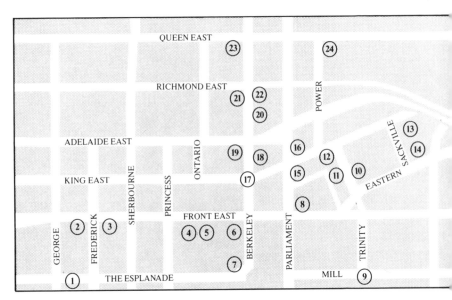

2 *139-145 Front St. E.*

6 *239 Front St. E.*

4 219–221 Front St. E. (factory), 1885.
More yellow-brick decoration in brisk splashes across the front, with waves of round-headed Renaissance Revival windows lighting deep interiors. Originally woollens were made at no. 219; cigar boxes at 221.

5 Joey and Toby Tanenbaum Opera Centre/originally Standard Woolen Mills, 223–237 Front St. E. (factory), possibly E. J. Lennox, 1882; three-storey addition, 1893; additions, including fourth storey, 1904; rehabilitated, Arcorp Associates, 1984–87.
How lovingly detailed the 19th century made a factory: curved relieving arches accenting windows, prominent piers standing out from walls, decorative brick panels, corbelled friezes. And how lovingly detailed the 20th century has rehabilitated it: conscientious cleaning, accurate restoration including black creosote highlighting yellow brick, sparky 1800s-looking sign. Inside all are spanking new offices, archives, and library for the Canadian Opera Company [see 2/6].

6 Joey and Toby Tanenbaum Opera Centre/originally Consumers' Gas Co. purifying house, 239 Front St. E., probably David B. Dick, 1887–88; rehabilitated, Arcorp Associates, 1984–87.
Consumers' Gas Company began generating coal gas here in the late 1860s, eventually occupying all the Front Street blocks between Berkeley and Trinity Streets. Most of the complex has been demolished, but these buildings remain as striking reminders of how architecturally accomplished utilitarian factories can be. Rows of great stone-capped piers, pinnacles, fancy brickwork, stepped gables— none of these were necessary to make gas, but they did announce corporate pride and confidence. No less so for the Canadian Opera Company, whose architects have orchestrated here one of Toronto's grandest comebacks. Rehabilitated as a huge, handsome rehearsal hall, no. 239 stars again as a significant building in the life of the city.

7 Berkeley Castle/originally Toronto Knitting and Yarn Factory/formerly Toronto Storage Co., 2 Berkeley St. and 250 The Esplanade, c. 1866; additions, Charles J. Gibson, 1896, 1898, 1905, 1909, 1910; remodelled, A. J. Diamond & Partners, 1979–82.
Joseph Simpson brought his knitting and yarn works to this corner in 1874, expanding piecemeal over the next 30 years as the need arose, with scant interest in architectural uniformity. Today, the six-building complex is a congenial commercial and office addition to the St. Lawrence Neighbourhood, having been smartly homogenized by A. J. Diamond & Partners, who have their own new offices within.

8 Originally Consumers' Gas Co. purifying house, 45 Parliament St., Bond & Smith, 1898–99; additions, Frederick H. Herbert, 1902, 1904.
Another industrial stunner for the gas company.

9 *Gooderham & Worts Ltd., chromolithograph c. 1890*

The factory, the house, the school, the church, the tavern—in the 1800s, that was almost all a working-class family needed. Until recently this pocket of Toronto was unique in still having in original use all those items of the Victorian workingman's agenda. But now—for good or ill—the "white-painters" have arrived as well as the city planners, who propose to transform this sector of town into a new residential neighbourhood for 12,000 people at a cost of $1 billion. The goal of affordable housing is laudatory, all the more if new construction is integrated with existing historic structures. The distillery factory complex, however, should be sacrosanct—to walk inside those precincts with brick-paved street and polite buildings bordered with neat swatches of lawn is to leave the 20th century behind. A rare experience.

9 Gooderham and Worts Distillery, 55 Mill St. at Trinity St. (mill and distillery), David Roberts Sr., 1859; rebuilt after fire, 1870; malthouse and store-house additions, Gundry & Langley, 1863–64; five two-storey tank-house additions, David Roberts, 1906; warehouse addition, Victor L. Gladman, 1927; processing plant addition, 1929.

Begun on this site in 1832, the Gooderham and Worts Distillery is not only a going concern but also one of the best-preserved 19th-century industrial complexes in Canada. It numbers some 45 buildings, the oldest being the 1859 limestone grist mill and distillery, the exterior of which survived an 1869 fire.

Direct descendant of early 19th-century English factories, this massive unadorned box with evenly spaced Georgian windows relies on fine stonework and perfect proportions for its enduring worth. Later buildings are similarly plain, depending for aesthetic effect on sleek brickwork and regular fenestration, with only the cupolas of Gundry & Langley's malting kiln and warehouse betraying any obvious "architectural touch." Gooderham and his relative Worts had come from Britain to grind grain here, and the company's windmill was long a landmark on the shoreline. The lucrative switch from milling to distilling was common in the 19th century, and by the 1860s spirits headed the Toronto manufacturers' list of income producers (soap and candles came next).

10a 105–109 Trinity St. (three-house row), 1885.

Workers' cottages built in Second Empire style and delightful for their immodest—and successful—aims at all the grand effects: decorative slate roof, sawn curlicues in dormer pediments, yellow brick patterning the red.

10b 115–127 Trinity St. (seven-house row), 1886–87.

A very old-fashioned Georgian style for this late date, but two full storeys high and all of brick. Today just starting to be gentrified, some units more successfully than others. Single-pane windows inserted into Georgian fronts, as here, are as disquieting as the fake multi-panes snapped into new rowhouses across the street at no. 94–98.

11 *Enoch Turner Schoolhouse*

12a *Little Trinity Church*

11 Enoch Turner Schoolhouse/originally Trinity Street School/formerly Trinity Church Sunday School, 106 Trinity St., 1848.
Spunk and charm in soft yellow banding and exclamation-point Gothic windows, this is Toronto's oldest standing school building. The Protestant Irish in this working-class district were too poor to send their children to the school at St. James', and the city council balked at public education, so a beneficent neighbourhood employer, the brewer Enoch Turner, paid for Trinity Street School to be built on the grounds of Little Trinity Church. When free education was finally instituted, the school board took the facility over in 1851. Never happy with its coeducation and church-related programs, however, the board built Palace Street School in 1859 and in fact as well as deed this became Trinity Church Sunday School. Today it is a living museum of the time for school children and history buffs.

12a Little Trinity Church, 425 King St. E., Henry Bowyer Lane, 1843–45; restored after fire, F. Hilton Wilkes, 1961.
Built after Anglicans in this neighbourhood complained that they could not afford pew rents at St. James', and without any great Ecclesiological pretensions, Little Trinity turns out to be one of our most captivating churches. The building is beautifully proportioned, but it's the scenic Tudor Gothic details that really make it sparkle: octagonal corner buttresses, crenellated tower, energetic wishbone drip-moulds.

12b Little Trinity Church rectory, 417 King St. E., Cumberland & Storm, 1853.
A Georgian box lightly dusted with Gothic details. With the church, an idyllic setpiece.

13 21–33 Sackville St. (seven units of original eight-house row), 1890.
Another row of Second Empire cottages for workers, radiantly strung together by yellow-brick necklaces. Though flatter and less sculptural than many "French-roof" houses, they are exciting for their colour contrast. A knifed-off eighth house originally completed the ensemble.

14 Inglenook Community High School/originally Sackville Street Public School, 19 Sackville St., William G. Storm, 1887.
Unadorned yellow brick, tall light-giving windows, girls on one side, boys on the other—what could be simpler?

16 *334–344 King St. E*

19 *Alumnae Theatre*

15 Derby Tavern, 393 King St. E., 1846–47. 399–403 King St. E. (three-house row), 1855.

The roughcast façade of the Derby Tavern has been "modernized" many times over but it manages to carry on without much ado. On the other hand, the chunky Georgian buildings next door—all once doubled as shops—are much as they always were, including two original doors with tiny cast-metal letter slots.

16 Originally Aluminum and Crown Stopper Co., 334–344 King St. E. (factory), Frederick H. Herbert, 1911–12.

Ornamented industrial for the early 20th century, with a lovely Edwardian entrance sited to take advantage of the angled street corner. The company made "wood bungs, tops, spikes, caps, bottling wire, wax cork," and their own invention, the Crown Stopper.

17a Originally Reid & Co. Lumber, 359 King St. E. (commercial block), 1891–92; renovated, Peter Hamilton, 1984.

A great red-brick construction assembled with a sparkling assortment of window types—Gothic, Romanesque, Queen Anne—strings of swirling Victorian ornament, and tilehangings galore. This was all surely wonderful advertisement for the first owner, a purveyor of building supplies. Newly renovated to once again capture this corner.

17b Originally Small row/formerly James Greenshields Grocery, 298–300 King St. E. (two units of original three-house row), 1845.

A very old red-brick Georgian row, featuring yellow-brick quoins and belt courses, stone lintels and sills, and huge double chimneys. The row was owned by Charles Small, son of Simcoe's fellow officer, Major John Small. (Their large family villa, Berkeley House, stood across King Street from the early 1800s until 1891 when no. 359 [2/17a] was built.) Charles Small's first tenants in this grand three-storey ensemble were Henry Sullivan, professor of anatomy at King's College; John Marling, a "gentleman"; and brother James Small, provincial solicitor-general. In 1879, no. 300 was enlarged by thrusting the front wall out to the sidewalk, at which time the houses acquired their shopfronts. Greenshields purveyed groceries to the carriage trade from here then until 1956, one of the city's longest-lived enterprises.

17c Originally Garibaldi House, 302 King St. E. (commercial block), 1859.

In the 1800s, this jogged corner signalled the last street in town and the point at which travellers headed their horses northeast along the road to Ottawa. Many an inn and tavern stood nearby to help ease the arduous cross-province journey. No. 302 was a roughcast hotel called Garibaldi House in the 1860s.

21 *106–108, 110–112 Berkeley St.*

18 55–79 Berkeley St. (thirteen-house row), 1871–72; renovated, Joan Burt, 1969.

These simple 19th-century workmen's cottages were among the first in Toronto to be recycled. Architect Burt has since become known for her rehabilitated grey-stucco rows [see also 3/12].

19 Alumnae Theatre/originally Firehall No. 4, 70 Berkeley St., 1859; rebuilt, A. Frank Wickson, 1903; remodelled for theatre, Ron Thom, 1971.

The once-familiar firehall tower has been missing since 1952, but probably the boldest window in Toronto is still here, bursting with stone voussoirs and crowned with a boisterous shaped gable. Quite appropriate for Canada's oldest theatrical company, the University Alumnae Dramatic Club, which now runs the place.

20 Originally Christie, Brown & Co. stables, 95 Berkeley St., 1906.

A brash early 20th-century stone and brick composition that once stabled the horses used to deliver Mr. Christie's biscuits. (A hay pulley still dangles at the side.)

21 106–108 and 110–112 Berkeley St. (two double houses), 1886.
111–113 Berkeley St. (double house), 1882.

Three splendid examples of Toronto's native Bay-n-Gable design, an inspired marriage of bay windows and gingerbread gables that was consummated all across the city in the late 1870s and early 1880s.

22 Originally Sheldon Ward house, 115 Berkeley St., 1845; altered, 1881.

The 1880s remodelling, which altered this large Georgian-chimneyed single house to resemble its neighbours, has long hidden the fact, but this is one of the oldest houses standing in Toronto. It was put up as his own showy bichrome house by Sheldon Ward, a brickmaker and prominent city councilman. Poor Ward only lived here one year. In 1846, he "lost his life by a scaffold on a building in process of erection giving way with him."

23a Berkeley Studios/originally Berkeley Street Wesleyan Methodist Church/formerly Berkeley Street United Church, 315 Queen St. E., Smith & Gemmell, 1871–72.

A bulky Methodist "preaching box" spiked with energetic Gothic windows and drip-moulds that are especially crisp for being rendered in cast iron. The building now houses the United Church's audio-visual studios.

24 *St. Paul's Church*

23b 319 Queen St. E. (commercial block), c. 1888; altered, Landau Partnership, 1988.
This building, just celebrating its 100th birthday, seems to break all rules for preservation practice, but the sheer panache of inserting a sleek modern glass curtain wall between florid historic masonry front and back so sparks the imagination it makes us take notice in ways we might not otherwise have done. (In fact, the building was not on the Toronto Historical Board preservation list; the architects salvaged it because they liked it.) And the fearless rehabilitation—even though adding a fourth storey—does respect original scale and context. Corner-store architecture at its evolutionary, adventurous best.

24 St. Paul's Roman Catholic Church, 93 Power St. at Queen St. E., Joseph Connolly, 1887–89.
One is not prepared to come across the serene grandeur of a Renaissance basilica in Toronto—the Roman Catholics were the only denomination to try it—and that St. Paul's is such a poised version complete with 129-foot bell tower is all the more remarkable. This church has been likened to the 15th-century Santa Maria Novella in Florence, with the green and white marble of that edifice re-created here in rough Credit Valley stone and smooth Cleveland limestone. The light-filled interior displays all the lucidity and sense of visual order inimitably associated with the Renaissance: a barrel-vaulted nave separated from the aisles by a graceful Ionic arcade; short mural-graced transepts; and a lovely triple-apsed chancel. The church we see today replaced an earlier St. Paul's built for this working-class community in 1826. Power Street was named for Bishop Michael Power, first Roman Catholic bishop of Toronto, who died in 1847 while nursing the sick in a cholera epidemic.

Area II

Walk 3: New Town
Walk 4: King Street West

Area II

In 1793, the Town of York was born: ten modest square blocks laid out by the provincial governor, John Graves Simcoe, at the eastern end of the harbour [*AREA I*]. Four years later, a new administrator, Peter Russell, extended the town by jumping over the swamp that later would become Yonge Street [*AREA III*], and creating new streets to the west, including York, Simcoe, John, and finally namesake Peter. In this western sector, there grew up a stylish "New Town," with the architecturally distinguished buildings of Upper Canada's provincial government all coming to be located at its centre around John and King Street West by the 1830s. These included new parliament buildings (replacing those that had burned, twice, in Old Town), the lieutenant-governor's residence, Upper Canada College, and the general hospital. Front Street West, at this time still fronting the lake, became *the* residential street for Toronto's fledgling aristocracy with large and impressive houses for such as the Anglican bishop, receiver-general, and chief justice.

Beyond the Peter Street town limits, open spaces of the military reserve and garrison common stretched farther west—as far as today's Dufferin Street. But in the 1830s, when military exigencies no longer threatened as they had in war-plagued settlement years, the government released a section of this property for residential development. It was laid out following one of those elaborate urban sequences that were the glory of British colonial planning, with Clarence Square [3/12] connected to Victoria Square [3/20] via wide, boulevarded Wellington Place [3/14]. This ambitious residential district was to include a new government house, the garrison church, and a military burial ground in Victoria Square. Building never took off as anticipated, however, and in the 1850s these visions died with the arrival of that miracle of 19th-century progress, the railroad.

The railroads imposed their own dreams on New Town, extraordinary schemes that crisscrossed the waterfront and progressively cut off the city from the lake. Noise and congestion drove away owners of the fine houses—actual and anticipated—to be replaced by hotelkeepers attracted by proximity to the railroad. Hotel activity in turn stimulated building of Victorian amusements: Toronto's first zoo on the northeast corner of Front and York Streets, and a cyclorama across from that. As commerce increased, the lake was persistently filled in to accommodate more enterprise, chiefly foundries, fuel companies, and lumber yards. Eventually, the government institutions moved out too, opening the way for warehouses and factories. King Street, originally occupied by modest Victorian houses at its western reaches, developed into a notably busy thoroughfare lined with factories of every late 19th/early 20th-century architectural stripe. Other main streets might host the butcher and the baker, but the candlestick maker was to be found on King. (Literally. The renowned Toronto Silverplate Company started up in 1882 in premises which still stand at 572 King Street West [4/3a].) Employees could take the horse-drawn street railway to work. In service since 1861, it ran on King Street between the Don River and Bathurst Street.

The proliferation of factory buildings coincided with development of new construction methods. To support the structure, cast-iron framing began to replace load-bearing brick and stone walls after 1855; steel frames appeared in the 1880s; reinforced concrete about the turn of the century. Toronto builders often remained faithful to tried-and-true methods, however, and it is impossible to tell from looking whether a building is supported by masonry, iron, steel, or concrete. Cladding materials can be confusing as well. After Toronto's Great Fire of 1849 [see Introduction, *AREA I*], the city council began enacting a series of bylaws that imposed strict building regulations on the town. The result is that throughout the second half of the 19th century, central Toronto was a city of brick and stone with relatively few wooden or roughcast structures. In 1904, Toronto's second major fire occurred, levelling whole blocks of Front Street West as well as large chunks of Wellington and Bay Streets. After this conflagration, terracotta became more and more important as a cladding material. Not only had terracotta proved more fire resistant than stone, it could be made to look like stone and it was cheaper. Because of superstition about "artificial" building materials as well as the militancy of bricklayers' unions, concrete was slower in being accepted. But its demonstrated fire resistance eventually led to concrete's use as both a structural material (when reinforced with iron or steel), and an ornamental one, as it too could be precast or poured in place to resemble stone.

The design and decoration of these early manufactories was done with much personal concern. Victorian and Edwardian captains of industry hired the best architects they could afford to create for them images of solidity and richness, usually with their names writ bold on the façade. By the 1890s, Toronto could boast architects capable of turning out accomplished Richardsonian Romanesque and Second Classical Revival compositions. Later, in the 1910s and '20s, when manufacturing buildings became larger and housed more than one company—the open-plan, multi-use rentable loft building—a different look was expected, but it could be equally impressive. Toronto's garment district located on and around Spadina Avenue [see Introduction, *AREA VIII*] can claim buildings in this genre as good as any in North America. Lofts were often the building type where new land-, time-, and cost-saving technologies were tried.

The King Street West/Spadina Avenue manufacturing

Toronto waterfront, c. 1875, already becoming industrialized with lumber yards and grain elevators.

district remains much as it was in the early decades of this century, and as such is a fascinating and important chapter in the city's architectural history. The southern sector of this area, however, is today in the throes of massive redevelopment that will eventually encompass the railroad lands and waterfront. Although Walk 3 ends now with some secluded corners (and takes in four pre-1834 buildings), for the most part furious construction on a scale undreamed of in this city punctuates the route. The verdict is not yet in. Let us hope for amenities with the mammoths, in what truly will be Toronto's "New Town."

Walk 3: New Town

1 Osgoode Hall, 116–138 Queen St. W.

East wing, John Ewart, 1829–32; altered, Henry Bowyer Lane, 1844; law school addition, William G. Storm, 1880, 1890; interior altered, Burke & Horwood, 1899; interior altered, Vaux and Bryan Chadwick, 1925; rear additions, 1937, 1958.

Centre block, Henry Bowyer Lane, 1844; rebuilt, Cumberland & Storm, 1856–61; rear additions, 1910, 1923.

West wing, Henry Bowyer Lane, 1844; additions, Kivas Tully, 1883; interior altered, Burke & Horwood, 1897; rear addition, 1910; renovated and rear addition, Page & Steele, 1972–73.

Fence and gates, William G. Storm, 1866.

Built at the head of York Street north of Queen Street, then the town limits, Osgoode Hall was a harbinger of New Town's architectural eminence. In 1832, it consisted of the front east wing only, a small portion of the grand building we see today. Nevertheless, it was an ambitious showcase for Toronto's elitist colonials (specifically the Anglican, Tory governing class, many of whom were lawyers). Osgoode Hall was built as headquarters of the Law Society of Upper Canada, the lawyers' fraternity, and duly named for the first chief justice of the province, William Osgoode. Today it still serves the society, and houses the Supreme Court of Ontario as well.

Three architectural firms contributed to the design before 1860. Surprisingly, the result is a classical building of great presence, though an architectural hybrid. The scheme of temple-fronted wings flanking a centre pavilion is that of a Palladian villa. The central façade ornamented with rooftop urns owes much to the garden front of Versailles. And the interior vestibule, glass-roofed court, and paired stairway resemble nothing so much as an Italian Renaissance *palazzo*—a form then being explored in London for aristocratic clubhouses. In fact, even though Osgoode Hall has been official home of the provincial courts since 1846, the building preserves the air of a private club about it, rather forbidding behind that impressive iron fence. Actually, the fence is only gated against wandering cows—a problem in the early years—and visitors are welcome to look inside and visit the library, perhaps the noblest room in Canada. Beautifully proportioned, it is 122 feet long with a 40-foot-high vaulted and domed ceiling that virtually dances with rich plasterwork.

Additions and alterations since 1860 have been many. The west wing was extended in a sympathetic classical mode in

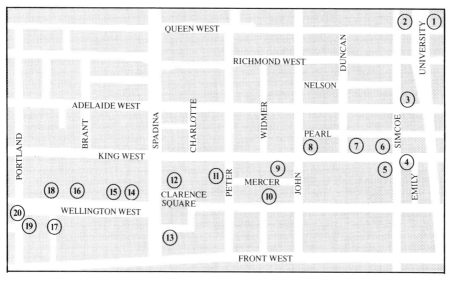

1 *Osgoode Hall*

1883, and again—not so sympathetically—in 1910, the same time the rear of the centre block was enlarged. A Romanesque law school was appended to the east wing in 1880, then hidden by nondescript cast-stone extensions in 1937 and 1958, the former lightly dusted with Moderne detail. Classical forms were also used for the final northwest addition, part of massive renovations completed in 1973.

The Law Society originally had its own Osgoode Hall Law School in this building, which moved and amalgamated with York University in 1958. In recent years, the society has tried to retrieve the name, citing "progressive" practices at the university inconsistent with Osgoode's 150-year-old traditions. *Plus ça change . . . .*

2 Campbell House, 160 Queen St. W., c. 1822.

William Campbell came out from Scotland to fight in the Revolutionary War, after which he settled in the Maritimes. After being named a judge in frontier Upper Canada in 1811 and transferred to York, the man who was later to become chief justice and the first Canadian judge to be knighted built himself a large Georgian house overlooking the harbour from high ground at Frederick and Adelaide Streets in the heart of Old Town [*AREA 1*]. One of the earliest houses built of brick in Toronto, it boasted such late Georgian refinements as a fanlighted doorcase, oval-windowed pediment, and elegantly tall windows ornamenting the front. Threatened with demolition in 1972 (before Old Town began its resurgence), the 300-ton house was put on wheels and moved with great fanfare to its present, not entirely inappropriate site, for other such fine Georgian houses stood in New Town in the 1830s and '40s. Campbell House has been renovated and partially restored and furnished by the Advocates' Society, a group of 600 courtroom lawyers who use part of it as a clubhouse. The house may be visited 9:30-12:30 and 2:00-5:00; weekends, 12:00-5:00.

3 Originally Bishop's Buildings, 192-194 Adelaide St. W. (two units of original five-house row), 1833.

These two 1830s brick and stucco row houses are Toronto's oldest example of the genre, though now sadly bereft of their three original sisters and most of their Georgian dignity as well. Joseph Bishop was a butcher who built these houses for speculation.

The corner of Simcoe and King Streets was the heart of Toronto's extravagant New Town in the early 19th century. Here, in the block north of King Street, stood Upper Canada College (1829-1900); Government House (1815-1862 and 1866-1912) was in the next block south between King and Wellington Streets; and south of that, covering the whole block between Wellington and Front Streets, stood the third Parliament Buildings (1829-1900).

3 *Bishop's Buildings, c. 1890*

4 St. Andrew's Presbyterian Church, 189 King St. W., William G. Storm, 1874-75. St. Andrew's Manse, 73 Simcoe St., 1873; condominium addition, Northgrave Architect, 1988-89.

Looking more florid every day as sleek new structures rise all around it, St. Andrew's poses theatrically in a Romanesque Revival costume borrowed from medieval Scotland. Typical of this "Norman Romanesque" are the arcaded corbel tables, tower finished off with parapets, broad stone wall surfaces, and novel decoration—the name and date interspersed on protruding stone bosses along the west façade for instance.

This revival style, which adherents pronounced more "democratic" and less ostentatious than Gothic but equally picturesque, would have held special appeal for this congregation, for it was they who counselled moderation in the split—over organ music for one thing— that saw a few of the members break off to build their own (organless) St. Andrew's on Jarvis Street [12/9].

Once dependent on Sunday guests at nearby hotels, St. Andrew's is an energetic centre-city church whose future was ensured when Sun Life Centre across the street [7/6] bought their "air rights." Sun Life gained permission to build higher than the law otherwise would have allowed, and St. Andrew's got $4.1 million. A deal was also made for ground below and air above the manse, which has been dug under, shored up, and cantilevered over to accommodate a 25-storey condominium. At least it's all still there.

5 Roy Thomson Hall, 60 Simcoe St., Arthur Erickson with Mathers & Haldenby, 1982.

Toronto's new concert hall, named for the donor who gave the most money, gets mixed reviews. This is one of the city's most arrogant buildings, a Neo-Expressionist extravaganza that integrates with the urban streetscape not at all. It could be argued that buildings designed for entertainment—"theatrical" buildings —have reason for not blending in, witness the grandiose opera houses of Europe, or even New York's Lincoln Center. But to be successful, exhibitionist buildings require harmonious shape and ceremonial setting. Arthur Erickson's hall suggests neither. The building, with its 40,000-square-foot circle of mirror glass, has been likened to a mushroom, a chunky inverted cupcake, and a ballerina's tulle tutu. Its siting, smack on the sidewalk along the side-street entrance and defending itself behind a moat-like sunken court on the main street, is anything but grand and inviting.

The interior is something else again. Arriving, mingling, and departing in a lobby of ramps, mirrors, and high spirits is as glamorous as listening to a performance in the elegant and muted champagne-coloured auditorium. Here Erickson has made moulded concrete balconies look like sensuous sculptures of floating marble, and dangling plastic acoustic disks like luminous effervescent bubbles. Why then, in this de luxe showcase, put two tiers of seats *behind* the stage, like last-minute rush seating, destroying the dramatic sight of performers spotlighted alone? Like the final design

7 *Royal Alexandra Theatre*

9 *24 Mercer St.*

for the exterior, this may have been an economy-minded alteration, and like the exterior, it is a compromise that didn't work. The public, and the Toronto Symphony Orchestra and Medelssohn Choir whose new home this is, are the poorer for it.

6 Union Building, 212 King St. W. (office building and warehouse), Darling & Pearson, 1907.

Built for the Canadian General Electric Company, this is a fine and pleasing example of the miniature Classical Revival palaces which prosperous manufacturers were erecting all along King Street in this period [see also Walk 4]. The moulded terracotta window surrounds, stone portico, and elaborate pressed-metal and terracotta cornice are all remarkably well preserved. The 1980s mansard added on top is suitably subtle.

7 Royal Alexandra Theatre, 260 King St. W., John M. Lyle, 1906-07.

Built as a series of three graduated boxes (lobby, auditorium, stage), it is the small first box that catches the eye with elegant balustraded windows and paired pilasters sparkling across the front beneath a crested stone parapet—a fine legacy of Lyle's Beaux-Arts schooling and his Carrère & Hastings' training. The Royal Alex was rescued from demolition in 1963 and restored to its original Edwardian splendour by merchant-restaurateur "Honest Ed" Mirvish—a rare gesture for a rare building.

8 Originally Eclipse Whitewear, 322-324 King St. W.
(See Walk 4/9.)

9 Originally John B. Reid house, 24 Mercer St., possibly John Tully, 1859.

One of Georgian Toronto's few Greek Revival strays. Characteristic Greek Revival features are the attic-storey half-windows in a "frieze" above the ornamental brackets (which likely terminated an applied cornice), the crisp rectangular windows with stone lintels and sills, and the sharply cubistic look to the whole. When built, this was the only brick house on a street of one- and two-storey roughcasts. Reid was a lawyer; his neighbour one door down was John Tully, a well-known architect.

10 Originally Verral Cab, Omnibus and Baggage Transfer Co./formerly Pilkington Bros. Ltd., 15-31 Mercer St. (originally stables), Langley Langley & Burke, 1878; addition, David B. Dick, 1894; factory and warehouse addition, Burke Horwood & White, 1909; office building addition, 1938-39.

Pilkington Brothers, manufacturers of "Polished Plate and Window Glass, Plain and Bevelled Mirror Plates, Rolled Plate, Fancy Cathedral, Colored Glass etc.," came to Mercer Street in the early 1900s, first occupying the two-storey brick stables building to the east, later enlarged with a four-storey addition. The real excitement, however, is the two-storey Art Moderne office building they appended in 1939. Befitting a maker of glass, it boasts a streamlined glass-block exterior and the best mirrored Art Deco lobby in town.

12 *Clarence Terrace*

11 50–52 Peter St. (double house), 1833–34; remodelled as school, c. 1880; remodelled as cartage company, c. 1930; remodelled with additions, Thomas Marzotto, 1988–89.

No. 50–52, an exceptionally large red-brick rectangular-windowed Georgian double house, has figured prominently in Toronto history. Records reveal it was built by the provincial receiver-general, George Crookshank, who had an estate a little south at the foot of Peter Street, then the last street in the west of town. Many illustrious tenants rented these two semi-detached houses located near the early parliament buildings, including statesman Edward Blake [see 12/14c] and other judges and lawmakers, before the neighbourhood slipped into decline. In 1878, Mrs. Mary Nixon conducted a ladies' boarding and day school here, eventually taking up both no. 50 and 52. It's likely the third storey was added then. Dr. Bernardo's Homes, an agency for destitute children, took over in 1915, and the 1930s saw possession by a storage and cartage company. The most recent remodelling is "preservation" at its most peevish: Crook-shank's fine double house is virtually lost inside a glass façade to the front, concrete extension to the rear, and brick addition to the top. The Toronto Historical Board was not amused.

Clarence Square is a lovely, Londonish 19th-century oasis still holding firm in the midst of a 20th-century manufacturing mêlée. Its English pedigree is legitimate, for it was laid out by British military engineers in the 1830s as the focus of a posh new residential district, which unfortunately came to little.

12 Clarence Terrace, 5–16 Clarence Square (twelve units of original sixteen-house row), 1879–80; renovated, Joan Burt with Douglas Swan, 1964.

Building did not begin around Clarence Square until the late 1870s, and these middle-class row houses are certainly less than the 1830s planners had in mind. Nevertheless, the long Second Empire ensemble was distinguished enough to make it a candidate for one of Toronto's first downtown rehabilitation projects—a program that still looks good, though today's purists may not be as keen about the grey stucco and solid windows as renovators were in the 1960s.

18 *488 Wellington St. W.*

19 *517 Wellington St. W.*

13 Originally Steele, Briggs Seed Co. Ltd., 49 Spadina Ave. (factory and warehouse), Sproatt & Rolph, 1911.

This neighbourhood began skidding from residential to industrial in 1911 when the Canadian Pacific Railway built a spur to Simcoe Street. Steele, Briggs were among the first manufacturers to take advantage of the change, building this unobtrusive five-storey red-brick commercial box. Growers and importers/exporters of seeds since 1873, the company is still in business, though no longer in this building.

This stretch of Wellington Street West, originally called Wellington Place, was designed as a stylish residential avenue formally linking Clarence Square to Victoria Square. It never became as fashionable as expected, however, and beginning in the 1910s it was built over with factories.

14 Originally Smith/Powell house, 422-424 Wellington St. W., 1889.

A last reminder of Wellington Place's residential intentions, this mighty Queen Anne double house still manages to hold its own amid factories and warehouses. Originally at no. 422 was John C. Smith of Cooper & Smith Boots and Shoes [for Mr. Cooper, see 11/22a]; at no. 424 lived Charles Powell, manager of the Temperance Colonization Company, whatever that was.

15 Monarch Building/originally Croft Building, 436-438 Wellington St. W. (factory), 1914.

William Croft & Sons manufactured something enigmatically listed as "small-wares" in the city directories, but there is nothing small about this precise six-storey red-brick cube with its simple but well-placed stylized classical ornamentation.

16 Originally Houlding Knitwear, 462 Wellington St. W. (factory), Yolles Chapman & McGiffin, 1916.

More "modern classical" decoration with smooth stone base and the slimmest of capitals at the top fifth floor to turn piers into square columns. Very handsome.

Draper Street, chock-a-block full of winsome mansard-roofed and Bay-n-Gable houses, is one of the city's little-known treasures. Just starting to be gentrified.

17a 20-24, 26-28, 30-32 Draper St. (one triple and two double houses), 1890.

Late-blooming Bay-n-Gables, with solid, squarish forms derived from Queen Anne style. Closely built and looking at first blush like a row, these are actually three separate buildings.

17b 4-6, 8-10, 12-14, 16-18 Draper St. (four double houses), 1882-83.

Second Empire cottages, 1½ storeys high and sweetly detailed with bay windows and panelled brick.

20 *Victoria Memorial Square, CN Tower*

17c 3–5, 7–9 Draper St. (two double houses), 1882–83.

More of the same.

17d 11–13, 15–17, 23–25, 27–29 Draper St. (four of original five double houses), 1881–82.

The expansive Second Empire mansard provided much needed space to attic bedrooms in small houses such as this, not to mention an eye-appealing roofline. (Transmogrified no. 27 seems a bit perverse, but hopefully under the ersatz beats a heart of Napoleonic fervour.)

18 Originally M. Granatstein & Son Ltd., 488 Wellington St. W. (warehouse), Hynes Feldman & Watson, 1918.

A Commercial Style stunner much talked about in its day. Decoration is minimal but bold and incisive. Note how piers rise to little Aztec observatory domes instead of cutting off at the roof, for example. In 1918, the real news, however, was those steel-sashed windows occupying the entire space between piers on all four sides of the open-plan building.

19 Copp, Clark Publishing Co., 495 Wellington St. W. (factory), Wickson & Gregg, 1912.

Copp, Clark Publishing Co., 517 Wellington St. W. (factory), Wickson & Gregg, 1928.

Smooth red brick for two early Commercial Style buildings, one decked out in classical detail, the other lightly streaked with stylized Gothic. Unfortunately, the industrial sash windows—which originally set the tone for both these buildings— have been removed.

20 Victoria Memorial Square, located near Fort York and the centre of the large military reserve which ran from Peter to Dufferin Streets, was the site of the military cemetery. Today, some of the old romantically weathered grave markers form a base for a stirring memorial in the centre of the square dedicated to those who served in Upper Canada in the early years. Created by Walter S. Allward, it was erected in 1902 at a time when the original square had already been cut in half by the advance of Wellington Street.

This is as good a place as any to peer at another Toronto commemorative—the CN Tower. The CN Tower is a monument to monumentality. It was built to serve the function of being the tallest free-standing (no guy wires) structure in the world and, at 1,815 feet, it is. Not everyone is impressed. We are fascinated by bigness and the enormity of the effort involved in creating bigness, but with similar urban landmarks knifing the sky around the world, the result does not seem to be the engineering marvel it was when, say, the Egyptians constructed the pyramids, or Mr. Eiffel put up his tower in Paris in 1889. Many Torontonians are embarrassed by the touristy boosterism. The tower's owners, the federal Canadian national railroad and telecommunications agency, argue that "almost" all the height is necessary for adequate communications facilities (transmitters of five television stations and FM radio are located on the mast). Critics don't like the unimaginative shape of the tower either. But then the Eiffel Tower was also criticized in its day, called a "gigantic black factory chimney, overpowering with its barbaric mass ...." One wonders.

Walk 4: King Street West

1a Originally Mason and Risch Piano Manufactory, 642 King St. W., 1879.

Mason and Risch projects a neat, conservative, almost domestic image with its four storeys of carefully laid red Georgian brick picked out with yellow-brick quoins, relieving arches over windows, and string courses between storeys. The company, with a combined annual output of 4,000 instruments, was one of ten in Toronto making pianos and organs in the 19th century. This enduring little manufactory employed 45 hands in woodworking, varnishing, and finishing; actions and keyboards were imported. The building, which still uses its original dray entrance, was heated by coal-fuelled steam and gas-lit. Mason and Risch are going strong in Scarborough; they only quitted this site in 1950.

1b 636 King St. W. (office building), c. 1955.
Sandwiched into the site with no acknowledgement of neighbours, two-storey no. 636 is typical of the post-World War II building boom when architects were crazy to try out new technologies and materials: glass curtain walls, black-glazed brick, decorative *red* panels. Actually, the most interesting feature here is the stylish *retardataire* Art Deco steel stair rail glimpsed inside.

2 Originally Beatty Manufacturing Co., 600 King St. W., Chadwick & Beckett, 1900–01.
Subtle red-on-red brick with crisp details woven in like a piece of fine damask worthy of Mr. Beatty's bindings, tapes, and braids which were made within. The Classical Revival composition proceeds with a base of horizontally rusticated brick for the first storey; a middle of two many-windowed floors; followed by a top attic storey decorated with columns blocked in brick; the whole finished off with a deep cornice, elliptical pediment, and finally, a flagpole. A majestic little factory.

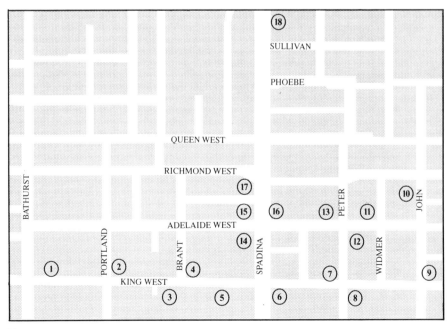

2 *600 King St. W.*

5a *469 King St. W.*

3a Originally Toronto Silverplate Co., 572 King St. W. (factory), 1882; ground-floor addition, 1983.

One-hundred-years old and tarnished by time and tampering, the Toronto Silverplate factory nevertheless manages to raise a bright gabled red-brick head above the street. The building was ahead of its time in 1882, its neat many-windowed façade suggesting the multiple-sashed loft look of the next century.

3b Originally American Watch Case Co., 511 King St. W. (factory), George W. Gouinlock, 1893.

Polished Richardsonian Romanesque in a pliant design with vertical banks of deep-set windows diminishing in size upward. The self-supporting cast iron, framing and making possible large first-floor windows, is handsomely decorative and out in the open here.

4 Originally E. C. Gurney & Co. Stove Foundry, 500–522 King St. W., 1873.

Behind the greige paint of no. 522 breathes Mr. Gurney's High Victorian stove works. This was the first factory on King Street West, its various buildings covering more than half the block. An experienced hand was at work here, enlivening the façade with a buoyant moulded impost course following the curve of windows and an extravagant brick corbel table at the cornice, the whole punctuated by brick piers every two windows. The resulting bas-relief is infinitely more successful than the fretful phony front now covering no. 500–510.

5a Originally Dominion Paper Box Co., 469 King St. W. (factory), George W. Gouinlock, 1903; addition, J. Francis Brown, 1907.

Classical Revival, but with too many fussy light-coloured "stone" details, all looking as if they were pasted on to the red brick. In contrast to the busy base, the attic storey and roof line look unfinished, as if the architect were worn out by the time he got up there. No denying, though, the charm of winged cherubs decorating Ionic capitals at the entrance.

5b Originally Toronto Lithographing Co./formerly Stone Ltd. Lithographers/formerly Salada Tea, 461 King St. W. (factory), Gouinlock & Baker, 1901.

A firm red-brick factory building with Classical Revival details massively and organically in place. Though the Dominion Paper Box building [4/5a] is a failure compared to this, the two together—joined by common scale and a decorative iron fence—do create a Beaux-Arts *environment entire*, something sadly missing on most of the street.

8 *355 King St. W.*   **10** *Turnbull Elevator Co.*

6 Originally Warwick Bros. & Rutter Publishers, 401–409 King St. W. (factory), George W. Gouinlock, 1905; addition, 1913.
The ubiquitous Gouinlock, calmed down with an elegant composition using less flashy brownstone details on red brick in place of the bright white beloved of the Beaux-Arts. The 1913 addition is almost an exact copy, except it is two storeys too high. Warwick Bros. & Rutter were printers, bookbinders, and stationers.

7 Originally National Drug & Chemical of Canada Ltd., 388 King St. W. (factory), 1941; altered, 1986.
No. 388 was one of Toronto's rare low-slung Art Moderne buildings, suavely steering rounded corners, see-through glass blocks, smooth unornamented walls, and horizontal ribbons of windows into a streamlined whole (see photo, page 20). Sad to say, renovation has managed to mangle the flow. Those responsible for the new verticality—the three-part windows, for example—should be cited for building abuse.

8 Originally Canadian Westinghouse Ltd., 355 King St. W. (factory), Bernard H. Prack, 1927; addition, Prack & Prack, 1934.
This looks like a very daring design with the building visually cut through the centre by the company name in lovely 1920s lettering. Actually, it was a case of necessity for the top three storeys were a later addition, but that should do nothing to diminish our admiration for the rich terracotta that separates the vertical banks of windows into showy picture frames.

9 Originally Eclipse Whitewear, 322–324 King St. W. (factory), Gregg & Gregg, 1903; renovated, A. J. Diamond & Barton Myers, 1970.
Probably more and bigger window openings than Toronto had ever seen in 1903, fenestration *is* the design here. This building, wherein was first manufactured ladies' and children's underwear, was notable for its two-foot-thick brick bearing walls with very large interior timber supports and heavy mill-construction timber flooring (revealed afresh with the 1970s "exposed services" renovations). Someone should have told new owner Ed Mirvish that consistency—i.e., the feckless signature white paint—is the hobgoblin of little minds. Is his Royal Alex Theatre [3/7] next?

10 Turnbull Elevator Manufacturing Co./ originally John Burns Carriage Works, 126–132 John St., 1886; addition, Wickson & Gregg, 1906; additions, 1909, 1919.
Turnbull Elevator moved into John Burns's factory building in 1900 when it consisted only of the smallish Renaissance Revival structure to the south, and they've been there ever since, now occupying several additions as well. This factory, with heavy base and weighty piers, seems plainer and more substantial than kindred buildings such as those on Front Street East [1/12]. Still, the three different window treatments, one for each floor, and ornate cornice with segmental pediment are true to picturesque form. In 1900, this was one of four companies in Toronto making elevators.

14 *Darling Building*

15 *Tower Building*

11 Manufacturers Building, 312–318 Adelaide St. W. (loft), Baldwin & Greene, 1927–28.

Hailed at the time as the "greatest year in the history of Canadian construction," 1928 saw hundreds of open-plan Commercial Style loft buildings spring up. Flat roofed and forthright, their primary feature was abundant light-giving windows. (In buildings where decorative fenestration seemed desirable, it usually appeared only on front or corner walls, with large industrial sash covering less conspicuous sides.) Stylistic touches were minimal, here no more than a streamlined steel and glass door and some Deco lettering.

12 Commodore Building, 317–325 Adelaide St. W. (loft), Benjamin Brown, 1929.

The metal-frame technology that made tall, many-windowed Commercial Style buildings possible, in large part determined their aesthetic as well—precise, regular, clean, and mechanistic. In the hands of the best architects, however, this characteristic façade was never less than human: the scale of the individual window was that of the worker inside; the base storeys that of the pedestrian on the street. Here Benjamin Brown has created a fine, inviting, vaguely historical—and thereby reassuring—ground storey and portal. A graduate in architecture at the University of Toronto in 1913 and member of the Ontario Association of Architects, Brown designed many of the distinguished loft buildings in the garment district in this period.

13 Capitol Building/originally Hobberlin Building, 366 Adelaide St. W. (loft), Yolles & Rotenberg, 1920.

In 1920, this seven-storey structure for the garment industry was one of the ten largest loft buildings ever constructed in Canada. It remains among the most outstanding. It used steel columns on side walls and the lightest possible brick bearing piers on front and rear to provide the absolute maximum of light—90 percent of the walls are glass. It also featured four high-speed elevators, a sprinkler system that lowered the insurance rate, one of the fastest construction periods on record—78 days—and terracotta Gothic detailing handsomely capping the top. (Sad to say, ghostly new glazing has taken some of the life out of it.)

14 Darling Building, 96–104 Spadina Ave. (loft), 1909.

One of the area's first lofts, this nine-storey Commercial Style building is remarkable for its balanced vertical/horizontal design with large regularly placed steel-sash windows and practically no ornament, not even a cornice. The battlemented projections at the corners might be rooks on an empty chess board.

15 Tower Building, 106–110 Spadina Ave. (loft), Benjamin Brown, 1928.

A carefully composed loft building with design devices marshalled to accentuate the ten-storey height: tall windows with long narrow triple sash; shallow unbroken piers rising the height of the building; spikey Gothic ornament around the

18 *241 Spadina Ave.*

entrance; and of course that landmark pyramidal-roofed tower (really a disguise for roof-top mechanicals).

16 Balfour Building, 119–121 Spadina Ave. (loft), Benjamin Brown, 1930.
Another loft by Brown, this time 12 storeys spelled out with geometric zigzags, fans, and lettering of the Art Deco vocabulary. The building was named to honour British Prime Minister Arthur James, the Earl of Balfour, who in 1917 pledged his government's support for a Jewish homeland in Palestine.

17 Fashion Building, 130 Spadina Ave. (loft), Kaplan & Sprachman, 1927.
More vague medieval details for the garment makers, especially in the lobby and heavily encrusted base storeys. Above rise six floors of what might be mistaken for a yellow-brick apartment building. The individual street-level shop entrances here, as on other loft buildings, were not there in the beginning.

Many more 1920s and 1930s lofts can be viewed in the blocks to the north on Spadina, plus one of the finest early 20th-century small factory buildings Toronto ever produced.

18 Originally Consolidated Plate Glass Co. Ltd., 241 Spadina Ave. (factory), William Steele & Sons Co., 1910; altered, 1982.
This small five-storey factory is something to feast your eyes on, one of the city's most appealing creations. There is a rousing firm base with lovely iron grill-work at the entrance, a simple smooth shaft, and most wonderful elaborate cornice, all the more extraordinary for having been done in moulded and carved warm red brick and terracotta. These were materials of the picturesque, but the idiom here is clearly classical. This building is also a lesson in sympathetic alteration: stores have been slipped into the ground floor, but without cutting big jarring windows in the façade, thereby amending hardly at all Spadina Avenue's most stunning architectural essay.

Area III

Walk 5: Yonge Street

Area III

Yonge Street is Toronto's principal thoroughfare, th geographic centre from which the city's cross street busily march east and west, and—with subway, automc biles, and pedestrians—the most-trafficked route to the downtown core. It is also something of an architectural wonder, for unlike similar concourses in major urban centres, Yonge Street (at least the part we are concerne with) retains a narrow width and preponderance of 19th-century buildings of Victorian scale and sensibility The reasons are many, none definitive, none planned.

At first Yonge Street was not part of the town at all. Conceived as a military road leading north to Lake Simcoe and the wilderness beyond, it was named by the provincial governor, John Graves Simcoe, for Sir George Yonge, the British secretary of war. Simcoe had his military corps, the Queen's Rangers, start blazing th path soon after they arrived in 1794. The Rangers begar in the vicinity of present-day Eglinton Avenue and moved north. In 1796, William Berczy and his contingent of German settlers also worked on the road (which they needed to connect them with their promisec lands near Markham), including the stretch south from Eglinton to just north of Bloor Street. There was a section south of Bloor, but it was too swampy for vehicular traffic and was commonly referred to as the "road to Yonge Street." This extended only as far soutl as Queen Street, below which were private lands. Traffi therefore had to detour on the way in and out of town to avoid both swamp and private property.

Yonge Street was finally opened through to the bay sometime after 1812, and the wet section firmed up witl gravel in 1828. Below King, it began to sprout warehouses and banks [*AREA IV*], and north of King, retail shops. By mid century Yonge Street had become second only to King Street in importance, but a far second it seems. A writer in the 1870s commented that "the buildings on King Street are greater and grander than their neighbours on Yonge; the shops are larger and dearer; and last, but not least, King Street is honored by the daily presence of the aristocracy, while Yonge is given over to the business of the middle-class and the beggar."

Yonge Street's architecture was indeed motley, and it stayed that way. Squarish two- and three-storey Georgian commercial blocks built in the 1850s and '60s were joined by more flamboyant four- and five-storey structures in sundry styles popular in the city as the 19th century wore on: Renaissance Revival, Second Empire, Queen Anne, Richardsonian Romanesque.

Nevertheless, at the turn of the century, Yonge began to supplant King as Toronto's equivalent of Main Street, abetted in party by King's declining Old Town neighbourhood [*AREA I*]. Finally when two long-time Yonge Street dry goods merchants, Robert Simpson anc Timothy Eaton, risked altering traditional small-store

Commercial blocks on Yonge Street looking north from Queen in a motley of styles, c. 1885.

shopping patterns and successfully recast their enterprises as large single-stop "departmental" stores, Yonge Street's primacy was ensured. In the next decades, smart specialty shops such as Fairweather's [5/1c] and Ryrie Brothers [5/3b] also appeared on the thoroughfare. These sophisticated new stores were not overly large, however, having little inclination or wherewithal to challenge the scale and scope of Simpsons and Eaton's, which by the 1920s had come to own a good deal of Yonge Street property. At the same time, branch banks were cropping up on corners and vaudeville theatres mid block, but these too were only three or at most four storeys high. (The theatres were deceptive, for their low narrow Yonge Street frontage was only a corridor which led to the bulk of the building situated on the street behind.)

Yonge Street north of College Street was not at first part of this downtown commercial development. This stretch of Yonge was dotted with handsome landscaped residences, much like those on nearby Church and Jarvis Streets [AREA VII]. As more and more houses were built in those areas, however, Yonge Street began to assume the role of neighbourhood shopkeeper, with row houses and shops going up apace for grocers, druggists, and the like. In the 1860s and '70s, these were two- and three-storey late Georgian designs. The following decades saw slightly larger, more obviously commercial buildings constructed, but there was still a residential overtone that attracted, for example, fraternal lodge buildings and dentists' offices.

Yonge Street at Carlton, 1900, still featuring a quiet residential overtone.

An attempt to change all this was made with the opening of Eaton's College Street department store in 1930 [5/24]. Eaton's had banked that College Street could replace Queen as Toronto's major east/west shopping thoroughfare and to this end donated land around their new store for the widening of Yonge and College and the curving of the latter to meet Carlton in an easy jog. The city widened Yonge Street one more block south to Gerrard and it was anticipated the widening would continue. The Depression and then World War II stalled such plans, however. In the meantime, Bloor Street [AREA IX] was quietly developing as *the* carriage trade avenue; after all, it was that much closer to the "carriages"—to Rosedale, the Annex, and Forest Hill. And the status addresses for office towers had become Bay Street [AREA IV] and University Avenue [AREA V], which connoted finance and government. Finally, there was suburbanization, which simply ignored downtown. Yonge Street stayed much as it was, except it was now one continuous Main Drag, for along with shoppers on foot, there were automobiles (a staggering number of them on weekend evenings). To the window signs designed for pedestrians were added larger ones, elevated and perpendicular to the street, to entice motorists.

The next phase of the Yonge Street saga began in the 1960s when Eaton's announced plans for large-scale redevelopment of its property between Queen and Dundas Streets. The initial schemes were utterly insensitive to the cityscape and heritage concerns, and would have levelled not only the old Eaton's buildings, but Old City Hall [7/11], the Salvation Army building, Trinity Square, and Holy Trinity Church [5/13a]. Resulting public clamour delayed the Eaton Centre project for years and necessitated a string of architectural firms and any number of plans before an acceptable design was achieved. In the meantime, uncertainty encouraged many legitimate storekeepers to move away from Yonge Street and buildings deteriorated from indifferent maintenance. Sleaziness set in, along with big buzzing signs to advertise it. Yonge Street had become Toronto's Strip.

The completion of the first phases of Eaton Centre [5/12], renovation of Simpsons [5/7], Confederation Life [6/14], and a few other major buildings, as well as political pressure and new laws (no more body rub parlours), have to some extent cleaned up Yonge Street. But the enthusiasm for signs—ever-larger areas of moulded plastic, pressed metal, and glowing light—continues. In some instances, a building's entire façade is sign, as at no. 347, Sam the Record Man [5/19].

Main Street, Main Drag, Strip—Yonge Street seems comfortable performing all these roles. It is nothing if not hospitable, and soon it seems likely the thoroughfare will be asked to also host the giant structures it has up to now had little interest in. A tourist mega-complex, incorporating hotels, theatres, and restaurants, is planned for the easterly block between Queen and Shuter, for example. How graciously such new guests are made to fit in with the existing liveliness and human scale will be a real measure of Toronto's urbanity.

Walk 5: Yonge Street

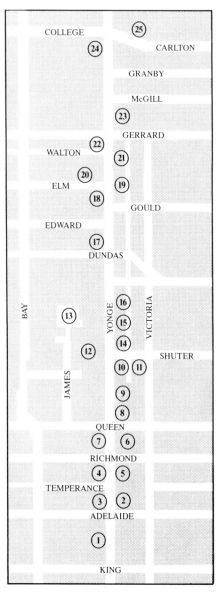

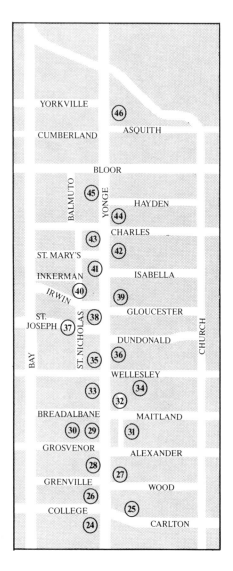

1a Originally Hiram Piper & Brother Hardware/formerly Toronto World Newspaper, 83 Yonge St. (commercial block), probably Joseph Sheard, 1857; addition, Charles J. Gibson, 1895.

Yonge Street's earliest shop buildings were simple Georgian boxes, most now gone. The next generation of stores aspired to a more eleborate and commercial look. No. 83, almost the last of this genre, surely stood out even in its own day. The cut-stone capitals on the pilasters and radiating brick lintels over the windows rank among the city's finest. The Pipers became prominent businessmen and politicians, and one family member ran Toronto's first zoo. The city's third morning daily, the conservative *Toronto World*, took over the building in 1892.

1c *100 Yonge St., 1980*

3a *118 Yonge St., 1980*

1b 85–107 Yonge St. (commercial block and office building), Page & Steele, 1988–89.

To accommodate this new mega-development, an eclectic but harmonious mix of shop buildings dating from the 1850s through about 1915 was torn down. The façade of no. 85, pledged for retention, was nevertheless demolished and then "replicated" as part of what we now see. Though the architects' attempt to recreate original scale and eclecticism is praiseworthy, new is new.

1c 100 Yonge St. (office building), Quadrangle Architects, 1988–89. Incorporates front façade of Fairweather Building, Charles S. Cobb, 1918–19.

102–104 Yonge St. (commercial block and nursery school; part of Scotia Plaza), Webb Zerafa Menkes Housden, 1988–89. Incorporates front façade of Bible & Tract Society Building, Gordon & Helliwell, 1885–86; altered, Burke Horwood & White, 1910.

Champions of one-wall preservation call it "better than nothing"; detractors, "façad-ism," "façadectomy," or "façadomy."
We preserve old buildings to impart a sense of the past, which should help us to understand the present and future. But what precedent, what inspiration is provided by these token remnants slapped onto new construction? What consolation? Are we reminded here of Robert Fairweather's ultra-sophisticated ladies' fine furs and specialty shop, of a time when coming downtown to buy a pair of gloves, not to mention a fur, was an act of some occasion? Is there anything left to signal the Bible & Tract Society's rousing

mansarded, proselytizing presence on 1880s Yonge Street? And how can we begin to appreciate the sense of place these structures once evoked when their historic neighbours have been levelled? As to their *new* neighbours, no. 100's 15-storey granite-clad office tower looks to be spare and elegant, making the attached historic façade all the more incongruous. New construction behind the façade of no. 102 will fortuitously be hidden; no. 104 is pathetic Post-Modernism. As seen in this whole sequence, façadism makes for superficial preservation; flawed new design; and an incoherent, deceptive streetscape.

2a Lumsden Building, 2–6 Adelaide St. E.
(See Walk 6/10a.)

2b Ontario Heritage Foundation, 8-12 Adelaide St. E.
(See Walk 6/10b.)

2c 20 Adelaide St. E.
(See Walk 6/10c.)

3a Originally Holt, Renfrew & Co., 118 Yonge St. (commercial block), James L. Havill, 1910.
This has long been an illustrious address for Toronto commerce. In the late 1800s, Ryrie Brothers displayed their jewellery here before moving north one block [5/3b]. Then the Savoy Tea Room fortified shoppers with scones and Salada from this corner. In 1909, the Savoy was demolished to make way for Holt, Renfrew, another purveyor of furs in these

7 *Robert Simpson Co.*

precincts. Their impressive four-storey brick emporium is still with us, its classical cornice gone but its stalwart double chimneys still standing sentinel along Adelaide Street.

3b Originally Ryrie Brothers/formerly Ryrie-Birks/formerly Henry Birks & Sons, 134 Yonge St. (commercial block and office building), probably Burke & Horwood, 1905; altered, Burke Horwood & White, c. 1925; altered, Horwood & White, 1950–55.

Rather inelegant today, but upper storeys still reveal some turn-of-the-century classical dignity and display windows a little '20s Deco verve. A few classical and Deco details remain in the interior as well.

4a Dineen Building (Shorney's Opticians), 140 Yonge St. and 2 Temperance St.
(See Walk 6/12a.)

4b Aikenhead's Hardware, 17–19 Temperance St.
(See Walk 6/12b.)

5 Originally R.S. Williams Building, 145 Yonge St.
(See Walk 6/13.)

DEMOLISHED

6 Confederation Square, 2–14 Richmond St. E.
(See Walk 6/14.)

7 Robert Simpson Co., 160–184 Yonge St. (department store), Edmund Burke, 1894; rebuilt after fire, Burke & Horwood, 1895–96; addition, Burke Horwood & White, 1907; addition, Horwood & White, 1923; restored and entrance remodelled, 1977.

Richmond/Bay addition (store and office building), Chapman & Oxley, 1928.

Simpsons Tower, 401 Bay St. (office building), John B. Parkin Associates with Bregman & Hamann, 1968–71.

Robert Simpson began selling dry goods in Toronto in 1872, moving to this corner in 1881 where his two-storey business could claim 13 clerks and two display windows. Today Simpsons' buildings blanket the block. The most stunning is

8a *Bank of Montreal*

the six-storey structure at Queen and Yonge which was put up as the city's first entry in a daring new enterprise: the high-rise "departmental" store. Not only was the idea revolutionary, so was the architecture—a polished native-son translation of avant-garde modes then being explored in the United States by Louis Sullivan and other express-the-steel-skeleton pioneers. The steel skeleton bore the weight of the building and permitted open interior spaces as well as large light-giving windows—perfect for a department store. Torontonians loved Simpsons, not least for its new-fangled escalators, baby-minding facilities, "writing rooms, waiting rooms, and toilet rooms." With the 1907 nine-storey addition along Queen Street, it became the largest retail establishment in Canada.

The 1928 Art Deco addition at Richmond and Bay Streets influenced store-wide alterations, including creation of a broad interior concourse lined with Moderne display windows. A remnant of this glamorous indoor street exists today as the hexagonal vestibule inside Simpsons' Richmond/Yonge entrance, its Deco metals and etched glass of interest still.

Parkin's 1971 tower at Queen and Bay is unassuming, with only an illuminated top floor to set it apart from other high-rises. Happily its aluminum and glass skin was not stretched around the other buildings as planned. Instead, Simpsons had restored the older exteriors (while handsomely updating interiors), and adroitly opened up the main Queen/Yonge entrance to create a store as handsome today as it was 90 years ago.

8a Bank of Montreal, 173 Yonge St., Darling & Pearson, 1909–10.

Classicism gone "sweet," via wreaths, cartouches, and garlands edging round-arched windows and entry. This Edwardian approach was seldom historically precise, but it did look stylish, especially when detailed in terracotta by Doulton & Company.

8b Elgin Theatre/originally Loew's Yonge Street Theatre and Wintergarden Theatre, 189–191 Yonge St., Thomas W. Lamb with Stanley Makepeace, 1913–14; interior remodelled, H. N. Stillman, 1934.

Swathed in Adamesque plasterwork, gold leaf, and red plush, Loew's Yonge Street originally exuded vaudeville house opulence galore. The upstairs Wintergarden was even more enticing: one of the world's first "atmospheric theatres," decked out with a ceiling of real leaves, supporting columns in the form of tree trunks, and trellised walls. After minor remodelling, the Yonge Street was able to continue as a motion picture house; the movies, however, closed the Wintergarden (who needs atmosphere in a dark room?). These theatres are now owned by the Ontario Heritage Foundation, which will open them as live theatre houses again.

12 *Eaton Centre*

8c Originally J. F. Brown Furniture/formerly Heintzman Hall, 193 Yonge St. (warehouse and commercial block), Henry Simpson, 1903; altered, J. Wilson Gray, 1910.

This is probably the closest Toronto ever came to the spacious, crisp vocabulary of Frank Lloyd Wright and his followers. Buff-coloured brick, three-part Chicago windows, horizontal banding, and the pendant-like ornament dangling down the front are all lessons learned from the Prairie School master.

9a Originally Canadian Bank of Commerce, 199 Yonge St., Darling & Pearson, 1905.

The hefty columned and pedimented portico of this branch bank is similar to that on the Commerce's Montreal headquarters. Such family resemblances were bankerly attempts to create recognizable images, in this case a very solid and earnest mien.

9b Toronto-Dominion Bank/originally Bank of Toronto, 205 Yonge St., E. J. Lennox, 1905-06.

A small lavish Pantheon, squeezed onto the site with the same energy as is that colossal model of antiquity in Rome. Lennox's interest in organic, integrated detail seems to have deserted him in this florid number (really more Greek than Roman), but one can't help admiring the panache with which he goes at it. If the bank doesn't look entirely prudent, it certainly looks prosperous.

10 Originally John Catto Co. Ltd., 221–223 Yonge St. (two-unit commercial block), 1920.

Very modern for its day, there is no question here where the supporting steel piers are located, nor that the wall of glass is a curtain hung between those piers, bearing no weight but its own and admitting as much light to the interior as possible.

11 Massey Hall, 15 Shuter St., Sidney Rose Badgley with George M. Miller, 1889-94.

Massey Music Hall was built as a gift to the city by farm machinery magnate Hart Massey. Today looking the worse for wear and safety regulations which have draped ever-larger fire escapes across the front, the hall is still renowned for its superb acoustics. Actually, the flat-chested red-brick exterior never had any great architectural pretensions; it was criticized from the first (chauvinistically, in part, because the plans were by an architect practising in Cleveland). Long the home of the Toronto Symphony Orchestra, Massey Hall (the word "Music" was dropped in the 1930s when "music hall" began to convey more salacious interests) continues as a redoubtable Toronto institution even with the symphony ensconced elsewhere [see 3/5].

12 Eaton Centre, Queen to Dundas St., Bay to Yonge St., Bregman & Hamann with Zeidler Partnership, 1975–ongoing. (E. L. Hankinson with Parkin Millar & Associates for Eaton's store; Parkin Partnership for Bell Trinity Square.)

Completed in 1979, Phases I and II of Eaton Centre embrace the six-storey

13a *Church of the Holy Trinity, c. 1875*

buff-porcelain T. Eaton flagship department store, two hexagonal mirror-clad high-rise office towers, and a five-level shopping/office arcade. Phase III will introduce more buildings, including residences, facing on Bay Street as well as around a newly designed Trinity Square (the ten- and 15-storey towers of Bell Trinity Square have been completed).

To most people, however, Eaton Centre spells the glass-roofed arcade—the world's busiest indoor shopping complex. The Yonge Street exterior of this two-block-long phenomenon is a high-tech version of the street itself, with the scale, colour, and signs of Yonge Street all visually re-created in the slick vocabulary of the exposed-services, industrial school of architecture. One thing the exterior does not re-create is Yonge Street's lively welcome. Up close, the menacing aspect of tech looms, with doors that don't open, balconies leading nowhere, and spare display windows that have the unused look of obsolescence. This is all fake front; the real action is inside the arcade. There pedestrian life energetically reappears on stacked indoor streets animated by trees, benches, even widened junctures or "cross streets." A festive atmosphere pervades, and for many people just being in Eaton Centre is an event. The actual shops are mostly humdrum, although the multi-arched, two-level store designed for Henry Birks is not bad. All in all, there are telling contradictions at Eaton Centre, but in that too it shares the legacy of commerce and of Yonge Street.

13a Church of the Holy Trinity, Trinity Square, Henry Bowyer Lane, 1846–47; Sunday school addition, William Hay, 1856–57.
Set against Eaton Centre's high-tech glitter, stout, corner-buttressed Holy Trinity looks more impressive today than it did even a century ago when it was the centrepiece of Macaulaytown, a working-class community on the outskirts of Toronto. The church was built with funds donated anonymously by a woman in England who, the story goes, greatly admired Toronto's visiting Bishop Strachan. Rather plain Gothic Revival, Holy Trinity nevertheless manages a good measure of finesse thanks to its cruciform plan and distinct chancel—supposedly a requirement of the gift, as was free seating. How misguided was Eaton's plan to demolish this church; it forms one of the most appealing vistas in the centre.

13b Church of the Holy Trinity rectory, Trinity Square, William Hay, 1861.
Looking as comforting and picturesque as a Victorian parsonage should, the rectory and garden of Holy Trinity today provide a setting of enviable repose for lunch-hour office workers and weary shoppers.

13c The Rev. Henry Scadding house, originally at 10 Trinity Square, William Hay, 1857; third-floor addition, c. 1875; moved and restored, 1977.
Henry Scadding was the first rector of Holy Trinity and well-regarded author of two early histories of Toronto. His eclectic Georgian/Gothic house originally stood east of the rectory where Eaton's

16a *Pantages Theatre, 1920, front and rear elevations*

store now sits. The mansarded top floor containing Scadding's study was probably added in the 1870s; its intriguing balcony is said to have commanded a view down to the harbour and all around the town in the reverend's day.

14 Ryrie Building, 229 Yonge St. (commercial block and office building), **Burke Horwood & White, 1913–14**; ground floor and basement remodelled for Muirhead's Grille and Cafeteria, **Norman A. Armstrong, 1934.**

A dull five-storey brick cube saddled with all the tentativeness architects were experiencing at the beginning of the 20th century in efforts to amalgamate new methods and ideas. (The project was actually a modernizing re-do of two existing 1891 structures.) This building was an investment venture for Ryrie, Toronto's major jeweller, whose own store was farther south on Yonge Street [5/3b]. The Silver Rail Tavern on the corner is named for its jazzy Art Deco stair rail, a remnant of Muirhead's Grille and Cafeteria, which graced this space in the 1930s.

15 Originally Art Metropole Ltd., 241 Yonge St. (commercial block), **Mitchell & White, 1911.**

Yonge Street's narrow frontages were parcelled out with modest Georgian shops in mind. When later builders wanted to put much taller structures on the same narrow lots they were hard put to create buildings of similarly pleasing proportion and grace. Mitchell & White admirably met the challenge here, however, treating their four-storey curtain wall like a blank canvas on which to sketch elaborate and lovely windows and classical details. Inside, Art Metropole ran a picture gallery, blue-printing facility, and art supply store.

16a Pantages Theatre/originally Pantages Theatre/formerly Imperial Theatre/formerly Imperial Six Theatre, 263 Yonge St. to Victoria St., Thomas W. Lamb, 1920; remodelled, Mandel Sprachman, 1972; restored, David K. Mesbur, 1988–89.

The vicissitudes of the Pantages echo those of many theatres in North America in the 20th century. When built, it was the largest vaudeville house in the British Empire, a lavish place of plush upholstery and Adamesque detail. Then with the advent of talkies and huge Depression-era audiences, it became a grand picture palace. When double features disappeared and large crowds with them, it was divided into six theatres fronted by a sleek "stripscape" façade of video machines on Yonge Street. A real estate battle of two giant distributors had it severed in half for a time until one of them acquired the whole for come-full-circle restoration to a legitimate theatre once again.

16b Originally Childs Restaurant, 279–283 Yonge St. (commercial block), **John C. Westervelt, 1918.**

Childs was a large New York chain with a reputation for simple but stylish premises where the average wage-earner could sit down to a speedy, reasonably priced meal. Designed by Childs's New York architect, this Toronto branch (there

19 *347, 349, 351 Yonge St., 1984*

were eventually three) was typical of Manhattan restaurants of the era with its many windows and bold white terracotta face. In 1918, Yonge Street office workers and shoppers would have found the interior equally direct and sparkling.

17a Atrium on Bay, 320 Yonge St. to 595 Bay St. (commercial block and office building), Page & Steele, 1982–83.

The Atrium on Bay—actually three atriums (atria?) on Bay, Dundas, Yonge, and Edward—is a good place to examine this skylighted phenomenon which wells the interior of so many multi-storeyed office buildings these days. In early Roman architecture, an atrium was an outdoor courtyard in the centre of a house. Modern-day architects have adapted the concept as a way to increase the number of naturally lighted offices available in a building. Because they don't have a view of the out-of-doors, workers toiling in core offices are presented with a decorated atrium view, often one replicating nature, using trees, plants, waterfalls, etc.

The possibilities for creating dramatic and convivial indoor public spaces in these atriums are great, but not many Toronto developers have risen to the challenge. (The Royal Bank atrium is a banking hall; the A.E. LePage Building atrium, an information booth!) With their trees, seating, food facilities, shops, and inviting traffic courses, the Atrium on Bay atriums have the right social idea, though their execution does leave something to be desired. The place looks a little tacky.

On the other hand, the exterior of this three-unit structure—two 13-storey cubes connected by one of nine storeys—is extremely handsome. Files of polygonal bays are clad in silvery mirror glass, creating a sculptural composition with a kaleidoscope of reflected images that mitigates against the boredom of many glass-clad buildings.

17b 335–339 Yonge St. (three-unit commercial block), 1888–89.

Rowdy red brick with late Victorian variety and flair fancifully planting a Renaissance tower to guard the corner site. In 1889, no. 335 was a butcher shop; no. 337, a variety store; and the corner, no. 339, an undertaking establishment over which operated the Empress Hotel. The hotel business must have been better than the funeral business, for the next year the Empress occupied the entire corner.

18 Toronto Camera Centre/originally Thornton-Smith Co., 340 Yonge St. (commercial block), John M. Lyle, 1921.

One of Toronto's most amiable small shop buildings. Lyle won first place in an Ontario Association of Architects' competition for this "modernized Italian" treatment, complete with red-tile roof. The large display windows on two floors were a requirement of the client, an antiques dealer and interior decorator.

19 Sam's, 347–349 Yonge St.; A&A, 351 Yonge St. (commercial blocks), all c. 1870–80; all remodelled, c. 1970–80.

The sign as architecture, and very good signs they are.

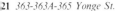

21 *363-363A-365 Yonge St.*   22a *Toronto-Dominion Bank*

Named for a solitary elm tree that once dominated the corner at Yonge, Elm Street is still of interest for its landscaping. An attractive row of recently planted ash trees and the widened and handsomely paved sidewalk make this a very appealing detour.

20a Barberian's Steak House, 7–9 Elm St. (double house), 1868.

Georgian, the first style to enjoy favour in colonial Toronto, featuring a carefully proportioned, formal façade invigorated with picturesque round-arched windows and a brick cornice. These were built as dwellings, but the style served equally well for shops, a few of which still survive on Yonge Street.

20b Arts and Letters Club/originally St. George's Hall, 14 Elm St., Edwards & Webster, 1891; interior remodelled, Sproatt & Rolph, 1920.

A late Victorian smorgasbord with enough Old World historicizing to make members feel right at home. (The St. George's Society was founded to foster British traditions in Canada.) Inside is the *pièce de résistance*, a wood-panelled Tudor dining hall with great baronial fireplace and fanciful heraldic crests invented in 1920 for members of the Arts and Letters Club.

20c Elmwood Club/originally YWCA, 18 Elm St., Gordon & Helliwell, 1890–91; rear addition, André Ostiguy, 1982.

A rich and rotund Richardsonian Romanesque club building with fine detail outlining the mass. The new addition in

the rear for a women's health and social club is first-rate: large, but not overpowering; modern, but not incompatible.

21 363-363A–365 Yonge St. (three-unit commercial block), Denison & King, 1890.

Part Moorish, part Richardsonian Romanesque, part Commercial Style, this is among the most attractive façades on Yonge Street. Despite the variety of windows and all kinds of applied ornament—don't miss the terracotta lions' heads at the second-storey cornice—the overall impression is one of harmony and splendour.

22a Toronto-Dominion Bank/originally Dominion Bank, 380 Yonge St., John M. Lyle, 1930.

In the 1920s and '30s, John M. Lyle was the architectural master of the Canadian branch bank, his Moderne designs dressing up street corners all across the land. Working within the banks' mandate for classical detailing but eschewing Greek acanthus leaves and Roman ox skulls, he tried to create a distinctively Canadian "modern classical" idiom and crowned his columns with stylized native produce and his pilasters with Deco cows and geese. This bank was highly praised when built, but there was concern that it would be "mutilated" when the "inevitable" widening of Yonge Street proceeded south of Gerrard. The inevitable has yet to happen, and Lyle's bank continues to spill forth its Canadian cornucopia undisturbed.

24 *Eaton's College Street, as proposed 1928*

22b Originally Gerrard Building, 385–395 Yonge St., Sproatt & Rolph, 1924.

This is one of the earliest of many fine, firm commercial/office blocks with which Sproatt & Rolph adorned Toronto in the 1920s and '30s. No doubt spurred by anticipated development of Eaton's College Street [5/24], they drew on splendid proportions and simple carved detail to create a "modern Gothic" building of great presence on this corner. First tenants included IBM and the Olympia-Gerrard bowling alley, this latter replaced in the 1950s by Bassells Restaurant, a popular family eatery of the era.

23 401–405 Yonge St. (three-unit commercial block), 1873.

Much taller than Georgian-style predecessors and employing all the facile shadow-producing details of the Renaissance Revival, these row shops must have appeared very grand in their day.

24 College Park/originally Eaton's College Street, 444 Yonge St. (department store and office building), Ross & Macdonald with Sproatt & Rolph, 1928–30.

Apartment house and office building additions, Allward & Gouinlock, A. M. Ingleson & Associates, Joseph Bogdan, Webb Zerafa Menkes Housden, 1977-ongoing.

The seven-storey 1920s Art Deco building is a fraction of the 40-storey-plus skyscraper that Eaton's expected would replace its hodgepodge of Queen Street stores, workrooms, and offices. The Depression and construction difficulties interfered and the building never proceeded

further than this, but monumental scale, superb materials, and distinctive detailing made it an architectural event anyway. (Contemporary writers dubbed the stylized half naturalistic/half classical ornament "floral Ionic.")

When the first stage of Eaton Centre opened in 1977 [5/12], Eaton's sold this facility to developers who have turned it into individual shops and offices. Much of the Art Deco interior in the shopping levels designed by French architect René Cera is in place, as is an extraordinary seventh-floor Deco concert hall and restaurant created by another Frenchman, Jacques Carlu. Adjacent new buildings on the College Park site are huge but forgettable, neither enhancing nor detracting from the 1920s centrepiece, although the ice rink/reflecting pool in the rear is quite handsome.

25 Toronto Hydro-Electric System, 14 Carlton St. (office building), Chapman & Oxley, 1931–33.

Built as the head office of the city's hydro system in what was considered Toronto's up-and-coming business section, this ten-storey skyscraper was the last word in suave Deco styling. Even today's glassy towers are little match for the smoothness of its meticulously laid limestone face, sleekly graced with Moderne bas-reliefs and four female heads peering precipitously down over the sidewalk—the building was in fact planned to be much higher. Inside, Hydro ran a Home Institute featuring lectures on "the use of electrical appliances for interested housewives."

26a *2 College St.*

College Street, like University Avenue
[*Walk 7*], was originally a private road
leading to the university grounds, complete
with pre-emptive gate at Yonge Street. The
area south of this road was the site of the
Hon. J. B. Macaulay estate built in 1841. It
later served as Bishop Strachan School
from 1870 to 1915, at which time Eaton's
acquired the land for their new store
[*5/24*]. To the north another solitary villa
dominated until 1881 when the O'Brien
house was constructed [*5/26d*]. The university removed its gate in 1882 and officially
conveyed the thoroughfare to the city as
a public street in 1889.

**26a Originally Oddfellows' Hall, 2 College
St. (commercial block and office building),
Dick & Wickson, 1891–92.**

The Independent Order of Odd Fellows
owned and met in this building, and there
certainly is a feeling that mystical rites were
carried on behind the elaborate chateau-
roofed, Gothic-ornamented fourth storey.
"Going to lodge" was a popular leisure
activity in Toronto at the turn of the
century, with scores of branches of various
fraternal societies located around town,
some in money-making edifices such as
this.

**26b Originally Upper Canada Bible Society,
14 College St. (office building), Gordon &
Helliwell, 1910.**

The Bible Society unabashedly borrowed
an Ionic portico from the repertoire of
the banks to front this building. The
office block atop is a later addition.

**26c Superior Loan/originally Canadian
Order of Foresters, 22 College St. (office
building), William R. Gregg, 1908–10.**

Comfortable buff-brick Classical Revival,
following no rigid rules but coming
together in a pleasantly dignified structure. The quasi-residential character of
College Street at this time seemed to
appeal to fraternal societies.

**26d Originally Lucius R. O'Brien house/for-
merly Jenkins Antique and Art Galleries, 32
College St., possibly Darling & Curry, 1881;
remodelled as commercial block thru to 23
Grenville St., Sproatt & Rolph, 1917; street-
front addition, c. 1975.**

**26e Metropolitan Toronto Police Headquar-
ters, 40 College St. (office building), Shore
Tilbe Henschel Irwin Peters, 1987–88.**

If it had been sited as a flags-flying beacon
atop a mountain, cascading down its glassy
office boxes to succour citizens in the city
below, Metro Police Headquarters might
have worked as a kind of Big Brother
protectorate. But on this tight, complicated
lot, the design looks chaotic and inflated.
The entrance is stagey (especially with that
enshrined remnant from a former building
here), and the interior a glitz of high-style
lobby devices: atrium, waterway, bridges,
broadloom. Seeming to be accessible is one
thing; setting up as a Sheraton hotel quite
another.

28b *488 Yonge St.*   **29a** *496 Yonge St.*

27 Loew's Westbury Hotel/originally Hotel Torontonian, 489–493 Yonge St., Page & Steele, 1956.

An artful postwar high-rise with pattern parts hung on a steel cage in the eye-catching systems mode that Page & Steele—with the help of their controversial British emigrant partner Peter Dickinson—were unleashing in the 1950s. Dickinson's expressive, sometimes flamboyant structures are often denigrated these days, but they should be appreciated as among Toronto's first inventive forays into International Style modernism, the heroic departure from which architecture is still evolving.

28a 480 Yonge St. (detached house), 1864.

Initially the home and office of a "corn dealer," this was among the first buildings erected on Yonge Street north of College. In the 1870s, it served as an inn, and the unusual pliant-looking stone quoins and window surrounds may have been affixed at that time.

28b Originally site of Firehall No. 3, 488 Yonge St., James Grand with William Irving, 1870–72.

The shingled Victorian tower rising above glitzy stores below is all that remains of an 1870s firehall, but even after 110 years, it is still the eye-catcher on this stretch of Yonge Street. In some firehalls the tall towers were used to drain and dry hoses, but here the picturesque pile with bell-cast roof and open beaming was solely a reassuring civic landmark.

29a Bank of Montreal, 496 Yonge St. (originally two-unit commercial block), 1886–87; remodelled as bank, 1928.

A very distinguished commercial building for 1887, with imposing pedimented roof dormers and assured details. No wonder the Bank of Montreal was attracted in 1928, a period when branch banks seemed to be taking over half the street corners.

29b Originally Clarke's Buildings, 502–508 Yonge St. (four units of original six-unit commercial block), 1860.

These were the first three-storey brick shops on this stretch of Yonge. One unit served as a boarding house, another a saloon, and the others as places of work and living for an organmaker and stonecutter. The showy Renaissance Revival pediment and cornice window heads are later additions intended to give a second generation of stores a sophisticated, up-to-date character.

29c 526–528 Yonge St. (two-unit commercial block), McCaw & Lennox, 1881.

Looking very ancient to our eyes with its frilly towered mansard, this pair of shops in fact replaced a brick house put up on the site only ten years prior. Yonge Street's burgeoning commercial potential made rebuilding desirable, and the flashy Second Empire style was just the ticket to attract customers. The first shopkeepers sold furniture and stationery and lived upstairs. This is one of E. J. Lennox's first-known buildings, designed early in his career when he was in partnership with William F. McCaw.

30 *YMCA of Metropolitan Toronto*

30 YMCA of Metropolitan Toronto, 20 Grosvenor St. thru to 15 Breadalbane St., A.J. Diamond & Partners, 1984.
Sleek with rosy-red brick, trim stonework, smooth glass blocks, and bold muscular shapes, the new YMCA building glows with health and vigour. The materials and aesthetic are assuredly those of the 1980s, but this is no flimsy Post-Modern exercise. It is a challenging, meticulous balance of cubes and spheres, flat planes and curves, all rendered with extraordinary skill. The building is large but never overwhelms its through-block site, and the composition is as intriguing viewed from the rear street or even through the parking lot from the side street as from the front. One has the feeling this building will still be winning kudos 100 years from now.

31 Originally William Galbraith house, 37 Maitland St., 1868.
Flour merchant Galbraith built himself one of the most radiant houses in Toronto. He must have liked it too, for he lived here 30 years, 1868–1898. The well-laid courses of red brick, handsome chimneys and hipped roof, the contrasting yellow-brick quoins, string courses, and relieving arches all make for a beautifully articulated and civilized composition.

32 527–529 Yonge St. (two-unit commercial block), 1876.
531 Yonge St. (commercial block), 1883–84.
533 Yonge St. (commercial block), 1880–81.
535 Yonge St. (commercial block), 1881–82.
These five shops were variously owned and rented out by the four Sharpe sisters, spinsters whose family had held the land hereabouts from before 1834. While the different styles may point to varying proclivities among the Misses Sharpe, they also indicate the period's rich architectural repertoire: Second Empire, Renaissance Revival, Queen Anne. In 1883, shopkeepers were, south to north: a druggist, spice dealer, furniture dealer, butcher, and marble worker.

33a 546–550 Yonge St. (three-unit commercial block), 1885–86.
Instead of peas in a pod, we have a nimble orchestrated arrangement here, focused on a very decorative centre unit. The cut stone, terracotta, and rich brick detailing are typical of the Queen Anne ornament that began to grace the city in the 1880s.

33b 564–568 Yonge St. (three-unit commercial block), 1874.
Decorative brick quoins at corners and raised arches over windows; otherwise it's our old friend, the simple dormered-roof Georgian row shop. First tenants were a cabinetmaker, tailor, and grocer.

34 Originally "Somerset House" (residence of Hon. James Cox Aikens)/formerly J. W. L. Forster house, 27 Wellesley St. E., 1876; apartment house addition, Jerome Markson, 1979.
Wellesley Street was originally lined with fashionable residences, much like those on nearby Church and Jarvis Streets. One of the few to survive the later redevelopment of this busy thoroughfare was Somerset House, the home of James Aikens, secretary of state under Sir John A. Macdonald until 1873 when the Pacific Scandal booted the Tories out of power. When Sir John A. returned to Ottawa in 1878, Aikens rejoined him. It was in the interim that the Hon. Aikens built himself this tall-gabled country-looking manor. Later it was the home of Canadian portraitist J.W.L. Forster, who had married Aikens's daughter. Today it fronts a popular pub and neatly appended low-rise apartment building.

35a 570–584 Yonge St. (eight-unit commercial block), 1876; nos. 574, 578, 580 rebuilt, c. 1890.
Appearing only two years after the reticent Georgian trio to the south [5/33b], this buoyant Second Empire octet must have made quite a splash on Yonge Street in 1876.

35b 588 Yonge St. (commercial block), 1879.
Big roof, little window; but the bracketed cornice is lively enough to handle any deficiencies. Charles Barnsley, a wig-maker, had these premises in 1879.

35c 590–596 Yonge St. (four-unit commercial block), 1888.
There's no question here that these are anything but commercial buildings, and very smart and sprightly ones too with crisply detailed cornice and pilasters. An unusual touch is the alternating wide and narrow bays and windows. In 1892, no. 596 was a "locksmith and bell-hanger's" store and works.

36 565–571 Yonge St. (four units of original six-unit commercial block), 1887–88.
Today bleakly "blackwashed," this commercial block was once as ruddy as its Richardsonian Romanesque details suggest. Such a weighty look was not much used for shops; its massive rough-cut ashlar and deep-set windows were just too expensive for speculative builders.

St. Joseph Street, like other saintly thoroughfares in this neighbourhood, was laid out and named by John Elmsley, a wealthy landowner and Roman Catholic convert. The rise of sandy ground which dominated his holdings and accounted for the curve of St. Joseph Street as well as Irwin Avenue (originally St. Charles) one block north, he called Clover Hill. In the early 1850s, Elmsley donated a choice parcel atop Clover Hill for the building of St. Basil's Church and St. Michael's College [8/36a].

37a 6–14 St. Joseph St. (five-house row), 1879.
A proud and brassy Second Empire quintet, built when the mansard-roof style was at the peak of fashion in Toronto. Usually Second Empire houses were of yellow brick, not the red seen here, but all the other rich effects are typical.

37b *5 St. Joseph St.*

37e *Cloverhill Apartments*

37b Originally Marmaduke Rawlinson Storage, 5 St. Joseph St., Wickson & Gregg, 1905–07.

Hiding behind the appearance of a medieval fortress, with broad walls, few windows, pointy portal, and metal bars, this meticulous four-storey brick warehouse surely inspired confidence among those who stored goods with Mr. Rawlinson. Long in the express, cartage, and storage business, Rawlinson was a two-time Toronto alderman and relative of cabinetmaker Lionel Rawlinson [5/42]. The company continues in business in suburban Mississauga.

37c Originally Marmaduke Rawlinson Storage, 11–19 St. Joseph St., Dick & Wickson, 1895–96; fourth-storey addition, A. Frank Wickson, 1898–99.

This earlier Rawlinson warehouse, built farther from Yonge Street amid residences, utilizes a pleasing stepped arrangement, large windows, and decorative detailing for a more neighbourly look.

37d Canadian Music Centre, 18–20 St. Joseph St. (double house), 1892.

A Queen Anne/Romanesque medley in a form that Toronto made its own, especially in the Annex [Walk 19]. This harmonious gable/turret duet now enlivens Chalmers House, the Canadian Music Centre.

37e Cloverhill Apartments, 26 St. Joseph St., J. Gibb Morton, 1939.

Art Moderne curves, steel-sashed windows, and glass blocks in ornamental forms that are finding favour anew.

38a 620–632A Yonge St. (eight-unit commercial block), 1877.

A Second Empire octet of shops by builder Thomas Bryce, also responsible for those at 570–584 Yonge Street one block south [5/35a]. Details such as cornice brackets are identical in the two rows, indicating that standardized parts and the speculative builder's penchant for cost-cutting repetition is nothing new.

38b 634–644 Yonge St. (six-house row), 1860; remodelled as commercial block, c. 1870–80; nos. 642 and 644 renovated with rear addition, G.S. Baldine Associates, 1983–84.

Wooden sills and six-light sash windows betray the early date of these simple two-storey brick row houses, built in a period when Yonge Street was still partly

39 *Gloucester Mews*

residential. They had all probably been converted to shops by 1880. The most noteworthy thing about this row, however, is the recent rehabilitation of the two corner units. Not only has their Yonge Street façade been meticulously renovated with specially made yellow brick duplicating the original and a Mr. Submarine outlet somehow unobtrusively inserted, but a bit of Post-Modern verve has also been produced for the Irwin Avenue face in the form of an eclectic classical portal leading to second-floor offices. First rate.

39 Gloucester Mews/originally Masonic Hall, 601 Yonge St. (commercial block and office building), 1888; renovated with rear addition, Adamson Associates, 1972.

For many years the tallest building on Yonge Street north of Dundas, this handsome red-brick and stone five-storey structure stands as one of Toronto's best late 19th-century commercial blocks, bringing dignity *and* energy to the street. The whole building is well represented by the complicated yet clean-looking wood and iron shopfronts with rope-turned posts. The architect has not been identified, but there were a number of designers practising in the city in this period capable of such refined work, and the Masons—Toronto's second largest fraternal group after the Orangemen—no doubt could afford the best. They met here in a hall on the fourth floor for 33 years until 1921 when a new Masonic building was

constructed at Davenport and Yonge.

Adamson Associates' immaculate renovation in 1972 included a Bay-n-Gable house on Gloucester Street sensitively linked to the Masonic Hall by a modern but complementary two-storey glass structure. Though still called Gloucester Mews, the shops-around-a-courtyard mews plan was early abandoned to allow Fenton's Restaurant to fill the glass-covered interior space as well as the old house. The architects occupy the top floors.

40a 6–14 Irwin Ave. (five-house row), 1892.
A Queen Anne quintet nimbly grouped around a central tower for added pizzazz on this curved street.

40b Originally See & Duggan Motors, 18–30 Irwin Ave. (factory), Mathers & Haldenby, 1929.

Though now virtually abandoned, this industrial-looking 1920s affair is the sort of building a clever Post-Modernist might turn into trendy flats. Ford dealers See & Duggan had their primary showroom nearby on Yonge Street; in 1931, they advertised this building as a "Ten-Minute Car Wash."

40c 45–63 St. Nicholas St. (ten-house row), 1884–86.

Situated on what was once a back lane, this delightful row of small houses—each with a name marker for a different tree or flower—is unknown to most Torontonians. Bargeboarded Bay-n-Gable was unusual for such a long terrace, but it works just fine.

41 *664-682 Yonge St.*

44 *675 Yonge St.*

41 664-682 Yonge St. (ten-unit commercial block), E.J. Lennox, 1883.

These shops rival Lennox's gracious houses, except that they are splendidly bigger and bolder. Architecturally, they mark a short but interesting interval between a time when Yonge Street stores could pass for houses and when they became no-nonsense commercial fronts. Lennox designed this row for the Scottish Ontario and Manitoba Land Company, a name recalling days when developers forthrightly spelled out their auspices—no "Fairviews" or "Cadillacs."

42 Originally Schomberg Furniture/formerly Rawlinson Furniture, 647-649 Yonge St. (two-unit commercial block and factory), 1878; altered c. 1910.

An 1870s three-storey factory showroom brought up to 20th-century snuff by new crisp yellow-brick cladding and an oak-panelled shopfront, all done for Lionel Rawlinson, one of Toronto's leading furniture makers and dealers at the turn of the century.

43 Coles Book Store/originally Robert Barron Provisions, 726-728 Yonge St. (two-unit commercial block), 1889.

Lavish Richardsonian Romanesque arches and terracotta detail plus an elegant Queen Anne oriel window hanging over the corner. Toronto provisioners—they sold liquor and wine as well as foodstuffs in those days—often seemed to command the handsomest building on their blocks.

44 Originally Postal Station F, 675 Yonge St., Samuel G. Curry, 1905-06.

Though more than 75 years have elapsed since its construction, this three-storey former post office is still one of the most imposing buildings on Yonge Street. In contrast to the thoroughfare's more usual brick, terracotta, and ground-level entries, here massive rock-faced ashlar, cut-stone Ionic columns, and a stepped-up first floor were used to signify the postal station's important civic function. The early 1900s date would also have dictated such formal, classical architecture.

45a Burger King/originally Rising Sun Hotel, 752-754 Yonge St., 1890.

A bold pediment abloom with finials to set the hotel apart from surrounding stores.

45b Uptown Theatres/originally Loew's Uptown Theatre, 764-766 Yonge St. thru to Balmuto St., Thomas W. Lamb, 1918; remodelled, Mandel Sprachman with Marvin Giller, 1970.

This is said to have been the first theatre in Canada to sport a V-shaped marquee. A clock sat at the apex telling unreliable time and inside was a 2,000-seat vaudeville house. Sprachman and Giller turned it into five separate cinemas: three fill the old auditorium; two more are squeezed into what was the original stage. These latter two, entered from the street behind and appropriately called Backstage 1 and 2, are enlived with some of the best supergraphics in town. Lamb's lovely plasterwork is in place in the original foyer, now brightly painted.

46 *Metropolitan Toronto Library*

45c 774–776 Yonge St. (two-unit commercial block), 1884–85.
This is surely among the most flamboyant commercial buildings on Yonge Street. Windows grouped in pairs within busy brick frames dangle from a dazzling brick-corbelled cornice like pendants from a richly encrusted necklace. Earliest shop tenants sold shoes, and, yes—jewellery.

45d Stollery's, 790 Yonge St.
(See Walk 18/13).

Yonge Street north of Bloor Street was part of the independent Village of Yorkville [see AREA IX], dominated by the Yorkville Town Hall which stood just north of Yorkville Avenue until 1942. The block between Cumberland and Yorkville Avenues is notable for its Victorian variety—look to the upper floors—and as a relatively intact parcel of 19th-century streetscape. In the 1880s, the shops purveyed groceries, dry goods, drugs, and the like. No. 828 was a Bell Telephone Company branch (telephones had been introduced in 1877); no. 842 was a hardware store.

46 Metropolitan Toronto Library, 789 Yonge St., Raymond Moriyama, 1973–77.
From outside, the Metropolitan Toronto Library is good urban architecture. Not great, but good. Its stepped mass, setback from the street, red brick, and ground-level "shop window" façade all fit in with surrounding buildings, never overpowering them. Yet the building *is* big. And that's really what keeps it from being truly distinguished. One remembers a friendly hulk of a library on Yonge Street, but it's difficult to recall just *exactly* what it looks like. Perhaps unobtrusiveness can go too far after all. Not hard to guess that this was a compromise design.

We do remember the interior though because it's so different from most libraries. It is bright and inviting with warm orangey carpeting, light wood tables and carrels, wicker-backed chairs, and everywhere plants. There are large banners proclaiming subject areas, glass elevators, ponds and running water, and a one-million-foot fibre sculpture by Aiko Suzuki. The place is laid out with a variety of "environments" from quiet solitary carrels to communal lounge areas. The public loves the library; architects are divided—Buckminster Fuller called it a preposterous Sheraton lobby; and librarians bemoan nooks and crannies that allow lazy "scholars" to rip and snitch rather than to read and write. (As a reference library, virtually no books may be checked out.)

Area IV

Walk 6: Financial District

Area IV

T oronto's financial district is an indefinite square half-mile or so at the base of the downtown core. From the intersection of King and Bay Streets—its symbolic as well as geographic centre—rise the monolithic namesake towers of four of the country's five national banks (the fifth looms two blocks south). Marching out from this mythic crossroads are buildings containing offices of the country's major loan, trust, insurance, brokerage, and legal firms as well as the largest stock exchange—in short, the repositories of the financial claims of the nation.

Toronto's financial and business community early made this area its own. Though the city's first bank, the Bank of Upper Canada founded in 1822, was in the Old Town of York [*AREA I*], banks that followed were centred not in Old Town nor New Town [*AREA II*], but here in this midtown district amid wholesale commercial establishments whose credit-based enterprise had created a need for banks in the first place. In the single year 1845, three distinguished stone-faced bank buildings were constructed in the vicinity of Wellington and Yonge Streets: the Renaissance Revival Bank of Montreal [see 6/1], the Greek Revival Commercial Bank of the Midland District [6/4], and the Neo-Classical Bank of British North America [see 6/5]. These were followed in the 1850s and '60s by other banks, erected side by side with equally handsome commercial warehouses, and what was then a new building type, office chambers. (Heretofore offices had been located on upper floors of Georgian houses and shops.) Once concentrated along Wellington Street just east and west of Yonge, almost all these structures have been lost to us, but vintage photographs reveal they were an architecturally rich array and included palatial edifices for such as the Toronto Exchange (1855), Edinburgh Life Assurance Company (1858), Ontario Bank (1862), Bank of Toronto (1863), Ontario Chambers (1866), and Royal Canadian Bank (1871).

With no real product to sell other than "image," bankers and other owners of offices placed great emphasis on an imposing and up-to-date look for their buildings, scrapping outmoded ones with a rapidity unheard of for houses, churches, or civic structures. More to the point, as years went by, expanding business and rising land values set the stage for such buildings to be replaced again and again—no matter how fashionable or worthy—by ever-taller edifices providing greater floor area and larger rental income. (Technical barriers to tall buildings had effectively been removed with development in the United States of the wall-supporting steel skeleton in 1885 and the electric passenger elevator in 1887.)

Escalation of building height was not entirely foreordained here, however. True, by 1890, Toronto could point to four buildings dotted about the financial district that were each a remarkable seven storeys high:

the Canada Life Building on King Street West [demolished], the Board of Trade Building on Front Street East [demolished], the Canadian Bank of Commerce on King Street West [demolished], and Confederation Life on Richmond Street East [6/14]. And ten years later, the celebrated Temple Building [demolished] at Richmond and Bay rose to a headline-grabbing ten storeys. But the prospect of taller skyscrapers—a term coined in the United States some 20 years earlier—did not meet with unbridled enthusiasm, many critics voicing concern for sanitation, safety, and traffic. (Paris at the time had a limit of six storeys and London too spurned the new architectural giants.) In 1905, however, Toronto's city council finally assented to 15 storeys for the Traders Bank [6/6], as it did six years later for the Canadian Pacific Building [6/7]. Only then—with public acceptance—did the modern high-rise city really begin.

The design of Toronto's first skyscrapers followed the lead of the United States and traditions that dictated an orderly beginning, middle, and end to composition. Their form has been likened to the base, shaft, and capital of a classical column: weighty entrance floors provide the base, repetitive floors rising above are the shaft, and cornice-topped attic floors create the ornamental capital. Decoration of these early high-rises was classical too, with temple porticoes gracing many a façade. The theory seemed to be that conservative imagery would impart to the radical new structures a sense of permanence and humanity. Although Bay Street could boast the aforementioned Temple Building and the towered new city hall of 1899 [7/11], the geographic centre for the 1910s wave of skyscrapers was still Yonge Street, with the corner of King and Yonge soon to become Canada's busiest street crossing.

Canadian Pacific Building under construction adjacent to the Traders Bank on Yonge Street, 1912, the city's first two skyscrapers.

Toronto's next series of skyscrapers, those of the 1920s and '30s, had a quite different look. Critics had begun to question the validity of the richly sculpted classical column as a paradigm for tall buildings; the early towers did not adequately express their function, they argued. Architects responded by contriving structures that boldly announced their skyscraping verticality. Façades became smooth and taut, with windows stretched heavenward in dynamic strips uninterrupted by the heavy cornice which had served to emphatically terminate previous compositions. Some of the more adventurous buildings paraded picturesque stepped profiles to upper storeys, a design influence which originated in New York as a way of complying with that city's 1916 zoning resolution—America's first—restricting bulk in relation to height. Decoration too was influenced by New York, where the geometrical vocabulary of Art Deco was being explored along with abstract interpretations of classical, Gothic, and Romanesque motifs—all of which found their way onto Toronto skyscrapers.

This second wave of tall buildings did spring up on ripe-for-development Bay Street, and it was at this time that local boosters began to compare the thoroughfare with the canyons of Wall Street. Toronto high-rises did not entirely echo those of New York, however. None attempted the fantastic spires that were so exciting atop the most famous New York skyscrapers such as the Empire State, Chrysler, and Woolworth Buildings. On the other hand, these 1920s and '30s Toronto buildings were like their relatives in being firmly rooted at the lot line to provide definition, continuity, and scale to the street, a distinction that was as meaningful for life in the city as the new skyline they created.

Firmly rooted at the lot line, these skyscrapers help create the Bay Street "canyon."

Toronto's next important cycle of skyscrapers followed the post World War II International Style: flat, unadorned slabs of gargantuan proportion scored by layer upon layer of income-producing office floors. Toronto's first major entry was the Toronto-Dominion Centre [6/29], predictably followed by other modernist "skyboxes" clustered around the by-now emblematic crossroads of King and Bay: Commerce Court [6/28b], First Canadian Place [6/30a, /30b], and Scotia Plaza [6/27b].

Early formulas for the towering modernist box included showing it off away from the street in the middle of an open plaza. The wisdom of these wind-swept barren spaces, as well as the isolation of the buildings that sit on them, is being questioned by Late-Modernists concerned with the architectural context of urban life. By the same token, Toronto should examine the urbanist thrust of the below-street-level shopping malls which burrow underneath these buildings in complicated underground networks. However practical for winter-weary shoppers, these concourses effectively sap streetlife, leaving the mighty towers to stand alone against the sky—solemn and detached symbols of financial power in the city.

Walk 6: Financial District

Much is in flux in the financial district. It appears that entries 1–4 will soon form an "historic district" for new mega-development of this block (52- and 43-storey towers, 6-storey galleria). The Bank of Montreal [6/1] is slated to become the Hockey Hall of Fame; the Yonge and Wellington Street warehouses [6/2, /3] will be rebuilt as shops; the Commercial Bank [6/4] will be moved into the galleria! How successful these shuffles prove, both as preservation and as innovation, awaits completion of the project.

---

1 Bank of Montreal, 30 Yonge St., Darling & Curry, 1885–86.

This rich and lovely rococo gem is surely the most spirited, self-assured building erected in 19th-century Toronto. Put up in a prosperous period of national optimism, it abounds with vigorous stonework, grand plate-glass windows, and exuberantly carved trophies announcing verities to make the country great: Agriculture, Architecture, Music, and Commerce on the south side; Science, Industry, Literature, and Art on the east. The interior, considered "the finest of any banking institution in the Dominion" at the turn of the century, boasts a 45-foot-high banking hall topped by a vibrant stained-glass dome depicting more allegory: a dragon guarding gold from an eagle! The wing to the west housed the manager's office, boardroom, and private apartment. This bravado building, which replaced a restrained straight-fronted High Renaissance-style bank put up in 1845, was the Bank of Montreal's head Toronto office until 1949, then its most magnificent branch until 1982.

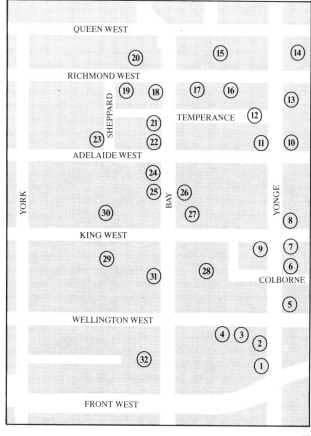

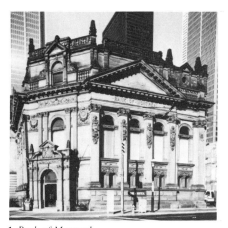

1 *Bank of Montreal*

5 *Bank of British North America*

2 36 Yonge St. (warehouse), 1844; altered, 1928.

38–40 Yonge St. (two-unit warehouse), 1852; no. 40 altered, c. 1865.

42–44½ Yonge St. (two-unit warehouse), 1850; altered, c. 1880–85.

Originally Argyle Hotel, 46 Yonge St., 1844; altered, Frederick H. Herbert, 1901.

Once repositories for dry goods and groceries, these are the earliest commercial warehouses to survive in Toronto. Originally all would have resembled the upper storeys of no. 38–40, with neat Georgian brickwork, precise stone lintels and sills, and simple brick corbel table at the cornice. Ground floors would have been similarly trim with small windows and a single office behind the front door. Later "modernizations" include a shop-front with cast-iron foliate columns to no. 40, a towered mansard to no. 42–44½, and "modern classical" stone facing and Doric columns to no. 36. No. 46 on the corner was the Argyle Hotel, built even earlier than the warehouses. Its classical reworking dates to 1901.

---

3 5 Wellington St. W. (warehouse), 1858–59.

7 Wellington St. W. (warehouse), Smith & Gemmell, 1871.

9 Wellington St. W. (warehouse), Smith & Gemmell, 1871; altered, Bond & Smith, 1919.

11 Wellington St. W. (warehouse), possibly William Hay, 1854–55.

Another bevy of warehouses, more ornamental than those at 36–44½ Yonge Street [6/2], thanks to burgeoning Victorian interest in florid, shadow-provoking forms: articulated cornices, foliated capitals, giant keystones, arcades, prominent sills, raised brick panels. Though all different one from another, and even with altered, industrially sashed no. 9, the height of the storeys and similar scale link these buildings in a harmonious ensemble.

---

4 Originally Commercial Bank of the Midland District/formerly Merchant's Bank/formerly Clarkson Gordon, 13–15 Wellington St. W., William Thomas, 1845.

Simple and solid, this dignified stone bank meticulously ornamented with refined Greek Revival details must have projected a persuasive image of security, solvency, and conservative stylishness in early Toronto. Designed by one of the foremost architects of the day, it is the second oldest bank in the city and a gracious last reminder of the 1840s and '50s when handsome buildings such as this lined Wellington Street. Originally, two pedimented doors graced the front. The entrance on the east led to the banking chambers, that on the west to a second- and third-floor apartment used by the bank manager. The accounting firm of Clarkson Gordon occupied the premises from 1913 to 1969.

5 Originally Bank of British North America, 49 Yonge St., Henry Langley, 1873–74; altered, Burke & Horwood, 1903.

Henry Langley brought the sophistication of Baron Haussmann's Parisian boulevards to Toronto with this richly decorated Second Empire bank of Ohio sandstone. Langley had introduced the French-derived style to Toronto with his 1866 Government House and it took the city by storm, but nowhere was the style's message of grandeur and power more appropriate than here, the most prestigious corner of the financial district at the time. (The segmentally pedimented doorway originally stood on Wellington, but after Yonge Street became the more important thoroughfare it was moved without any loss of splendour to that façade in 1903.) Recently cleaned and the sumptuous interior refurbished, the building is again an impressive sight on this corner. Langley's bank replaced a sedate Neo-Classical original erected in 1845.

6 Originally Traders Bank of Canada, 61–67 Yonge St. (office building), Carrère & Hastings with Francis S. Baker, 1905.

Designed by New York architects Carrère & Hastings, this 15-storey tower was Toronto's first real skyscraper. The architects would later create such extravagant Beaux-Arts masterpieces as the New York Public Library, but here they are responding to more cautious concerns with a conservative three-part classical composition that emphasizes horizontal movement and hides the uppermost floors behind a deep cornice, thus diminishing any visual sense of height. "A virtue of the projecting cornice for the people of Toronto," wrote a contemporary skyscraper-shy critic, "is that it will reduce the building in appearance to 12 storeys." The building was planned with the main banking hall on the second floor, a concept new to Toronto but thought to be very sensible, for the centrally located stairway led the public into the middle of the floor space and kept tellers together around the window-lighted perimeter. The hall was long ago demolished, but recent renovation has resurrected the dignified exterior of this benchmark tower.

7 Canadian Pacific Building, 1 King St. E., Darling & Pearson, 1911–13; altered 1929.

Built for the Canadian Pacific Railroad with a grand marbled and columned ticket office on the ground storey and floors and floors of rentable offices above, this building replaced the Traders next door as "The Tallest Building in the British Empire." At the time, it was one of some 200 structures in North America with 15 storeys or more. Frank Darling, who only 15 years prior had been doing such rococo palaces as the Bank of Montreal [6/1], seemed right at home with skyscraper style, creating a skeletal vertical composition that lifts the eye upward from a granite base via emphatic ribbons of double windows, piers, and corner end bays that rise uninterrupted through arcaded attic storeys until they are capped at the top by shapely cupolas. The original cladding was a more exuberant terracotta; it was replaced in 1929 with the bland limestone we see today.

8 Royal Bank, 2 King St. E. (office building), Ross & Macdonald (banking hall, Carrère & Hastings with Eustace G. Bird), 1913–15.

The 20-storey Royal Bank building (also called the Guardian Realty Building for its co-backers) quickly upstaged the Canadian Pacific structure as "The Tallest Building in the British Empire." Headquartered in Montreal, the Royal selected hometown architects Ross & Macdonald, who perhaps relied on Carrère & Hastings (credited with the interior of the banking hall) for the magnificent Corinthian-columned granite and limestone base. By contrast, the shaft is stark with plain windows set into smooth terracotta cladding and the crowning attic storeys hardly noticeable. (The top two were occupied by the Toronto Board of Trade which made use of the 20th-floor setback for a "lounging promenade.") One reached Carrère & Hastings' ornate main-floor banking room (with ornamented columns of black and gold and tables in a style borrowed from the Vatican) by walking up a short marble stairway. Steps descended to the savings department on the King Street side and to four retail shops on the Yonge Street elevation. This banking hall ensemble was demolished by the Royal in 1964 when they moved their Toronto headquarters to 20 King Street West, and 2 King became just another branch.

6, 7, 8, 9a *Traders Bank, Canadian Pacific Building,
Royal Bank, and Toronto-Dominion Bank, c. 1920*

**9a Toronto-Dominion Bank/originally
Dominion Bank, 1 King St. W. (office building), Darling & Pearson, 1913–14.**
The banking hall of this one-time head
office of the Dominion Bank (before it
merged with the Bank of Toronto) is not
to be missed. As one enters the gleaming
bronze and marble foyer, a wide central
stair flanked by majestic classically
inspired lamp standards leads dramatically down a few steps to the savings
department and its monumental centre-
stage vault. (At the time, this was the
largest vault in Canada and was said to
be protected by the heaviest doors—30
tons—ever built. The bank's literature
explained that the vault was equipped
with a telephone for anyone accidentally
locked in at night!) At the west end of the
foyer, off which originally was a ladies'
waiting room, an even more ceremonial
marble stair with bronze balustrade beck-
ons to the main banking hall on the floor
above. Two storeys high, ringed by an

18-pier arcade, and lined with sumptuous
marble from floor to ceiling, every detail
offers visual pleasure, from the ceiling of
soffited panels decorated with provincial
coats-of-arms to the brass cheque-writing
calendars.

The Dominion Bank, 50 feet shorter
than the Canadian Pacific Building across
the street, never achieved the "The
Tallest, etc. etc.," but its architectural
reputation was assured by the sophistication and beauty of its Renaissance Revival
design. Here classical detail has been put
in the service of perpendicular grace with
the delicate, precisely placed mouldings of
the shaft effortlessly leading the eye up to
handsome Ionic attic storeys. The granite
base is bold and firm, with windows and
King Street entrance set deep into the
wall. That entrance, a grand Doric
portico with columns 25 feet high and
three feet thick, should never have been
encased in such a trivializing glass front.

9a *Toronto-Dominion Bank*

10b, c *8–12, 20 Adelaide St. E.*

9b Originally Hiram Piper & Brother Hardware, 83 Yonge St.
(See Walk 5/1a.)

9c 85–107 Yonge St.
(See Walk 5/1b.)

9d 100 Yonge St.
(See Walk 5/1c.)

10a Lumsden Building, 2–6 Adelaide St. E., John A. Mackenzie, 1909.
In 1909, this extraordinary waffle was the largest concrete-faced building in the world, an unusual application in an era when structural steel skeletons were clad in brick or terracotta, with stone-looking concrete restricted to selected ornament. That the architect so dramatically expressed the decorative possibilities of his material with a modular repetition of husky blocked window surrounds makes the essay all the more interesting. Built as a profit-making venture by the Lumsden Estate of Ottawa, the rental units were identical, including striped awnings at each window and a wash basin in each office. Whether tenants could equally avail themselves of the swimming pool and Turkish baths in the basement is unknown. Such amenities are long gone, as is, unfortunately, the rich modillioned cornice which handsomely completed the original composition.

10b Ontario Heritage Foundation and Royal Canadian Academy Building/originally Canadian Birkbeck Investment & Savings Co., 8–12 Adelaide St. E. (office building), George W. Gouinlock, 1907–08; renovated, 1986–88.
Lavish classical pomp for a five-storey miniature treasure by one of Toronto's master Beaux-Arts evocateurs. Thanks to consummate restoration, the radiant exterior as well as rich banking hall and other interior spaces gleam anew for many of the province's cultural organizations which now inhabit the place.

10c 20 Adelaide St. E. (office building), Francesco Scolozzi and Page & Steele, 1987–88.
A dashing standout in the cityscape, no. 20 Adelaide is Toronto's best Post-Modern office building to date. A concise formalistic design of the early skyscraper kind (weighty base, long smooth shaft, ornamental crown), it is extraordinarily well crafted (though materials are not especially luxe they look to be), with artful contextual qualities to boot (the inimitably Toronto yellow of the implied stone, for example). With its polychromy, sleek surfaces and segmentally, curved pediment, the building has an air of the 1920s about it, but even more of the Renaissance (whose rigorous geometry was the touchstone for Art Deco). The lobby reinforces the concept: scenographic but humanistic; stately yet intimate.

12b *Aikenhead's Hardware*

13 *145 Yonge St.*

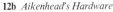

11a 11 Adelaide St. W. (office building; part of Scotia Plaza), Webb Zerafa Menkes Housden, 1988–89. Incorporates front façade of original John Kay Co./former Wood Gundy & Co., 36–38 King St. W., Samuel G. Curry, 1898; altered, Ferdinand H. Marani, 1922.

Its wealth of Renaissance Revival terracotta detail made the John Kay carpet store worthy of preservation. Critics are uncertain of the value of transporting its front wall here to the back of Scotia Plaza [6/27b], however, especially as the façade we see is a confusing mix of two architectural impulses anyway. The ground "floor" owes its staid investment-banker classicism to a 1922 remodelling.

11b Originally Holt, Renfrew & Co., 118 Yonge St.

(See Walk 5/3a.)

Temperance Street was laid out and named by Jesse Ketchum, a Toronto pioneer who owned the land from just north of King all the way to Queen between Yonge and Bay Streets whereon was located his profitable tannery and large house in the 1830s. A political reformer, temperance advocate, and generous philanthropist, he later donated much of his land to "worthy causes," including the Yonge Street tannery plot to the Bible & Tract Society [5/1c], and here on Temperance Street, a large lot for a temperance hall [demolished]. Ketchum's deed covenants on Temperance Street forbade licensed inns or other places where "spiritous liquours" might be sold, a restriction that remained until the 1960s.

12a Dineen Building (Shorney's Opticians), 140 Yonge St. and 2 Temperance St., Frederick H. Herbert, 1897.

Late Victorian picturesque by Toronto's king of the eclectic façade, who sprinkled his zany details here no less than on suburban houses. As well as renting out office space, W. and D. Dineen sold furs from the ground-floor corner.

12b Aikenhead's Hardware/originally Comet Bicycle Co., 17–19 Temperance St. (factory), E.J. Lennox, 1894–95; remodelled as commercial block, E.J. Lennox, 1905.

Where Herbert's decoration on the Dineen Building [6/12a] is so much flimsy accumulation, Lennox has gone far the other way to create a meticulously integrated composition with the building elements—deep-set, precisely placed windows for example—creating their own vivid ornament.

The Comet Bicycle Company building was erected during the 1890s North American cycle craze. Thanks to the introduction of a low-seated safety bicycle in 1887 and the pneumatic tire in 1891, the two-wheeled vehicles were finding an ever-growing number of enthusiasts. In 1895, there were 19 companies in Toronto manufacturing bicycles, and a traffic count that year recorded 395 cyclists in one half-hour passing the corner of Yonge and King. Enthusiasm didn't last, however, and faced with competition from the U.S. many Canadian companies folded. In 1905, Lennox remodelled his bold bicycle building for a hardware merchant who's been here ever since.

14 *Confederation Life Building, chromolithograph 1890*

---

13 Originally R.S. Williams Building, 145 Yonge St., Chapman & McGiffin, 1912.
In 1912 the building code didn't cover a structure 23 feet wide and over 100 feet high faced in glazed terracotta with reinforced-concrete bearing walls, no matter how classical the decoration might appear. Somehow the Williams Building got built, and it is still a standout on this block. (Chapman was one of those architects able to bridge the gap between Beaux-Arts tradition and Moderne innovation.) Williams sold pianos and other musical instruments from his ten-storey premises, symbolized by the monogrammed lyre serving as rooftop pediment.

---

14 Confederation Square/originally Confederation Life Building, 2–14 Richmond St. E., Knox Elliot & Jarvis, 1890–92; altered, J. Wilson Gray, 1898–1900; addition, J. Wilson Gray, 1908; renovated, Thom Partnership, 1981–82.
The fairy-tale Confederation Life Building has held Toronto's imagination from the day the design competition was announced in 1889, through completion in 1892 when its six storeys plus towers marked it as one of the city's four tallest, to the fire that almost destroyed it in 1981, and now in its recent splendid restoration that signals new life for lower Yonge Street. Adding towers, steep hipped roof, wishbone window surrounds, and other chateauesque touches to the period's popular Richardsonian Romanesque style, Knox Elliot and Jarvis came up with a bold, massive structure enlivened with the sort of fanciful detail that was being lavished on Fifth Avenue millionaires' mansions at the time. Confederation Life loved the image of solidity plus richness, and publicized it widely.

The structure is actually two units, separated by the middle tower, which stood originally over an open carriageway leading to a lane behind. In 1900, the ground floor of the Yonge/Richmond unit was altered considerably to provide larger window openings and a prominent corner entrance, a transformation that entailed prodigious shoring and balancing of the weighty upper floors. The more conventional-looking office block along Victoria Street was appended in 1908. The recent renovation is laudatory, not least for having uncovered from under mid-century "modernizations" beautiful Sullivanesque carved ornament. The building does cry out, however, for its original pyramidal roofs now missing from the towers. The Fidinam Group ownership plans instead to put its money into two 30-storey-plus mirror-glass slabs to go up behind Confederation Life.

18 *Sterling Tower*

20 *Victory Building*

15 Robert Simpson Co., 160–184 Yonge St. (See Walk 5/7.)

16 Silver Crown Tavern/originally Paterson Building, 25 Richmond St. W., Sproatt & Rolph, 1928.
Offices for stockbroker D.S. Paterson posing as a Jacobethan manor house. A very luxurious use of expensive land, this was the last two-storey structure constructed in the financial district.

17 Central Building, 45 Richmond St. W., Baldwin & Greene, 1927–28.
A rather tepid try at 1920s streamlining, the 12-storey beigy-brick Central Building ends up looking too washed out to convey the necessary zip, even with enigmatic hieroglyphs stitched up the sides. The grotesques issuing forth from the corners, like so many genii from Aladdin's lamp, do add the exotic Deco touch though.

18 Sterling Tower, 372 Bay St., Chapman & Oxley, 1928–29.
Twenty storeys of smooth height with the squared mass of the building stepped at the top in an arrangement of setbacks, Bay Street was getting into 1920s skyscraper swing here. Narrow piers provide vertical oomph, and stylized Gothic quatrefoils, exotic dragons, and similar appliqués perk up the ground and attic storeys. Though the big-windowed base still makes use of classical square columns, they are so zingy as to thrust antique impulse into the jazz age.

19 Graphic Arts Building (Hy's Restaurant), 73 Richmond St. W., Francis S. Baker, 1913.
A beauteous Greek temple built to house not commerce but culture, this was the home of *Saturday Night*, the debonair magazine intent on bringing insight and wit to Canada in the 1910s, and still at it, though no longer from this three-storey Ionic palace. Properly cultivated refinements remain intact in the marble and wood lobby: "Saturday Night" inscribed on bronze wreaths set into stair railings, elaborately carved wooden doors sporting knights and damsels, deep coffered ceiling.

20 Victory Building, 80 Richmond St. W., Baldwin & Greene, 1929–30.
An inventive Art Deco version of a traditional three-part skyscraper, the Victory Building uses contrasting brown brick in horizontal bands at the second and top floors to create a veritable base and cornice for its 20 stretched storeys of tan brick. Especially zippy are elongated pyramids decorating spandrels and the Art Deco chrome and marble lobby. Baldwin & Greene had come a long way from their mushy Central Building of two years earlier [6/17].

23 *Concourse Building*

21a National Building, 347 Bay St., Chapman & Oxley, 1925–26.
An early 1920s high-rise by the architect/engineer team of Chapman & Oxley, responsible for many Toronto skyscrapers in this period. The use of extensive plain wall surfaces to highlight selected decorative detail was typical of Chapman's work.

21b Originally Atlas Building, 350 Bay St., S.B. Coon & Son, 1928.
The façade sports a little of the old heavily classical skyscraper vocabulary and some of the new vertical emphasis, but most noteworthy here is the splendid 1930s elevator lobby glowing with polished brass roped columns and a frieze of half-lion/half-eagle griffins.

22 Originally Northern Ontario Building, 330 Bay St., Chapman & Oxley, 1924–25; addition (incorporating street façade of Savarin Tavern), Webb Zerafa Menkes Housden, 1982.
With the exception of exotic griffins (again griffins?) flanking second-floor windows, the Northern Ontario Building is an unassuming 1920s skyscraper: just a dab of classical detail to ornament the ground floor (originally six separate-entry shops), only darker-coloured spandrels to relieve the clean-limbed shaft, and the slightest of cornices "waving" along the broken-cornered eaves course.
The 1982 addition to the north, housing Banco Central of Canada, is interesting for its stepped horizontal profile in contrast to the verticality of the Northern

Ontario Building. It is not a bad marriage. The famous Savarin Tavern designed by Norman Armstrong—called Toronto's most palatial eating house in the 1930s—fell victim to the new construction, but after preservationists' prodding, its two-storey 1929 Romanesque façade was reassembled as three walls in the new building's atrium restaurant. The recreated eatery bears no relation to the old Savarin, and the walls (unidentified) are lost behind chi-chi 1980s restaurant decor. A meaningless gesture.

23 Concourse Building, 100 Adelaide St. W., Baldwin & Greene, 1928.
This 16-storey paean to verticality is Toronto's jazziest Deco skyscraper. From a cubist three-storey stone base springs a shaft of office floors dramatized by jutting wide and narrow piers that shoot up without interruption to the parapet, where they fly still higher in the form of pinnacles glinting with brightly coloured tiles. Tile mosaics sow verve over tympanum and soffit of the tall entrance arch as well. Designed by J.E.H. Macdonald, one of the nationalist Group of Seven painters, and his son, Thoreau Macdonald, the mosaics depict Canadian airplanes, ploughs, furnaces, sailing ships, and the like to symbolize the coming together or "concourse" of elemental air, earth, fire, and water. The lobby once featured Canadian verse chiselled on the walls and Canadian flora and fauna emblazoned on the ceiling. That is now gone, but wonderful Art Deco brass lettering which proclaims building name and address still animates the Adelaide façade.

24 *Canada Permanent Building*

26 *National Club, left, c. 1912*

24 Canada Permanent Building, 320 Bay St., F. Hilton Wilkes with Mathers & Haldenby and Sproatt & Rolph, 1928–30.

The architect said he wanted to avoid "restless outlines," and by combining massive bulk with delicate ornament, that is exactly what he did. He also avoided any possibility of architectural distinction. The two design impulses cancel one another and the Canada Permanent Building ends up with neither power nor grace—a stout matron in too-thin ingenue's finery. Only the deeply vaulted entrance and its bold coffered ceiling speak with any vigour, pronouncing the solidity and weightiness that "The Permanent," by its very name, undoubtedly hoped to evoke. The interior lobby and banking hall are another matter—rich extravaganzas of satiny marble and burnished metal in the best Art Deco manner. Don't miss the extraordinary bronze elevator doors whereon are portrayed kneeling antique figures, one holding out a model of the company's medievally quaint former headquarters and another a replica of this skyscraper—self-congratulatory offerings to the gods of commerce.

25 Originally Trust and Guarantee Co. Ltd./formerly Crown Trust, 302 Bay St. (office building), Curry & Sparling, 1916–17; addition, 1929.

Looking slightly schizophrenic, this building is a lesson in skyscraper design as it was conceived before and after 1920. The sculptural Corinthian temple front shows the rich classicism characteristic of the earlier period; the attic storeys added 12 years later are in the smooth, angular, stepped fashion then popular. The exquisite marble and plasterwork banking hall is from the earlier period before 1920, when fine craftsmanship and materials were still the order of the day.

26 National Club, 303 Bay St., Curry Sproatt & Rolph, 1906–07.

The four-storey red-brick Neo-Georgian National Club, with its self-consciously domestic air, probably appeared less alien to its surroundings in 1907, when Bay Street still consisted mainly of 19th-century commercial blocks, houses, and churches. The National Club was founded in 1874 as a counter to growing sentiment for union with the United States.

27a Bank of Nova Scotia, 44 King St. W. (office building), designed, John M. Lyle, 1929; built, Mathers & Haldenby with Beck & Eadie, 1949–51; altered, 1988–89.

Office buildings erected in Toronto after World War II took up where their pre-war brethren left off. The Bank of Nova Scotia was built using actual pre-war Deco plans (shelved first during the Depression). Lyle had been a prolific

28a *Canadian Bank of Commerce, c. 1935*

architect of banks notable for their crisp planarity and stylized decoration based on Canadian themes: native flora and fauna, Indian motifs, local industry and historical events. His mountainous 23-storey Bank of Nova Scotia rises resolutely on this key corner, its massive smooth stone base punctuated by elegant metal-mullioned Deco windows and 1930s style bas-reliefs (executed by Fred Winkler). Lobbies and banking hall are further decked out in Moderne streamlining, marbles, metals, and Lyle's iconography (north-wall mural by Jacobine Jones). Lately "opened up" as part of the Scotia Plaza complex [6/27b], this muted banking hall is slated for aggressive alteration. But at one time demolition of the whole building was considered, so who can carp!

27b Scotia Plaza, 30 King St. W. (complex of office and commercial buildings), Webb Zerafa Menkes Housden, 1985–88.
The last of the five major banks to build a less-is-more tower in the financial district, Scotiabank opted for red cladding in contrast to the black, white, silver, and gold of the others'. It is not a boring box; it's a 68-storey boring trapezoid, with two of its parallel sides stepped. (Read, more corner offices.) Actually, at ground level the project is in many ways commendable. It fits into the tight site elegantly and the forecourts on King and Adelaide Streets are ceremonial and gracious. The legible punched windows, referencing '20s and '30s skyscrapers, add human scale to the monumental. The fact that older buildings were retained [6/26, /27a] makes the block seem more alive and natural. The façade shenanigans [5/1c, 6/11a] are definitely unreal, however.

Toronto bank towers, 1985

28a Canadian Imperial Bank of Commerce/originally Canadian Bank of Commerce, 25 King St. W. (office building), York & Sawyer with Darling & Pearson, 1929–31.

After more than 50 years, this is still the best bank building *and* the best office tower in the financial district, combining mighty monumentality and soaring grace in a 34-storey structure of unquestionable presence. York & Sawyer were New York's leading bank architects, and they obviously knew a thing or two about image-making as well as composition. If one's money isn't safe inside that awesome Romanesque block of seemingly solid stone that forms the building's base, where then? If that massive, smooth shaft gliding upward in a series of subtle setbacks does not connote architectonic movement and skyscraping height, what then? And at the top, if that Romanesque diadem-cum-observation-deck thrusting gigantic heads over the city of Courage, Observation, Foresight, and Enterprise is not the way to pronounce richness and bold endeavour crowning the Bank of Commerce, how then? Similar grandeur

suffuses the interior of the ground-floor banking rooms and lobbies, especially the immense main banking hall. Executed in roseate stone with gilt mouldings and roofed with a deep blue coffered barrel vault, there is a dusky, hushed tone of reverance here that is the closest the financial district comes to ecclesia.

28b Commerce Court, 243 Bay St. (complex of office buildings), I.M. Pei & Partners with Page & Steele, 1968–72.

Commerce Court comprises York & Sawyer's 1931 skyscraper [6/28a], two five- and 14-storey modular limestone buildings, and, on the fourth side of the plaza, a slick 57-storey glass and stainless-steel towering box. The tower is International Style at its cleanest and most rational, with horizontally emphasized layers of office floors rising one atop another, unadorned, undifferentiated, and precision-perfect. Pei's tower is distinguished from similar packages by its fragile-looking three-storey clear-glass base, a telling contrast to the impenetrable stone of the adjacent 1931 building. In

30b *Toronto Stock Exchange*

fact, contrast and contradiction are the name of the game at Commerce Court: old and new, high and low, steel and stone, void and solid, axis and cross-axis. Unfortunately, the cerebralizing doesn't add up to hot architecture, but to cold plazas—the chilliest corner in Toronto, they say.

29 Toronto-Dominion Centre, 55 King St. W. (complex of office buildings), Ludwig Mies van der Rohe with John B. Parkin Associates and Bregman & Hamann, 1964–71; 4th tower added, 1985–86.

A guiding light of the international Modern Movement, Ludwig Mies van der Rohe came to America from Germany in the late 1930s. In 1958, he designed the Seagram Building on Park Avenue as New York headquarters for the Canadian distillery giant. One of the most influential pieces of architecture ever built, it became a model for all the reductivist glass slabs that still rise from plazas around the world. The towers of the Toronto-Dominion Centre—the tallest is 56 storeys—are similar to Seagram. Heroic scale is reproduced, even magnified by having multiple towers instead of one. Sophisticated materials are repeated in the form of bronze glass set in a black metal web of I-beams. Mies's meticulous proportions are duplicated. And like Seagram in New York, the T-D Centre remains the most renowned of the seemingly omnipresent form in this city.

Miesian buildings are under attack these days, not only because so many are cheap copies—such refinement and dignity are not easy to come by—but for their unused plazas and disengagement from the fabric of the city. Legitimate as these concerns are, Toronto's Miesian masterwork continues to reward us with its dark, austere beauty.

30a First Bank Tower, First Canadian Place, 50 King St. W. (office building), Edward Durell Stone Associates with Bregman & Hamann, 1972–75.

Built for the Bank of Montreal, this endless ladder to heaven is the sort of "boring box" that gives International Style towers a bad rap. That the shaft is clad in august marble counts for little because its flush smoothness and division into small tiles serve to deny our Michelangelesque notion of that sculptural material. An attempt at outsize vigour has been made at the base, which looks weighty and three-dimensional with pillars and landings marching in and around as well as out to meet the street. The complex improves inside, where commercial concourses are mostly above ground, daylighted, spacious. Here all that marble is almost glamorous.

30b Exchange Tower, First Canadian Place, 140 King St. W. (office building), Bregman & Hamann, 1981–83.

Connected to First Bank Tower by a pleasant small park strung out along King Street, Exchange Tower uses similar white marble but stretches it vertically instead of horizontally and sets silvery mirror glass behind pronounced mullions for a more elegant façade. This building now houses the Toronto Stock Exchange, which occupies the third through sixth

31 *Toronto Stock Exchange*

32 *Royal Bank Plaza*

floors. In addition to muted plush public rooms and the latest in paraphernalia for traders, the new facility boasts two large-scale works by avant-garde artists General Idea and Robert Longo, as well as a replica of the frieze on the former building [6/31].

31 Originally Toronto Stock Exchange, 234 Bay St., George & Moorhouse with S.H. Maw, 1937.

With the Concourse Building [6/23], this is the city's most evocative Art Deco setpiece. A smooth cube of hazy pink granite and beige limestone is spotlighted by five stage-centre columnar windows below which the action is played out on a 74-foot carved stone frieze designed by Charles Comfort and depicting toilers in Canadian industry (or at least those industries with stock handled on the exchange). Inside is an equally dramatic three-storey-high trading floor of Art-Deco-detailed marble, metal, and wood.

Since 1983 when the traders moved to Exchange Tower [6/30b], this fascinating structure has stood empty. It is owned by a neighbour on this block, the Toronto-Dominion Bank. The T-D likes consistency. In 1986, to Mies's original pavilion and three towers [6/29], they added an identical fourth on Wellington Street. The T-D now proposes to do it again here—Tower Five it's to be called. And the Stock Exchange? It'll stay in place, a five-storey beige limestone cube encased in 31 storeys of Miesian black glass and steel. This is yahoo compromising, neither good architecture nor good preservation. Ludwig Mies van der Rohe was acclaimed

for his almost fanatical discipline, the absolute precision of his proportions and details. Mies's plans for the Toronto-Dominion Centre were meticulous in placement and size of structures. He never would have countenanced more towers on this site, let alone constructing one atop an historic building! The ultimate irony of this loutish scheme is that the preserved Stock Exchange is destined to become a centre for the display of outstanding Canadian design. Keep your eyes on that trading floor.

32 Royal Bank Plaza, 200 Bay St. (office building), Webb Zerafa Menkes Housden, 1973–77.

Any building in Toronto that makes it look as if the sun were shining on a dreary winter day has a lot going for it. The faceted gold-enriched mirror-glass of Royal Bank's Late-Modern jewel seems to reflect a warm sunny glow no matter what the weather. This is a very showy building all around. The triangular 41- and 26-storey gold-glass towers are linked by a 12-storey clear-glass atrium, in the midst of which a theatrical circular ramp leads to underground commercial concourses, the whole centred by an island of tropical plants. There *is* something amiss about making the atrium into a dour banking hall, however; the space is deadening. Otherwise the building is lively hi-jinks on the skyline as well as in the streetscape, and best of all, it manages its *joie de vivre* with respect for very proper dowager neighbours [*AREA V*]. An actual plaza at Royal Bank Plaza is yet to be found.

Area V

Walk 7: University Avenue
Walk 8: University of Toronto

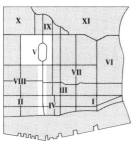

Area V

Today it is celebrated as one of Canada's foremost educational institutions, but the University of Toronto has had a patchy history, one marked by false starts, tenuous endorsements, changes of course, but ultimately world accolades. Its huge sprawling centre-city campus haphazardly punctuated by very good *and* very mediocre architecture in a hodgepodge of styles, materials, and shapes echoes that history.

The young province of Upper Canada took first steps toward establishing an institution of higher learning in 1827. Endowed with a royal charter and a governing council drawn from members of the Church of England, the new university was inevitably christened King's College. A large parcel of 160 acres was assembled, virtually the campus we know today, though then at some remove from town. Two further strings of land were therefore acquired as long drives connecting town and campus: College Street [5/26] and University Avenue (originally called College Avenue).

It was at the head of University Avenue, where it crossed College Street, that King's College was to be built. A three-storey Doric-columned stone building, one wing of an ambitious complex, was completed in 1845. University Avenue was laid out as a suitably auspicious approach, with a wide carriageway flanked by treed walkways. Though fenced and gated university property, the fine avenue soon became a fashionable promenade, where Torontonians in pursuit of seeing and being seen daily enjoyed its amenities.

Felicitous as that may seem, some powers-that-be were not keen that a government-funded university should be Anglican. By the Act of 1849, the legislature reconstituted King's College as the nondenominational University of Toronto. The classical plans and formal siting were scuttled in favour of more adventurous designs and a fresh location farther west on campus. University College, the first building of the reborn university, was begun in 1856 and completed in 1859, notable from the start for its spectacular visage [8/1].

For a university in the mid 19th century to have no church affiliation was very radical. Bishop Strachan thought the new school a "godless imitation of Babel" and forthwith built Trinity College on Queen Street [demolished] to educate Anglican gentlemen properly. Catholics, Methodists, Presbyterians, and Baptists also stayed away, continuing to support their own institutions of St. Michael's, Victoria, Queen's, Knox, and McMaster. It is not surprising then that nonsectarian University College, even though its faculty was outstanding, did not exactly sweep the province of students. By 1887, there were but 500 (including nine women) roaming the large picturesque campus of winding lanes and flowing creek.

With so many schools vying for so little largesse, it finally became clear that the only hope for higher education in the province lay in unification. One after another, the sectarian schools—save for Queen's and McMaster—joined with University College as partners in the University of Toronto and proceeded to settle on the U. of T. site. This expansion coincided with a terrible fire that destroyed much of University College. Thus it was that in the 1890s a wave of building overtook the campus. University College was restored more or less to its original Romanesque Revival look, while designs for a library [8/4], since-demolished science buildings, and newly ensconced Wycliffe [8/30] and Victoria [8/35] all followed similar Romanesque style, although some of a more ruddy Richardsonian stripe. This was the last time the campus was to enjoy such visual cohesiveness.

Buildings constructed from the turn of the century up to World War I reflected varying architectural taste: "Collegiate Gothic" was hands-down choice for the Oxbridgian residential colleges and halls, as well as for the ambitious men's activity centre, Hart House [8/3]; Classical Revival was called up for administration buildings; and a few classroom facilities experimented with a free, modern Romanesque. Buildings of the 1920s and '30s were mostly Neo-Georgian. Construction since World War II has added Bauhaus and other variants of International Style, Neo-Expressionist, and even Brutalist structures to the already heady mix.

Construction through the 1950s was centred on the Front Campus, its picturesque byways straightened and macadamized by 1910; the East Campus, outposts of St. Michael's and Victoria; and the north sector above Hoskin Avenue. In the 1960s, buildings burst onto a new West Campus to meet tremendous enrolment pressures of that era, though not without repercussion for it meant incursion into a residential neighbourhood west of St. George Street. Ironically, the original King's College section of the campus has never been built on by the University of Toronto. When they recast the university in 1849, the provincial legislators craftily expropriated this commanding location as a site for their own new parliament building. In 1859, they offered it to the city for parkland, and a year later, it was rechristened Queen's Park by the visiting Prince of Wales. The orphaned King's College building served briefly as a provincial lunatic asylum before finally being torn down in 1886 to make way for the long-promised new Provincial Parliament Building [7/26].

At about the same time, magnificent houses were going up on large lots laid out on university property ringing the park. The university hoped to foster a high-class residential environment for the campus as well as increase its coffers from ground leases. The same was true of university property on and around St. George Street. The Queen's Park enclave, especially,

Picturesque U. of T. campus east of University College, with Taddle Creek and McCaul's Pond adding bucolic atmosphere c. 1868.

was one of the city's best addresses until the 1920s, when the mansions fell to institutional use or were demolished. The park itself, though now tamed and manicured, remains a lovely green oasis in the city.

The course of development of University Avenue has been quite different. As early as the 1850s, it seemed clear the genteel promenade could not last, with the municipality showing increasing unhappiness with this private swath interrupting the flow of the city grid. Peevishly, it built a public road flanking the avenue to the east, and finally took the whole thing over as a public right-of-way. Though the combined width of the two roadways made for an impressive avenue, it was not a useful thoroughfare for it dead-ended at Queen Street. Nor did it have any particular architectural distinction. Houses on the west side fronted on Simcoe Street, showing their backs to University Avenue; those on the east were dwellings of a large working-class district known variously as Macaulaytown, or "The Ward." With completion of the Provincial Parliament Building in 1892, however, the character of University Avenue began to change, a change that by 1910 was focused on grand new possibilities for the area.

In those first prosperous decades of the 20th century, Toronto was eager to embrace the City Beautiful Movement then sweeping North America. As elsewhere, civic art guilds and improvement leagues formulated comprehensive Beaux-Arts plans that had parkways radiating in all directions from an ennobled city centre. One sequence envisioned a huge railway terminal on Front Street linked to the city hall on Queen Street [7/11] via an expansive concourse and plaza laid out between York and Bay Streets. Thus was begun magnificent Union Station [7/2]; World War I stalled the remainder of the scheme. In the late 1920s, Beaux-Arts visions were revived with a plan that included University Avenue as a great ceremonial motor way linking Union Station to the Provincial Parliament Building lined with massive uniformly styled architecture. The centre median was spruced up and formalized, sidewalks were widened, the parliament building landscaped to focus the dramatic vista, and the broad thoroughfare extended south to meet Front Street in a bold sweep. The imposing Dominion Public Building was begun on Front Street [7/1], while on University Avenue, Canada Life proceeded to put up a majestic street-defining structure for the Beaux-Arts avenue [7/14]. Then the Depression intervened, and that was the end of that. Today a miscellany of buildings and mini-plazas sit uneasily on Toronto's half-baked grand boulevard. Whether we would have liked such a monumental office-towered traffic artery any the better had it been completed as planned is another question.

Walk 7: University Avenue

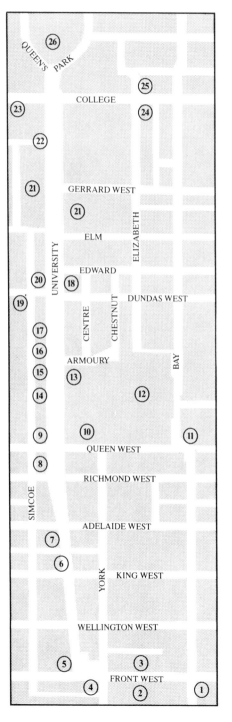

1 Dominion Public Building, 1 Front St. W., Thomas William Fuller, east and centre blocks, 1926–31; west block completed, 1935–36.

The starting point of the grand Beaux-Arts scheme planned for Front Street and University Avenue in the late 1920s, the Dominion Public Building is typical of hundreds of buildings whose impressive classical countenances were sent marching across North America in the service of monumental public architecture in the early years of this century. The monumentality of this, Toronto's customs house, is additionally enhanced by the sweeping arc of its Ionic-columned front, rhythmically keeping step with the curve of the street.

---

2 Union Station, 65–75 Front St. W., Ross & Macdonald with Hugh G. Jones and John M. Lyle, 1915–20; opened, 1927.

With this grandiloquent Classical Revival building, a style then synonymous with progress and prosperity, Toronto architecturally entered the new century. It was not an easy birth, nor has its life since been secure. Begun in 1915, the building was not opened until 12 years later, construction having been thwarted first by World War I and then a bureaucratic feud over a planned viaduct in what became a great local joke. Threatened demolition in the early 1970s inspired no laughter, however, and the community efforts and, finally, political responsibility that saved the station remain a high point for preservationists.

If any building in Toronto can be described as monumental, this is it. Over 750 feet long and set well back along its Front Street block, Union Station borrows from antiquity its elongated form and colossal colonnade to create a magnificently powerful yet simple structure. Though the building is entered directly at ground level, the exterior is as impersonal and awesome as any elevated classical temple, a fitting gateway for a great metropolis. (Recent efforts to "humanize" the front with planter boxes and a kitschy multicultural monument miss the point.)

As mighty as the exterior is, the architectural glory is the interior, the Great Hall. Considered by many the finest room

2 *Union Station, 192?*

in Canada—and at 260 feet still the largest some 60 years after it was built—this
majestic space features a vaulted ceiling
that gently curves down to rows of clerestory windows which bathe the hall in natural light, illuminating walls of sand-
coloured Missouri Zumbro stone and a
floor paved in muted grey and pink Ten-
nessee marble. The impression is of soft
light and serene surfaces, a tranquil back-
ground for the bustle of arrivals and de-
partures yet one suitably grand to the excitement of travel. Union Station was
innovatively designed to separate incom-
ing and outgoing passengers and avoid
congestion. Below the main departure
concourse is another of equal floor space
for arrivals. It is now given over to com-
muter trains, our new paeans of progress.

**3 Royal York Hotel, 100 Front St. W., Ross
& Macdonald with Sproatt & Rolph,
1928–29.**
Skyscraper-cum-chateau overlooking not
the Loire, but the railways, which took
their role most seriously. If the railways'
stations resembled classical temples
through which travellers were intended to
enter the city like Caesars, their hotels
became fairy-tale castles in which guests
were invited to live like kings. (In fact,
members of the Royal Family do often
stay here when they visit Toronto.) The
Canadian Pacific Railway's "castle"
mode—a pleasing but vague mix borrowed from 16th-century France, Venice,
and Lombardy—was used by other hotel
builders in North America, but the Royal
York is an especially refined version. For
many years, it was the largest hotel in the

British Commonwealth, and its picturesque verdigris-tinged roof still contributes
a note of grace to Toronto's skyline.

**4a University Place, 123 Front St. W. (office
building), Parkin Partnership, 1983.**
Twenty clumsy storeys of missed opportunity. Closing the vista at the end of
University Avenue where it flows into
Front Street, this should have been one of
the city's most exciting compositions, a
triumphant counterpoint to the dramatic
site and noble neighbours. As it is, this
glass and steel hulk ignores them, its
ungainly shape connected to nothing but
itself. It all seems so mean and unambi-
tious, without the sense of grandeur that
the railway—yes, they are landlords here
too—was able to summon for its station and
hotel.

**4b Metropolitan Place, 1 University Ave.
(office building), Brisbin Brook Beynon,
1985–86.**
A wise and gentle comment upon the
nature of this site and of University
Avenue, this building avoids aggressive
gestures but has its own monumentality.
The real mark-the-corner edifice here is of
course the Royal York Hotel [7/3], and
by using airy glass and subtle shape, this
19-storey structure does not compete,
knows its place, but suffuses that place
with rare elegance. The overall impression
of lightness and grace is enhanced by the
serenely stepped landscaping which floats
the building above the busy intersection,
and by the sensuous bluey-green glass and
oxidized metal materials.

4b *Metropolitan Place*

6 *Sun Life Centre*

5 142–144 Front St. W. (warehouse), Symons & Rae, 1903.

Built 28 years before the curved extension of University Avenue even existed, and one of the few survivors of the 1904 fire which levelled much of the area, this seven-storey red-brick warehouse fortuitously enhances the sweeping juncture today.

6 Sun Life Centre, 150 and 200 King St. W. (two office buildings), Webb Zerafa Menkes Housden, 1983–84.

A giant matched pair that brings to University Avenue a vision more grandiose than any the wildest Beaux-Arts dreamers could have conceived. In some ways, the structures are praiseworthy: the two towers sit firmly on their corner sites flanking the avenue; stepped setbacks, used to such dramatic effect by 1920s skyscrapers to lighten their tops, do the same for Sun Life's shafts; the envelopes are handsome, with small-gridded glass skins and precisely grooved elongated shapes. It's just that the two buildings are altogether too big. Sun Life gained its extraordinary size in a density trade with St. Andrew's church [3/4]. It may have been fiscal sense, but it makes for flawed scenery.

7 Reynolds Building/originally Parker Fountain Pen Co., 154 University Ave., 1933.

This was the first building to go up along the leg of University Avenue that extended the thoroughfare south from Queen to Front Street in 1931, and it remained virtually the only structure here until after World War II. A punchy-looking, modest Art Deco study, it is firmly placed at the lot line to help define the street, although one suspects it was meant to be taller; there's something of an unfinished quality about it. The bas-relief around the doorways is unusual for its delicacy and sinuousness.

8 Bank of Canada Building, 250 University Ave., Marani & Morris, 1955.

Whether Toronto was trying to resuscitate its late 1920s scheme for University Avenue, or wasn't yet ready for the sleek International Style boxes with which other cities in North America were experimenting, this is a very *retardataire* composition. Rounded cornice and attic storey, tinted green glass, and chunky sculptural reliefs are all memories of the Art Moderne style. "A bulwark of banking... with a solidity that matches the half-yearly dividend," grumbled one disappointed critic.

9 Campbell House, 160 Queen St. W.
(See Walk 3/2).

10 Osgoode Hall, 116–138 Queen St. W.
(See Walk 3/1).

11 *Old City Hall, 1912*

11 Old City Hall, 60 Queen St. W., E.J. Lennox, 1889–99.

This is one of Toronto's most rousing architectural testaments, expressing not only the confidence of the late 19th-century city but also the prowess of one of its most accomplished architects. In the 1890s in North America, the style of public dignity was unshakeably Richardsonian Romanesque, with courthouses and town halls rising all across the continent in the massive, robust solidity of Henry Hobson Richardson's seminal 1884 Allegheny County Court House in Pittsburgh, Pennsylvania. When it came to building a new courthouse here, Toronto chose native-son E.J. Lennox's own bold Romanesque design. By the time construction started in 1889, city hall functions had been added and the plan much expanded. The basic form of the building resembles Richardson's—both are designed with rough masonry of immense scale, legible corner pavilions, and great mansard roofs ranging around a courtyard—but Lennox's building is no mere imitation. Old City Hall is pictorial and ornamental in ways not found in Richardson's more intellectual, abstract granite composition. Here the bell tower,

placed to terminate the vista up Bay Street, is off centre, and the façade is handled as a surface to be decorated, either by contrasting textures and colours of brown and beige sandstone or by intricate foliate and grotesque carvings.

The interior is equally picturesque, featuring intricate bronze and iron detailing, painted murals by George Reid, as well as a huge allegorical stained-glass window by Robert McCausland. Such elaboration was not without cost: the resulting $2.5 million figure brought the architect lawsuits, investigations, and untold imbroglios, the most notorious being the affair in which his name was revealed carved in corbels below the eaves. The letters, interspersed along the sides, spell out "E J LENNOX ARCHITECT."

When New City Hall [7/12] was opened in 1965, there was much concern about the future of this older building. But as demolition seemed imminent, the Friends of Old City Hall rallied enough support to ensure preservation of this distinguished Romanesque building, a campaign that was instrumental in developing Toronto's awareness of its architectural heritage.

12 *New City Hall*

12 New City Hall, 100 Queen St. W., Viljo Revell with John B. Parkin Associates, 1965.
Selected in international competition, New City Hall represents a very daring look for Toronto. It is a monumentally sculptural design, with two tall curved towers of unequal height embracing a low saucer-shaped council chamber, the whole sitting on a two-storey podium. Such a Neo-Expressionist concept is not often advanced in this city of strict rectangularity, but the Finnish architect's extravagant scheme is superbly executed with clean-lined simplicity. And the plan eloquently acknowledges citizens' role in government, with the metro chairman's and mayor's offices visible in windows above the main entrance and the council chamber set out in the form of a participatory amphitheatre. For all its showiness, New City Hall is also dignified and accessible, and these are characteristics of which Torontonians are immensely proud.

Integral to this concept of New City Hall is Nathan Phillips Square in front of it, named for the Toronto mayor who encouraged the competition. A grand sweeping plaza introduced by a large reflecting pool that becomes a skating rink in winter, the square is both inviting and formally ceremonial. Some controversy surrounded installation in 1965 of the smallish, friendly Henry Moore sculpture, *The Archer*, an artwork that today seems almost inconsequential. A much

more bold endeavour on the square is the 1984 Peace Garden. With its symbolic "half-hut" and Oriental serenity, it is in keeping with the concept of invitation, formality—and daring. New City Hall with its square remains a noble space, and deservedly Toronto's most famous landmark.

13 Metropolitan Toronto Court House, 361 University Ave., Marani Morris & Allan, 1964-66.
Understated, formal modernism in an appealing composition with wide plaza that bows both to the scale and classical façade of Osgoode Hall [3/1] and the Neo-Expressionism of New City Hall [7/12]. The polygonal tunnel that directs pedestrians between University Avenue and Nathan Phillips Square is an interesting architectural conceit, accommodating a courtroom above. It should be noted, however, that this "artistic" ensemble does neglect its street-affirming duties to University Avenue. A memorial plaque in front of the courthouse commemorates the largest armoury in Canada which stood on this site from 1890 to 1963, once an architecturally distinguished and important building in the life of the city.

15 *University Club of Toronto*

14 Canada Life Assurance Building, 330 University Ave., Sproatt & Rolph, 1929-31.

Rising resolutely from the street line to a cornice height of 100 feet and formally framed by swatches of manicured lawn, Canada Life was the first—and only—building constructed on University Avenue in accordance with visions of 1929 Beaux-Arts planners. As originally designed, the "tower" was to have climbed higher in a series of dramatic setbacks, which probably would have made the solid, almost excessively scaled bulk of the Classical Revival "base" less formidable. The deepening Depression cut back on the height and other construction on the avenue as well. Even truncated, the tower with its neon weather beacon has become the company's trademark: a steady green beacon predicts fair weather, red means cloudy skies; white flashes are for snow, red flashes for rain.

15 University Club of Toronto, 382 University Ave., Mathers & Haldenby with F. Hilton Wilkes, 1929.

The University Club was founded in 1906 in premises near King and Bay Streets. Members, who had to be university graduates, were mostly from the nearby business and legal communities but also included several prominent architects. After purchasing land on University Avenue for a new building, the club was able to restrict the design competition to architect-members, drawing six entries. Mathers & Haldenby won with this elegant Palladian-windowed Neo-

Georgian design borrowed from the illustrious clubhouses of London. F. Hilton Wilkes came a close second, and the comradely jury named him associate. When built in 1929, the University Club was flanked by office buildings of comparable scale and style.

16 Travelers Tower, 400 University Ave. (office building), Page & Steele, 1970.

The Travelers is like a big dark rain cloud hanging over University Avenue—the company's red umbrella trademark at the top of the building is more appropriate than ever they knew. But the design program to insinuate a tall tower between low-rise club buildings was awesome to begin with. The octagonal shape with angled setbacks to either side is as accommodating as possible to the Travelers' neighbours but it does little for the streetline, and the bronze-glass and brown-concrete cladding is too muddy and cheerless to provide the clarity the avenue requires.

17 Royal Canadian Military Institute, 426 University Ave. (house), c. 1890; altered, Chadwick & Beckett, 1907, 1913; altered, Mackenzie Waters, 1930; altered, Fisher Tedman Fisher, 1955.

More classical swagger than rational architecture, this clubhouse for officers of His/Her Majesty's Forces has a lengthy history of alterations and additions. The institute was formed in the late 19th century by officers of the Toronto garrison who in 1905 bought a Victorian house on Simcoe Street for their club. Architect-

19 *Metropolitan Toronto Police*   **20** *Global House*

member Capt. Vaux Chadwick added the Tuscan columns and two-storey swelling bay to the *back* of the Simcoe Street house, turning it into an appropriately dignified classical front for University Avenue. A few years later he added another bay to the south from the rear of a second adjacent house. Architect-member Lt.-Col. Mackenzie Waters moved the entrance from the north bay to the south, and Blake H.M. Tedman finished up the campaign by enclosing second-storey sunporches and providing a Neo-Georgian façade to the Simcoe Street elevation. The RCMI, which today includes officer-members of both sexes, boasts a rare collection of military artifacts and memorabilia and a 25,000-volume library unique in Canada.

18 McClelland and Stewart Building/originally Maclean Publishing Co., 481 University Ave. thru to Centre St. (office building), Sproatt & Rolph, 1911; addition, Marani & Morris, 1961; altered, William Strong Associates, 1984.
210 Dundas St. W. (printing plant), probably Murray Brown, 1928.
The Maclean Publishing Company moved to University Avenue in 1911. Theirs was the first commercial building on the street, situated among houses and a few churches. The rear of that original building still shows off striking red-brick and stone buttresses along Centre Street. The

front was consumed in 1961 by the *retardataire* Moderne edifice that now occupies the University Avenue frontage, lately updated with a sassy Post-Modern entrance. The 1928 eight-storey printing plant at Dundas and Centre Streets still intrigues for its fine "modern classical" details and handsome tall ground-storey windows—unusually high to accommodate printing presses.

19 52 Division Headquarters Metropolitan Toronto Police, 255 Dundas St. W., Shore Tilbe Henschel & Irwin, 1977.
Looking zippy, with 1930s Deco glass blocks and ocean-liner dash, 52 Division Headquarters was one of this city's first Post-Modern quotations of earlier styles, and, with its dignifying plaza, an intriguing contribution to the curved Dundas streetscape, Post-Modern or no. It seems obvious the police station was trying to appear accessible—light and shadows show through the glass blocks—but also solid and secure. It works.

20 Global House, 480 University Ave. (office building), Webb Zerafa Menkes, 1968.
Marked by precise International Style rectangularity with elegantly slim concrete arches patterning the rectangles, Global House is a good example of a decorative, sculptural variant of the form. Rising a modest—by today's standards—18 storeys and graciously filling its site, this beautifully proportioned formal-looking building is an asset to its owners, the Global Group of Insurance Companies, and to University Avenue.

22a, b, c *Hydro buildings*

21a Queen Elizabeth Hospital/originally New Mount Sinai Hospital, 550 University Ave., Kaplan & Sprachman with Govan Ferguson Lindsay Kaminker Maw Langley & Keenleyside, 1952.

Mount Sinai Hospital, 600 University Ave., Bregman & Hamann, 1974.

Hospital for Sick Children, 555 University Ave., Govan Ferguson Lindsay Kaminker Maw Langley & Keenleyside, 1949.

Hospitals have come to dominate the upper precincts of University Avenue, although "dominate" is hardly the word, for most of the buildings are as bland and pasty as the diets they prescribe. Such seems to be the architectural way with hospitals these days, but for all that, Toronto hospitals can claim some very impressive medical achievements. Toronto General installed the world's first heart pacemaker and administered the first shot of insulin; Sick Children's pioneered facilities for children; and Mount Sinai is a leader in geriatrics.

21b Toronto General Hospital, 101 College St., Darling & Pearson, 1909-19.

Though later additions along University Avenue and elsewhere in the huge complex look as antiseptic as other hospitals in the neighbourhood, the original College Street building, decked out in friendly beigy-brick Georgian Revival, is really very warm and welcoming. Interestingly, the facility was described as "severely plain" when new, but with long classically detailed wings flanking an elegant domed centre pavilion, today it can be seen to have an intimate scale and graciousness lacking in newer hospital buildings.

22a *610 University Ave.*   **22b** *620 University Ave.*   **22c** *700 University Ave.*

Electricity came to Toronto in the early 1880s with salesmen offering illumination to householders for 8 cents a night and electric arc lamps erected on a few streets. The power source was dynamos operated by wood or coal, but they were not that effective and eventually water power was perfected. By the beginning of the 20th century, the possibilities seemed enormous, though private companies were charging very high rates. The creation of a public utility, the Hydro-Electric Power Commission of Ontario, brought cheap power to the province and instant prestige to the government responsible. By 1914, Hydro was supplying 69 municipalities, and the next year built the first of its three buildings on University Avenue, each designed to convey the importance of the commission in the province.

22a Hydro-Electric Building, 610 University Ave., George W. Gouinlock, 1915.

This first structure put up by the Hydro does not appear very auspicious today, but at the time its stylish classical colonnade loomed large on University Avenue. The shield in the segmental pediment of the portico bears the arms of the commission, designed by the provincial archivist with suitable symbols: wheels for power, wavy chevrons for running water, stars for light, a locomotive for electric railways. In placing contracts for the steel and reinforced-concrete building, the commission specified that where possible materials should be manufactured in Canada by hydro-electric power.

22b Ontario Hydro Building, 620 University Ave., Sproatt & Rolph, 1935; ten-storey addition, Sproatt & Rolph, 1945.

Hydro's architectural message of corporate greatness in the 1930s was just as up to date as their Classical Revival image had been in 1915. The vocabulary was now streamlined Art Deco and the building's smooth, vertical look is unrelieved except for narrow horizontal bands of fluting and a hydro-electric dam stylization on the piers flanking the entrance. Originally, no. 620 was but six storeys; its ten-storey addition of 1945 certainly overpowers the earlier building at no. 610. That aside, this handsome 16-storey tower taken alone—unequivocally planted at the lot line and graced with a series of pleasing setbacks at the top to lighten the skyscraper mass—is probably the single best building constructed on and *for* University Avenue.

22c Hydro Place, 700 University Ave. (office building), Kenneth R. Cooper, 1975.

Unfortunately Hydro has not come up such a winner with its latest eye-catching effort. The building's smooth, zero-detailed glass skin, huge size, curved shape, sunken forecourt, and virtually hidden entrance are all at odds with University Avenue. The energy-saving virtues of mirror glass as well as its intriguing reflective qualities should be noted, but in this case, mirrors alone can't do the trick.

23 *149 College St.*   **25** *College of Physicians and Surgeons*

23 Ontario College of Art/originally Toronto Athletic Club/formerly Stewart Building/formerly Central Technical School/formerly Police Department, 149 College St., E.J. Lennox, 1891–94.

Round-arched Richardsonian Romanesque without the usual rugged sandstone, but still a very stalwart building and a tribute to 19th-century brickwork. Lennox lavished a good deal of care here, the subtle incline or batter of the west tower and taut equilibrium of disparate window shapes and sizes, for example. Successive renovations have destroyed most of the interiors, but the newly cleaned exterior—despite revamped entry—continues to parade Lennox's masterliness.

24 Victoria Hospital for Sick Children, 67 College St., Darling & Curry, 1889–91.

This hospital was the first in North America designed exclusively for children. It began in a nearby house and after several moves settled in this brawny Richardsonian Romanesque structure all of its own, in large part thanks to the philanthropy of John Ross Robertson, owner-editor of Toronto's *Evening Telegram* [see also 11/9]. It boasted a deft E shape to provide cross-ventilation and maximum light to wards, as well as a pace-setting rooftop playground. Though the building is compact and tightly packed onto its city lot, the façade is energetic, almost playful. The cheery carved angels above the round-arched entry set the tone. Since 1949, when the world-famous hospital moved to quarters on University Avenue [7/21c], no. 67 has been desultorily used; its future is uncertain.

25 College of Physicians & Surgeons of Ontario, 80 College St. (office building), Zeidler Roberts Partnership, 1983.

One of Toronto's first full-blown Post-Modern tableaux and an inviting grab bag of architectural remembrances from medieval turrets to Renaissance pillars to Art Deco keystones. The slightly roughened rosy-red brick is just the right contrast to the slick aesthetic, and the cater-corner entrance neatly accommodates the sloping site, providing Post-Modern symmetry to what is really an asymmetric building. The interior—wherein the province's medicos are licensed to practise—is 1980s Deco.

26 *Provincial Parliament Building, c. 1900*

26 Provincial Parliament Building, 1 Queen's Park, Richard A. Waite, 1886–92; west wing rebuilt after fire, E.J. Lennox, 1910; library addition, George W. Gouinlock, 1913.
Torontonians don't take this amiable Richardsonian Romanesque building as seriously as they should. Perhaps it is the usual city slicker disdain for the country bumpkin—the Ontario legislature has historically been associated with rural interests—and there *is* something slightly cloddish about this reddish-brown behemoth. But the monochromatic palette hides a wealth of beautiful carved detail, and the interior boasts exquisite decoration. The grand ceremonial staircase leading from lobby and entrance vestibule to the legislative chamber above is of delicate ornamental iron, and the red, blue, and cream chamber itself is adorned with bronze-coloured ironwork and intricately carved woodwork. In the rebuilt west wing, grey and white marble piers and balustrades grace walls and stairwells. And the white and gold library wing in the rear introduces luxurious marble detailing. (On the exterior as well these two additions, though generally following Waite's Romanesque, can be seen to display their architects' own distinctive imprint.)

The Provincial Parliament Building was surrounded by controversy from its beginning, possibly because its architect was not only English born and Buffalo based, but also had been one of the judges in the inconclusive design competition that at first had awarded the commission to a Canadian firm. Or possibly because it was so expensive. Waite's building eventually cost nearly $1.3 million, well above his estimates. But this edifice and Lennox's city hall of about the same date [7/11] are undeniably the two buildings that carried Toronto out of the small town category architecturally and gave the city the imprimatur of an urban metropolis.

Walk 8: University of Toronto

1 University College, 15 King's College Circle, Cumberland & Storm, 1856-59; restored after fire, David B. Dick, 1892; Laidlaw Library addition, Mathers & Haldenby, 1961.
Part Romanesque cathedral, part Ruskinian college; part picturesquely medieval, part symmetrically classical; part colourful and flamboyant, part commanding and formal—University College confounded reviewers from the start. (At the unveiling, the *Globe* reporter surmised that the tower was unfinished and would soon acquire three additional turrets, to this day asymmetrically graced with but one.) The architects had first drawn an English Gothic design, but the governor-general of the provinces, perhaps mindful of Gothic's ecclesiastical flavour and the new university's avowed secularism, countered with something more "Italian." Back and forth they seem to have gone, with one of

the most exciting, inventive structures ever created in Canada the magnificent result.

Dick's restoration after the devastating fire of 1890 is evident only in the interior where brightly tiled floors and robust wooden gargoyles speak of the late 19th-century Arts and Crafts Movement. On the exterior the superb carved stone details—no two alike—and grand stone masses and profile of 1859 stand much as before. Unfortunately, the library wing added to the north in 1961 to close the quadrangle is nondescript if not a little lumpish. But even recent renovations which have introduced unlovely interior "modernizations" cannot detract from the essence of University College, which will always reside in Cumberland's beautiful Norman portal, image of all that is graceful, human, and ennobling in college life.

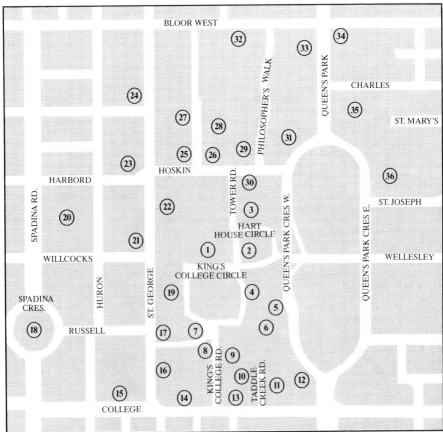

1 *University College, c. 1885*

2 Students' Administrative Council Building/ originally Toronto Magnetic and Meteorological Observatory/formerly Stewart Observatory, 12 Hart House Circle, Cumberland & Storm, 1857; reconstructed, 1908.

A charming Victorian miniature, this towered relic incorporates the stones as well as style of the 1857 Toronto observatory which was one of three in the world established by the British government for geodetic survey in the mid 19th century. The building was moved from its original site on the other side of the Front Lawn in 1908 to make way for new university buildings, at which time Louis Beaufort Stewart was professor in charge.

3 Hart House, 7 Hart House Circle, Sproatt & Rolph, 1911–19.

Soldiers' Memorial Tower, Sproatt & Rolph, 1924.

Hart House was a gift to the University of Toronto from the Massey Foundation. Named for company founder Hart Massey and intended as an undergraduate men's activity centre, it originally embraced "common room, reading room, music room, lecture room, sketch room, photographic dark room, Great Hall, chapel, gymnasium, squash courts, swimming pool, running track, rifle range, billiard room, library and theatre." It was designed in the Late Gothic Revival style then in favour for "scholastic work," admired for its evocation of ancient centres of learning, specifically the English universities of Oxford and Cambridge. Hart House is very good Late Gothic Revival. Often such buildings, with prag-

matic 20th-century emphasis on mass rather than picturesque silhouette, end up monotonous and dry. Henry Sproatt, who counted this his masterpiece, has given Hart House a bold, undulating façade with strongly defined fenestration.

In recent years, many former recreational facilities have been turned to other uses: a handsome new art gallery to house Hart House's distinguished Canadiana collection for example. The biggest change occurred in 1972 when women students were automatically admitted to membership along with men. They do not seem to have disturbed the Oxbridgian decorum and the Great Hall still stands resplendent in its double hammerbeam roof and stained glass windows.

Soldiers' Memorial Tower was added to Hart House to commemorate students and alumni who lost their lives in World War I (and later World War II). It is a fine, firm tower that turns what might have been an uneasy meeting between Romanesque University College and Gothic Hart House into an exciting architectural juncture.

6a *McMurrich Building*

6b *Medical Sciences Building*

4 Departments of French and English/originally University of Toronto Library, 7 King's College Circle, David B. Dick, 1892; south wing addition, Darling & Pearson, 1912. Sigmund Samuel Library, 9 King's College Circle, Mathers & Haldenby, 1953–54.

Dick's library for the University of Toronto is Richardsonian Romanesque but with a crispness of detail that ties it to the more brisk 1850s Romanesque of University College. Darling & Pearson's addition to the south of a few years later echoes Dick's work, and Mathers & Haldenby's 1950s expansion to the north paid for by wealthy businessman Sigmund Samuel tries not to be disruptive, especially of the picturesque apsidal termination of the original building.

5 Canadiana Building of the Royal Ontario Museum, 14 Queen's Park Crescent W., Mathers & Haldenby, 1951.

Donated by Sigmund Samuel along with his extraordinary collection of Canadian prints, paintings, maps, and documents, this building is interesting for its 1950s modern treatment of cut grey stone and its stone wall sculptures depicting Champlain, Wolfe, Simcoe, and Brock.

6a McMurrich Building/originally Anatomy Building, 12 Queen's Park Crescent W., Darling & Pearson, 1912–22.

Darling & Pearson's distinctive latter-day Romanesque, designed to harmonize with the 1890s university buildings, but, somehow, with characteristic rough stone and round-arched windows looking 1920s taut and streamlined. The Anatomy Building,

constructed behind the medical building of 1885 [demolished], contained large lecture rooms and, in the basement, a "suite of rooms for experimental surgery"! J. Playfair McMurrich was professor of anatomy from 1894 to 1939, celebrated for his definitive study of *Leonardo da Vinci, the Anatomist.*

6b Medical Sciences Building, 1 King's College Circle, Govan Kaminker Langley Keenleyside Melick Devonshire & Wilson with Somerville McMurrich & Oxley, 1966–69.

A giant assemblage of Brutalist parts neatly insinuated into a skinny site between Queen's Park and the Front Lawn. The sculptural pick-up-sticks of precast concrete that enliven the façade have mellowed gracefully with time—so many 1960s motifs look dated and shoddy to 1980s eyes.

7a Convocation Hall, 31 King's College Circle, Darling & Pearson, 1906–07.

"Not particularly in harmony with the University," wrote the prestigious *Canadian Architect and Builder* in 1907. But this domed, Ionic-columned circular hall seemed to be what was expected at a time when more picturesque forms suddenly appeared outdated and fussy. Unfortunately, Convocation Hall has not improved with age; if anything it is more lifeless and inert, its yellow brick darkened by dirt and lumpish mass surrounded by asphalt.

7a *Convocation Hall*

7b *Simcoe Hall*

7b Simcoe Hall, 27 King's College Circle, Darling & Pearson, 1923–24.

Simcoe Hall is the school administration centre, named for John Graves Simcoe, founder of Toronto, who in 1793 first suggested the establishment of a university. Eschewing the Edwardian pomp of Convocation Hall to which it is attached, Simcoe Hall is a gracious 1920s translation of yellow brick and classical motifs. The delicate Corinthian-columned entrance is one of the most inviting portals on campus.

8 Sandford Fleming Building/originally Physics Building/formerly McLennan Laboratories, 10 King's College Rd., Darling & Pearson, 1907; restored after fire, 1977.

Another dry Second Classical Revival building for what was then touted as the "most fully equipped physical laboratory on the continent." The building was designed to get students in and out quickly—ten minutes between classes—but the multiplicity of entrances is at odds with the theatricality of the form. For most of its life called McLennan Laboratories, after John McLennan, a distinguished physics professor and discoverer of cosmic rays, the building became Sandford Fleming in 1967 when physics moved elsewhere. Fleming is remembered as the inventor of standard time zones.

9a Mechanical Engineering Building, 5 King's College Rd., Darling & Pearson, 1909; new wing, Allward & Gouinlock, 1947–48.

Darling & Pearson's energetic yellow-brick Romanesque sits to the rear, its grand three-storey arches of glass as powerful as the machinery glimpsed inside. By contrast, the very smooth yellow-stone walls and slim ribbons of industrial sash employed by Allward & Gouinlock for the street addition of 1948 appear unusually sleek and serene. That date makes of their structure one of the very first Modern Movement buildings in Toronto. The clockface set on a protean tower was a trademark of this utilitarian Bauhaus factory look.

9b Haultain Building/originally Mill Building, 170 College St. (rear), Francis R. Heakes with Frank Darling, 1903; rebuilt, Craig & Madill, 1930–31.

Originally one storey, the Mill Building served the mining engineering department under Prof. H.E.T. Haultain. The 1930s reworked it into four storeys of Georgian red brick, and changed its name.

10 Rosebrugh Building/formerly Electrical Building, 4 Taddle Creek Rd., Darling & Pearson, 1921.

Ravishing, slimmed-down 20th-century Romanesque and one of the most delightful buildings on campus, with springy arches leaping all over the taut façade in an eye-catching display of energetic brickwork. T.R. Rosebrugh was founding head of electrical engineering at the university.

15 *Public Reference Library, postcard c. 1913*

11 FitzGerald Building/originally Hygiene and Public Health Building, 150 College St., Mathers & Haldenby, 1927.
Behind this unassuming red-brick Georgian Revival façade some of the most notable advances in the history of Canadian public health were achieved. Under the direction of Prof. J.G. FitzGerald, work leading to the virtual extinction of diphtheria and other contagious diseases was carried out, and from 1937 to 1969, the entire nation's insulin was produced. The top floor and gently balustraded roof originally contained houses and runs for rabbits, cats, and guinea pigs.

12 Botany Building and Greenhouse, 8 Queen's Park Crescent W., Mathers & Haldenby, 1931-32.
A rather overwrought classical stone pastiche, but with an angled shape that clearly understands the Queen's Park Crescent site. And who couldn't love the airy glass greenhouse, a Crystal Palace descendant that is probably the most interesting structure on this intersection.

13 Institute for Environmental Studies/originally School of Practical Science (Chemistry and Mining Building), 170 College St., Francis R. Heakes with Frank Darling, 1901-05.
Paid for by the province to help further the advance of Ontario's burgeoning mining industry, this beautifully executed red-brick structure with imposing elevated Ionic portico well illustrates the high seriousness placed on science and technology in the period. The interior is as finely detailed as the exterior.

14 Wallberg Memorial Building, 184-200 College St., Page & Steele, 1947-49.
A simple modern red-brick façade with smooth stone details and dignified twin entrance-pavilions disconcertingly bombarded by a fusillade of roof-top mechanicals.

15 Koffler Student Services Centre/originally Public Reference Library, 214 College St., Alfred H. Chapman with Wickson & Gregg, 1906; addition, Chapman & Oxley, 1928-30; altered, Howard D. Chapman with Howard V. Walker, 1985.
One of the best Second Classical Revival buildings in Toronto, rich in sculptural stone ornament but poised and firm with graceful large windows set deep into smooth yellow-brick walls and a gradually stepped approach to dignify the entrance. The City of Toronto accepted $350,000 from library benefactor Andrew Carnegie to build this reference facility, albeit reluctantly; one Canadian scion thought the offer from an American "impertinent." Nevertheless, the gift was approved, a site chosen (near the university and far from the recently ravaged downtown "fire zone"), and an architectural competition held. This enlightened Beaux-Arts composition by Alfred Chapman, newly returned to his hometown after studies in Paris and New York, was the distinguished choice. Chapman's son, Howard, working with Howard Walker, did the sympathetic update.

19 *Knox College*

20 *New College*

16 International Student Centre/originally "Pendarvis" (Frederic W. Cumberland residence), 33 St. George St., Frederic W. Cumberland, 1857–60.

Architect Frederic Cumberland built himself this refined residence at the same time he was working on spectacular University College [8/1]. The style is indeterminate, but forms and details are very pleasing. (The principal façades were originally those looking south and east; a long front path ran south to College Street.) This became the official home of Ontario's lieutenant-governors in the 1910s at a time when St. George Street was primarily residential and the large lots were held by well-to-do Torontonians on 21-year renewable leases from the university.

17 Forestry Building, 45 St. George St., Darling & Pearson, 1925.

A handsome red-brick Georgian cube with, as reported at the opening, "no suggestion of extravagance." The building was moved some feet south in the 1950s to make way for the Galbraith Building.

18 Originally Knox College, 1 Spadina Crescent, Smith & Gemmell, 1875.

Knox College was established in Toronto in 1844 as a Presbyterian theological seminary. After several changes of venue, this churchy-looking High Victorian Gothic Revival edifice was built, punctuated with pointy windows, wall dormers,

turrets, and gables. Conspicuously sited in an ornamental crescent and closing the vista up wide Spadina Avenue, Knox College took its formal, symmetrical responsibilities perhaps too seriously. What should have been an exciting picturesque form ends up not a little boring. Knox federated with the University of Toronto in 1890, occupying this fortuitously nearby building until 1915 when it moved into 59 St. George Street [8/19].

19 Knox College, 59 St. George St. thru to 23 King's College Circle, Chapman & McGiffin, 1911–15.

A typical North American Collegiate Gothic building of the period, with blocky, rather dry forms in a quadrangular plan that encompasses library, chapel, dining hall, and student residences. Rough sandstone walls and leaded casement windows are quite appealing though, and the Gothic-detailed interiors among the most evocative in all the university.

20 New College (Wetmore and Wilson Halls), 300 Huron St., Fairfield & DuBois, 1964 and 1967.

Constructed to meet the exploding university population of the 1960s, this was the first new undergraduate college built on campus in 40 years. Its two residence halls rimming the block look regular and foursquare from the street, but seen from inside the interior well, they surprise and delight with undulating walls and contoured grounds spiritedly nudging our idea of the traditional "quadrangle."

23 *John P. Roberts Research Library*

21 Sidney Smith Hall, 100 St. George St., John B. Parkin Associates, 1961; cafeteria addition, Irwin Beinhaker Associates, 1984.
Employing a spare International Style look of implied stone and glass modules, this arts and sciences building was the first to go up on the new West Campus. Its program of rationality and contextualism dictated two wings: a two-storey block of easily accessible lecture rooms related in scale to buildings on the east side of St. George; and a six-storey tower containing more privatized faculty offices placed on axis with the street to hide height and cut down noise. The high-tech ruby-red-brick and glass-block cafeteria addition to the south is intriguingly scooped into the site. Sidney Smith was one-time Minister of External Affairs and president of the university.

22 Sir Daniel Wilson Residence, 73 St. George St., Mathers & Haldenby, 1953–55.
Whitney Hall, 85 St. George St., Mathers & Haldenby with John M. Lyle, 1930–31.
Two self-conscious Neo-Georgian ensembles erected in this century for the men's and women's residences of University College [8/1], to which they relate not at all. Wilson was an early president of University College; Whitney, a wealthy benefactor and brother of the premier.

23 John P. Roberts Research Library, 130 St. George St., Warner Burns Toan & Lunde with Mathers & Haldenby, 1968–73.
Called "intimidating," "ponderous," "pompous," and "arrogant," this is the one building in Toronto everyone loves to hate. It was named for the province's incumbent premier and designed by an eminent New York firm of library architects who began with a master university plan that called for large-scale buildings to cover this northwest sector as well as contouring of the site. But, with 100,000 cubic yards of poured-in-place and precast Brutalist concrete, it would have taken a heap of hills and high-rises to integrate this mass. The composition is interesting and functional, however, with a 14-storey triangular-shaped unit containing stacks and reading rooms linked to two vari-shaped satellites, one of seven storeys for library science studies, and another of six floors for rare books. It looks great from a helicopter, they say.

24 Innis College, 2 Sussex Ave., A.J. Diamond & Barton Myers (designed by A.J. Diamond), 1975.
A reevaluation of the goals of higher education in the province, public outcry over behemoth Roberts Library [8/23], neighbourhood agitation about continuing encroachment, and budgetary crisis—all contrived to change the university's grand plans for this neck of the campus. Unpretentious, low-scale, meld-into-the-environment Innis College, appropriately named for pragmatic philosopher Harold Innis, was the thoughtful result.

24 *Innis College*   25 *Massey College*

25 Massey College, 4 Devonshire Pl., Ron Thom (for Thompson Berwick Pratt), 1963.
Medieval ideas and forms translated into the best of modern taste. Massey College was conceived by Vincent Massey, the farm machinery scion and one-time governor-general, as an interdisciplinary men's graduate centre in the form of an exclusive monastery for an intimate community of scholars. Quadrangular and inward-looking in plan, richly textured and elegant in stance, permanent and symbolical in mood, Thom's fastidious design must have pleased Massey mightily. Whether we should have been building Neo-Gothic Revival men-only educational institutions at all in the late 20th century is another matter. Massey College has been co-ed since the mid '70s.

26 Devonshire House, 3 Devonshire Pl., Eden Smith & Son, 1908–09.
Jacobethan "period houses" for resident men.

27 St. Hilda's College, 20 Devonshire Pl., George & Moorhouse, 1938; addition, 1982.
In the allotment of architectural styles, women's residences seem habitually to receive neat domestic Georgian. This one serves the ladies of Trinity.

28 Gerald Larkin Academic Building, 15 Devonshire Pl., Somerville McMurrich & Oxley, 1961.
A quietly modern version of Trinity stone and stance, without the flounces but with all the flair. Beautifully sited and landscaped, it is home to the George Ignatieff Theatre, offices, and a buttery.

29 Trinity College, 6 Hoskin Ave., Darling & Pearson, 1925; residence wing addition, George & Moorhouse, 1941; chapel addition, Sir Giles Gilbert Scott, 1955; residence wing addition, Somerville McMurrich & Oxley, 1961.
Romantic evocation of England's ivied halls, this stone building is a copy of the original Trinity College of 1851 on Queen Street [demolished], which in turn had borrowed its Tudor Gothic garb from Oxford and Cambridge. Trinity did not affiliate with the University of Toronto until 1904 and did not arrive on campus until 1925. Of special note is Trinity's distinctive chapel, designed in 1955 by Sir Giles Gilbert Scott of Liverpool Cathedral renown. Built of bright, crisp stone with luminous clear glazed ornamentally leaded windows sparked by brilliant touches of colour, the chapel is almost mystically "light."

29 *Trinity College*   30 *Wycliffe College*

30 Wycliffe College, 5 Hoskin Ave., David B. Dick, 1888–91; refectory and library addition, Gordon & Helliwell, 1906; chapel addition, George M. Miller, 1911; Leonard Library addition, Chapman & Oxley, 1929–30.

Founded in 1877 as a "low church" Anglican college to train clergy in the evangelical ways of John Wycliffe, the school ironically sits directly opposite Trinity [8/29], representative of the ritual-istic Anglo-Catholic "high church." Wycliffe federated with the U. of T. in 1890 and its unpretentious but well-made building was one of the many harmonious Richardsonian Romanesque structures designed by Dick to grace the early campus. Interestingly, the Leonard Library addition to the rear ignores Wycliffe's red-brick richness, lining up instead with stony Late Gothic Revival Hart House [8/3].

Running from Hoskin Avenue to Bloor Street, Philosopher's Walk follows the course of Taddle Creek, which once mean-dered through these fields. Until recently it represented a tranquil vestige of the pictur-esque 19th-century campus, but recent uprooting of trees and rude construction (garage for Trinity, retaining walls for Laskin Library) are creating mayhem in this grove of academe.

The iron and stone Alexandra Gates at the north end originally stood at Bloor and Queen's Park. Designed by Chadwick & Beckett for the International Order of the Daughters of Empire, they were officially opened by Queen Alexandra's son, the future King George V, and his consort on their visit in 1901.

31 Flavelle House/originally "Holwood" (Sir Joseph Flavelle residence), 78 Queen's Park, Darling & Pearson, 1901–02; addition for Faculty of Law, Hart Massey with Wil-liam J. McBain, 1961; altered with addition, Moffat/Kinoshita, 1988–89.

Using a Second Classical Revival vocabu-lary including monumental Corinthian porticoes but arrayed on the sloping site in picturesque manner with wings off in several directions, Flavelle House is a spirited *tour de force* and probably the most publicly grand mansion in all of Toronto. It was built by Joseph Flavelle, wealthy president of the William Davies Co., forerunner of Canada Packers, at a time when Queen's Park was a very prominent residential quarter. Today the house is centrepiece of the university's Faculty of Law and most of the rooms have been institutionalized, but the fine Georgian hall with Art Nouveau ceiling painted by Gustav Hahn remains intact.

Massey and McBain's red-brick addi-tion of 1961 once felicitously joined Flavelle House on the sloping site. But now—enlarged, terraced, glassed, and contextually nil—the "reconfigured" extension seems to have lost interest in a proper marriage here. (The new liaison is down the walk, with the look-alike ROM infill of 1983 [8/33].)

32 Royal Conservatory of Music/originally Toronto Baptist College/formerly McMaster Hall, 273 Bloor St. W., Langley Langley & Burke, 1880–81.

Bristly High Victorian verve for the Baptists, rich with sky-shooting dormers and chimneys, corbels and panels, stone

33 *Royal Ontario Museum*

nd brick. The individualistic denomina-
on decided not to federate with the U.
f T., and in 1930 moved away to
lamilton to settle McMaster University,
amed for the Toronto dry goods mer-
hant and senator who financed it all [see
lso 14/28].

**3 Royal Ontario Museum, 100 Queen's
'ark, Darling & Pearson, 1912–14; east wing
ddition, Chapman & Oxley, 1930–32; infill
dditions, Moffat Moffat & Kinoshita with
Mathers & Haldenby, 1978–83.**

'ommissioned by the province but early
nder the supervision of the university,
he Royal Ontario Museum was designed
·y Darling & Pearson using the exuberant
·ee Romanesque style they were
xploring elsewhere on campus [see 8/6a,
a, 10]. The façade of their building (now
ne west wing on view from Philosopher's
Valk) is one of the architectural gems of
ne city. Using buff-coloured brick and
·rracotta, the architects wove an exotic
orgeously rich Venetian Byzantine tapes-
·y of corbels, fretwork, arcades, and
·iezes to play over an elevation of great
rched windows and bold projecting bays.
　Chapman & Oxley's east wing addition
f 18 years later along Queen's Park (con-
ected to the west wing to form an H)
·as from a sterner Byzantium, a flat Art
)eco Romanesque with sculptures almost
·ding in the stone walls.
　The latest expansion has unobtrusively
lled the spaces between the bars of the
: a plain six-storey office building for
·rators to the south; a glazed terrace
allery for the world-famous Chinese col-
ction to the north.

**34 Provincial Ombudsman/originally Lillian
Massey Department of Household Science,
157 Bloor St. W. at Queen's Park, George M.
Miller, 1908–12.**

A very distinguished example of Neo-
Classical Revival, this building features a
colossal pedimented Ionic portico centring
beautifully proportioned wings with giant
engaged columns, all of gleaming smooth
Indiana limestone. A donation to the
university from Lillian Massey Treble of
the farm machinery family [see 12/19], the
facility was intended to educate young
women in the scientific running of a
household and thereby it was hoped
alleviate some of the period's social ills!
Interior fittings of marble and oak were
as fine as the exterior, with the domestic
training suite outfitted with Limoges
china. A gymnasium and swimming pool
in the basement were designed to serve
women students from across the campus,
just as the Masseys' Hart House donation
[8/3] served the men.

**35 Victoria College, 73 Queen's Park Cres-
cent E., William G. Storm, 1892.**

**Annesley Hall, 95 Queen's Park, George M.
Miller, 1901–03.**

**Burwash Hall, 89 Charles St. W., Sproatt &
Rolph, 1909–12; additions, Sproatt & Rolph,
1930.**

Birge-Carnegie Library, 75 Queen's Park, Sproatt & Rolph, 1908–11.

Emmanuel College, 75 Queen's Park, Sproatt & Rolph, 1929–31.

E.J. Pratt Library, 73 Queen's Park Crescent E., Adamson Associates, 1961.

Northrop Frye Hall/originally New Academic Building, 73 Queen's Park Crescent E., Adamson Associates, 1967.

Singly and as a group, the buildings of Victoria University are probably the best of their type on campus. Certainly the Brobdingnagian creation that is Victoria College—hard to believe this giant is only three storeys high—is as solid, as rich, as consummately crafted, and energetically balanced as any Richardsonian Romanesque structure in the city. It doesn't look like an institutional building at all, more like a colossal house eager to shelter its 1890s family of scholars.

Burwash Hall, the Late Gothic Revival 1910s assembly of men's residence houses that rims the site to east and north, is superb, neither stiff nor quaint, with fluid ashlar walls and clean stone window surrounds. It was paid for by the Masseys, as was the earlier domestic-looking Jacobethan Annesley Hall for women residents located on Queen's Park.

American library benefactor Andrew Carnegie and Canadian steel magnate Cyrus Birge were responsible for endowing the 1930s Late Gothic Revival building on the northwest corner of the site. Originally the college library, this romantic church-like edifice now houses the central archives of the United Church of Canada—a luminous place to dig for facts. The United Church's divinity school, the 1931 Emmanuel College, compatibly finishes off the west wing of Victoria's Gothic quadrangle.

The Pratt Library and Northrop Frye Hall, exquisitely terraced and sited to border Victoria College to the south, are quiet, immaculate 1960s boxes floating in space, never obtrusive to the grand mansion that still towers over the elegant ensemble. When Methodist Victoria College elected to federate with the University of Toronto and left its Cobourg home in 1890, it was a grand day for scholastic architecture in Toronto.

36a St. Michael's College, 50 St. Joseph St., William Hay, 1856; additions, William T Thomas, 1862; addition, 1872 (demolished), addition, 1903 (demolished).

St. Basil's Church, 50 St. Joseph St., William Hay, 1856; sanctuary additions, 1876; vestibule and choir loft additions, Joseph Connolly, 1886; spire addition, Arthur W Holmes, 1895.

Queen's Park Building (Pontifical Institute for Mediaeval Studies, More House, Fisher House, Teefy Hall), 53–59 Queen's Park Crescent E., Arthur W. Holmes, 1935–36.

Brennan Hall, Elmsley Place, Arthur W Holmes, 1938; north wing addition, Frank Brennan, 1967.

Carr Hall, 100 St. Joseph St., Ernest Cormier, 1954.

St. Basil's College, 95 St. Joseph St., Ernest Cormier, 1951; addition to fourth storey, John J. Farrugia, 1982.

John M. Kelly Library, 113 St. Joseph St., John J. Farrugia, 1969.

Alumni Hall/originally Ontario Research Foundation, 121 St. Joseph St., 1929; two-storey addition, c. 1955; renovated, 1983.

Situated on a quietly dignified site east of Queen's Park, the buildings that make up the University of St. Michael's College seem unlike any others on the U. of T. campus, beginning with French Gothic St. Basil's Church and attendant college buildings designed by William Hay in 1856. In fact, it was only coincidental that St. Michael's was located hard by the University of Toronto campus at all. The Basilian Fathers, who had come to Toronto from France to found the Catholic school, objected to the obvious east-end location around St. Paul's [2/24] because of its proximity to the unhealthy Don River [see Introduction, *AREA VI*], and accepted instead this commanding site atop Clover Hill proffered by wealthy landowner and Roman Catholic convert John Elmsley [see 5/37]. Propinquity undoubtedly influenced St. Michael's early decision to affiliate with the U. of T. in 1881, the first outside school to do so.

St. Michael's College, then, can claim the oldest buildings on the U. of T. campus, predating completion of University College [8/1] by three years. It was supposedly at donor Elmsley's request that a parish church was put up here along with school buildings, perhaps so he wouldn't have to walk as far as St. Michael's Cathedral [13/3] for his daily devotions (Elmsley's house, also called

35 *Victoria College*

36 *St. Basil's Church*

Clover Hill [demolished], was situated within a stone's throw). St. Basil's is a fine Gothic Revival church: lithe, tense, almost prickly-looking. The attached St. Michael's wing displays some of the same energy, with pointy dormers and lovely spired turrets sprouting along the high roof. But there is also a cautious, flattened dignity here, characteristics that reappear in later college buildings as well. Subsequent easterly additions to St. Michael's were expropriated by the city and demolished in the 1920s during Bay Street's northward march.

Holmes's Queen's Park Building and Brennan Hall are 1930s Late Gothic Revival, built of limestone and stone-textured light-coloured cement blocks. Again picturesque Gothic detail is rendered cooly French and precise, an impression reinforced especially at the Queen's Park Building with its formal open quadrangle and decorous "stone" and iron fence. A world centre for medieval studies, this building also contains student residences (More and Fisher Houses) and classrooms (Teefy Hall). Brennan Hall, named for Father Laurence Brennan, who was pastor of St. Basil's, 1880–1889, 1891–1904, is a student and faculty activity centre.

Carr Hall, the classroom building added along St. Joseph Street in 1954, was designed by Montreal architect Ernest Cormier of Art Deco renown. Cormier's Gothic is definitely cool, if not cold, with a façade of cheerless window slits punctuated by a bulging pentagonal stair tower. Father Henry Carr is remembered as president of St. Michael's College,

1915–1925, and founder of the Pontifical Institute.

Architect John Farrugia's Post-Modern efforts to animate Cormier's plain yellow-brick St. Basil's College by adding some vigorous concrete columns to the front, plus an overhang to the fourth storey, are not without merit, but they have created a top-heavy look for this theological seminary. Farrugia was also responsible for the typical 1960s waffled precast concrete John M. Kelly Library.

36b Originally George W. Ross house, 1 Elmsley Pl., Langley & Langley, 1896.

Originally William Chalcroft house, 3 Elmsley Pl., Langley & Langley, 1896.

Formerly Sir Bertram Windle house, 5 Elmsley Pl., possibly John M. Lyle, 1896.

Maritain/Gilson House, 6–8 Elmsley Pl., A. Frank Wickson, 1904.

Originally Gibson/Gibson house, 2 Elmsley Pl. and 96 St. Joseph St., Marshall B. Aylesworth, 1892–93; additions, Burke & Horwood, 1897.

Now part of St. Michael's campus, Elmsley Place was laid out in 1890 by Remigius Elmsley, son of John Elmsley, as an exclusive residential precinct. The land was conveyed by leasehold, and in the 1920s, St. Michael's was able to buy up the attractive enclave with its bevy of distinguished turn-of-the-century houses, most of which stand now as student residences. Illustrious early residents included a famous portrait painter, a university president, and an Ontario attorney-general, senator, judge, and premier.

Area VI

Walk 9: Don Vale
Walk 10: "Old Cabbagetown"

In the beginning, this area was known simply as "on the Don." The provincial governor, John Graves Simcoe, had named the picturesque stream flowing from the north into the bay east of town after the Don River in Yorkshire, England. Simcoe fully appreciated the value of this strategic waterway running through a steep valley. When he parcelled out the town of York and surrounding concessions in 1793, he set aside the large tract south of present-day Carlton Street between the town and river for a government reserve, the King's Park. Here he planned a naval shipyard which would draw timber from surrounding forests to build a protective fleet for the new province. The wooded acreage north of this, running to today's Bloor Street, he took for himself in the name of his infant son, Frank, who had come with Simcoe and his wife to the new land. Then, as a means of finally securing the river, Simcoe granted the 250 acres east of the Don between the bay and Bloor Street to his trusted aide, John Scadding.

A qualification for landholding was erection of a dwelling on one's property. The governor was no exception and the Simcoes soon commenced to put up on their son's land a small house which they dubbed "Castle Frank." Located on a bluff overlooking the river and then some hours' journey from town, this forest retreat was not finished until 1796, a few months before Simcoe was recalled to England. Left derelict, Castle Frank burned down in 1829, but the name lingers for a short street and high school in the area. John Scadding built his required dwelling in the verdant valley, where Queen Street now crosses the river. Scadding returned to England with the Simcoes, but he came back to York in 1818 and built a larger, more substantial house farther north and east of his first. (That earlier cabin of 1794 now sits in the Canadian National Exhibition grounds, billed as Toronto's oldest building.)

Other pioneer buildings in the Don Valley can be seen at Todmorden Mills, a small museum village that commemorates early enterprises located along the Don: sawmills, grist mills, paper mills, brickyards, breweries, and distilleries. Simcoe's shipyard was never put into operation, but a need for house-building materials depleted the tall stands of pine soon enough. The valley then began to attract a few farmers and market gardeners.

Starting in the 1850s, the City of Toronto began assembling land in and around the Don Valley. Here they erected institutions that would benefit from the remote locale: the isolation hospital [demolished], city jail and industrial farm [9/20], and poorhouse or "house of refuge" [demolished]. In 1875, a public park was begun which was officially opened as Riverdale Park five years later. By the turn of the century, it was the second largest park in Toronto and the locus of great sports activity: lacrosse, football, baseball, tennis, sledding, skating, and swimming in the Don.

But the sylvan environment was not to last. In 1886, voters were persuaded to pass a bylaw for straightening and deepening the Don River to accommodate industrialization of the lower valley and a new railway line into Toronto. And although the 1918 Prince Edward Viaduct spanning the valley at Bloor Street helped remove traffic for a time, the expressway now streaking through its centre has turned the Don Valley into little more than an automobile track despite efforts of conservationists.

P roximity to the Don influenced building in this part of Toronto in several ways. Take Cabbagetown. (Though the name Cabbagetown is sometimes used— especially by real estate agents and local businessmen— to include all of *AREA VI*, historically Cabbagetown was the portion between the Don Valley and Parliament Street, Queen Street to Gerrard.) This had originally formed part of Simcoe's government reserve, but the land was opened to subdivision as early as 1819. At first it attracted only a few squatters' huts. Townsfolk talked of the unhealthy effluvia of the marshes of the Don, and development moved in other directions away from the stagnant waters. Then, beginning in the 1840s, great waves of immigrant Irish began to find their way to Toronto. If other citizens did not think this neighbourhood congenial, it looked fine to those fleeing potato famines back home. Speculative builders jumped in with rentals for the unskilled labourers, who planted cabbages in their front yards, enjoyed free recreation aplenty in swimming and skating on the Don, and never felt it necessary to move. One hundred years later it remained a poor but lively working-class community of small houses and corner stores. Today the cabbages are gone, and most of the houses as well. After World War II when city fathers had a chance to take a careful look at the burgeoning metropolis, they decided Cabbagetown was a slum ripe for that great preoccupation of North American cities in those postwar years: urban renewal. They also decided this was just the place to introduce another municipal mainstay of the era: public housing. Within the area are four government-subsidized housing projects: three clearance, rebuilding-from-scratch blockbusters; and one rehabilitation, infill scheme [10/30, 31, 32, 33].

The land north of Carlton originally belonging to Simcoe was managed by John Scadding on his return to York, and later purchased outright by John junior after the elder Scadding's death. In 1844, young Scadding and his wife Amelia donated a large tract near Bloor Street for St. James' cemetery [9/1]. Parliament Street (so called because the first parliament buildings had been located at its foot) functioned primarily as the "sad road to the cemetery." By the mid 1850s, the

SAND OR FLINT PAPER.

TWO QUALITIES, viz.:
FLINT PAPER, } ALL NUMBERS
X X FLINT PAPER, }

CRYSTALIZED FLINT,

Chains, Hubs, Spokes, Fellors, Lasts, Handles and Oxcake, also, for Ivory, Brass and Marble Workers, Machinists, Cutlery Manufacturers, &c.

Put up in Numbers 00 FINISHING, 0, 0, 1, 2, 3, 4, 5, 6, 7d, 8, 1 being Finest, No. 9 Coarsest.

Blacking, Water-proof Leather Preserver, Snow Blacking, Harness Oil Blacking.
Neat's Foot Oil, Ivory Black, Super-Phosphate of Lime for Manure, Animal Charcoal, Sand Paper, Ground Bone for Manure, Glue.

A business card of Peter R. Lamb company whose large factory complex was located in Don Vale at the end of Amelia Street, 1848-88.

Toronto Necropolis [9/17] had also found its way to these remote precincts, along with the Lamb glue and "blacking" factory, virtually an animal crematory [see 9/13]. Add to this the unhealthy reputation of the nearby Don, and it is little wonder that residential development was sluggish. As late as 1891, a guidebook dispatched the whole of this corner of town with a single line, noting it was the site of the "city's cemeteries overlooking the beautiful vale of the Don." (Since about 1970, the hill area east of Parliament Street and north of Gerrard has been called Don Vale, a misnomer given it by city planners.) Although some streets had been laid out for residential subdivision in 1851, an atlas of 1858 shows only about 50 houses east of Parliament Street and north of Carlton, one of which still stands more or less with its original look [9/30]. The area remained in semi-rural torpor until the late 1870s/early 1880s when another swell of immigrants from the British Isles arrived. Some were headed for Cabbagetown, but others, including the more affluent, began to settle here, making this part of Toronto unusual in not following the late 19th-century pattern of residential segregation by class. Workers' cottages were built side by side with more generous double houses for the middle class. Some large single houses were even put up by well-to-do Torontonians at this time, witness the fine Gothic Revival and Second Empire residences which still garner attention on Carlton Street. Finally, the building boom that overtook Toronto in the late 1880s/early 1890s gobbled up all the empty lots in Don Vale for impressive Queen Anne designs, and there was no more talk of "sad roads to the cemetery." Both Carlton and Parliament Streets—which had become quite commercial with shopfronts pasted onto former houses—had horse-drawn streetcars, and by 1902, the electric street railway was carrying hundreds of Torontonians to the Riverdale Zoo at the end of Winchester Street.

This area deteriorated in the years between the wars much like the blocks to the south. Unlike them, however, it has been rehabilitated not through slum clearance and public housing, but gentrification, which has brought its own rewards and penalties. It is estimated that 80 percent of the houses in Don Vale have been renovated one way or another. The area west of Parliament Street included in *AREA VI* was never "on the Don," taking its cues more from residential development along Sherbourne Street [Walk 11]. Today, however, it is very much part of what passes for "Old Cabbagetown," Toronto's emblem of renewed downtown living.

Walk 9: Don Vale

1a St. James' Cemetery, 635 Parliament St., John G. Howard (grounds), 1845; Darling & Pearson (fence and gate), 1905.
A 19th-century guidebook called it a "garden of graves," and the meandering roads and lush landscaping designed by Howard for the rolling, heavily wooded site still make for a richly scenic spot. The first graveyard for the Anglicans had been adjacent to St. James' Church on King Street [1/8], but by the 1840s, that was filled and this remote site acquired on the hills overlooking the Don Valley. At 65 acres, this was the largest cemetery in Toronto, and it was here that the leading families came to rest. Tombs of architectural and historical interest listed by the Toronto Historical Board are: Austin, Brock, Gooderham, Gzowski, Howland, Jarvis, Manning, and Severs.

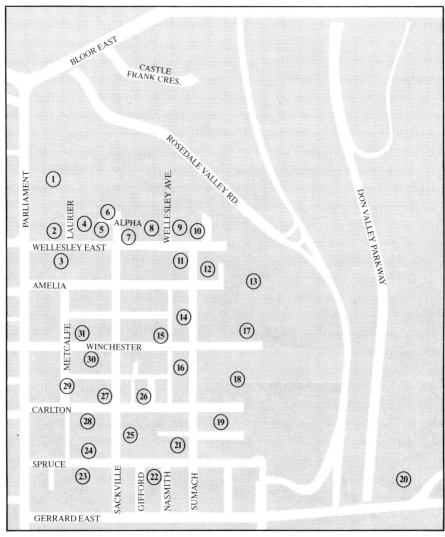

1b *St.-James-the-Less*

2 *314 Wellesley St. E.*

1b St.-James-the-Less Chapel, 635 Parliament St., Cumberland & Storm, 1858.

Built in that decade when many superb structures designed by immigrant British architects were rising in the city, this is one of the choicest buildings in Toronto, if not in all of Canada. Although it may suggest a simple 13th-century English parish church, there is nothing primitive about the bold massing and tense outlines seen here, with a squat masonry base playing against the swoop of a steep roof punctuated by a sharp, soaring spire. Intended only as a mortuary chapel, St.-James-the-Less did hold public services for a period in the mid 1860s before nearby St. Peter's [10/6] was built.

2 Originally Thomas Harris house, 314 Wellesley St. E., 1889–90.

This joyful, informal house is emblematic of Don Vale's Queen Anne architecture of delight, with irregular massing and fenestration, a variety of materials, ingenuity of shapes, and lively surprises, provided here by a veritable catalogue of terracotta and carved stone ornament. Mr. Harris was, appropriately, proprietor of a stone-cutting firm. As a result of new row houses sneaked in behind, no. 314 gained a garage but lost some garden.

3 Originally Arthur Henry house, 327 Wellesley St. E., 1875.

Mr. Henry was a carpenter and he built his 1½-storey cottage to last; save for added insul-brick siding, no. 327 appears perfectly intact. This symmetrical design with barge-hung gable centred over a front door was typical of small dwellings built across Ontario from earliest days well into the 1870s.

4a 316–324 Wellesley St. E. (five-house row), 1888–89.

326–334 Wellesley St. E. (five-house row), 1888–89.

Many Don Vale houses were built in a rush of speculation by a few contractors, offering an unusual opportunity to create large and ambitious ensembles. These spirited twinned five-house rows with bristling corner towers keeping watch over Laurier Avenue, itself created as part of the composition, have few equals in Toronto for bravura planning.

4b 1–21 Laurier Ave. (ten-house row), 1889.

2–22 Laurier Ave. (ten-house row), 1889.

Queen Anne row housing that is repetitious but never static. Working with a basic repertory of factory-made parts—unpierced bargeboards, wooden slatted porches, stained glass windows—Toronto builders were somehow able to adapt features of a style known for variety and asymmetry to long Bay-n-Gable rows of look-alike houses. Part of the trick was the exuberant sunbursting detail that went with the style, part was the undulating rhythm of the façade.

5 *1-7 Wellesley Cottages*

5 1–7 Wellesley Cottages (seven-house row), 1887; rear additions, 1985.

Don Vale is unusual for its deep lots and back alleys which once accommodated stables and other outbuildings, and sometimes, as here, actual houses. Until 1980, these gentle gabled cottages were occupied by long-time tenants paying low rents to a single landlord. Sold to a developer and in his words "revitalized," they are very fashionable now. Picket fences are grace notes to be seen throughout the area.

6 1–17 Alpha Ave. (nine-house row), 1888.

2–18 Alpha Ave. (nine-house row), 1888.

After the peaked-roof 1½-storey cottage came the mansard-roof 1½-storey cottage. Although these variously painted houses are very ornamental, unpainted ones show that the brick itself was meant to be decorative with yellow bands stringing the red. Alpha Avenue was another instant 1880s street, which, it has recently been discovered, the residents in fact own. One of them balked at paying taxes, but then the city stopped collecting their garbage!

7 483–485 Sackville St. (double house), 1889–90.

376–380 Wellesley St. E. (triple house), 1889.

These dwellings sitting around the corner from one another are uncommonly commercial-looking, flaunting flat roofs, pressed-metal cornices, and brick belt courses. Potential residents didn't much take to them either and they stood vacant for many years, even though they were expensively built entirely of brick instead of the roughcast with brick front more usual in this area. The owner was Nathaniel Baldwin, who ran a dairy store on the corner between the two.

8a Owl House Lane, 390 Wellesley St. E. (complex of twenty row houses and one rehabilitated house), Peter Turner, 1978–79.

An unobtrusive condominium development boasting underground parking and an 1892 "theme" house tucked in the northeast corner of the complex that was once home to artist C.W. Jefferys and his parents and brothers. When Jefferys knew this house, it sported a gabled roof and third storey, but insurance atlases indicate it never covered more ground than the small parcel it does today. It was built by Jefferys's father, a contractor. The small owl and other terracotta devices on the Jefferys house are typical Queen Anne ornament. An identical serpent as well as much larger owl can be seen at 314 Wellesley Street East [9/2], probably also designed and built by contractor Jefferys.

8b 398–402 Wellesley St. E. (three-house row), 1886.

This trio well represents the eager Bay-n-Gable houses that rose in great numbers across Toronto in the 1870s and early 1880s. The curved bargeboard embroidering the gable, polygonal bay window, and red brick sparked with yellow continue to spell picturesque at its most sprightly.

8b *398 Wellesley St. E.*

14a *420-422 Sumach St.*

9a 414-416, 418-420, 422-424, 426-428 Wellesley St. E. (four double houses), 1887-88.
Displaying vigorous patterns and textures associated with the burgeoning Queen Anne style, these slam-bang double houses are later versions of Toronto Bay-n-Gable. Tall and flat with dynamic rectangular bays and boldly geometric ornament in the gable, they loom large and loud in the streetscape.

9b 1-3, 5-7, 9-11, 13-15, 2-4, 6-8, 10-12, 14-16 Wellesley Ave. (eight double houses), 1888.
17-19, 18-20 Wellesley Ave. (two double houses), 1889.
Wellesley Avenue was created by developer Frank Armstrong, also responsible for the houses framing it on Wellesley Street [9/9a] and the similar Laurier Avenue project [9/4a, 4b]. Armstrong was an inventive speculative builder, deploying prefabricated parts and forms in different combinations. Here the double houses feature a single, centred gable; on the corner at Wellesley Street, each double house is assembled with two side gables. The land at the end of this narrow cul-de-sac did not belong to Armstrong; the two double houses there were built in a different style one year later.

10 438-444 Wellesley St. E. (four-house row), 1883-84.
"French-roof" cottages, small but spirited with an animated curve to the mansard and busy patterns of yellow brick playing over the red. Early tenants were a cabman, an organmaker, a widow, and a "labourer." The houses were valued by their first owner, tax collector Mungo Nasmith, at $400 each.

11 442-444, 446-448, 450-452, 454-456 Sumach St. (four double houses), 1886-87.
The Second Empire mansard roof was practical for providing space to attic bedrooms and these straight-sided mansards were the most practical of all, but they are not nearly as attractive as the concave curves gracing the cottages across the way on Wellesley Street [9/10].

12a 437-439 and 441-443 Sumach St. (two double houses), 1892.
Weighty Richardsonian Romanesque loners in this nimble precinct, these double houses parade the heavy stone bases and voluminous round-arched windows of houses built in Toronto's Annex neighbourhood during this period.

12b 425-435 Sumach St. (six-house row), 1904-05.
An idiosyncratic row still enjoying a Victorian passion for the strange and exotic. The half-timbered oriels suggest medieval England; the lilt to the gabled dormers is almost Chinese.

17 *Toronto Necropolis Chapel*

13 About Wellesley Park and Hillcrest Avenue abutting the Toronto Necropolis

originally stood some dozen factory buildings of Peter R. Lamb & Company, makers of glue, ground bone, lime, animal charcoal, and a popular shoe and stove lustre known as Lamb's Penny Blacking. Begun here in 1848, this was Don Vale's first and only real industry, and while it may have drawn some settlement to the area, it is likely the sooty, malodorous enterprise kept more potential development away than it attracted. The main building burned down in 1888 and the factory was never rebuilt, although the family retained this large parcel of land until it was built up with houses and the park created in the early 1900s.

14a 420-422 Sumach St. (double house), 1886.

Sporting four sprightly pointed dormers skipping across a mansarded roof and a harmonious ornamental porch, this redbrick Second Empire pair makes a handsome contribution to the streetscape.

14b 410-412 Sumach St. (double house), 1884.

Well-made Bay-n-Gables with pleasantly curved yellow-brick details sparking the red. The half windows at ground level were where coal went in to fuel the furnace.

14c 404-408 Sumach St. (triple house), 1902.

The English cottage found its way to Toronto in the early 20th century. Its fresh, quaint half-timbered look was typically used—paradoxically enough—for large, expensive single-family dwellings, but it also worked well for this winsome miniature triple house.

15 Originally Daniel Lamb house, 156 Winchester St., 1867; altered and major additions, 1877.

Daniel Lamb was the son of Peter Lamb, founder of the glue and blacking factory at the end of Amelia Street [9/13]. When Daniel moved into no. 156 on his marriage in 1867, it was a single-storey frame dwelling and one of only ten houses on Winchester Street. Over the years, many additions and a few subtractions led to the substantial, albeit picturesque Victorian mien we see today. Daniel, who was alderman for this area 1885-86 and again 1892-1902, lived here until his death in 1920. The house with its large garden and handsome fence then fell on hard times, but it has been thoughtfully refurbished by recent owners.

16 384 Sumach St. (detached house), 1866; altered, later.

Locally called the "Witch's House" for reasons unknown, no. 384 is showcased as the quintessential "Victorian" house with its wooden gingerbread and Eastlake bric-a-brac. Ironically, such flavour was achieved over many years, the house having been much added to and altered.

17 Toronto Necropolis Chapel, 200 Winchester St., Henry Langley, 1872.

The Toronto Necropolis cemetery dates from the early 1850s when a group of concerned citizens banded together in search of a new site for the town's nonsectarian burying ground and potter's field, which then stood dangerously close to the burgeoning Town of Yorkville [see Introduction, *AREA IX*]. (Graveyards were considered unhealthy, and indeed did pose a threat to the water supply.) The solicitous band paid the City of Toronto $16,000 for these 18 acres and proceeded to transfer the remains from potter's field. In the mid '60s, they purchased an adjacent 15 acres, but the municipality bought them back when landowners in the area objected to expansion by the necropolis—a spreading "City of the Dead" was little spur to real estate development.

Langley's High Victorian Gothic mortuary chapel ensemble with porte-cochère and superintendent's lodge was added in 1872, today one of the city's unspoiled architectural treasures. Elaborated with all the panoply of the decorative style—multi-coloured and patterned slate roof, complicated tracery and bargeboards, crockets, finials, ironwork—the chapel also manages a quality of ground-hugging repose, even simplicity, that admirably suits its function and site.

18 Riverdale Park, Carlton to Winchester St., Sumach St. to the Don Valley, opened, 1880; zoo addition, 1898.

The City of Toronto created Riverdale Park from sections of the former Simcoe/Scadding landholdings which it had begun purchasing in the 1850s. At one time, the park encompassed 162 acres on either side of the Don River. Today, much diminished in size and beauty by the noxious Don Valley Parkway, it is still a pleasant outing for its terraced site and historic associations.

The zoo, brainchild of Alderman Daniel Lamb, got off to a slow start in 1898 with only two prairie wolves and a few deer. In 1901, a polar bear was added. One year later, however, success seemed within reach with the donation of an elephant plus the exotic-looking, slightly Richardsonian Romanesque Donnybrook Pavilion. These were gifts of the Toronto Street Railway, which not incidentally was

the means by which most visitors would travel to park and zoo.

In 1978, with the opening of a new metro zoo, the Riverdale facility was transformed into a bucolic farmyard zoo with capacious 19th-century barns removed from Markham, Ontario, and a replica of a Markham farmhouse, called after its architect, Napier Simpson House.

19 Originally James Reeve house, 397 Carlton St., 1883

Though not built until 1883, this was the first house on the block. Its expansive Italianate villa style had long passed out of fashion in more built-up areas of the city, but the appealing form seemed appropriate for this still-countrified neighbourhood. Reeve was a barrister.

20 The Toronto (Don) Jail, 550 Gerrard St. E., William Thomas, 1858; rebuilt after fire, William T. Thomas, 1865.

The earnest Victorians, dedicated to such humanitarian issues as imprisonment and reform, took their prison buildings very seriously. Leading architects were called upon to design them, expensive materials and methods utilized, and every care given over to functional concerns of security, supervision, ventilation, and heating. Such was the case with Toronto's stately Don Jail. Designed by William Thomas, who also created triumphant St. Lawrence Hall [1/2], the classically inspired Don Jail sits serenely on its rise of ground like a grand palace, entered by one of the noblest doorways in the city. Manipulating vermiculated quoins, piers, half columns, and cornice window heads, the architect has made four storeys appear as two, a complicated façade look calm, a massive building seem human. The precisely fitted courses of fine Queenston and Ohio stone, the neatly laid brick, the beautifully carved stone details are all superb.

The layout followed 19th-century thinking in putting accommodations in wings radiating from a service core, the west wing for women inmates, the east for men. Thomas's three-storey wings, almost factory plain, lack the graciousness of the centre pavilion, but contemporary critics who have been appalled at the tiny cells

20 *The Don Jail*

may not realize that correctional philosophy of the time called for many small cells where prisoners could solitarily "think upon" their transgressions.

The Don Jail—it was really a maximum penalty prison with hangings taking place until 1962—is presently out of business, except for a banal 1960s addition which still serves as a detention centre. Slated for demolition in the late 1970s, this architectural gem was rescued by preservationists and is now awaiting some adaptive brainstorm.

21 Spruce Court Apartments, 74–86 Spruce St., Eden Smith & Sons, 1913; additions, Mathers & Haldenby, 1926.

This trim, spacious two-storey complex was the city's first government-sponsored housing project, built to provide decent accommodation for low-income families at reasonable rents. Enjoying many salutary features associated with the period's experimental housing—grassy communal courtyards, private entrances, intimate scale, plenty of windows for air and light—it also respects the street and neighbourhood. A similar experiment, Riverdale Courts, was designed by Eden Smith one year later at 100 Bain Avenue on the other side of the Don Valley.

22 Gifford and Nasmith Streets were laid out in the 1920s following demolition of Toronto General Hospital which had occupied the four-acre site between Sumach and Sackville Streets from 1855 to 1913. The two short streets were built up with simple, unassuming bungalows typical of the period throughout North America. The style was very popular in Southern California and should be familiar to Hollywood movie buffs of the era. Early 20th-century bungalows line many a street in the near suburbs of Toronto as well.

23a Trinity Mews, 41 Spruce St. (complex of seven row houses and rehabilitated Trinity College Medical School), Ferdinand A. Wagner, 1979.

Established in 1859 as part of Trinity College on Queen Street [see Introduction, *AREA V*], Trinity Medical School moved to this bold red- and yellow-brick facility close to the general hospital in 1871. In 1903, the school was absorbed by the University of Toronto Faculty of Medicine and this building fell to a variety of owners over the years, including a maker of mattresses, before it was salvaged as the showpiece of Trinity Mews. Though the gawky newcomers tried to replicate the original building, the best part of Trinity Mews is the neatly laid brick that patterns the courtyard.

23b Originally Charles B. Mackay house, 35 Spruce St., 1867.

An early house endowed with the dignity of a deep setback and orderly red-brick Georgian façade, although the front

25 *377 Sackville St.*

27d *280-282 Carlton St.*

gable is unusual for a Georgian design. Mackay clerked at the customs house on Front Street [demolished], and so lived a long way from work at a time before the horse-drawn street railway ran up dirt and gravel Parliament Street.

24 56 Spruce St. (attached house), 1872; restored, 1983.

A simple roughcast cottage of the 1870s, more endearing than ever thanks to its honest restoration, a pleasant surprise in this era of glitzy gentrification.

25 Originally Francis Shields house, 377 Sackville St., 1876; altered, later.

Mr. Shields, a drover, first had a brick and frame place, probably resembling the double house next door at no. 373–375, which parades identical Second Empire top and fenestration. The ballooning mansard style brought cachet to these houses in a primarily pointy-gable precinct, but adding pseudo-dignity with a facing of stone was really one-upping the neighbours. There is not another house like it in the city.

26 Originally Benjamin Brick house, 314 Carlton St., 1874.

A neat mansard-roof brick cottage enjoying formal repose and grandeur more typical of its larger Second Empire brethren. At the time he built his house, Mr. Brick was listed in the assessment rolls as—what else?—a bricklayer. He later became a full-time contractor for several fine houses on this street.

27a 294–296 and 298–300 Carlton St. (two double houses), 1889.

Late Bay-n-Gables plumbing all the diverse details the Queen Anne style had to offer. The double doors and stained glass transoms are stunners, never mind that they were repeatable prefabs. The porches contribute to the happy scale. Modern-day renovators who shear off porches on Victorian houses willy-nilly are making a big design mistake, as well as a practical one.

27b Originally William Lumbers house, 288 Carlton St., 1881.

A formal 1880s Second Empire house built for a medicine manufacturer, today looking a little silly with the addition of a 1980s Second Empire garage! The smooth stone window lintels set flush with the wall seem to have been popular in this neighbourhood for all manner of houses.

27c Originally Frederick Nicholls house, 286 Carlton St., 1884.

Bowed bay, end-wall porch, and gabled slate roof for a merchant, whose original front door is now "boxed" and daintily bracketed.

27d 280–282 Carlton St. (double house), 1886.

As close as Toronto comes to Eastlake architecture, that extravagantly decorative version of late Victoriana that gloried in the products of the woodworker: spools, spindles, lattice, posts, knobs, and brackets. Porches were perfect places to turn it all out.

29e *37 Metcalfe St., 1892*

28a 297 Carlton St. (detached house), 1892.
A sober late Queen Anne house whose narrow, frontal emphasis is misleading; the house is huge. The reticence is real, however, signalling new turn-of-the-century Classical Revival architectural directions.

28b Originally Hugh Neilson house, 295 Carlton St., 1878.
A handsome Gothic Revival survivor with fine details. The bargeboards edging a perfectly proportioned gable borrow from church tracery for their trefoil profile, which is scrupulously repeated in cresting atop the bay. Neilson, who was associated variously with the Dominion Telegraph Company and the Telephone Dispatch Company, had installed in this house one of the first residence telephones in the city. (Telephones were first used in Toronto in 1877. In 1883, there were 700 lines from 14 switchboards, and records indicate approximately 3,400 telephones were in service by 1890.)

28c 287–289 Carlton St. (double house), 1878.
A big yellow-brick, slightly Gothic double house enjoying the gracious siting of a single house. Semi-detached houses were always popular in Toronto, even in neighbourhoods with abundant land. Pattern books touted their value for a single owner who could rent out one-half, preferably to a relative! The owner/occupant here was Christopher Wilson, a scale maker; the relation to his tenant is unrecorded.

Sloping, narrow Metcalfe Street is surely one of the city's loveliest, graced with a series of gentle late Victorian rows, all tied together with new delicate iron fencing and a renovation concern for the streetscape.

29a 1–3, 5–7 Metcalfe St. (two double houses), 1889.

9–11, 13–15 Metcalfe St. (two double houses), 1885.
A long, neat Queen Anne string of houses put up in two different years. Builder Thomas Bryce did the assembling here, shopping for doors, windows, and other parts at the same factory from whence had come 294–296 and 298–300 Carlton Street [9/27a]. The roof-like projection overhanging the first storey, called a pent eave, is a distinctive feature of this neighbourhood.

29b 17–25 Metcalfe St. (five-house row), 1888–89.
A neatly composed all-red row with two bowed bays framing three straight arrows.

29c 6–18 Metcalfe St. (seven-house row), 1883.
A Bay-n-Gable row with three curious eyelid dormers winking from the roof and lighting what must be a shared attic. Removal of shadow-producing details and new homogenizing stucco covering the brick reveal how much these Victorian abodes need those eye-catching furbelows.

30 *85 Winchester St.*

31a *92 Winchester St.*

29d 20–32 Metcalfe St. (seven-house row), 1886.

Bay-n-Gable details in the service of congenial urban housing: red- with yellow-brick trim, polygonal bays, peaked gables, and scroll-sawn gingerbread.

29e Formerly James L. Morrison house, 37 Metcalfe St., 1875; remodelled, J. Wilson Gray, 1891; altered, 1912.

What's going on here? This looks like a showroom for decorative mouldings, or maybe an over-zealous movie set. To start at the beginning. In 1875, Capt. John T. Douglas owned the southeast corner of Metcalfe and Winchester Streets, on which he built a large rambling Italianate villa facing north onto Winchester. He rented and then sold it to Joseph Reed, an insurance man, who enjoyed the comfortable house, spacious grounds, and quiet neighbourhood until 1882. Enter a new owner, James L. Morrison, one-time president of the Brilliant Sign Company. Morrison expanded the Victorian villa into a much grander mansion complete with the latest classicizing details: modillioned cornice, dentils, Ionic columns, foliated consoles, leaded glass transoms, scrolled pediment, even carved lions. Then in 1910, a new owner sold the front lawn and Winchester Street venue for an apartment building, leaving the house with little land and an address on Metcalfe Street. Not wanting to waste any of Morrison's expensive touches, however, he transferred those hidden by the apartment to the new Metcalfe Street front, ergo the lately spruced-up Classical Revival billboard on view today.

30 Formerly Charles Parsons house, 85 Winchester St., 1857.

Formal Georgian proportions and decorous deep setback mark this as one of the first houses in the area; in fact it is Don Vale's oldest building still with its original bearing. This was a gentleman's house, and its three doors opening onto an inviting veranda speak of a more leisurely time when Mr. Parsons, a leather merchant, could step out upon his block-square grounds and survey the vista north to the rolling, landscaped hillocks of St. James' Cemetery, south to the manicured grounds of the general hospital, and east to the wide Valley of the Don.

31a 92, 94–96, 98 Winchester St. (two single and one double house), 1898.

After the fidgety demeanor of so many Victorian houses, the passive mien of these turn-of-the-century abodes comes as a welcome relief. With barn-like girth and a great roof sliding down and enveloping all, they epitomize "hearth and home."

31b Toronto Dance Theatre/originally St. Enoch's Presbyterian Church/formerly St. Enoch's United Church/formerly Don Vale Community Centre, 80 Winchester St., Gordon & Helliwell, 1891; Robert Pogue Hall addition, Molesworth West & Secord, 1927.

Designed in monochromatic Romanesque Revival style, St. Enoch's is undramatic but decent in the manner of many Presbyterian churches of the time. The building is almost a square, with identical end walls coming together at the compulsory, and here perfunctory, corner tower.

Walk 10: "Old Cabbagetown"

This stretch of Carlton Street was laid out in the late 1850s, shortly after which modest frame and roughcast cottages began to sprout. More ambitious dwellings followed, Georgian in style and set out along the street in a tidy urban string. Later Gothic Revival and Second Empire neighbours did not detract from the mannerly streetscape, and today, though some houses have become offices or shops and the street has been widened, an air of courteous restraint continues to prevail.

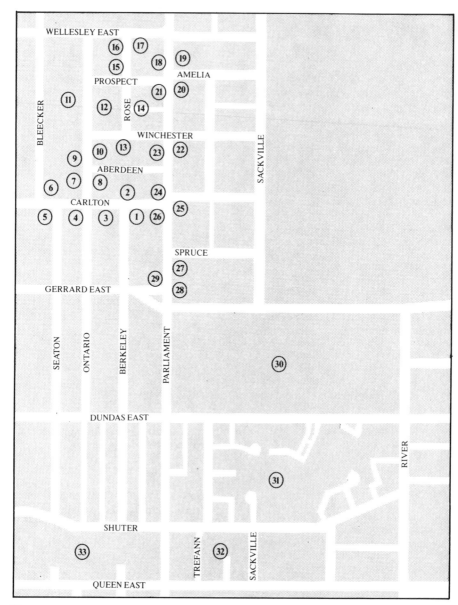

1 *219 Carlton St.*

2b *226-228 Carlton St.*

1 219 Carlton St. (detached house), 1882.
Big bay 'n little gable in exuberant red
and yellow brick with a pointy High
Victorian Gothic air. Look to the side for
other well-executed, well-cared-for details.
Stone lintels were much favoured in this
neighbourhood.

2a 230–232 Carlton St. (double house), 1864.
Rather awesome looking these days with
tall mansard addition looming on top,
this double house started out as a tasteful
two-storey Georgian rectangle, undoubtedly with a low pitched roof and dormer
or two. Yellow brick—called white when
new—was popular in Toronto in this
early period. The owner, jeweller James
Ellis who lived in a large house on the
street behind, tore down two frame
dwellings which had been constructed
only four years earlier to put up these
more stylish and remunerative rentals.

2b 226–228 Carlton St. (double house), 1879.
Gorgeously decorative Second Empire,
built when the style was at its peak in
Toronto. Yellow brick lost out to red in
the early and mid 1870s, but it returned
to popularity with Second Empire when
red was reserved for glittery accents. Bold
wooden trim provided further drama. The
arcaded second-floor sunporch with
starchy rope-turned mouldings and bent
corner windows looks extremely inviting.

2c 218, 220, 222–224 Carlton St. (two single and one double house), 1877.
Variations on a yellow-brick theme, some
houses subtly changed over the years,
some seemingly not at all. When Oscar
Wilde, the "Apostle of Aestheticism,"
lectured here in 1882, he remarked on
Toronto's "horrid white brick with its
shallow colour spoiling the effect of the
architecture." Yellow (white) brick was
equal in price and availability to red, so
its use was simply a matter of fashion.

3a 205–207 Carlton St. (double house), 1879.
Bowed Bay-n-Gable with rather skimpy
gables and windows for that brawny
front. Latter-day owners may have taken
a lesson from Mr. Wilde: the dark paint
covers yellow brick.

**3b Originally William Foss house, 203 Carl-
ton St., 1879.**
A fat and sassy house with buxom bay
dominating the front. Corresponding
polygonal rooms inside should be delightful, though hard to furnish. Foss was a
barrister.

**4a 195 Carlton St. (one-half of original dou-
ble house), 1858.**
This was among the first of the Carlton
Street buildings, originally a roughcast
double house with straight-headed six-
light sash windows. Storefront appendages
work particularly well on these ancient
Georgian boxes, so it seems misguided
that half this building was recently
replaced.

4c *185 Carlton St., 1984*

9 *484-490 Ontario St.*

4b 191 Carlton St. (detached house), 1892.
Virile brick and stone in the city's *last* Victorian style, the Queen Anne/Romanesque hybrid that filled up empty lots across Toronto in the 1890s.

4c Originally William Jamieson house, 185 Carlton St., 1861; altered, 1988.
Hipped-roofed and quietly formal, with an assured repose typical of early Georgian houses in this district. The splendid wooden doorcase was fitting for Mr. Jamieson, a lumber dealer.

5 187–189 Carlton St. (double house), 1878.
181-183 Carlton St. (double house), 1878.
Chamberlin Block, 165–179 Carlton St. (eight-house row), 1877–78.
A bevy of townhouses assembled by builder Charles Chamberlin in the best richly sculptural tradition of Second Empire. The concave curve of the mansards is properly animated, and window and other details refined and sophisticated. Chamberlin, who liked to attach his name to buildings, was also responsible for Chamberlin Terrace nearby on Parliament Street [10/18a].

6 St. Peter's Church, 188 Carlton St., Gundry & Langley, 1865; transepts addition, 1872; Sunday school addition, 1880.
High Victorian multi-coloured verve for a perky parish church. Especially interesting is the west front, where a neat gabled porch leads the eye up to a handsome rose-windowed central bay, which in turn highlights a lofty, confident bellcote.

7 First Church of the Christian Association, 474 Ontario St., Frederick J. Bird, 1905.
This red-brick Gothic charmer for a one-of-a-kind Toronto congregation still shows off the sweet and simple proportion and details that made it a perfect reflection of its religious founders. The Christian Association worshipped here until the 1970s.

8 481–483 Ontario St. (double house), 1877.
Pointed arches and lacy bargeboard for an appealing yellow-brick Gothic Revival number, straight out of a builder's pattern book, which probably would have labelled it a "double-detached villa."

9 484–490 Ontario St. (four-house row), 1877.
A handsome yellow-brick Bay-n-Gable row still boasting heavy hammerbeams in gables and peaked overdoors for entrances. Only blank new windows detract from the overall felicity. The less said about the gauche new pastiches next door, the better.

10 497–503 Ontario St. (four-house row), 1885.
505–511 Ontario St. (four-house row), 1884.
Two identical Bay-n-Gable rows seasoned with spicy details: polygonal bays, rickrack trim, stained glass transoms, creosoted black bricks to pepper the front. No. 503 retains its vestibule and inner transomed double doors.

11a, b *Winchester Square and Hugh Garner Co-op*

The superblock bounded by a line north of Carlton, and Wellesley, Bleecker, and Ontario Streets has been the occasion of probably Toronto's most bitter redevelopment struggle, an acrimonious ten-year battle that pitted local residents and aldermen against the giant Meridian Corporation, developers of St. James Town to the north [11/17]. Originally Meridian had its high-rise sights on a much larger area, to be called South St. James Town, and it had begun to accumulate—and demolish— Victorian houses on Prospect, Rose, and Wellesley Streets as well. However, public outcry combined with a reform city council slowed matters down and eventually achieved a compromise of sorts whereby Meridian got only this block and the city assumed still-standing Meridian-acquired neighbourhood properties for conversion to city-run housing. The city also staked a claim in Meridian's superblock for subsidized housing. The project is still aborning along Wellesley Street, but Meridian says it plans at least three rental or condominium buildings there, one as high as 30 storeys.

11a Winchester Square, 55, 85, 101 Bleecker St. (housing complex), Klein & Sears, 1980–81.

Not as high as high-rises can get, nor as charmless as government-run housing can be, Winchester Square manages a decent, European matter-of-factness. The complex weaves unassuming red-brick buildings of differing heights and small details in a casual layout that is quite inviting. Covered pedestrian bridges linking the taller buildings are practical and pleasing.

11b Hugh Garner Housing Co-operative, 55 Ontario St., Klein & Sears, 1981–82.

Named for the Canadian novelist who made Cabbagetown his special purview, the Hugh Garner Co-op was built at a moment when safe and serious architecture would no longer do. Whether this colourful orange and blue ornamentalist design will continue to hold our attention is hard to say, but right now its looks are intriguing.

12 *Winchester Street Jr. School*

12 *Winchester Street Sr. School*

12 Winchester Street Junior Public School, 15 Prospect St. thru to Winchester St., Charles H. Bishop, 1898, 1901.

Winchester Street Senior Public School, Frederick Etherington, 1959.

"Massive dignity and good old-fashioned academic atmosphere" was the description in the early 1900s, and it still rings true. The secular Queen Anne style was popular for public school buildings; not only did it seem "democratic," but those many tall windows gave perfect light for studying. A school has stood on this block since 1874. This particular building began in 1898 as a preliminary one-storey red-brick affair. So rapid was student population growth, however, the slowly staged expansion was accelerated and completed in one fell swoop three years later. Illustrious graduates include artists C.W. Jefferys and Fred H. Brigden, and actor Walter Houston.

The senior school stretched out along Prospect Street shows off its own 1950s dignity with a ribbon of regular fenestration and evenly spaced turquoise and yellow corrugated panels. The mosaic tile mural is also very much of the period, and very nice.

13a 7–11 Winchester St. (triple house), 1885; porch additions, c. 1900.

Heavy stone lintels and sills, as well as the stone bases and capitals of the square pillars gracing the front, make this Queen Anne triple house an unusual standout.

13b 13–15 Winchester St. (double house), 1880; porch additions, c. 1900.

Textbook-perfect Second Empire with an imposing central pavilion breaking from a symmetrical façade, all enlivened with bold window heads, bonnet dormers, quoins, and coupled brackets at the eaves. Porches are later additions.

13c 17–19 Winchester St. (double house), 1878; additions, later.

Big and rigid Second Empire-cum-Queen Anne with little of the pliant flamboyance associated with the style, although some of the classicizing details are very fine.

13d Formerly the Rev. Samuel Boddy house, 21 Winchester St., 1858.

This is what is left of an early tall-chimneyed Georgian house that for many years served as rectory for St. Peter's on nearby Carlton Street [10/6]. Despite disfiguring surgery as well as grafts, it remains appealing for its English garden and inviting setback from the street.

14a Winchester Block, 1–11 Rose Ave. (six-house row), 1879; demolished no. 5 replaced, 1979.

A creative 19th-century brickmason was at work here, with a lovely border of yellow brick embroidering the red on a six-house row built for John Winchester, a local landowner. A fine latter-day brickmason has been at it as well, seamlessly stitching in a new no. 5 to replace that torn out by Meridian in its redevelopment manoeuvres.

15b *56 Rose Ave., c. 1880*

14b Originally Charles Mitchell house, 23 Rose Ave., 1880.

A distinctive Italianate detached house with stilted arches ornamenting openings and red brick covering all four walls. Mitchell was a conductor on the Nipissing Railroad which in the 1880s was helping to open up the Ontario hinterlands.

15a 44–46 Rose Ave. (double house), 1887.
48–50 Rose Ave. (double house), 1885.

Two woodworkers' showcases, one parading big and bold fixtures, the other light and spindly accoutrements. Such prefabricated details were favourites of the busy builder Thomas Bryce.

15b Originally John Kesteven house, 56 Rose Ave., 1858; tower addition, 1878.

Now mostly hidden by later construction, this hipped-roof brick house was among the first in the area. Once enjoying a long veranda and large gardens to the south, it was built by a contractor as his own residence. Superb details are still impressive over 100 years later—the carved stone sills are truly fine. The mansarded tower to the rear was added in 1878 when round-arched windows were stylishly replacing foursquare Georgian.

16 257–263 Wellesley St. E. (four-house row), 1878.

Second Empire symmetry and formality somewhat diminished by haphazard front gardens. No denying the outsize vigour of keystoned window surrounds though.

17a 265–271 Wellesley St. E. (four-house row), 1876.

A straight-sided mansard quartet, with a 1970s paint job punching up the Second Empire exterior—brown arched window heads, sills, and roof details against yellow walls. This row introduced the patrician alternating segmental and triangular dormers also seen at no. 257–263 [10/16].

17b 273–277 Wellesley St. E. (triple house), 1887.

Tall, narrow Bay-n-Gables built to fill a gap site. Double front doors deeply recessed in a room-like porch are congenial exceptions to an otherwise nondescript front.

18a Chamberlin Terrace, 568–582 Parliament St. (eight-house row), 1876.

Eight Second Empire row houses appealing for the indifference of their frankly appended commercial fronts.

18b Darling Terrace, 562–566 Parliament St. (triple house), 1877.

A lively trio still boasting original Victorian accoutrements, including iron cresting atop generous bay windows and William Darling's self-aggrandizing name stone. "Terrace," a British usage for imposing block-long residential ensembles, seems a little over-blown for a pocket of three houses.

19 583–585 Parliament St. (two-unit commercial block), 1889.
With corner oriel, finialed tent-roofed tower, and big broad gables, this building looks more like a lavish Queen Anne house than a retail block. It was probably trying to be a good neighbour on its then residential street. Originally at no. 583 was Arthur Squires, a butcher; at no. 585, Benjamin Playter sold shoes. Brass letters still imbedded in front of the entrance to no. 583 remind us that this was Barr's Dairy from 1912 to 1925, the Mac's Milk of its day.

20a Cabbagetown Texaco Self-Service, 581 Parliament St. (automobile service station), c. 1970.
A Second Empire gas station. Terrific.

20b Brougham Terrace, 549–563 Parliament St. (eight-house row), 1875–76.
Comfortably plump red- and yellow-brick row houses, now mostly with ground-floor shops. The wishbone sweep of the bargeboard edging the gables is grand.

21 542–544, 546–548, 550–552 Parliament St. (three double houses), 1886–87.
Bay-n-Gable with a zesty spindled porch at no. 542 and the dean of Cabbagetown realtors at no. 552.

22a Hotel Winchester/formerly Lake View Hotel, 531 Parliament St., Kennedy & Holland, 1888.
A tavern and/or hotel has stood on this site since the 1860s when an establishment called the Santa Claus held sway. The present three-storey building was constructed in 1888 for the Lake View—a belvedere once perched atop the corner tower and one could indeed view the lake from that aerie. The Lake View was highly recommended in guidebooks of the era. It was at the end of the omnibus route and advertised a bucolic resort atmosphere with a "good lawn" and beer garden, plus "electric bells and bathrooms" on every floor. Nothing to write home about today, though the old fire escape is wonderfully decorative.

22b Maple Terrace, 519–527 Parliament St. (five units of original six-house row), 1875–78.
Gracious gables and serviceable stores.

23 502–508 Parliament St. (four-house row), 1879.
An exuberant, larger-than-life Second Empire quartet that still enjoys a deep front garden on this now-commercial street. The richly detailed wooden window surrounds could be the most vivacious in Toronto. Earliest tenants were a jeweller, a "gentleman," a minister, and Flavius P. Stiker, superintendent of the Grape Sugar Company.

24 242–250 Carlton St. (five-unit commercial block), 1889.
A theatrical three-storey commercial row, richly tapestried with stone sills and lintels, semicircular-arched windows, keystones, panel brick, and lots more. No. 244 retains its original shopfront.

25 489–491 Parliament St. (two-unit commercial block), 1889.
An early business block, bringing the authority and three-storey presence of commerce to Parliament Street.

26 Canadian Imperial Bank of Commerce/ originally Canadian Bank of Commerce, 245 Carlton St., Darling & Pearson, 1905.
Auspicious Classical Revival with weighty Doric columns framing a deep vault-like entrance; above, a domestic Queen Anne bay window—curtains and all. These small branch banks were often built with residential flats on the second floor.

27 Lepper's Block, 433–443 Parliament St. (six-unit commercial block), 1885–86.
Flat roof and bracketed projecting cornice to signal another early commercial entry on Parliament Street. Originally were purveyed, south to north: groceries, barbering, hardware, plumbing, stationery, and more groceries. Lepper was vice president of Union Loan & Savings Company with a large house on Winchester Street.

28 411½–415 Parliament St. (three-unit commercial block), 1889–90.
A slightly askew Richardsonian Romanesque trio, with no. 411½ stepped slightly forward. All three boast the style's pink-coloured stone dressings and round-arched windows. Earliest tenants were J.A. Carveth, selling medical books; a branch of the Canadian Bank of Commerce; and Fred J. Vose, a butcher.

30 *Regent Park North*

31 *Regent Park South*

29 Lorne Terrace, 284–296 Gerrard St. E. (seven units of original eight-house row), 1879.

One of the city's most picturesque rows, with pointy little windows strutting smartly along the second floor. Pyramidal-capped pavilions give the mansard a distinctive roofline.

30 Regent Park North, Gerrard to Dundas St., Parliament to River St. (housing complex), John E. Hoare Jr., 1947.

This is Canada's oldest and largest public housing development. It is so fastidiously bland and spartan, one suspects the housing authority of purposely setting out to forestall any glimmer of aesthetic or social pleasure. (Don't make the buildings more attractive than homes of surrounding taxpayers, the architect was supposedly cautioned.) Le Corbusier's cruciform plan, beloved of public housing developers, is here repeated again and again and again (though laudably without the French planner's heaven-thrust visual effect—the buildings are a more humane three to six storeys high). Constructed of brackish, mean red brick and without serious architectural embellishment, to this day the buildings have not been enlivened by any sort of foundation planting. There is no surprise or drama anywhere except in the impulse to leave, but the "streets" end only in one of the myriad automobile lots which are as monotonous in this "park" as are the buildings. The name is derived from nearby Regent Street, not because there is anything regal here.

31 Regent Park South, Shuter to Gerrard St., Parliament to River St. (housing complex), Page & Steele (apartment houses) and John E. Hoare Jr. (row houses), 1957.

Again an island in the city, with buildings standing solitarily in a "park" planted with more cars than foliage and no through streets to continue the urban flow. Here the authority did succumb to prevailing public housing practice of stacking families in high-rise cabinets—five 14-storey slabs score the development. Today we believe that filing families in the sky is not the best way to ask people to live, but at the time—at least by designers—Page & Steele's colourful, complicated towers with their two-storey apartment units (bedrooms one floor up or down from the living room floor) were much admired award-winners. Thirty years later we realize it is John Hoare's rather comfortably banal rows of housing which meander about the site that should take the prize for amiable accommodation. Close to 10,000 people live in Regent Park, North and South. They seem happy about their new community centre coming in; unhappy about banks and supermarkets going out to reap bigger profits in the suburbs.

32 *Trefann Court*   33 *Moss Park Apartments*

32 Trefann Court, Queen to Shuter St., Sumach to Trefann St. (complex of row houses and rehabilitated houses), 1971, 1973, 1978.
Rehabilitation of a run-down area by renovating existing houses, where possible, and filling in gaps with compatible new ones, where it's not, is a star urban renewal turn these days. When the Trefann Court area was first threatened with slash-and-burn tactics by zealous planners, however, neighbourhood preservationists had a long, hard haul of it. The restored 19th-century charmers and zesty low-scale newcomers lining these streets all attest to the final count in favour of human relevance. The larger new houses contain one-, two-, and three-bedroom rental units, 25 percent subsidized.

33 Moss Park Apartments, Queen to Shuter St., Sherbourne to Parliament St., Somerville McMurrich & Oxley with Gibson & Pokorny and Wilson & Newton, 1961.
Neither as unfocused nor as vast as Regent Park, this medium-rent redevelopment project manages architectural delicacy despite its 15-storey height. About two-thirds back on the superblock, with parking space behind to the north, three identical V-shaped buildings sit in a row, though differently oriented to give a variety of exposures. A large area to the south is thereby available for imaginative landscaping, incorporating artificial mounds, paths, seating, and sculptured play areas.

Area VII

Walk 11: Sherbourne Street
Walk 12: Jarvis Street
Walk 13: Church Street

Area VII

Toronto's distinctive north/south residential corridors developed as a consequence of John Graves Simcoe's scheme to compensate his senior provincial officials for their dreary life in "Muddy York" with gifts of 100-acre "park lots." Thirty lots were set out along present-day Queen Street in narrow 1/8-mile strips running north 1¼ miles to Bloor Street. Simcoe planned that the officials would create English-style country estates on these properties, helping to set the stage for a Canadian aristocracy, or at least landed gentry. A few recipients did indeed construct grand landscaped manors, but mostly these enterprising gentlemen traded the parcels among themselves and then broke them up into streets and residential building lots to be sold for easy profits when the town began to boom in the 1830s and '40s (it grew from a population of 700 in 1815 to 30,000 by 1851).

Typical of this process was the park lot strip presented to the first provincial secretary, William Jarvis. Jarvis's son and heir, Samuel P. Jarvis, who was superintendent of Indian affairs, had built a brick manor house, "Hazelburn," on the Jarvis grant. When his reputation and fortunes began to ebb as a result of alleged mismanagement of government funds, however, he resorted to tearing down his house and selling off the land. In 1845, Jarvis hired well-known Toronto architect John G. Howard to lay out a model subdivision. Howard conceived a wide tree-lined avenue—not surprisingly to be called Jarvis Street—running through the park lot rimmed with small plots at the south end for workers' cottages, somewhat larger lots in the centre for middle-class dwellings, and large tracts at the top near Bloor Street for mansions of the rich.

The two park lots that came into the hands of Surveyor-General Thomas Ridout and Postmaster William Allan became the site of the Sherbourne Street corridor. The Ridouts were responsible for naming the thoroughfare (after the birthplace of the first Ridout in Sherbourne, Dorset, England), but it was the Allans who influenced development. William Allan, who had become a wealthy merchant as well as postmaster, built a large mansion on his land called "Moss Park" [demolished], and his son, George William, was ensconced farther north on the property at "Home-wood" [demolished]. But after William died in 1853, George William too began dividing the bulk of his father's park lot into building sites, with one exception. He held out a large parcel on which to indulge his very Victorian fancy for things botanical. Set smartly in the middle of his family inheritance, Allan's horticultural gardens [11/1] became a glamorous centrepiece for his residential development, especially after the touring Prince of Wales endorsed the site in 1860 by formally planting an oak tree. (A year later, in 1861, Allan deeded the gardens to the Toronto Horticultural Society; in 1888, the society sold the bequest to the city.)

From its earliest days, Church Street has been called Church Street, after St. James' Church [1/8]. Simcoe granted the choice park lot to the north of Church Street to Capt. John McGill, a loyal Queen's Ranger who had fought with him in the Revolutionary War. Simcoe also gave the captain a plum job in the government of the new province, that of commissioner of stores. McGill built a modest 1½-storey Regency cottage on his park lot, but he set it in the centre of the impressive grounds that came to be called McGill Square. McGill's park lot was subdivided by his estate in 1836, at which time the line of Church Street was extended northward, prophetically continuing its descriptive appellation: the Roman Catholics decided to locate their cathedral church in this neighbourhood in 1845 [13/3]; and the Methodists selected it in 1870, acquiring the whole of McGill Square for their church [13/1].

Each of these corridors eventually evolved its own ambience, but settlement on all three was more or less similar. Dressmakers and dairymen with large families rented quarters in the simple gabled cottages and boxy row houses that went up along the southern peripheries. A growing middle class of clerks, accountants, and "travellers" settled into more commodious single, double, and triple houses in the centre of the tracts. And finally, the city's merchant princes and reigning politicians found their way to the upper reaches, vying with one another in the voguishness of their sumptuous houses, manicured grounds, and ornamental fences.

A narrower, boulevarded Jarvis Street in its heyday.

The first houses, large and small, were in the Georgian architectural mould that was Toronto's colonial inheritance. Later, these thoroughfares and their side streets began to borrow from the expansive catalogue of evocative Victorian styles: Gothic manor houses, Italianate villas, Second Empire palaces, Queen Anne cottages, and Romanesque abbeys. Often houses were an eclectic mix of several styles. They were by no means all architect-designed; by mid century, many Toronto housewrights were making use of American and British pattern books to guide and inspire them.

Punctuating the tree-lined residential streets were the big Victorian churches for which the city was becoming famous. Although some detractors complained that "Toronto the Good" had too many half-filled meeting houses built to please each and every Protestant sect, the "City of Churches" was widely praised for the architectural beauty of its myriad houses of worship.

In the mid 1880s then, this district was heralded in a guidebook of the day as Toronto's most fashionable neighbourhood: "Of all the avenues extending south from Bloor Street to the Bay, the noblest are Church, Jarvis and Sherbourne Streets. Church Street is somewhat less aristocratic....Jarvis and Sherbourne are lined on either side through most part of their extent by the mansions of the upper ten."

By the turn of the century, however, fickle fashion had begun to desert these environs. The area's pre-eminence had already been challenged in the 1890s by the Annex [*AREA X*], and soon other new suburbs such as Parkdale and Rosedale [*AREA XI*] began to beckon. Architectural change was in the air, and Victorian villas looked less and less appealing. Some large mansions were sold to institutions; others were torn down and replaced by three- and four-storey apartment buildings designed in the Classical Revival style popular in the 1910s and '20s [13/21, for example], or in the new Art Moderne idiom [12/7]. Apartments were intriguingly new, but after an initial flurry of enthusiasm, they were slow to take hold in Toronto, considered by many as habitats suitable only for the "newly wed or nearly dead." By the time of the Depression, many buildings in this quarter were rooming houses or worse, and the area had completely lost its tone.

The decline of this district was not reversed until the mid 1950s when giant apartment blocks such as City Park [13/18] began to appear. Although these have taken further toll of the original housing stock, an enlightened appreciation of the area's Victorian extravaganzas has more recently witnessed much sympathetic renovation. Today this gentrification is a potent drawing card for a new wave of homeowners eager to return to the central city, and despite a recent increase in high-rise apartment construction, it seems safe to hope the legacy of low-scale and humane Victorian housing will continue to define the fundamental character of this area of Toronto.

Walk 11: Sherbourne Street

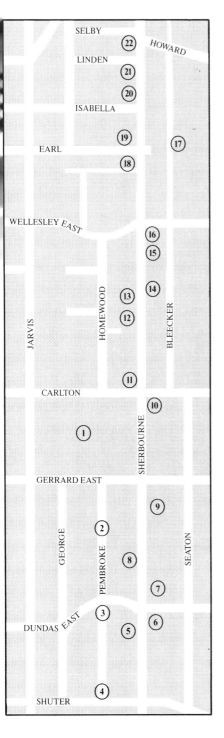

1 Allan Gardens, Gerrard to Carlton St., Jarvis to Sherbourne St., opened, 1860; Palm House, Robert McCallum, 1910, 1913.

In true botanical gardens fashion, there has always been an eye-catching pavilion here. The first, a large open-air affair of rough-hewn logs, was erected in 1860, the year the gardens were formally opened. The second, a more ambitious endeavour put up in 1878, was an exotic pagoda-like extravaganza that boasted the late 19th-century city's finest ballroom and concert place. Destroyed by fire in 1902 along with its extensive greenhouses, it was replaced in 1910 by the present structure designed by the official city architect, Robert McCallum. McCallum's Palm House, which borrows both construction and name from British prototypes, is a bubble of glass and metal tracery in the grand tradition of such pavilions, few of which have survived in North America. It is open daily 10 to 5.

Though the Palm House with its changing displays of seasonal flowers is the main attraction, the park surrounding the building is a most inviting and genteel place, notwithstanding occasionally ungenteel inhabitants. One wonders what the area might be like today had a 1955 recommendation of the Parks Department been accepted. The department suggested demolishing the blocks between Allan Gardens and Moss Park to create here one sweeping "Central Park" for Toronto, around which, they had forecasted, would rise luxurious New York-style apartment houses.

2c *78 Pembroke St.*

3b *École Publique Gabrielle Roy*

Pembroke Street, as an avenue linking two important early parks, was once considered one of the city's finest residential streets. Today it is a bit of a backwater, not to mention the site of some of the daffiest renovations in town. But don't overlook the architectural gems.

2a Originally Bernard B. Hughes house, 104 Pembroke St., 1873.

Gothic Revival at its most attractive, with lovely, delicate gingerbread edging the gable and a voguish L-shaped plan that highlights sunporch, vestibule, and stunning doorway. Hughes was a merchant who lived here with his family of six.

2b Originally John Reid house, 87 Pembroke St., 1872-73.

Another picturesque Gothic Revival villa of the 1870s complete with original iron railing bordering a large garden. Reid, a merchant, headed a family of seven. The house currently serves as Street Haven, a women's hostel and drop-in centre.

2c 78 Pembroke St. (detached house), 1886.

Handsome Queen Anne displaying an unusually subtle composition with fine details and restful scale appropriate to the original tenant, the Rev. Alexander T. Bowser, pastor of Jarvis Street Unitarian Church. Today, reverently renovated for apartments, though the bricks look as if they might have been cleaned with brimstone!

2d Originally W.J. Davis house, 67 Pembroke St., Langley & Burke, 1885-86.

Typical Queen Anne, built when the style was the height of Toronto fashion, with a rich variety of shapes, materials, textures, and colours. Davis was co-owner of Davis and Henderson, wholesale stationers.

The bend of Dundas Street here—first named Wilton Crescent—was an aesthetic touch laid out by the Allans and balanced by Wellesley Crescent to the north. Among the few curves in foursquare Toronto.

3a Originally William Pearson house, 35 Pembroke St., David B. Dick, 1881.

High Victorian at its most theatrical, with an imposing pyramidal-roofed three-storey tower unique in Toronto. Pearson was secretary of Consumers' Gas, for which the architect was also busy designing offices and works [1/23b, 2/6].

3b École Publique Gabrielle Roy/originally Duke of York Public School, 14 Pembroke St., C.E.C. Dyson, 1929.

An enlightened building by the board of education's architect which deftly integrates chateauesque detail with expansive 1920s metal-framed fenestration. More recent enlightenment has seen this become Toronto's French-language elementary school, wisely with a change of name.

5 *230 Sherbourne St.*

6 *All Saints Church*

4 142-152 Shuter St. (six-house row), 1871; altered, 1985.

138-140 Shuter St. (two-house row), 1987.

122-136 Shuter St. (eight-house row), 1876-77.

112-120 Shuter St. (five-house row), 1891.

Shuter Street between George and Sherbourne is lined with row houses of all persuasions. No. 142-152, built during the 1870s economic slump, is the simplest of two-storey rows embellished only with gently curved windows, and doorways with rectangular toplights. (Renovations have removed some of the original modest charm.) No. 122-136, slightly later and more ambitious, demonstrates how ideal the newly popular Second Empire mansard style was for row housing, providing an animated and inexpensive third storey. No. 112-120 follows the Queen Anne prescription that each house in a row have an air of exciting individuality. New no. 138-140 should be noted for its very plain—and therefore comparatively dull—face.

5 230 Sherbourne St. (double house), 1871; remodelled as single house, Langley & Langley, 1895.

With its lovely glass toplight and sidelights and intricately carved oak surround, this remains one of the most inspired classical doorways in town. It was part of an 1890s remodelling that turned a two-family house into an elegant single dwelling, at the same time introducing similar classically derived moulded brick and terracotta decoration.

6 All Saints Anglican Church, 223 Sherbourne St., Richard C. Windeyer, 1874; Sunday school addition, Richard C. Windeyer, 1883.

The rector had been to England and knew the score—not only was democratic ecumenism favoured, so was High Victorian Gothic. Inspired by the writings of John Ruskin, whose models were Italian buildings of multi-coloured marble, High Victorian churches flaunted smooth, highly decorated surfaces, most typically red with black or yellow with red brick. All Saints perfectly captured their effect, which—depending on one's bias—was dubbed either "constructional polychromy" or "streaky bacon."

The church was equally adventurous in its ministry. An accommodating spirit in the 1870s mixed high and low church practices and welcomed parishioners of whatever means by offering free seats in an age when pew holders paid for their spaces. Today this self-same attitude has removed some of the pews to accommodate a drop-in centre for the neighbourhood needy, but all the other splendid fittings remain: double hammerbeam chancel roof, pink granite columns, Minton tiles, beautiful brass lectern, and much more.

7 Sherbourne Lanes, 241-285 Sherbourne St. (complex of four apartment houses and twelve rehabilitated houses), A.J. Diamond & Barton Myers (designed by Barton Myers), 1975.

A municipal experiment in urban surgery still alive and doing well. In 1973, this

7 *241 Sherbourne St.*   9a *283–285 Sherbourne St.*

ailing 19th-century block was slated for demolition to make way for two 24-storey apartment buildings. Roofs had been razed before neighbourhood preservationists and the innovative architects persuaded city fathers it was possible to rehabilitate the old houses and infill behind them with low-rises for the same bottom-line profit and space as high-rise towers. The four new seven-storey apartment buildings complement the old houses in their use of brick and stone, animated recesses and projections, and similar scale. The 12 old houses themselves are an intriguing representation of 19th-century styles (made a little more "colourful" than necessary recently by garish paint jobs). The mansard roof Second Empire double houses were constructed in the 1880s; the Queen Anne designs date from the 1890s. The oldest and most interesting of the houses are two examples of Georgian, no. 241 [11/7] and no. 283–285 [11/9a].

Although there is a feeling in places that the complex is congested on this narrow plot, the larger issues triumph: humane subsidized housing and a resuscitated Victorian block.

7 Originally "Allendale" (Enoch Turner residence), 241 Sherbourne St., 1856.

This glowing gem was the home of Enoch Turner, a successful and beneficent brewer who paid for beer for his horses and the city's first school for the poor [2/11]. His fine-looking red-brick Georgian house is bedecked with quoins and cornice of yellow brick, a showy bichrome effect that was repeated again and again in Toronto.

8a 260–262A Sherbourne St. (two attached houses), northern house, 1872; altered and southern house added, Knox & Elliot, 1889–90.

Stones and bricks, semicircles and rectangles, towers and gables, carved panels, finials, even an emblematic carved stone crane for a striking example of Richardsonian Romanesque. Architects Knox & Elliot, newly arrived from Chicago, created this extraordinary amalgam for Edward Hewitt, an alderman and busy speculative builder.

8b 280 Sherbourne St. (complex of eleven row houses and one rehabilitated house), Ferdinand A. Wagner, 1979.

A new "Victorian" pastiche, taking its red and yellow bichrome cue from the Enoch Turner house across the street at no. 241 [11/7], but here the effect is gaudy baubles rather than polished gemstones.

8c 284 Sherbourne St. (detached house), 1877–78.

Deft Gothic Revival more associated with the Ontario countryside than the city: pointed windows, vigorous bargeboard, and picturesque quatrefoil doo-dads. Its one-time twin, no. 282, now bereft of these niceties, forms an endpost to the new terrace at no. 280 [11/8b].

9a Originally Ritchie/Forneri house, 283–285 Sherbourne St., 1856–57.

A row should be more than two houses, but this large handsome pair clearly bears the imprint of decorous English or New York rows with its flat blocky shape, neat multi-light sash windows, and low-pitched roof. These were expensive houses, but well-to-do Torontonians—unlike their fellows in Montreal—did not much take to row houses and no. 283–285 stood alone, unimitated and surrounded by vacant land for almost two decades. Earliest residents were John Ritchie, a merchant; and James Forneri, professor at University College [8/1].

9b Formerly "Culloden" (John Ross Robertson residence)/originally Capt. John T. Douglas house, 291 Sherbourne St., 1875; stable and coach house addition, 1882; veranda addition, Samuel G. Curry, 1903.

This much modified, vaguely Italianate house is primarily of interest as the home from 1881 to 1918 of John Ross Robertson, muckraking publisher of the Toronto *Evening Telegram*, liberal philanthropist who endowed the first hospital in North America for children [7/24], and ardent compiler of six volumes of Toronto history. Robertson also owned the house at no. 295, which he made available to the Toronto Graduate Nurses Association. Both buildings now serve as hostels.

10 Saint Luke's United Church/originally Sherbourne Street Methodist Church, 355 Sherbourne St., Smith & Gemmell, 1871; Sunday school addition, Langley Langley & Burke, 1876; remodelled, Langley & Burke, 1886; porch and south wing addition, Parrott Tambling & Witmer, 1960.

Sherbourne Street Methodist started out in 1871 as plain brick Gothic. Enlarged and re-dressed in grey and brown sandstone in commanding new Richardsonian Romanesque style in 1886, the church was called "the handsomest in central Toronto" at the turn of the century. Admiring its carefully wrought checkerboard stonework and dramatic tiled conical tower, one can envision what a rich and powerful presence it must have been on this corner before the nondescript porch and south wing were grafted on, insidiously sapping the strength and integrity of a bold composition.

11 Originally Abram M. Orpen house, 380 Sherbourne St., Henry Simpson, 1900.

A perfect turn-of-the-century expression, this large house sophisticates 1890s picturesque (rough-cut stone, round arches, decorated brackets) by smoothing out the edges with smart 1900s classical (Palladian windows, keystones, dentil mouldings). Orpen was president of a contracting and paving company in 1900. In 1899, he too seemed to have had a more picturesque profile; the city directory listed him as a "book maker."

12 Originally Kerr/Boyd house, 416–418 Sherbourne St., 1881.

A rotund, smooth Second Empire double house with unusual shared entry. Kerr was listed in city directories as a clerk; Boyd was one of the brothers in Boyd Bros. & Co. dry goods wholesalers.

13 Originally the Rev. Hoyes Lloyd house, 422 Sherbourne St., 1871–72.

More intriguing than the one entrance for two families at no. 416-418 [11/12] is no. 422's two entrances for one family. The appealing design with wraparound porch and centre-stage chimneys seems to be unique in Toronto. When he built this house, Lloyd was listed in city directories as an insurance agent. He also built the house next door at no. 432, which dates to 1875. These houses now function as C[ommunity] R[esource] C[entre] Bunton Lodge, a facility for men run by the Salvation Army.

14 Originally the Rev. Alexander Sutherland house, 437 Sherbourne St., 1878.

Victorian eclectic and showily painted to highlight Gothic gables, Italianate eyebrow window heads, and Eastlake spools and spindles. Sutherland was with the Methodist Missionary Society.

17 *St. James Town*

15 Rosar-Morrison Funeral Residence, 467 Sherbourne St. (detached house), possibly David B. Dick, 1877–78.
Classical frets and pilasters, even leaves on the Corinthian capitals, rendered in picturesque red and yellow brick. Dick is known to have designed a house of the same date that once stood next door, and he may have been responsible for this handsome, playful endeavour as well. Rosar-Morrison have occupied the premises since 1929. With records to 1861, they are one of Toronto's oldest firms.

16 Ernescliffe, 195 Wellesley St. E. (apartment house), Redmond & Beggs, 1913–14.
Designed in the Classical Revival style of the moment, the Ernescliffe took the axiom of "building as column" more literally than most, with a rusticated cast-stone base at ground storey, modillioned cornice capping the top, and giant Ionic pilasters at every turn of the five storeys of shaft. The double entrances on Wellesley Street are grand little temple fronts.

17 St. James Town, Wellesley to Howard St., Sherbourne to Parliament St. (housing complex), George Jarosz with James Murray 1965–68.
The east side of Sherbourne Street north of Wellesley is dominated by the 15 somber apartment towers of St. James Town, cheerlessly extruding a population of 15,000 souls 16 to 33 storeys into the sky. Begun in the mid 1960s when a serious housing shortage was looming and existing Victorian houses on the 32-acre site were crumbling into decay, this private developer's project was welcomed by the city as an urban godsend. (After all, they had paid for the same concept themselves ten years earlier in Regent Park [10/30, 31]. Billed as a "city within a city" and with its own network of meandering streets, St. James Town remains visually and practically isolated from the surrounding neighbourhood. At the same time, the complex lacks adequate shops, cafés, and street life—amenities we associate with the public fabric of a community. Having become neither a city nor integrated within a city, St. James Town is a good example of how developments never develop at all.

18 *Our Lady of Lourdes Church, c. 1890*

18 Our Lady of Lourdes Roman Catholic Church, 520 Sherbourne St., Frederick C. Law, 1884–86; remodelled, James P. Hynes, 1910.

When built, this was considered a most glorious jewel: the only domed church in the city and a worthy commemorative to the first Roman Catholic archbishop of Toronto, John Lynch. Lynch was credited with helping quell much of the religious prejudice then prevalent in the province, and in recognition of this and as part of the 25th anniversary of his appointment as archbishop, a fund was raised to build a small memorial church at his official summer residence, St. John's Grove, located near Sherbourne and Wellesley. The Renaissance Revival church which Frederick Law built directly beside the Gothic Revival residence (still visible in the rear) consisted of what is today the wing along Earl Street. The altar was situated to the west beyond the domed crossing and a portico fronted the east entrance. When it came to enlarging Our Lady of Lourdes in 1910, James Hynes was forced to do some juggling. The only space for a new nave was running north/south along Sherbourne Street, and accordingly the altar was moved to the centre of the original structure with the side spaces becoming east and west choirs. Hynes also moved Law's portico to adorn his own new entrance. Unconventional but impressive, outside and in.

19 Earl Court, 30–38 Earl St. (complex of ten row houses and three rehabilitated houses), Peter Turner, 1982.

Well detailed and constructed, the new houses are a felicitous match for the old. In the best tradition of such "mixers," they are not slavish copies but capture the general forms and spirit of the originals, which date to 1879 and 1885. Very nice.

20a John Howard Society, 168 Isabella St. (detached house), 1891.

A multiplicity of stones, bricks, and tiles in a stoutly serious manifestation of Queen Anne style. Any hint of pomposity is quickly dispelled, however, by the sprightly angels and mustachioed gentlemen peering out from atop porch columns. One of the city's little-remarked architectural highs.

20b Isabella Hotel/originally Mrs. Mary Northrop house, 556 Sherbourne St., 1890–91.

Though now fused with the larger hotel and ignobly covered in painted pebbles— a kind of modern-day "roughcast"—what remains to be seen of the three-storey house with its grand pentagonal tower is still an eye-catcher here. Mrs. Northrop was the wealthy widow of a patent medicine manufacturer.

21 570–578 Sherbourne St. (five-house row), 1887–89.

"Simplicity, health, practicality and beauty are one and the same" pronounced the 1880s Aesthetic Movement.

22a *582 Sherbourne St.*

These five houses are very "aesthetic" with fine but modest decoration, U shape to accommodate many windows giving light and fresh air, and compact yet individual design. One can imagine that the builder, Edward Hewitt [see also 11/8a], advertised all these singular qualities for his little terrace along with its high-toned neighbourhood. Assessed at $1,000 each, these units were assuredly in good company with the $20,000 mansion across the way at no. 582 [11/22a].

22a Knights of Columbus clubhouse/originally James Cooper house, 582 Sherbourne St., 1880–81; recreational addition, Charles J. Read, 1911.

The finest Second Empire house remaining in Toronto and a preserved glimpse of just how grand the 19th-century city was, at least on posh avenues such as Sherbourne. The style was then the rage in Toronto, after sweeping Montreal and the United States, and aspiring and wealthy gentlemen such as the owner of no. 582, a boot and shoe manufacturer, would have been well aware of the aura of power and privilege such a palatial house could convey. The design boldly contrasts red-brick walls with light-coloured wood, metal, and limestone details (the pilasters

imaginatively issuing from quoins and window surrounds are a very sophisticated bit of sculptural frosting worthy of the best Second Empire buildings anywhere). Today enjoyment of this desirable domicile owes as much to careful custodianship as it first did to caring connoisseurship. Since 1910, the Knights of Columbus have respectfully maintained the whole, including first-floor interiors.

22b Selby Hotel/originally Charles H. Gooderham house, 592 Sherbourne St., David Roberts, 1883.

Large and typical Victorian picturesque with fanciful sawn bargeboard, tall two-pot chimneys, and informal windowed sunporches. One of the eight sons of the founder of the Gooderham and Worts Distillery lived here for many years with his family, unembarrassedly staying on even when the mansion next door at no. 582 [11/22a] briefly served from 1900 to 1905 as the Keeley Institute, a "Sanitarium for the Scientific Treatment and Cure of Liquor and Drug Addiction. Lady Patients Treated Privately."

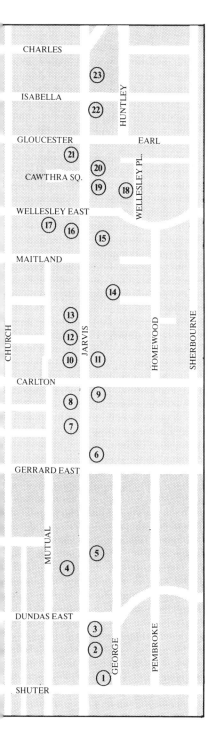

CHARLES

ISABELLA

GLOUCESTER   EARL

CAWTHRA SQ.

WELLESLEY EAST

MAITLAND

HUNTLEY

WELLESLEY PL.

CHURCH

JARVIS

HOMEWOOD

SHERBOURNE

CARLTON

GERRARD EAST

MUTUAL

DUNDAS EAST

GEORGE

PEMBROKE

SHUTER

1 Originally O'Donohoe row, 104–110 Shuter St. (four-house row), John Tully, 1856.

Think of early 19th-century London or New York and blocks of identical attached dwellings—row houses—come to mind. Toronto followed the leaders, with Georgian-style brick rows beginning to go up here in the 1830s. Well-to-do Torontonians, however, came to prefer detached or semi-detached houses, and not many really grand rows were ever built and even fewer remain. One notable exception is this neglected but imposing quartet, which boasts three tall storeys, a beautifully proportioned façade, and exquisite details such as six-light sash windows, stone lintels and sills, and Flemish-bond brick. Well-known architect John Tully designed the handsome ensemble for John O'Donohoe, ward alderman in 1859. Let's hope a modern-day alderman takes these deserving derelicts in hand.

2a 207–213 Jarvis St. (four units of original six-house row), 1879.

An eye-catching ensemble newly "white-painted" in teal blue and mustard yellow. In the 1870s and early '80s, Toronto loved the Second Empire style and used it for everything from courthouses to row houses. The grandiose courthouses were massed around projecting centre pavilions; here the centrepiece is a double dormer in the convex-sloped mansard roof. The porch is a distracting but practical early 20th-century addition.

2b 215–219 Jarvis St. (three-house row), 1863.

A trio of row houses essaying what is probably the closest Toronto ever came to Manhattan's Italianate brownstones, sans the brownstone. Typical features include flattish roof, heavy cornice, round-headed windows with boldly protruding dripmoulds and sills, and prominent doorways with overdoors resting on pilasters (intact at no. 219). The exterior flight of steps leading to a raised parlour floor and the rusticated high basement with access from the outside are the most telling common denominators. Nineteenth-century builders' guides recommended "earthy" paint colours such as the rusty

1 *104-110 Shuter St.*   2b *215-219 Jarvis St.*

red and mustard yellow of these recent renovations, but evidence suggests Victorian Torontonians preferred white, dark green, or brown. Nevertheless, these are very special all around.

3 Royal Canadian Mounted Police, 225 Jarvis St. (office building), Mathers & Haldenby, 1972.
A formal, formidable building for the Mounties with windowless front façade and steep entrance. This raw concrete style is today called Brutalist.

4 Simpsons-Sears, 222 Jarvis St. (office building), Maxwell Miller, 1969–71.
Simpsons-Sears Catalogue Centre/originally Robert Simpson Co. Mail Order Building, Mutual St., N. Max Dunning with Burke Horwood & White, 1916; addition, 1930.
Daring? Bold? Futuristic? Yes, that's Simpsons-Sears on Jarvis Street. But the same words were used 60 years earlier to describe the building behind it. In 1916, Simpsons department store on Yonge Street [5/7] hired American architect Max Dunning to create the last word in a mail order house. And he did. Eleven storeys of precast reinforced concrete and light-refracting windows, the building featured such radical energy-, time-, and space-saving devices as openings in the floor slab under each parcelling bin to drop orders onto an endless conveyor belt running just under the ceiling of the storey below. The company advertised that without exception orders went out the same day they were received.
When the Simpsons mail order business

was merged with Sears in the 1960s, the company decided to build corporate headquarters adjacent to the older warehouse. The massive cantilevered brown-brick design by Simpsons-Sears' own architect is certainly a startling look for Jarvis Street, but it echoes the earlier building in its efficiency-conscious interior—modular planning, high-speed escalators, vertical conveyors moving paperwork from floor to floor—and in its thoughtfully detailed, gridded façade.

5 285–291 Jarvis St. (four-house row), possibly Knox & Elliot, 1889–90.
Row housing is cheaper and faster to build than detached units so it has always appealed to speculative builders, but this is Toronto's only known row using weighty Richardsonian Romanesque style, and a very skilful application it is. The developer here was Alderman Edward Hewitt, for whom architects Knox & Elliot had just created a distinguished Romanesque two-family house nearby on Sherbourne Street [11/8a], suggesting the talented pair may have also designed this virile composition which even years of neglect can't hide. It is unique and begs to be restored.

4 *Simpsons-Sears*

6a Jarvis Street Baptist Church, 130 Gerrard St. E. at Jarvis St., Langley Langley & Burke, 1874–75; renovated and altered, Horwood & White, 1938–39.

This Jarvis Street landmark was designed in Decorated Gothic Revival, considered *de rigueur* for ecclesiastical architecture in the 1870s. It boasts a wealth of fluid detailing and a complicated composition, with the animated cater-corner siting of the tower resonating in contours of rough brownstone walls and outlines of jagged buttresses. That these expressive gestures work in a relatively small church on a tight city lot is a measure of Langley's finesse. It was for this church that he designed the first amphitheatrical interior in Canada. The west doors, expressively flanked by grinning gargoyles, were inserted in 1939, part of massive renovations carried out by Horwood & White, Langley's ultimate successor firm.

6b Toronto Baptist Seminary/originally Samuel Platt house, 337 Jarvis St., 1849–50.

Mr. Platt, a brewer and distiller, must have been thumbing through some architecture books. The pointed detailing on his front door is Gothic; the capitals on the pilasters, Egyptian; the rectangular shape of the doorway comes from Greek Revival; and the symmetrical plan with low hipped roof looks Italianate. (The early 20th-century porch is not Platt's doing.) It all comes together in a very distinctive manner, however, and the seminarians really shouldn't have blandly painted over all the excitement.

7 Essex Park Hotel/originally Frontenac Arms Apartments, 300 Jarvis St., Joseph A. Thatcher, 1930.

The Frontenac Arms was the embodiment of a 1930s apartment building with romantic name, salubrious design, and stylish Moderne façade. This was the heyday of apartment construction in Toronto and keen competition flogged features such as superior ventilation, view, sun, and sound insulation. The ten-storey Frontenac boasted all these plus concrete-block construction and Deco decoration enhancing lower-floor spandrels. Unfortunately, it was too late to rescue Jarvis Street from its downhill slide, and the Frontenac never attracted the tenants it had hoped for. Ten years later, it was an apartment hotel and the sole example in this area of a 1930s high-rise.

8 314 Jarvis St. (detached house), 1865.

An early Jarvis Street house that has engaged not a few remodellers over the years, but with surprisingly handsome result. The below-ground "first" floor, which originally would have housed kitchen and family dining room, is unusual for Toronto.

9 St. Andrew's Lutheran Church/originally St. Andrew's Presbyterian Church/formerly St. Andrew's United Church, 383 Jarvis St., Langley Langley & Burke, 1878; Sunday school addition, Langley Langley & Burke, 1882.

At the turn of the century, Toronto historian John Ross Robertson confidently wrote, "St. Andrew's presents a uniform, substantial, real appearance that fittingly symbolizes the character of the religious faith in which it is enshrined." Langley's plain but pleasant façade of Credit Valley freestone has since been called upon to represent the Lutherans, after a 25-year stint for the Uniteds, but it seems to have adapted well enough.

10a 336, 338, 340 Jarvis St. (three units of original eight-house row), 1862; nos. 338 and 340 remodelled, 1882; no. 336 remodelled, 1886.

Once part of a Georgian row of two-storey houses that ran south to the corner, these three survivors only later took on mansard roofs, bowed bays, and other Second Empire trappings in what looks like loving-hands-at-home alterations. At one time, artist Frederick Bell-Smith lived at no. 336.

10b 342-344 Jarvis St. (double house), 1874.

The architectural amplitude of the Italianate—round-headed windows and doors, heavy shadow-producing quoins and drip-moulds, rich bracketed cornice—cleft in the centre by an anomalous gabled recess.

10c 346 Jarvis St. (detached house), A.R. Denison, 1899.

A diminutive French chateau trying on a small scale to live up to the hauteur of Jarvis Street.

11 Hampton Court Hotel/originally Four Seasons Hotel, 415 Jarvis St., Peter Dickinson Associates, 1960–61.

Three- and four-storey rectilinear blocks around a central landscaped courtyard in the best, crisply clean tradition of the International Style, with coursed, rough-cut ashlar serving as grounding pad for smooth white boxes floating above. In the early 1950s with Page & Steele and later as head of his own 100-member firm, Dickinson was hugely influential in bringing modernist method and materials to Canada, none better than this.

12a Originally Havergal Ladies College, 354 Jarvis St., George M. Miller, 1898.

At the time Miller designed this building, Jacobethan was favoured for private educational institutions, but it doesn't look as if the architect had his heart in it. Havergal wanted a large building packed onto a small city lot, which they got, but the no-nonsense visage could only have appealed to the young ladies' parents.

12b Originally "Northfield" (Oliver Mowat residence), 372 Jarvis St., Joseph Sheard, 1856.

A trim, symmetrical two-storey manor designed by eminent architect Joseph Sheard for a young Oliver Mowat, later a Father of Confederation and longtime premier (1872-1896) of Ontario. The house has had only five tenants: Mowat for six years when Jarvis was a dusty road and empty fields stretched northward; Edward Rutherford, president of Consumers' Gas, and his wife for 52 years when the street was in its heyday; Havergal Ladies College from 1913 to 1932 when it was used for boarders' rooms; the RCAF during World War II; and since 1946, the CBC for executive offices. It was the Havergal ladies who added wall dormers to light attic bedrooms, resulting in the curious pierced cornice. Presumably the CBC added the skimpy shutters and "modernizations" to the front door.

13 Originally Blaikie/Alexander house, 400–404 Jarvis St., Gundry & Langley, 1863–64; no. 404 remodelled, 1882; remodelled with additions, A.J. Diamond & Partners, 1987–88.

Even though land was plentiful, some well-to-do Torontonians were not averse to semi-detached houses. Pattern books touted their economy, especially when "people can agree and get along together." The first two owners here were partners in a brokerage firm, at which time the houses displayed similar Gothic Revival intentions. By 1882, however, the occupants seem no longer to have been in agreement and no. 404 received a fussy Queen Anne facelift. Today, their front exteriors have been meticulously restored while attaching to the rear a large but unobtrusive facility for the National Ballet School. New landscaping incorporating parking space and wheelchair ramp is very neatly accomplished.

12b *372 Jarvis St.*   **13** *400-404 Jarvis St., 1984*

14 Maitland Place, 445 Jarvis St. (complex of two apartment houses and four rehabilitated houses), Edward I. Richmond with Spencer R. Higgins, 1983–84.

The rehabilitation of these four fine Victorian houses as frontispiece offices for the new high-rise apartment development is unusually honest and well done.

14a Originally Alfred Mason house, 441 Jarvis St., 1881.

Vigorous High Victorian Gothic eschewing facile surface ornament for an organic decoration created by the structural bricks and boards themselves. No. 441 was built for the manager of the city's first savings and loan company, Canada Permanent.

14b Originally Edward F. Blake house, 449 Jarvis St., Knox & Elliot, 1891; north bay addition, David B. Dick, 1897.

Vaguely chateauesque, but really more Shakespearean stage set than serious style. Concern for invention did not preclude quality, however; both firms of architects were masters of their art and the house is flamboyant but never flimsy. Edward F. Blake was the Hon. Edward Blake's son [see 12/14c].

14c Originally Samuel Briggs house/formerly Hon. Edward Blake house, 467 Jarvis St., possibly Smith & Gemmell, 1871–72.

An eclectic 19th-century house mixing Second Empire mansard with Italianate tower and off-centre plan in a typical Victorian show of the practical and picturesque. No. 467 was bought by one of Canada's leading statesmen, the Hon. Edward Blake, in 1879, the year he became leader of the opposition Liberal party. The previous owner was a lumber merchant.

14d Originally Thomas Thompson house /formerly Alexander Morris house, 471 Jarvis St., Langley Langley & Burke, 1873–74.

Built for a dry goods merchant, this is very accomplished High Victorian Gothic, with emphasis on the whole cake— materials, colour, harmonic silhouette— and not just the icing. Tory bigwig Alexander Morris moved to the house in 1881 after serving as lieutenant-governor of Manitoba and the North West Territories. Instrumental in concluding Indian treaties that secured much of the Canadian West for Ottawa, he may have found Jarvis Street a bit tame, the only controversy being whether to pave with cedar blocks, macadam, or asphalt (asphalt won out in 1889, the year Morris died).

15 *Jarvis Collegiate Institute*

18b *4 Wellesley Pl.*

15 Jarvis Collegiate Institute, 495 Jarvis St., C.E.C. Dyson, 1922–24.

"Collegiate Gothic," the last, recumbent phase of Gothic Revival, is well represented by Jarvis Collegiate Institute with its horizontal solemnity and 20th-century "medieval" mouldings, parapets, and mullioned and transomed windows. Jarvis traces its lineage to Toronto's first secondary school, the publicly owned but tuition-funded Home District Grammar School of 1807.

16 C.M. Hincks Treatment Centre, 440 Jarvis St. (office and residential building), Shore & Moffat, 1967.

A splendidly designed small-scale psychiatric facility for adolescents and their families. The building's delicacy and reserve along with careful landscaping and large trees make it easy to miss, but this is one of the most thoughtful structures on Jarvis Street.

17 Originally H.D. Warren house, 95 Wellesley St. E., 1892; additions, c. 1900; additions, Symons & Rae, 1908.

A large, rambling, slightly Jacobethan manor, no. 95 is one of those houses that just grew, with additions sprouting every few years. Mr. Warren's profits from gutta percha (a 19th-century formulation akin to rubber) paid for it all, another instance of Victorians' longing to live in a picturesque past even as they worked to create the fantastic future.

Two of the best 19th–century houses in the city are to be found on Wellesley Place, hidden behind hospitals that long ago swept away their neighbours.

18a Originally R.M. Simpson house, 2 Wellesley Pl., Charles J. Gibson, 1899.

With its broad flat front elaborated with one finely wrought Richardsonian Romanesque detail after another, this is a virtuoso artist's canvas of plum-coloured stone and red-brown brick. The stepped gable of the stable in the rear (belonging to an earlier, demolished house) is studiously repeated in this house to the side.

18b Originally Mrs. Mary Perram house, 4 Wellesley Pl., 1876.

Reminiscent of Ontario farm houses, this is an Italianate villa minus the typical tall square tower, but all the rest of the picturesque panoply is here.

19 Keg Mansion Restaurant/originally Arthur R. McMaster house/formerly "Euclid Hall" (Hart Massey residence), 515 Jarvis St., probably Gundry & Langley, 1868; additions, Langley Langley & Burke, 1882; additions, E.J. Lennox, 1883–85; additions, George M. Miller, 1900–01.

The much publicized home of farm machinery magnate Hart Massey underwent accretions from several architectural firms before it came out looking like the quintessential Baronial Gothic ensemble that it is today. To the initial asymmetric Gothic composition of crenellated tower, bay windows, and high gables

19 *Hart Massey residence, c. 1890*

originally designed for a dry goods merchant prince, Langley Langley & Burke introduced interior Queen Anne fittings for the newly installed Masseys in 1882. Lennox added veranda and conservatory to the south (now ignobly gone). Miller's contribution included front porch, corner veranda, second-floor sunroom, and domed south turret. Inside the turret Miller assembled a Moorish-style smoking room, a favourite turn-of-the-century conceit commissioned after her father's death by Massey's daughter, Lillian Massey Treble. It is unlikely the abstentious Massey would have approved of this harbinger of things to come, for today his elegant house is one of Toronto's most popular saloons.

20 Originally Charles A. Massey house/formerly Chester D. Massey house, 519 Jarvis St., E.J. Lennox, 1883–85; additions, Sproatt & Rolph, 1907.

Another Massey mansion, but here too many cooks have spoiled the architectural broth. Lennox's basic recipe for a picturesque Queen Anne house using half-timbered gables, dormers, and decorative bargeboards has been considerably diluted by Sproatt & Rolph's classical additions: skylit picture gallery to the north (for Chester's collection of Dutch masters), and columned porte-cochere to the south (for his Packard and Peerless motorcars). Today the house is primarily of note as the boyhood home of brothers Vincent Massey, Canada's first native-born governor-general; and Raymond Massey, the Broadway and Hollywood actor.

The west side of Jarvis Street between Cawthra Square and Gloucester is a precious intact block of late Victorian houses, all built during the 1880s, all abandoned by original owners within a few decades following the street's changing character at the turn of the century, and today almost all enjoying renewed uses.

21a Originally George H. Gooderham house, 504 Jarvis St., David Roberts, 1889.

This house for the 21-year-old son and namesake of distillery magnate George Gooderham was architect Roberts's rehearsal for the more grandiose Richardsonian Romanesque house designed for father George a year later in the Annex [19/30]. A decorous pile of red brick and stone, it is like a Rubik's cube with all the parts twisting precisely into place. Not a bad first house for young George who had his initials entwined in the expertly carved frieze over the front door. Many of the splendid original interior fittings remain; the vulgar iron fence is new.

21b Originally John H. McKinnon house, 506 Jarvis St., Langley & Burke, 1888.

Toronto's late, frontal Queen Anne with first-rate details: moulded terracotta frieze, spooled porch balustrade, scalloped tilehangings, and masks of Tragedy and Comedy summing it all up from perches aside the large front window. McKinnon was in proprietary medicines.

21a *504 Jarvis St.*

21e *514 Jarvis St.*

21c Originally Thomas Taylor house, 510 Jarvis St., 1888.
Attractive scrolled brackets and an unusual stepped gable. The original owner was big in brewing and malting.

21d Originally Edward Gallow house/formerly Charles Band house, 512 Jarvis St., possibly E.J. Lennox, 1889–90.
Classical Revival touches for a late Victorian house: Doric columns, dentil mouldings, pedimented lookout. Gallow was a broker; Band a grain merchant well known for his collection of paintings by the Group of Seven (donated at his death to the Art Gallery of Ontario).

21e Originally Charles R. Rundle house, 514 Jarvis St., E.J. Lennox, 1889–90.
If the house at the other end of this block is like an earnest Rubik's cube, no. 514 is more akin to one of those agile wooden acrobat toys that tirelessly somersault down the upended ladder—quick and quirky but executed with supreme skill and confidence. The architect has manipulated the house on this small lot brilliantly, placing the entrance on the interior south side to permit a centre hall and to give over the principal façade entirely to windows and an abundance of lovely Romanesque/Queen Anne ornament. Rundel was a speculative builder for whom Lennox designed several houses in this neighbourhood, none finer than this.

22 Originally William R. Johnston house, 571 Jarvis St., Langley Langley & Burke, 1875.
Neither Italianate villa nor French chateau nor Scottish manor, this merchant's house was not specifically related to any style, but the imposing capped piers flanking the main entrance would have lent enough of an historicizing air to qualify it for this fashionable Victorian street. The coach house in the rear is a much later addition.

23 Queen's Court, 579 Jarvis St. (one-half of original two-unit apartment house), 1908–10.
Toronto began to build apartment houses after the turn of the century. Land in the city was becoming scarce and expensive and apartments such as the Queen's Court could provide residences for 14 families who wanted to live on prestigious Jarvis Street, instead of just one. In fact, several company presidents lived in this ostentatiously classical building when it was new.

Walk 13: Church Street

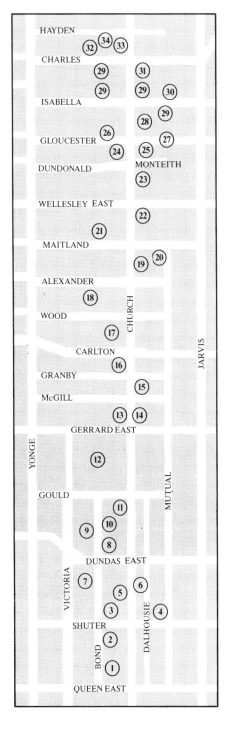

1 Metropolitan United Church/originally Metropolitan Wesleyan Methodist Church, Queen St. E. at Church St., Henry Langley, 1870–72; rebuilt after fire, J. Gibb Morton, 1928–29.

This majestic "Cathedral of Methodism" was in no small way a symbol of the commercial and social power of Toronto's Methodist community in the 1870s, raised as bold challenge to both Anglican and Roman Catholic cathedrals [1/8, 13/3]. All three have towers by Langley but Metropolitan's remains the best, its heroic proportions and firmness restored after a devastating fire of 1928. And even though the rebuilding did not make use of the same richly decorated High Victorian elaboration as the original, the deeply recessed windows, sharply contoured buttresses, and sweeping rhythm are in similar spirit and give Metropolitan a magnificent sense of space and volume. In 1925, with the union of Methodists, Congregationalists, and two-thirds of the Presbyterians, this centre-city church became Metropolitan United. It continues to enjoy a privileged site in the middle of a block-square park, now municipally maintained in part. Unfortunately, the cast-iron fence designed by Langley to complete the setting has been removed.

---

2 Metropolitan United Church parsonage, 51 Bond St., Curry Sproatt & Rolph, 1906; parish hall addition, J. Gibb Morton, 1929–30.

With its diminutive, rough-hewn character, this stone parsonage looks exactly as we have come to expect from our reading of English novels. The parish hall added to the east repeats the same forms in less vigorous brick.

---

3 St. Michael's Roman Catholic Cathedral, 57 Bond St., William Thomas, 1845–48; tower and spire additions, Gundry & Langley, 1865–67; dormer additions, Joseph Connolly, 1890.

Today, hemmed in by streets and adjacent buildings, St. Michael's lacks the expansive sites of both St. James' and Metropolitan United, and therefore the grand prominence of those two edifices. As well, too many fussy details appended later have sapped whatever drama the 14th-

1 *Metropolitan United Church*

3 *St. Michael's Cathedral*

century-derived church with its striking west façade might have originally enjoyed. Langley insinuated three detailed lancets in each face of the tower where Thomas had planned but a single traceried window, and the quirky dormers stapled onto the broad roof—though they do provide a light-enhancing clerestory—destroy the bold sweep of Thomas's roofline. The interior is appealing with lushly painted ceiling and exuberant Gothic arcades and clustered piers, but hardly the stuff of great cathedrals.

4 68-70 Shuter St. (two units of original four-house row), probably John Tully, 1855.

Another of Toronto's rare remaining examples of aristocratic Georgian row housing à la London or New York [see also 12/1]. The high parlour floor reached by a flight of steps can be traced to Georgian's Dutch ancestry where the threat of flooding made such townhouse elevation necessary. In other parts of the world, as here, the raised entry simply became an affectation of grandeur.

5 St. Michael's Cathedral rectory/originally Bishop's Palace, 200 Church St., William Thomas, 1845-46; north wing addition, Joseph Sheard, 1852; third-floor addition, Frederick C. Law, 1889.

The residence for the bishop uses the same stone-dressed brick as the cathedral [13/3], but here Thomas is flashier, employing decorative buttresses and pinnacles among other evocative medieval memories. The label-stops depict the heads of both bishop and architect.

6 191-197 Church St. (four-house row), 1852; rebuilt after fire, probably John Tully, 1856; demolished no. 195 rebuilt, Mekinda Snyder & Weis, 1981-82.

One of Toronto's finest remaining Georgian rows, actually highlighted by the new replacement at no. 195. Before the gap site was filled, it seemed only a faithful reproduction would do. But the properly scaled reinterpretation, announced by decidedly modern fixtures alongside the Georgian, has proved to be more interesting, both in itself and for its commentary on the whole. The wooden doorcases on

6 *191-197 Church St.*   7 *82 Bond St.*

these houses resemble those around the corner at 68-70 Shuter [13/4], and it seems likely both rows were designed by John Tully, who we know was responsible for similar 104-110 Shuter Street [12/1].

7 William Lyon Mackenzie house, 82 Bond St. (one unit of original three-house row), 1858.
This charming Georgian showplace, once part of a row, is something of an architectural rarity for Toronto with its high parlour floor reached by a flight of steps inside a vestibule. The lawned setback adds to the distinctiveness, as does the fact that this row house now stands alone. This was the last home of Toronto's renegade first mayor after he was allowed to return from sanctuary in the United States whence he had fled following an abortive rebellion against the ruling oligarchy in 1837. After Mackenzie's death in 1861, his widow and children stayed on, two of his daughters running the "Misses Helen and Elizabeth Mackenzie Ladies Boarding School" here. No. 82 is maintained as a fully furnished house museum by the Toronto Historical Board and is open daily 9:30 to 5; Sundays 12 to 5.

8 Doubleday Publishing/originally C. E. Goad Co./formerly Norris-Patterson Advertising, 105 Bond St. (office building), Curry & Sparling, 1912.
This three-storey structure isn't as old as it looks. The rusticated ground floor, stone string courses, and alternating segmental- and triangular-pedimented window heads were all part of the Second Classical Revival that around the turn of the century saw Italian *palazzi* again put in the service of private clubs, banks, and small office buildings. This particular palace was for a compiler of insurance atlases, C. E. Goad Company.

9a Originally Piper/Birnie house, 110–112 Bond St., 1862.
A fine early Toronto double house in the tall, blocky tradition of Georgian row housing [see also 11/9a]. Original owners were Noah L. Piper, a hardware merchant, and Mrs. Grace Birnie, who ran a girls' boarding school here. Perhaps that's why Mr. Piper later moved to Yorkville [17/2].

9b First Lutheran Church/originally St. John's Lutheran Church or German Lutheran Church, 116 Bond St., Charles F. Wagner, 1898–99.
Described in its time as "modern Gothic," this perky abstraction features smooth stucco walls and elongated windows, buttresses, and corner tower. The congregation, which was founded in 1851, replaced an earlier wooden meeting house on the site.

9b *First Lutheran Church*

12a *"Folly" of Normal School*

10 St. George's Greek Orthodox Church of Toronto/originally Holy Blossom Temple, 115 Bond St., J. Wilson Siddall, 1895; remodelled, 1938; renovated, Allan M. Young, 1982–84.

After centuries of emulating the architecture of the community in which they found themselves, Jewish congregations of the late 19th and early 20th centuries tried to develop a distinct synagogue style that they hoped would acknowledge their Middle-Eastern origins. Holy Blossom Temple on Bond Street, the second synagogue of the first Hebrew congregation in Toronto, was typical of these efforts. A Byzantine domed cubicle was given a Romanesque façade, then punctuated at the corners with stair towers topped by shaped domes. A large central dome is also the style of the Eastern Orthodox church and not a few downtown synagogues have converted to those houses of worship as the Jewish population moved elsewhere. No. 115 Bond Street was purchased by the Greek community in 1938 and is now their Toronto mother church. Recent renovations included installation of an intriguing mosaic of St. George and the dragon in the tympanum of the central arch.

11 Ryerson Polytechnical Institute Student Centre/originally "Oakham House" (William Thomas residence)/formerly Working Boys Home, 322 Church St., William Thomas, 1848; addition, David B. Dick, 1901; additions, George E. Kneider, 1977.

For his own house, Toronto's eclectic transplanted English architect William Thomas chose a romantic version of the medieval with an abundance of showy Gothic decoration: pointed arches, quatrefoil tracery, drip-moulds, pinnacles, crockets. The somber dark-brown-brick addition of 1901 was for working boys; the airy glass stairwell additions of 1977 for Ryerson students.

12a Normal and Model Schools, St. James Square, Cumberland & Ridout, 1851–52; all but folly demolished, 1963.

Founded by Egerton Ryerson, the Normal and Model Schools provided the first teacher-training facility in the province and as such became the cornerstone of the Ontario public school system. Housed in an imposing Victorian classical edifice situated in the centre of a landscaped square surrounded by handsome residences, the school was a distinguished Toronto landmark for many decades. Though the facility had become sorely antiquated by this century, it served briefly after World War II as a veterans' training school and later the first home of Ryerson Institute before it was finally demolished in 1963. A solitary span of porticoed wall was left standing in the middle of the Ryerson quadrangle, however, creating one of those architectural oddities referred to as "follies."

12b Ryerson Polytechnical Institute: Kerr Hall, 50 Gould St., Burwell R. Coon, 1954–63; Recreation and Athletic Centre, Lett/Smith, 1986–87.

Constructed around the old Normal School before it was demolished, Kerr Hall was the first new Ryerson building. It would be easily forgettable except for the stone bas-reliefs by Thomas Bowie that decorate its walls. Here are depicted Ryerson students in the guise of nude Art Deco style Greek gods and goddesses going about their scholarly and athletic activities: pony-tailed reader, crew-cut thinker, a gymnast, skater. Another delightful surprise is Ryerson's 1980s Recreation and Athletic Centre, an extraordinary high-style facility burrowed 2½ levels under the quad.

12c Ryerson Polytechnical Institute: Jorgensen Hall, 380 Victoria St., Webb Zerafa Menkes, 1968; Palin Hall, 87 Gerrard St. E., Crang & Boake, 1969; Photographic Arts Centre, 122 Bond St., Crang & Boake, 1969; Learning Resources Centre, 350 Victoria St., Webb Zerafa Menkes, 1971; Architectural Science Building, 325 Church St., Thom Partnership, 1979.

The various buildings put up by Ryerson since Kerr Hall [13/12b] are of a higher order. Including much older buildings in the area that the school has rehabilitated for its use, they form a dignified yet inviting inner-city college campus, the whole beautifully integrated by thoughtful landscaping, handsome signage, and pocket parks. Devonian Square, the skating rink/pond constructed in 1978 at the corner of Victoria and Gould, is one of Toronto's most sophisticated urban gestures.

13 62–66 Gerrard St. E. (three-house row), 1855; mansard addition, c. 1875.

The crisp rectangularity of an early Georgian row, with Flemish-bond yellow brick and stone lintels and sills. The Second Empire mansard was added later. In the mid 19th century, Gerrard Street was a prestigious residential thoroughfare.

14a Originally I. A. Smith house, 70 Gerrard St. E., 1847; remodelled, Langley & Burke, 1885.

A large red- and yellow-brick Georgian house for a dry goods merchant, niftily "modernized" in 1885 with Queen Anne orioles, porch, gables, and dormers.

14b 74 Gerrard St. E. (attached house), Langley & Burke, 1884–85.

A fine Queen Anne house designed by the town's leading architects, who obviously knew a good craftsman or two—the woodwork and brickwork are superb.

14c 76 Gerrard St. E. (attached house), 1878–79; rebuilt after fire, 1983.

A Bay-n-Gable of the 1870s laudably rebuilt after a fire in the 1980s to its original configuration, though with more Victorian bric-a-brac than it truly needs.

14d Originally Green/Green house, 78-80 Gerrard St. E., 1858.

This is one of Toronto's most interesting buildings, a handsome yellow-brick double house, unusual for its three-storey height and bay-windowed front. It does resemble some other early Toronto Georgian double houses, however, in that the units look more like row housing than semi-detached (the entrance to no. 80 has been bricked into a window), and in the high parlour floor reached by a steep flight of steps. At no. 78 lived Columbus H. Green, a barrister; at no. 80, the Rev. Anson Green.

15 375–377 Church St. (two-unit commercial block), 1876.

These blocky shops were probably among the last Georgian structures built in Toronto, a very, very old-fashioned look for 1876, even with the addition of a picturesque corbel table. Earliest tenants were grocer Donald Murray and butcher Frank Bilton.

16 Canadian Imperial Bank of Commerce/ originally Somerset House Hotel, 432 Church St., Frederick H. Herbert, 1895; remodelled as bank, Langley & Howland, 1930.

This branch bank began life as the Somerset House Hotel when Church Street, though a bit commercial with its streetcar tracks, was still a fashionable address. Hotel guests were no doubt attracted by the ample windows and finely detailed Richardsonian Romanesque character of the place as well.

18 *City Park Apartments*

20 *111 Maitland St.*

17 Maple Leaf Gardens, 438 Church St. (athletic hall), Ross & Macdonald with Jack Ryrie and Mackenzie Waters, 1931.

The language of a Deco skyscraper deftly translated to a colossal box with set-back angular façade and Art Moderne decorative touches. Some 700 construction workers toiled night and day to finish the reinforced-concrete building in time for the opening of the 1931 hockey season, a feat they accomplished in a record five months 12 days.

18 City Park Apartments, 484 Church St., Peter Caspari, 1954.

In the 1950s, City Park was famous as Toronto's first high-rise apartment complex, a daring three-building experiment in the vocabulary of the International Style. Today the precise modular patterning is no longer novel, but the simplicity of the design—which relies on little more than balcony shadows for ornament—remains distinguished. Cognoscenti also covet the quietude and unusually generous size of City Park's 774 units. Its European developers and their local architect used a combination of reinforced-concrete frame with poured reinforced-concrete carrying walls between apartments, and cut back by 375 the number of apartments allowed by city council. As with many International Style buildings, City Park's characteristic white-painted exterior plaster cladding deteriorated badly; it has since been removed.

19 467-475 Church St. (five-house row), George M. Miller, 1893.

No 19th-century row of houses could have been more picturesque than this bravura Queen Anne quintet. Symmetrically composed around a mountainous roof, this looks like nothing so much as Gulliver's house on a Lilliputian's street.

20 National Ballet School/originally Society of Friends Meeting House, 111 Maitland St., John A. Mackenzie, 1911.

An elegant Palladian surprise shining amid Victorian furbelows. With its pedimented Tuscan portico and round-arched multi-light windows, this building is a dignified study in classical simplicity that must have seemed especially appropriate to its Quaker congregation.

21 The Maitlands, 36–42 Maitland St. (apartment house), 1911.

A typical apartment block of the first decades of the 20th century when classical architecture was in vogue again, the orangey-brick Maitlands sports a handsome cornice at the top, portico of pressed metal and cast stone at the base, and jutting bays at the sides.

24 *580-582 Church St.*

25a *2-36 Monteith St.*

22 77 Wellesley St. E. (apartment house), Larremore V.V. Sweezy, 1926; remodelled, Jedd Jones, 1982.

This apartment building eschewed popular Classical Revival and Art Deco styles, opting for the Gothic touch—clues are "medieval" lettering over the door and the suggestion of a pointed gable at the roof. The remodelling which has introduced shops to the ground floor is sympathetic, with new slender windows of upper storeys more in the style and spirit of the original than most such rehabs.

23 519 Community Centre/originally Granite Club annex/formerly York Badminton Club and German Club Harmonie/formerly Ulster Athletic Club/formerly 48th Highlanders Hall, 519 Church St., Edwin R. Babington, 1906.

Conservative Scottish though they may have been, the founders of the Granite Curling Club did not intend to be remembered by a dour clubhouse such as this. As erected on the site in 1880, the Granite Club was an exuberant Renaissance Revival building with flags set flying from a high centre tower on skating days. What we see today was an attached addition of 1906, but when the principal building burned in 1913, this was left and subsequent tenants have made the best they could of it. Partial walls of the club's indoor ice rink still rim the northeast corner of the site, now a municipal park.

24 580-582 Church St. (double house), 1877-78.

A Second Empire double house at its dignified best, built when the style was at its peak in Canada. The gentle concave curve of the mansard roof, striking dormer windows, brisk classical window surrounds, and harmonious symmetry create a rich design that is both conservative and assertive. Not surprising that the first owner of no. 580 was Robert Simpson, whose dry goods shop at 184 Yonge Street still prospers, grown into a vast Canadian department store enterprise [5/7].

25a 2-36 Monteith St. (eighteen-house row), 1887-88.

When this row of economical brick houses was built in the late 1880s, Second Empire was no longer the height of fashion. Nevertheless, its dominant trademark—the mansard roof—was put to good use, providing a practical third storey and rhythmic roofline to the long row of working-class dwellings. The enterprising builder added further cachet to his development by naming the private lane on which the row was built after the Cawthras, then one of the wealthiest families in Toronto. The impulse was prophetic. Roy Thomson, who was born at no. 32 in 1894, the son of a barber and his wife, went on to become newspaper magnate Lord Thomson of Fleet, and his son and family, Kenneth Thomson, is reported to be Toronto's wealthiest man today. The street name was changed to Mulock in 1897 and Monteith in 1909.

29 *72 Isabella St.*

29 *40-42 Isabella St.*

25b 551-555 Church St. (triple house), 1888.
Displaying a sensitivity to proportion and materials that belies the charge of "frantic excess" sometimes levelled against late Victorian houses, this three-house ensemble projects a quality of repose that still draws attention on the street. Thoughtfully adapted for shops and offices.

Gloucester between Yonge and Jarvis is a street of Victorian single and double houses of the 1870s and '80s celebrating centenaries in various gentrification guises of the 1970s and '80s—a good downtown address again after years of rooming-house neglect.

26a 66 and 68 Gloucester St. (two detached houses), 1889.
Two blocky Queen Annes, more formal than most, thanks to noble stonework: lintels, keystones, sills.

26b 49-51 Gloucester St. (double house), 1881-82.
Dazzling Second Empire carefully restored to highlight yellow-brick necklaces stringing windows and doors.

27a 96 Gloucester St. (detached house), 1883-84.
Conspicuous among towering apartment buildings, this boxy Queen Anne might stand out anyway, but its whimsical turret—which looks as if it couldn't possibly be supported by that single lion-headed bracket—is the real attention-getter here.

27b 103-105 and 107-109 Gloucester St. (two double houses), 1887.
Twin double houses that vividly compare what happened to good Victorian design when the add-a-big-wooden-porch salesman came around in the early 20th century. A quick survey in this and similar neighbourhoods reveals that not a few succumbed.

28 Grace MacInnis Co-operative: 561-571 Church St. (six-house row), 1890.
573-575 Church St. (two-thirds of original triple house), 1889.
Six harmonious row houses and a building of grab-bag shapes, materials, and colours made more asymmetrically picturesque than necessary by the excision of its northern one-third, now a driveway to the mountainous condominium building at 86 Gloucester Street. The condos gained their extraordinary height in a trade with the city whereby the Church Street houses were renovated as low-cost housing and kept in place as a valuable segment of streetscape.

30a *90-92 Isabella St.*

29 The Merlan, 81–83 Isabella St. (apartment house), probably Norman A. Armstrong, 1927; remodelled, 1982.

Church-Isabella Co-operative, 72 Isabella St. (apartment house), 1917.

The Brownley, 40–42 Isabella St. (apartment house), 1931–32.

Star Mansions, 61–63 Charles St. E. (apartment house), 1931–32.

Like many apartment buildings of this period, The Merlan displays a ceremonious name on the front (often the date of construction is there too) and a deep light-giving U shape. Though the ends of the U sometimes presented dissimilar faces to the street, usually the decoration was classical in keeping with the fashion of the new century (try to forget the ugly 1980s windows). Other versions, that at 72 Isabella Street, for example, sported projecting bays duplicating those of a bay-windowed house. In a few years, however, to be stylish would mean to be Moderne. The Brownley is representative of many such 1930s apartment buildings

in which distinctiveness actually amounts to little more than Art Deco spandrels and entrance fixtures. Star Mansions is another such small Deco declaration.

30a Originally Foy/Smith house, 90–92 Isabella St., probably Langley & Burke, 1887–88.

Like a kaleidoscope stopped in mid-spin, this elaborate double house is a pretty Victorian picture of variegated, mirrored parts (save that no. 90 has an idiosyncratic classically detailed porch). Earliest residents were James F. Foy, barrister with Foy and Kelly; and Austin Smith, a "gentleman." The sand-coloured paint of the recent renovation very nearly matches the hue of the stone lintels and beautifully delineates lattice, lunettes, spools, and spindles against red brick. In the 1970s, eight new row houses were adroitly sneaked in behind no. 90-92 to share the urban glamour.

30b *94 Isabella St.*

30b Jesuit Fathers residence/originally Helen E. McMaster house, 94 Isabella St., Langley & Burke, 1884–85.

The widow of dry goods merchant Arthur R. McMaster built this exemplary Queen Anne after selling her Baronial Gothic mansion around the corner to Hart Massey [12/19]. Truer to textbook form than most Toronto Queen Annes, this really does look like a 17th-century manor house as reinterpreted by England's Norman Shaw or Boston's Peabody & Stearns. The architects here showed their expertise at manipulating materials and surface planes to capture the play of light and shade, a free but irreplaceable design ingredient.

31 Church-Isabella Co-operative, 589–595 Church St. (four attached houses), 1867, 1868, 1870, and 1878; altered, 1982.

Paxton Place, 71 Charles St. E. (apartment house), Edward I. Richmond, 1982.

Another height-for-heritage trade. The precise late Georgian attached houses have been conscientiously salvaged and homogenized and the new 16-storey condominium is slick with bronze glass and neatly hemmed precast panels. But, like the mouse and the elephant, they make uneasy neighbours.

32 66 Charles St. E. (detached house), 1874; remodelled, 1885.

62–64 Charles St. E. (double house), 1884.

The Second Empire had been around quite a while before the owner of no. 66 decided to enlarge his house and build matching semi-detacheds next door. The remodelling scheme—adding a mansard roof to a two-storey Georgian box—was a relatively easy and popular ploy in New York and was tried elsewhere in Toronto, but it didn't work too well here, the whole seeming a bit stiff with little of the pliant ornament associated with Second Empire. The trendy 1970s dark-coloured glass which cuts black holes into the façades doesn't help either. John Wilson Bengough, Canada's famous political cartoonist of the late 1800s, lived at no. 66 for a time.

33a Manhattan Apartments, 68–70 Charles St. E., James A. Harvey, 1909.

One of Toronto's earliest apartment buildings, cleverly consuming an existing house, the entrance of which is still used on Church Street.

33b 634–636 Church St. (double house), 1878.

Second Empire in an exuberant mood, with strongly articulated centre pavilion, flanking end bays, and lively mansard roof. Thanks to two of Toronto's more enduring restaurants, this fine double house still stands much as it was.

34 61 Hayden St. (detached house), 1868.

One of the first houses built in this district, quietly proclaiming its auspices with some neat Georgian details.

Area VIII

Walk 14: The Grange
Walk 15: Queen Street West

Area VIII

This area, like *AREA VII*, was originally part of Simcoe's string of 100-acre "park lots," the 30 1/8-mile-wide parcels running north from Queen Street to Bloor Street that were granted to government officials as sites for large estates intended to frame and enhance the new colonial capital. One of the grandest of these estates was The Grange, a Georgian mansion still gracefully holding court in Grange Park [14/1]. The Grange was built about 1817 by D'Arcy Boulton Jr., eldest son of the young province's solicitor-general and a prominent member of the town's conservative political, religious, and social elite. It was surrounded by sweeping lawns and gardens with a gatekeeper's lodge to the south, servants' cottages to the north, an orangery and grapery, and later tennis courts.

As was the case finally with all the park lots, the Boultons' 100 acres got smaller and smaller as the town began to expand and lazy country fields suddenly metamorphosed into lucrative "city" building plots. The Boultons began to sell off parts of their park lot (which ran roughly between McCaul and Beverley Streets) as early as 1828, when the north half above College Street went at £25 an acre for the new Anglican-affiliated King's College campus [see Introduction, *AREA V*]. Archdeacon John Strachan is reported to have been dismayed at the high price asked by a fellow member of Toronto's close-knit aristocracy (a group dubbed "The Family Compact" by its political opponents), but later the Boultons donated land from their park lot for the first west-end parish church in Toronto, St.-George-the-Martyr [14/2], as well as for St. Patrick's Market on nearby Queen Street [14/5]. This was probably a bit of opportunism along with the *noblesse oblige*, however, for Boulton must have anticipated that church and public market would help attract buyers to the residential building lots he was trying to sell. Buyers were slow in coming, but eventually the handsome house of worship became the centre of a healthy community.

The architectural character of the district as it developed was undoubtedly influenced by the family's continued residence in their fine house on wooded and manicured grounds. Beverley Street especially, next to The Grange and divided into large lots, became a fashionable address in the 1870s when mansions in the voguish mansard-roofed Second Empire style began to go up. Houses on surrounding streets were somewhat smaller; as in *AREA VII*, they were an eclectic mix of late Georgian, Gothic Revival, Italianate, and Second Empire, moving on to Richardsonian Romanesque, Queen Anne, and finally turn-of-the-century Classical Revival.

The three park lots to the west of the Boulton land (running approximately between Beverley and Augusta Streets) came into the hands of the less Tory but no less influential Baldwin family. Baldwin land stretched as far north as Eglinton Avenue and their estate, called "Spadina," was located on the crest of Davenport Hill. Beginning in the late 1820s, William Warren Baldwin, a doctor as well as lawyer by profession but architect by avocation, began carving up his park lots for a residential district south of Bloor Street. His plan was worthy of his talent. Spadina Avenue was laid out as the central thoroughfare with a double width of 132 feet (later increased to 160) and an ornamental garden crescent above College Street. Queen Street, where it ran east of Spadina, was similarly widened. The side streets, though at right angles to one another, broke with the even grid of most city streets and stopped dead-end or jogged, forming interesting blocks of unequal size. Baldwin gave his streets self-conscious British names such as Kensington, Oxford, and Cambridge, or named them after the family: Baldwin, Robert, Phoebe, and Willcocks.

St-George-the-Martyr church, 1868, with commanding spire that was the second highest in Toronto until it burned down in 1955.

The last park lot in this area (Augusta to just east of Bathurst) was owned by the Denisons, a military family who in 1815 built an estate, which they called Belle Vue, right in the centre of their 100 acres just north of today's Bellevue Square [demolished, see 15/18]. Not to be outdone by Boultons and their gift of land for St.-George-the-Martyr, Col. Robert Denison gave both land *and* building funds for St.-Stephen-in-the-Fields [15/20], in 1858 the first church in Toronto west of Spadina Avenue. And when it burned down in 1865, the Denisons came up with more money for a complete rebuilding. At mid century, they cut up their property, like so many others, for streets and residential lots, demolishing one large estate building in the process. A principal Denison house stood well into the 1890s, however. Street names associated with the family include Denison, Bellevue, Lippincott, and Augusta. Here too, the houses were stylistically eclectic, progressing through and mixing the panoply of Victorian designs as the 19th century marched into the 20th.

These architectural changes, however, were as nothing compared to the sweeping shifts of population and ambience. Through the 1890s, this area, like most of Toronto, was solidly British in character. Though varied in economic level and religious persuasion, English, Scottish, and Irish residents alike kept all tidily decorous. Then, at the turn of the century, those who could afford it began moving north to new districts such as the Annex [*AREA X*]. Their places were taken by recent immigrants from Northern and Eastern Europe. Many of these were Jews fleeing religious persecution. The influx reached its peak in 1914, and shortly thereafter—following traditions in the homeland—these Jewish immigrants set up stalls in front of their houses on and around Kensington Avenue and began to trade with one another. Thus was born the lively confusion of Kensington Market. In addition to palatial Goel Tzedic temple on University Avenue [demolished], other synagogues were established: in small houses such as 37 D'Arcy Street; in new buildings on Henry, Baldwin, and Denison Streets [15/18]; in a converted church on Cecil Street [14/19]. Spadina Avenue became—and remains—the centre of the garment industry, first with facilities in converted houses, and then in lofts erected during the high-rise boom of the early 1900s [see Walk 4].

In the 1930s and '40s, many of these Jewish families repeated the northward pattern of movement, this time to Forest Hill Village, North York, and Downsview, a migration which reached its climax in the 1950s, at which time most of the synagogues were sold. Postwar immigrants from the Ukraine, Hungary, Italy, and Portugal were waiting to take their place. But in the 1970s, except for the Portuguese, these waves too moved on, followed in their wake by a new influx of West Indians and Filipinos. Today well over half the residents of the area are Chinese, with cultivation of summer melon replacing fava beans in front gardens. The intersection of Dundas Street and Spadina Avenue now forms the heart of Toronto's Chinatown, home to long-established Cantonese as well as streams of Hong Kong newcomers who have brought modern Crown Colony architectural ideas to the new splashy commercial blocks.

Finally there are the artists. Most are to be seen on Baldwin Street east of Beverley in a granola and Birkenstock sandal mode, on Dundas across from the Art Gallery of Ontario [14/10] in an established gallery mode, or on Queen Street West in an avant-garde mode. And, as in New York's SoHo district, all around this area artists are discovering that Toronto's commercial buildings and factories make splendid places to live, work, and exhibit. With The Grange still at its core as a symbol of gracious hospitality, this quarter continues to welcome one and all.

Walk 14: The Grange

1 "The Grange" (D'Arcy Boulton Jr. residence), Grange Park at John St., c. 1817; bathroom wing addition, c. 1840; library wing addition, probably Walter R. Strickland, 1885; restored, Peter John Stokes, 1973.
One of the four oldest buildings in Toronto, The Grange was the quietly imposing residence of the pioneer Boulton family, who named it after their ancestral home in England. It was built of red brick at a time when most buildings in the town were of wood or roughcast plaster, and it took as its design the harmonious Georgian box that had been standard for the English gentry since at least 1760.

Though The Grange has undergone substantial alterations over its many years, there has been little change in its genteel character. D'Arcy Boulton Jr., who built it, later added a short wing to the west for indoor plumbing and turned three bedrooms into a music room on the second floor and two others into a breakfast parlour on the first. (When built, The Grange was far in the country and the many socially and politically important visitors often stayed overnight, ergo many bedrooms.) D'Arcy's son and next Grange occupant was William Henry Boulton, a sportsman and two-time Toronto mayor. William Henry let the house be, though he did cut up some of the 20-acre backyard for a racecourse. In 1875, a year after William Henry died, his widow married Anglo-American academic

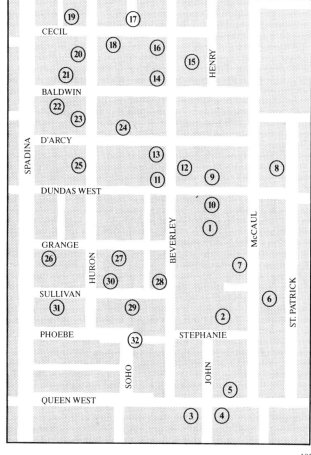

Goldwin Smith. Smith appended a sympathetic library wing, rebuilt the wooden portico in stone, and modernized—i.e., "Victorianized"—the colonial interiors. The Smiths willed the house to the Art Museum of Toronto, which exhibited here from 1913 to 1918, when a new gallery was built adjacent [14/10]. The Grange was then relegated to offices until 1973, at which time it was restored and opened as a house museum. The look-alike building to the east was the first Ontario College of Art on this site [14/7].

2 Church of St.-George-the-Martyr, 203 John St., Henry Bowyer Lane, 1845; Sunday school addition, Kivas Tully, 1857; all but tower and Sunday school destroyed by fire, 1955; parish hall addition, Gerald Robinson, 1987–88.

Dignified Perpendicular Gothic, attested by the bell tower of the steeple that alone stands after a devastating fire of 1955. Once celebrated for its beautiful stained glass windows and soaring spire atop the bell tower—it was the second highest in Toronto—St. George's was at the centre of a thriving west-end community. Today services continue in the former Sunday school and the orphaned tower carries on as bold symbol of church and district. The complex is completed by the rectory of 1865, a polite Victorian structure of a type common throughout Ontario, and a porticoed stone parish hall and cloister with ultra-modern "planter-columns" standing in for those of the church's burned nave.

3 315 Queen St. W. (office building), Zeidler Roberts Partnership, 1983.

Designed by high-profile firm Zeidler Roberts, this was among Toronto's first Post-Modern forays. Typical of the new play on past architectural modes are four-part square windows, colourful golden-hued square ceramic tiles, and a centre-stage Deco-curved bay of square glass blocks. (The square figures prominently with Post-Modernists.) The most self-conscious abstraction of historical forms are the "classical columns" ornamenting the ground floor which have been rendered as raw concrete "tubes" looking rather like fat lollipop sticks. The architects have their own offices on the mansarded top floor.

4 ChumCity/originally Wesley Buildings, 299 Queen St. W. (factory and office building), Burke Horwood & White, 1913–15; interior altered, Quadrangle Architects, 1986–87.

An early 20th-century contribution to the neighbourhood that seems to have strayed outside factory precincts to the south [Walk 4]. Built for the Methodist Book and Publishing Company (later Ryerson Press), the Wesley Buildings are garbed in Gothic fervour appropriate to the publishing company's early church association. The architects were not above a little Gothic fun as well, pinning grotesque readers and scribes along the second-storey horizontal band. Technology was all modern though: steel framing, terracotta cladding, and plenty of windows for air and light. Interior alterations in 1986 for ChumCity were even more avant-garde, creating the world's first television facility without formal studios.

5 Originally St. Patrick's Market, 234–240 Queen St. W., G.F.W. Price, 1912–13.

In 1836, D'Arcy Boulton Jr. of The Grange donated some of his park-lot land for a St. Patrick's Market, so-called because it was in St. Patrick's Ward, one of the five saintly political precincts created when the city was incorporated in 1834. The first market structure built by the city was a simple wooden Georgian design. Its replacement was more grandly brick Italianate. And the present building, now privately owned, is all utility, enclosing market space with long brick and wooden walls and the meekest of classical motifs.

6 Village-by-the-Grange, 49–105 McCaul St. thru to St. Patrick St. (complex of apartment houses and commercial blocks), Webb Zerafa Menkes Housden, 1980.

From its too cute name to its banal orange-crate façade, this condominium complex-cum-tourist mall is shoddy confusion. A ground floor jumbled with artsy-craftsy "shoppes" and fast foods from around the world borrows every decorating cliché going, from Early American gas lanterns to Broadway marquee lights. The lobbies of the condominiums opt for mirrored Louis XIV, and the body of the building is middle-brow modern though blessedly not overly tall.

3 *315 Queen St. W.*

4 *299 Queen St. W.*

7 Ontario College of Art, 100 McCaul St., George A. Reid, 1926; addition, Govan Ferguson Lindsay, 1957–61; altered, Moffat Moffat & Kinoshita, 1980–81.

The Ontario College of Art has been on this site since 1913, using part of the second floor of The Grange [14/1] until 1926 when its own new premises were constructed adjacent in complementary Georgian Revival style to designs by George Reid. Reid's two-storey red-brick structure now forms the northern rear wing of the OCA's large street-facing addition of 1957–61. That serviceable, institutional façade today hides much more exciting spaces created inside by Moffat Moffat & Kinoshita in 1980–81.

8 Our Lady of Mt. Carmel/originally St. Patrick's Church, 196 St. Patrick St., Gundry & Langley, 1869–70.

Redemptorist Fathers residence, 141 McCaul St., 1886.

St. Patrick's Church, 131 McCaul St., Arthur W. Holmes, 1905–08.

Named after the fifth-century cleric who carried Christianity to Ireland and only coincidentally after the political ward in which it was located, St. Patrick's was among the first Roman Catholic churches in Toronto. A small frame chapel stood on the site as early as 1860; when this burned in 1864, the amiable French Gothic house of worship we see today on St. Patrick Street was put up, followed by a schoolhouse to the north and the stolid Gothic priests' residence fronting on McCaul Street. The larger St. Patrick's was erected in 1908 in a placid Romanesque Revival of rather pasty stone, partly reclaimed by the vigorous arcaded portal and saintly niche at the top.

9 Dundas Street West between McCaul and Beverley was cut through The Grange back gardens in 1877 when the last acres from the estate were sold off. Among the first houses to go up in 1878 were paraphrases of the Second Empire mansions on adjoining Beverley Street. The superabundance of Second Empire wooden brackets at the eaves of the easterly houses is amusing, almost as if the contractor ordered too many but stuck them all on anyway. A number of 1870s houses in the centre of the block are remnants of Toronto Bay-n-Gable with fine sawn woodwork enlivening the gables. The most ambitious house is no. 344–346, a tall 1896 Queen Anne boasting lavish wooden detail and terracotta panels. No. 356–358, dating from 1877–78, has been slickly redone under the charitable auspices of the hamburger people and others as Ronald McDonald House, a hostel for parents of children undergoing treatment at the Hospital for Sick Children [7/21c].

10 *Art Gallery of Ontario*

11 *136 Beverley St.*

10 Art Gallery of Ontario, 317 Dundas St. W., Darling & Pearson, 1918; additions, Darling & Pearson, 1926, 1935; altered with additions, John C. Parkin, 1977; altered with additions, Barton Myers Associates, 1987-ongoing.

Founded in 1900 as one of the city's first cultural institutions, the Art Museum of Toronto, as it was then, made its first home in The Grange mansion [14/1]. In 1918, it moved into new galleries constructed in an austere Renaissance Revival style adjacent to the Georgian house. Enlarged in 1926 and again in 1935, this building, with its dignified, classically detailed Walker Court, served the city for close to 50 years.

In 1966, with provincial support and renamed the Art Gallery of Ontario, the institution turned to thoughts of expansion. The project was given definite shape four years later when Henry Moore was persuaded to donate a major collection of his work, then valued at $15 million. The Moore collection determined much of the interior design of the new building, but decisions to maintain a low scale by situating many facilities below grade were primarily prompted by streetscape concerns for the existing residential neighbourhood. The same impulse undoubtedly dictated much of Barton Myers's further expansion plans (laudably chosen in open competition), which extend the building to sidewalk line and festively deck it in towers, pyramids, cupolas, and such. One certainly can't accuse the AGO of not moving with the times; it seems to have produced a different building for every stylistic season.

11 Italian Consulate/originally "Chudleigh" (George Beardmore residence), 136 Beverley St., 1872; additions, Eden Smith, 1890, 1900, 1901.

The first of the Beverley Street mansions and still the most impressive house on the street, this is a bold asymmetric design accentuated by picturesque off-centre tower with oval picture-frame windows. Beardmore was a leather merchant with an equally striking warehouse on Front Street [1/15c]. No. 136 owes its distinction in part to its size—it was enlarged several times by Beardmore's son who joined old stables to the house; and to its spacious grounds ringed by an imposing stone, brick, and iron fence. In the 1930s, the house became the Italian consulate; it was confiscated during World War II; given back in 1958 to become an Italian language centre; and now, newly spruced up, serves again as consulate.

12 Beverley Mansions: 133–135 Beverley St. (double house), 1877.

137–139 Beverley St. (double house), 1876–77.

141 Beverley St. (detached house), 1877.

145–147 Beverley St. (double house), 1878.

The name seems a bit pretentious for this block renovated by the city's non-profit housing corporation as a 58-unit project, but in the 1870s these houses would have been thought quite grand indeed, if only for their expansive garden settings. No. 145–147 also boasts elegant one-storey mansarded kitchen pavilions to either side instead of more common rear service wings.

14 *186 Beverley St.*

15 *Beverley Place*

13 Originally John Cawthra house, 152 Beverley St., 1874; additions, Sproatt & Rolph, c. 1920; rehabilitated with additions, 1985–86.

Subdued Second Empire for a third-generation scion of the millionaire Cawthra family (grandfather Cawthra had come to Canada from Scotland in 1803 as an apothecary merchant and had gone on to become the principal importer of dry goods in the province). This house suffered a damaging fire in 1984 and although we should be thankful it is still with us and put to good use as city-sponsored housing, the "restoration" seems to have smoothed out all its character (the new windows are truly awful).

14 Originally "Lambton Lodge" (George Brown residence), 186 Beverley St., William Irving with Edward F. Hutchins, 1875–76; restored, 1987–88.

A formal red-brick mansard-roof house with powerful carved-stone portico and window surrounds, built for George Brown, founder of *The Globe* newspaper. Brown was also a Father of Confederation, having served in the United Provinces parliament from 1851 to 1865. In 1880, the high-principled radical was shot by a disgruntled *Globe* employee; the wound became gangrenous and he died in this house six weeks later. Used as a soldiers' rehabilitation centre by the Canadian National Institute for the Blind from 1919 to 1956, the place is now the property of that most conscientious restorer, the Ontario Heritage Foundation, which will use George Brown House for conference and office space.

15 Beverley Place, Baldwin to Cecil St., Beverley to Henry St. (complex of 152 units of row housing and nine rehabilitated houses), A. J. Diamond & Barton Myers (designed by A. J. Diamond), 1978.

This is another block of government-rehabilitated houses fronting new low-rise apartments by urban first-aid virtuosos Diamond & Myers [see also 11/7]. The most interesting of the older dwellings is no. 195–197 Beverley Street, an 1883 Second Empire double house with rare bowed bays. The award-winning new housing units are discreetly hidden from Beverley Street, unfolding in a crisp planar ribbon along Henry. Between the old and new runs a pleasant multi-level garden/recreation area.

16 196 Beverley St. (detached house), possibly George M. Miller, 1889.

198 Beverley St. (detached house), possibly George M. Miller, 1889; altered, David B. Dick, 1894.

200 Beverley St. (detached house), possibly George M. Miller, 1888.

Designed with true distinction, nos. 196 and 198 are outstanding examples of Richardsonian Romanesque style, with carved and moulded terracotta ornament among the most original in the city. The utterly powerful stonework and brickwork are enough to make one feel at once the weight and depth of walls and dark openings. They were built by James T. McCabe, also responsible for no. 200 in a somewhat less commanding idiom. We know Miller designed other, similar houses for this contractor, and it is conceivable he was the architect here too.

17 *24-26 Cecil St.*

21 *110-112 Baldwin St.*

17 20–22, 24–26, 28–30 Cecil St. (three double houses), 1881; demolished no. 24–26 rebuilt, Peter Turner, 1980–81.
Three trim Second Empire double houses of very congenial proportions attractively situated on generous–sized lots. Originally three more such houses ran to Huron Street, making these two blocks among the few in Toronto to approximate the expansive siting typical of American middle-class suburbs in this period. A close look at no. 24–26 reveals that it is a rebuilt copy of its neighbours, instructive for what the 1980s includes and what it omits of an 1880s house.

18 37, 39, 41, 43, 45 Cecil St. (five detached houses), 1886.
A quintet of speculatively built houses in decorative Queen Anne style making the most of irregular massing, rooflines, colours, textures, and elaborate *japonesque* woodwork, best preserved in no. 45.

19 Cecil Community Centre/originally Church of Christ/formerly Cecil Street Synagogue, 58 Cecil St., Knox & Elliot, 1890; remodelled, 1922; remodelled, Matsui Baer & Vanstone, c. 1978.
Built of sturdy brick and stone in Romanesque Revival, the original Church of Christ structure as designed by Knox & Elliot was dominated by an angled corner tower dramatically decorated with conical top and circular turret buttresses. In 1922, the building was bought by the Congregation Anshei Ostrovtze (Men of Ostrovtze) and became known as Cecil Street Synagogue. Several changes were made, including replacement of the Church of Christ's tower with one more in keeping with synagogue design [see 13/10]. The synagogue moved away in 1956 and after years of desultory use the building was skilfully altered to serve as a community centre.

20 122 Huron St. (detached house), 1889.
124–126 Huron St. (double house), 1889.
Queen Anne again, this time with characteristic tile-hung gables and walls the outstanding feature. The Queen Anne style enjoyed a long vogue in Toronto. That singularly American form, the Shingle Style, succeeded Queen Anne in the United States, but Toronto's fire regulations—which outlawed wooden shingles unless backed by brick—forestalled any tile-less tangents here.

21 110–112 Baldwin St. (double house), 1890–91.
A severe brick double house with one of the flossiest wooden porches in town—woodturning raised to art.

22 123–125 Baldwin St. (double house), 1873.
Like many in the area, this double house boasted expensive brick only on the front façade; the sides and rear were roughcast. The builder was not sparing in other niceties, however: vermiculated keystones, tall crest-like wooden finials, delightful knobbed pediment atop the porch.

25 *76-78 Huron St.*

27a *27-29 Grange Ave.*

23 106 Huron St. (detached house), 1873.

This was among the first houses in the district, but it's not as old as its style suggests. Building did not start hereabouts until the depressed 1870s and this cautious cottage opted for old-fashioned Georgian four-light sash windows and a Doric-columned veranda (now enclosed), though it did concede more contemporary Victorian vanities in its decorative chimneys and iron cresting. The owner was a bricklayer and the front and south walls are of brick—very posh for such a tiny abode. It was valued at $539 in 1873.

24 84–100 D'Arcy St. (nine-house row), Frederick H. Herbert, 1893.

Flamboyant anarchy and undeniably the city's most original row. During the 1890s and the height of the Queen Anne style in Toronto, the architectural rule was individuality and visual excitement. Insurrection against rectangular sameness was especially tested in a long row like this, but the ever-inventive Herbert met the challenge, creating an impression of nine distinct houses, each with its own peculiar bit of business.

25 109–111 D'Arcy St. (double house), 1874.
76–78 Huron St. (double house), 1877.
80 Huron St. (attached house), 1883.
82 Huron St. (attached house), 1875.

Built of lath and roughcast plaster, these charmers are the best examples remaining in Toronto of Georgian-style working-class habitations. Such houses easily

adapted to shops as at no. 109 D'Arcy Street, and the plan rarely changed, with side hall, two rooms per floor, and kitchen tail. No. 82, with a high raised first floor, would have had the kitchen in the basement.

26 Originally George M. Evans house, 69 Grange Ave., 1871.

One of the finest early houses left in the area and a good demonstration of how eclectic Toronto architecture could be. No. 69 handily mixes hipped roof, tall end chimneys, and brick quoins from Georgian ancestors with Italianate round-arched window heads and projecting bays. Evans, a popular Toronto lawyer and five-time alderman, lived here for 20 years until his death in 1891.

27a 27–29 Grange Ave. (double house), 1885.

Plastic, energetic Second Empire with not a few standout flourishes: convex curved mansard, bowed bays with Neo-Grec incised details, bold brackets, and busy dentil moulding. The front porches are later stick-ons.

27b 13–17 Grange Ave. (triple house), 1886.
19–21 Grange Ave. (double house), 1886.
23–25 Grange Ave. (double house), 1885.

Toronto's trademark Bay-n-Gable form is given idiosyncratic appeal on this string of houses by carved and knobbed wooden "jaws" angling the gables. The speculative developer, Alexander Mitchell, was a carpenter by trade.

28 *Baptist Church*

32 *Soho Square*

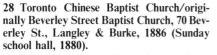

28 Toronto Chinese Baptist Church/origi-nally Beverley Street Baptist Church, 70 Beverley St., Langley & Burke, 1886 (Sunday school hall, 1880).

A neat, spikey composition with slender piers, narrow windows, and attenuated brick corbel table bringing zesty energy to this Baptist bastion, originally only the rear Sunday school hall. (There was even more verve before the yellow-dressed red brick was painted over.) Wealthy merchant William McMaster, a member of illustrious Jarvis Street Baptist [12/6a], donated land and money for this mission church, which counted Goldwin Smith of The Grange as an early member. The egalitarian Smith probably liked the idea that there were no pews to buy—Beverley Street Baptists sat on folding opera chairs.

In tandem with ethnic changes in the neighbourhood, the church has accommodated English, Swedish, German, Czechoslovakian, Hungarian, Finnish, Estonian, Russian, and Ukrainian congregations. At one time in the 1960s, there were four different congregations holding services in four languages. The church is now a focus of the Chinese community.

29 Originally Rubberset Co. Ltd./formerly RCMP building, 11 Sullivan St., 1919; remodelled as apartment house, Annau Associates, 1983.

About all that's left of the turn-of-the-century factory is the bold cast-stone classical entry, looking equally important and formal today as frontispiece for a 31-unit city-assisted housing project.

30a 24–26, 28–30, 32–34 Sullivan St. (three double houses), 1886.

These likeable ditties are from the hand of C.R.S. Dinnick, a dean of moderate-priced, standard-plan houses in Toronto.

30b 40–42 Sullivan St. (two units of original four-house row), 1872.

Two remaining units of an early dignified row with not a little classical finesse. The pediments of the dormer windows, pilastered doorcases, and delicate windows are all a neat carpenter's rendering of traditional forms.

31 53–83 Sullivan St. (sixteen-house row), 1880–81.

Even though individual units in this grand row have undergone idiosyncratic remodelling over the years, the effect is still one of dignified cohesion. Following the Second Empire style axiom of classical symmetry, the row is arranged about a centre pavilion with identical wings to the sides, except that on the east sits a single, useful grocery store instead of a residence.

32 Soho Square, Soho and Phoebe Sts. (complex of fourteen-, ten-, and six-house rows), Howard M. Greenspan, 1982–83.

14–24 Soho St. (six-house row), 1888.

In the late 1970s in Toronto it became chic to live in a Victorian house. Economics being what they are, developers started building new Victorian houses (with garages). Most of them are not as good as these red-brick numbers, whose inspiration can be seen a few doors south at 14-24 Soho Street.

Walk 15: Queen Street West

Queen Street West began in the early 19th century as a street of modest houses interspersed with small frame and rough-cast shops serving the residential enclaves that dotted its path. Later, these first buildings were replaced with more substantial, architecturally distinguished brick structures, though still only two, three, or at most four storeys high. Amazingly, most of these commercial blocks are still with us. We may be unaware of this at first because store fronts have been so bowdlerized, but the legacy of Victorian ornament and invention is usually intact on floors above— look up.

1 Black Bull Tavern, 298 Queen St. W., c. 1833; rear additions and alterations, 1886, 1889; altered, c. 1910.

An inn has stood on this site almost since York began and many an early traveller must have stopped the night at this unassuming roughcast structure before the last leg of the journey into town. By the 1880s, the town had spread to the tavern, but business was good and the proprietor built bold brick extensions to the rear and added a Second Empire mansard roof to the original two-storey front. (Hotels had discovered that a mansard was an easy and inexpensive way to create more

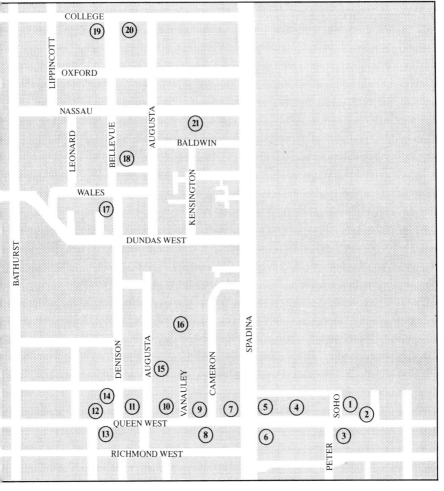

1 *Black Bull Tavern*

2 *280 Queen St. W.*

accommodations, and across North America the style survived for these buildings long after it had otherwise been abandoned.) Brick cladding and wooden pilasters were added to the front in the 1910s.

2 Originally Mara's Groceries and Liquors, 280 Queen St. W. (commercial block), 1881.

Making the most of this unusual "corner" site, no. 280 is a grand plastic composition of ornamental brick piers, bracketed cornice, mansard roof, dormer windows, and finialed spire. Mara's Groceries and Liquors was the first to display its wares behind the large plate-glass windows. The landlord was B. Homer Dixon, consul-general of the Netherlands in Canada and brother of Mrs. William Henry Boulton of The Grange, the former owner of this choice piece of real estate.

3 371–373 Queen St. W. (two-unit commercial block), 1890.

Two neat shopfronts with more 19th-century trim in place than most, including some nice stained glass. The trendy Peter Pan Restaurant was Bird's Provisions in 1890, incorporating a branch post office.

4a 328–330 Queen St. W. (two-unit commercial block), 1862.

A three-storey brick building whose early date is affirmed by dignified windows with stone lintels and sills, gently sloping roof with dormers, tall end chimneys, and yellow brick under the paint. The druggist and the milliner who first had the shops lived upstairs.

4b The Noble Block, 342–354 Queen St. W. (seven-unit commercial block), Smith & Gemmell, 1888.

356–356A Queen St. W. (two-unit commercial block), c. 1895.

A dazzling Victorian package ornamented with corbelled brick, Romanesque arches, classical keystones, and irrepressible oriel windows, among other flourishes. Until it mysteriously disappeared in the winter of 1981, a stone tablet atop the roof proclaimed this as the "Noble Block A.D.1888." Mrs. Emma Noble, widow, owned six units, and Mrs. Mary Ann Harvard, widow, held the last unit plus the property to the west. The widows must have planned a symmetrical nine-unit block, but Widow Harvard dropped out and the new owner didn't go along with the scheme, ergo the different look to no. 356 put up some time later. The first tenants purveyed, east to west: furniture, musical instruments, jewellery, barbering, men's clothes, tailoring, fruits, and drugs.

5 Canadian Imperial Bank of Commerce/ originally Bank of Hamilton, 378 Queen St. W., George W. Gouinlock, 1902–03.

Overbearing blocked rustication and exclamation-point stone keystones for a turn-of-the-century office/bank combo. Such decorative rhetoric was often marshalled by banks to convey their corporate message of wealth and permanence.

4b *The Noble Block*

6 *441-443 Queen St. W.*

6 Originally Devaney Bros. Dry Goods, 441–443 Queen St. W. (commercial block), Langley & Burke, 1886.

In the 1880s, this structure was illustrated in all the Canadian periodicals, acclaimed for its lush Victorian dome that still draws attention on this corner. Classical window heads and cornice were equally splendid. A delicious building.

7 388–396 Queen St. W. (five-unit commercial block), William G. Storm, 1881–84.

A workmanlike quintet with cleaned no. 388 giving some hint of original zest; the other units are too flattened by paint and grime. The mansard roof was mostly for show here, being too shallow and sloping to make a useful attic storey. First tenants were a druggist, bootmaker, provisioner, photographer, and grocer. The owner listed himself in assessment rolls as a "professor."

8 489–491 Queen St. W. (two-unit commercial block), 1890.

493–495 Queen St. W. (two units of original four-unit commercial block), 1889.

Semicircular Romanesque Revival parading a handsome arcaded fourth storey and arched oriel windows. Trophy panels at the third storey allegorize art and science, with lyres, compasses, gears, violins, and the like trying to lend a touch of class to original emporia: a billiard hall, barber shop, grocery, tailoring establishment, furniture store, and undertaking parlour.

9 Originally Dunn's Block, 440–450 Queen St. W. (six-unit commercial block), 1876.

An early mansard-roof composition featuring elaborate brackets at the eaves and classically distinguished open-pediment dormers (still intact at no. 444).

10 472–474 Queen St. W. (two-unit commercial block), Francis R. Heakes, 1893.

A tall, crisp commercial block embroidered with elegant Classical Revival ornament and delicate angled oriel windows. Two ladies first rented the shops: Mrs. Booth, millinery; and Mrs. Bachrack, dry goods.

11 484 Queen St. W. (commercial block), 1879.

An early, big commercial block, put up at a time when most of its neighbours would have been smaller and less formal. Deeply modelled pedimented window heads draw from the conservative Renaissance Revival, a refined rectangular-windowed style rare in Toronto. The owner-occupant George J. St. Leger first sold books here, adding shoes to the line the following year. Two years later, the shoes had completely replaced the books.

12c *506-514 Queen St. W.*

12a 486–492 Queen St. W. (four-unit commercial block), 1880.

Another unusually large commercial block for this date and district, displaying careful concern for distinguished detail. Note for example the incised stone capitals at the impost of the arcaded third storey, and how the mortar has been coloured to match the brick—red for red brick, yellow for yellow.

12b 500–504 Queen St. W. (three-unit commercial block), 1884.

A rousing Victorian trio decked out in enormous mansard, bursts of decorated dormers, and heroic cresting. The West Branch of the Ontario Bank did business at no. 500 for a time.

12c Originally Crocker's Block, 506–514 Queen St. W. (five-unit commercial block), William Stewart, 1874–75.

One of the first commercial blocks in Toronto to essay a Second Empire mansard roof, though Mr. Crocker must not have thought the new style entirely adequate for letting in light to the attic storey. Why else the row of glazed lunettes winking underneath?

13 Bank of Montreal, 577 Queen St. W., Frederick H. Herbert, 1899.

A splendidly enduring little corner bank, infused with robust details and crisp pressed brickwork and terracotta.

14 St. Stanislaus Roman Catholic Church/ originally West Presbyterian Church, 12 Denison Ave., Gordon & Helliwell, 1879–80.

Presbyterian churches often seem overly reticent, but this monochromatic broad and smooth Gothic/Romanesque design is theatrically saved by its octagonal spire, a vigorous statement on this corner and in the neighbourhood. This was the west end's second Presbyterian church on this site, serving until 1911 when demographic changes dictated a Polish Roman Catholic congregation.

15 Felician Sisters convent and day nursery/ originally Edward Leadlay house/formerly Salvation Army home, 25 Augusta Ave., 1876.

One of the most Victorian of Toronto's Victorian houses, with all the romantic bric-a-brac picturesquely in place: bonnet dormers, canopied windows, bracketed eaves, filigreed veranda, and gabled tower. Leadlay's was the single house of this size and grandeur built in the neighbourhood. A dealer in "Wools, Hides, Skins & Tallow" with a warehouse on Front Street [1/12a], he originally had his "sheepskin pulling" factory on this site. From 1906 to 1937, the house was used by the Salvation Army as an aged men's home. Since 1938, it has served an order of nuns who came to Toronto to work with the Polish immigrant community. The Sisters have been excellent custodians of the wool puller's palace, and interiors are as unblemished as exterior.

15 *25 Augusta Ave.*

16 Alexandra Park, Queen to Dundas St., Augusta to Cameron St. (complex of apartment houses and row houses), Jerome Markson with Webb Zerafa Menkes and Klein & Sears, 1967–69.

Metro Senior Citizens Building (apartment house), Adamson Associates, 1969.

Another government-subsidized mass clearance and building project, essayed two decades after Regent Park [10/30] introduced this as the way to wipe out downtown decay while providing needed low-income housing. This 18-acre, 430-unit development depends on a similar island-in-the-city concept, but with a variety of moderate-scale buildings, winding "Main Street," and tight-knit interplay of walls and open areas, Alexandra Park successfully re-creates the intimacy, privacy, human scale—and confusion—of the medieval town (it is difficult to find a way in, and once in, harder to figure the way out). The buildings themselves are a bit too stark for medieval vigour, but richly landscaped communal spaces and bountiful private gardens save all.

17 Originally Charles R. Peterkin house, 29 Wales Ave., 1884.

One of the Denisons' outbuildings stood on this site before the family began to parcel out their land for development. Peterkin, a fledgling lumber dealer, moved in in 1876 and eight years later built this stout house of his own. The bold wooden turnings of the porch bespeak his calling.

---

18 Kiever Synagogue, 28 Denison Square, Benjamin Swartz, 1927.

The currents of shifting population in this neighbourhood are especially vivid here. Where once dominated a grand manor of the pioneer Denison family, the vista up Denison Street is now commanded by the exotic synagogue of Congregation Rodfei Sholom Anshei Kiev (Men of Kiev, founded 1913). The building's pastel and white trim colours, geometric stained glass, and Byzantine stair towers recall a time when there were as many as 30

19 *Firehall No. 8*

20 *St.-Stephen-in-the-Fields, c. 1864*

synagogues in the area, each used by a homogeneous group from a particular part of Europe. Today Kiever Synagogue itself is an anachronism, almost the last of its kind in this quarter still used as a synagogue. Saved from adaptive use by the Ontario Jewish Archives Committee who have beautifully restored it, it is again attended by neighbourhood regulars as well as those who have moved up and out.

---

19 Firehall No. 8, 132 Bellevue Ave., 1877–78; rebuilt after fire, 1973–74.

The tall belvedere-capped towers of the city's fire stations, rising resolutely like medieval lookouts, must have been very reassuring to the fire-plagued Victorian city. One of the most evocative of these early fire houses is No. 8, a working station completely rebuilt in 1974 after a—fire! (An arsonist's sad joke, the station was empty and in the course of restoration at the time.) Today the interior of the crisp yellow- and red-brick structure is decked out in photographs and other mementoes of Toronto's fire department, and a fireman will be happy to show you around if he's not out blanketing a blaze.

20 St.-Stephen-in-the-Fields Anglican Church, 103 Bellevue Ave., Thomas Fuller, 1858; rebuilt after fire, Gundry & Langley, 1865; transept additions, 1878; parish house addition, Edwards & Saunders, c. 1910.

St.-Stephen-in-the-Fields rectory, 99 Bellevue Ave., Gundry & Langley, 1865.

The simplest and most primitive of revived medieval styles, Early English Gothic was recommended by the Ecclesiological Society for remote parish churches, and that's exactly what St. Stephen's was in 1858. But this is not just any country church. Its architect was soon to win the competition for the Houses of Parliament in Ottawa, and this sophisticated composition of sweeping roof and broad brick front broken only by a slim open belfry attests to his talent. (The gabled dormers were not part of the original plan.) In this century, the church was noteworthy as the "Radio Church," from whence in 1926 came the first regular religious broadcasting in Canada. The rectory, which has probably undergone as many alterations as the church, was originally roughcast.

---

21 Kensington Market is located here and there, Dundas to College Street, Augusta to Spadina. A wonderful, lively, intimate place to be, it is surely enhanced by the two-storey domestic scale of its hodgepodge of buildings, and the delightful surprise of its irregular, close-packed blocks.

Area IX

Walk 16: Old Yorkville
Walk 17: West Yorkville
Walk 18: Bloor Street

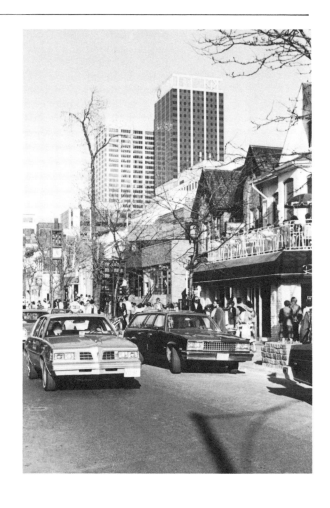

Area IX

Today the names Yorkville and Bloor Street are synonymous with Toronto's most de luxe consumer district, an area of expensive restaurants, trendy cafés, up-scale art galleries, chic boutiques, and glamorous high-fashion emporia. Architecturally, the district displays an intriguing combination of the spanking new, the new trying to look old, the old trying to look new, and a little of the old just looking like itself.

The history of the old goes back almost 200 years. Bloor Street was laid out by the provincial governor, John Graves Simcoe, as the First Concession Line—and so named—in York Township, the boundary separating the Town of York and Simcoe's "park lots" [see Introductions, *AREAS I, VII,* and *VIII*] from farm lands and wilderness beyond. Where Yonge Street [*AREA III*] crossed First Concession Line, a toll gate was erected in the early 1800s to tax farmers bringing produce to town from the north. Two inns to serve the travelling farmers, the Red Lion [demolished] and Tecumseh Wigwam [demolished], grew up nearby. From 1825 until about 1850 the Town of York's large nonsectarian burying ground and potter's field was also situated near these crossroads [see 9/17].

It was Joseph Bloor's brewery, located in the Rosedale Ravine [21/1], that first brought workers to the area in 1830, followed by Severn's Brewery near Yonge and Davenport Road in 1835, and then various brickworks at Blue Hill northwest of Yonge and Davenport. Framework for a community was set in place in the early 1850s when surrounding land was subdivided into streets and building plots by a number of speculators, chiefly John Elmsley.

The community was incorporated as the Village of Yorkville in 1853, occasioning erection in 1860 of a splendid High Victorian town hall at the corner of Yonge and Yorkville Avenue [demolished], and an impressive firehall in 1876 [16/3]. Village boundaries were First Concession Line to the south, the Canadian Pacific Railway tracks to the north, Sherbourne Street to the east, and a line near Bedford Road to the west—in other words, a much larger area than the Yorkville of today, including sections that are now manifestly parts of the Annex [*AREA X*] and Rosedale [*AREA XI*]. First Concession Line functioned as a true "division street" or no-man's land in this period. A reminiscence of the road circa 1850 speaks of its "solitariness and vacancy."

In the next decades, Yorkville prospered as a small "bedroom" community within convenient distance of Toronto. It had been supported as early as 1849 by regular omnibus service to and from the city, and later the horse-drawn Toronto Street Railway ran cars every 20 minutes from Yorkville Town Hall to St. Lawrence Hall [1/2]. In addition to labourers and shopkeepers, residents of more substantial means were attracted by

Yonge Street looking north to Yorkville Town Hall, c. 1860, with horse-drawn street railway on its way from St. Lawrence Hall.

the village atmosphere and low taxes, which were half those of Toronto. Architecturally, Yorkville was not unlike other Toronto neighbourhoods, with a variety of 19th-century designs built close to one another and to the street.

Yorkville managed to exist as a political entity for 30 years before those low taxes finally spelled inadequate municipal services. When the City of Toronto—in a move typical of expanding North American cities in the period—offered to annex Yorkville in 1883, the town was eager to accept. At the time, Bloor Street (by this date called after Yorkville's entrepreneurial brewer) numbered but scant buildings: on the south were St. Paul's Church [18/20] and a spotting of row and double houses, some functioning as laundries, groceries, and the like; on the north sat six largish houses across from St. Paul's plus a few others strung out between Sherbourne Street and Avenue Road, on the corner of which the Church of the Redeemer had settled in 1879 [18/4]. In the next ten years, this pattern greatly accelerated, with row houses filling in the south side, and grand houses with large grounds similar to those on upper Jarvis Street [AREA VII] completing the north. When the street railway, now electrified, added Bloor Street to its route in 1894, it took in "scores of the town's finest private mansions," according to a guidebook of the period.

By the turn of the century, however, the siren song of newer, more exclusive areas had begun to call the well-to-do. The mansions on Bloor Street were turned into osteopaths' and dentists' offices, along with premises for the occasional dressmaker, antiques dealer, and tearoom proprietor. And Yorkville itself quietly settled back as a working-class streetcar suburb, a role it was to enjoy through the 1940s.

For Bloor Street, however, the quiet was not to last. As a major cross street ripe for new development and strategically located between downtown and burgeoning suburbs, it looked very appealing to 1920s city planners. There was talk of widening the thoroughfare, and in anticipation of this, in what must have been a very daring gamble, Manufacturers' Life Insurance Company commenced to put up a majestic six-storey office building on regally landscaped grounds [18/19] across from St. Paul's Church in 1924. Other construction took off: apartment houses and medical buildings as well as the first Style Moderne harbingers of Bloor Street's commercial chic. The Helena Rubenstein Beauty Salon, Creeds Feminine Fashions, Bowles Lunch, Superior Optical, and Woolnough Corsetiere are all gone, but the Ashley & Crippin Building [18/9b] still shows off a sophisticated Art Deco façade from this period.

The street widening was completed in 1929 at a cost of $2½ million, but the Depression and World War II effectively stalled further building projects. Bloor Street again sat quietly, this time as a decorous carriage-trade shopping street, with the annual Easter Parade its most exciting event. (Things did liven up a little at night at the Embassy Ballroom on Bellair Street, where the big bands played.) The postwar years brought more metamorphoses. Coffee houses such as the Riverboat (located in two recycled Victorian houses on Yorkville Avenue) carried the village to the centre of the Canadian folk music scene, out of which came such luminaries as Gordon Lightfoot, Joni Mitchell, and Ian and Sylvia. By the mid 1960s, Yorkville had become a buzzword for the real and imagined excesses of Canada's hippy generation, with whole blocks of 19th-century houses sporting psychedelic shopfronts and the area's new subway stations a decidedly "sweetish" odour. Then in the 1970s, serious—and expensive—conversion of houses to shops and infilling with new commercial construction began taking over, and today on streets such as Yorkville and Cumberland it has largely been completed. At first, there were many who decried the tarting up of this area, but glitzy new Yorkville seems to have mellowed, and through it all the intimate scale of the original village has prevailed.

The bustling Bloor Street we know today began with construction of the Colonnade in 1965 [18/5], the city's first mixed-use building, combining residences, offices, shops, and restaurants. Its multiple function, relatively low but big size, and partial setback from the street set the tone and scale of Bloor Street for subsequent building through the 1970s. This decade has brought two less-positive developments: movement up as buildings rise higher and higher to take advantage of relaxed bylaws and expensive land; and movement down into underground shopping malls—Toronto's answer to the Canadian winter. Nevertheless, by virtue of its inviting and *visible* consumerism, along with a mix of uses, including residential, Bloor Street continues to encourage an energetic streetlife for most of this stretch. Like Yorkville, it is a lively, often idiosyncratic, always human place to be.

Walk 16: Old Yorkville

1 17 Yorkville Ave. (detached house), 1881; remodelled as commercial block, c. 1975.

The old trying to look new. A typical Toronto Bay-n-Gable of the third quarter of the 19th century, no. 17 is especially interesting for its 20th-century remodelling. The addition of a projecting glass bay to the second storey while leaving the original wall and fenestration visible and intact behind it perfectly expresses stylish modernizing efforts to be found throughout Yorkville.

---

2 Yorkville Public Library, 22 Yorkville Ave., Robert McCallum, 1906–07; addition and interior remodelled, Barton Myers Associates, 1978.

One of the hundreds of "Carnegie Classical" libraries built across North America in the early decades of this century with funds from the Andrew Carnegie Foundation. Though small in size, an appropriately bold porticoed entrance announces the civic importance of the library, as does its high first storey and foursquare

stance. Myers's 1978 remodelling program brilliantly lightened the interior—the space seems to literally glow—while leaving the public impress of the structure unchanged.

---

3 Firehall No. 10, 34 Yorkville Ave., Hancock & Townsend, 1876; all but tower rebuilt, Mancel Willmot, 1889–90; addition, 1975.

Though it might look like a child's anthropomorphic Lego-set creation with bright features of yellow and red brick smiling out at us, this firehall has served as a suitably serious hose house for over 100 years, with the high tower used to hang and dry fire hoses and to sound the alarm to volunteer fire fighters and community at large.

The coat-of-arms on the tower is that of the Town of Yorkville, removed to the firehall from the town hall when the latter suffered a fire in 1941 and was demolished. Represented are initials of the town's first councillors and symbols of their vocations: beer barrel for the brewer, jack plane for the carpenter, brick mould for the builder, anvil for the blacksmith, and bull's head for the butcher.

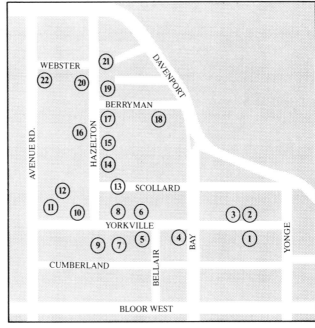

2 *Yorkville Public Library*

3 *Firehall No. 10*

4 61–63 Yorkville Ave. (double house), c. 1860; remodelled as commercial block, c. 1975.

One of the few early Georgian-style houses left in Yorkville, although few remember the formal façade once they peek inside at Lovecraft's sex super-market! Originally the abode of two farmer brothers, the house was later rented by William Willcocks Baldwin, who had just sold off the family manor "Spadina" [see Introduction, *AREA VIII*]. Excavating to uncover the basement has become a popular ploy today for increas-ing commercial frontage in old houses.

5 Originally John Daniels house, 77 York-ville Ave., c. 1867.

An early Yorkville cottage built by John Daniels, erstwhile saloonkeeper of the popular Tecumseh Wigwam inn which stood nearby at Bloor and Avenue Road in the mid 19th century. When he lived here, Daniels was constable of the village and tradition has it that his "overnight guests" were entertained in sheds at the back. Actually being constable was only a sometime job, although Daniels was empowered to carry a gun for six weeks in hot summer to shoot stray dogs. His house retains congenial Georgian propor-tions while introducing such zesty Victo-rian touches as curved relieving arches of slightly raised brick. The first-rate adapta-tion to present-day commercial use added an unobtrusive glass showroom of com-patible scale to the rear without at all diminishing the character of the house.

6 84 Yorkville Ave. (attached house), 1891.
A Queen Anne spooled and spindled porch holding its own on the third floor above new commercial glass and glitz.

7 Cumberland Court, 99 Yorkville Ave. thru to Cumberland St. (commercial complex), Webb Zerafa Menkes, 1973.
They're called courts, mews, squares, or lanes, and Yorkville abounds in them. Basically they're commercial complexes that contrive to combine shops and restaurants with landscaped outdoor spa-ces plus appealing traffic courses on several levels in an atmosphere that is variously described as lively, informal, and—at their worst—quaint. Cumberland Court gathers 19th-century gabled houses on Yorkville and Cumberland and boldly infills around them with a strikingly modern structure containing shops, cafés, art galleries, and on the top floor, the architects' own offices. The long, rela-tively narrow passage that angles in and out of doors through the complex is probably the most interesting in Yorkville for its variety and surprise.

8 Formerly Mount Sinai Hospital, 100 York-ville Ave. (detached house), 1871; remodelled, Benjamin Swartz, 1928; additions, Kaminker & Richmond, 1932, 1934; all but front demol-ished, 1988.
This was a residential street in 1922 when a group of Jewish women bought the large Victorian house-cum-private hospital at no. 100 and opened the first hospital in Toronto specifically to serve the Jewish community. It was at first slow to attract

7 *Cumberland Court*

11 *York Square*

patients even though attending Jewish doctors were not then accepted as full-time staff at Toronto hospitals. By 1928, however, Mount Sinai found it necessary to expand and began to build Georgian Revival additions to engulf the original house. When Mount Sinai moved to a big new hospital on University Avenue in 1952 [7/21a], this became a nursing home for a time before development pressures virtually destroyed the historic structure.

9 Old York Lane, 117 Yorkville Ave. thru to Cumberland St. (commercial complex), George A. Robb, 1963.

A discreet block of one-storey shops set along a brick-paved pedestrian way, Old York Lane was the first commercial complex in Yorkville. Its ground-hugging low-scale, contrasting surface textures, rhythmic façade, and inviting atmosphere still make it a standout.

10 116–134 Yorkville Ave. (five double houses), 1885–86.

Very new-looking old houses, just a touch too "artful" with machine-textured brick bubbling over the exterior. Originally five separate structures, commercial moderni-zation linked them in a row.

11 York Square, Yorkville Ave. at Avenue Rd. (commercial complex), A.J. Diamond & Barton Myers, 1968.

York Square does what a square is supposed to do: invites movement and communality in an easy grace true to European traditions. Seven Victorian

houses on Avenue Road and Yorkville Avenue have been remodelled as shops with signature round windows and ramped high-tech portals that lead to a comfortable backyard square that becomes an outdoor café in summer. Here the carefully staged informality is achieved by more steps and doors, an unobtrusive low-scale infill building to complete the square, and—of first importance—two venerable trees.

12 Hazelton Lanes, 55 Avenue Rd. thru to Hazelton Ave. (commercial complex and apartment houses), Webb Zerafa Menkes Housden, 1976.

Not bad, but not really good either. This ultra-posh development features two blocks of luxury condominiums rising stepped-fashion around an inner court-yard that becomes a skating rink in winter. The first two floors are given over to a *haute-monde* commercial complex that is so tortuously laid out it's almost impossible to find your way without dropping bread crumbs—or perhaps crois-sant crumbs, this being Hazelton Lanes. Although the labyrinth is handsome, with wood ceilings, quarry-tile floors, and brick walls punctuated by bay-windowed shop fronts, the plan is so disconcerting it discourages casual browsing, and business too, they say. The principal Avenue Road face of Hazelton Lanes is nondescript, but in the rear, tall round-arched windows handsomely tie the complex to Victorian houses on Hazelton Avenue.

14a *Hazelton House*

14b *Heliconian Club*

Scollard Street suffers some of the most insensitive and out-of-scale conversions in Yorkville. And yet many early houses remain relatively intact, giving a good sense of the intimate, democratic character of the 19th-century village that cheek-by-jowl built labourers' cottages, bank clerks' row houses, and "gentlemen's" semi-detacheds.

13a 94–104 Scollard St. (six-house row), 1893.

Rebuilding for speculation is nothing new to Yorkville. This cheerful Queen Anne row of 1893 replaced an 1871 sextet of 1½-storey cottages, each ensemble a rental enterprise of Larratt Smith, prominent Toronto lawyer and vice-chancellor of the university. The latest conversions to retail and office use have been unobtrusive, maintaining the picturesque rhythmic gables that still highlight this block.

13b 99–101 Scollard St. (double house), 1874.

Covering over deteriorated or unfashionable cladding is a quick way to spruce up old houses. One half of this double house was finessed with stucco in 1985, the other half with pressed-metal "bricks" c. 1890. Happily, though, no one has yet contrived to cover over the splendid Italianate porch posts.

13c 105 Scollard St. (detached house), 1872.
95 Scollard St. (detached house), 1871.

The cheeriest of peaked-gable cottages, both first owned by James Phillpot, a "travelling man."

13d 72–76 Scollard St. (triple house), 1888–89.

Triple houses are fun to puzzle out for the way they dosey-doo an unequal number of parts. Here the architectural dance choreographs identical end units with a flopped version centrestage. The builder seems to have been a little uncomfortable with his Second Empire mansard roof, altogether too high and stiff, and certainly on its way out of fashion at this late date.

14a Hazelton House/originally Olivet Congregational Church, 33 Hazelton Ave. at Scollard St., Dick & Wickson, 1890; remodelled as commercial block, Sheldon Rosen, 1972–73.

A 19th-century church alias 20th-century shops, galleries, and offices and a tribute to the recycler's art, in this case architect Sheldon Rosen who installed his own offices amid the attic boards.

14b Toronto Heliconian Club/originally Olivet Congregational Church, 35 Hazelton Ave., 1876.

A rare Toronto example of delightful Carpenter Gothic style wherein the humble woodworker is able to parade sophisticated medieval intentions. Using nail and board instead of mortar and masonry, Gothic details are invented anew: lancet arches become triangular; vertical buttresses, battens; bold decoration, filigreed. This church originally stood on the corner, but—being wooden—was easily moved when the congregation decided to build a larger,

15a *49-51 Hazelton Ave.*

15c *65 Hazelton Ave.*

red-brick edifice [16/14a]. The interior, today used by a venerable women's arts and letters group, is a simple auditorium with apsidal chancel.

Everyone peruses showcase Hazelton Avenue, even thundering tour buses which must shake the architectural survivors to their 19th-century posts and beams. It would be nice to report that these eye-catching charmers have been restored by loving owners; in fact, like much of commercial Yorkville, many of them were speculatively renovated by a single developer as high-rent properties. Some of the results are a little too precious all around, but many are worth a look anyway.

15a 49–51 Hazelton Ave. (double house), 1874.
Looking slightly unreal after recent remove-all-the-warts renovation, no. 49–51 nevertheless is one of Yorkville's most interesting houses, having dipped into the Victorian architectural costume box for seldom-seen Baronial Gothic accessories: bulbous-roofed tower, stringy drip-moulds, pointed-arch porches. The old iron fence is one of the city's best.

15b 53–55, 57–59, 61–63 Hazelton Ave. (three double houses), 1875–76.
After serious, boxy Georgian style [see 16/4], the next Yorkville double houses were playful, pointy centre-gable numbers, pleasing in their prickly insouciance. These variously clad free-spirits are typical.

15c Originally George Daws house, 65 Hazelton Ave., 1875.
This diminutive mansarded gem is one of Yorkville's most attractive houses, with its high parlour floor—and therefore high basement—reached by a tall flight of steps. The bell-cast roof and gingerbread of the bay window are especially appealing touches articulated by the first owner, a bricklayer and contractor. He probably looked through a builder's pattern book to find this "French-roof cottage."

16 Originally George Lee house, 68 Hazelton Ave., 1878.
A wonderful Gothic Revival house and garden built by the village registrar, and seemingly untouched by time. The centre gable with bargeboarded fascia, windows framed by shutters and raised brick, graceful iron-crested porch, and fine iron fence continue to spread Victorian delight, undaunted by anything the 20th century might bring.

17 77–81 Hazelton Ave. (triple house), 1881.
An engaging centre-gable trio of typical Yorkville houses sporting High Victorian red- with yellow-brick decoration.

16 *68 Hazelton Ave.*

18 *19 Berryman St.*

18 Originally Barton Myers house, 19 Berryman St., A.J. Diamond & Barton Myers (designed by Barton Myers), 1970.

In their conversions of 19th-century factories and warehouses to modern use, the firm of Diamond & Myers introduced Toronto to the "exposed services" style and Myers used the same expression here in his own small house. Though Myers's high-tech look was a shocker when new, his house does respect the scale and integrity of this street of simple cottages, a fact perhaps only appreciated now after the construction of glaringly large pseudo-Victorians across the street.

19 85 Hazelton Ave. (detached house), 1879.

This commodious-looking house planted firmly on the corner site is an eclectic design that marries ornament and form from several styles to come up with an engaging example of Victorian picturesque. Modern eclecticism has turned it into three separate units plus a boring attachment to the east.

20 88–90 and 92–94 Hazelton Ave. (two double houses), 1885.

Looking like delectable frosted cake with their white-painted trim, these late Bay-n-Gables parade sure proportion and fine detail. No. 88 alone of the four retains an appropriate bracketed overdoor.

21 101–105 Hazelton Ave. (four attached houses), 1880–81.

The slick modernization (which turned four houses into twice that number of apartments) has robbed this Second Empire ensemble of its resonance, but it is of interest for the arched carriageway that originally led to stables.

22 Originally St. Paul's Methodist Church/ formerly St. Paul's Avenue Road United Church, 121 Avenue Rd. at Webster Ave., Smith & Gemmell, 1887.

A large, unassuming Gothic church with an amphitheatrical interior that boasts the most elaborate Art Nouveau painted ceiling in the city—an extravaganza of angels, lilies, and trailing vines executed c. 1900 by Gustav Hahn of the well-known family of German emigré artists. In the 1960s, St. Paul's ministered to Yorkville's hippy population, but today it is without a congregation and the United Church of Canada has ominously sold the church with Hahn's masterpiece to developers.

Walk 17: West Yorkville

Cut off from the rest of Yorkville by traffic-choked six-lane Avenue Road, the enclave between Avenue and Bedford Roads exists more sensibly today as part of the Annex neighbourhood (AREA X). Nevertheless, the short east-west street layout, architectural styles, and construction dates all confirm this district's Village of Yorkville pedigree. Originally owned by the Anglican church and then sold by them to real estate speculators, the land had been carved out for streets and residential building lots by the late 1860s. Construction began on Avenue Road, Prince Arthur Avenue, and Lowther Avenue, followed by development on Elgin, Victoria (Boswell), Dufferin (Bernard), and finally Tranby—a narrow afterthought. In 1882, on the eve of annexation by the City of Toronto, this western section of the village contained approximately 100 dwellings, housing close to one-tenth of Yorkville's 5,200 population. Avenue Road remained residential and of moderate width well into the 1920s.

1 10 Bernard Ave. (detached house), 1881.
A firm Gothic Revival villa with fine proportions under a steeply pitched roof and pointed gable. Expensive detail is quiet but effective: stone lintels and sills bridging rectangular windows, bell-cast roof capping bay window, and raised brick quoins neatly turning the eye in to the tidy composition. The present doorcase is an alteration.

2 Originally Noah L. Piper house, 19 Bernard Ave., 1875.
One of West Yorkville's standout houses, this large, gracious Georgian box was the home of well-to-do Yonge Street hardware merchant Noah L. Piper. Very late for a Georgian design, the sedate style was enlivened with colourful High Victorian brick detailing. Piper moved to this then-bucolic precinct—his was the only house on this block for over two years—from "downtown" Bond Street [13/9a].

3 18–20, 24–26, 28–30 Bernard Ave. (three double houses), 1877–78; no. 18–20 remodelled, c. 1915.
When this section of Yorkville was developing in the 1870s, Second Empire was the height of fashion in Toronto. Described in periodicals of the day as befitting "aspiring gentlemen," it was a sophisticated urban style whose use for these handsome, plastic houses suggests that at least some builders had "citifying" ambitions for the area. Yellow brick—called white brick at the time—was preferred for Second Empire houses, perhaps to approximate the colour of expensive stone. The wood trim was probably originally painted creamy white or dark green.

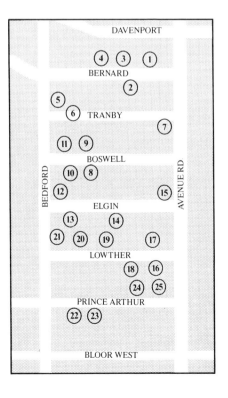

2 *19 Bernard Ave.*

3 *24-26 Bernard Ave.*

4 32–34 and 36–38 Bernard Ave. (two double houses), 1889.

In the late 1880s, the new Annex area west of Yorkville was in the throes of wholesale development in a Richardsonian Romanesque/Queen Anne mode; it is not surprising the activity filtered eastward into Yorkville. These identical double houses clearly draw from that massive, solid tradition, with cave-like round-arched entries and an intriguing trick of the form that sequesters one window of each of the polygonal bays inside the "cave."

5 123, 121 Bedford Rd. and 70 Tranby Ave. at Bedford Rd. (three detached houses), 1892–93.

Put up by one speculative builder, these three late 19th-century houses are instructive for the variety of ways they use similar brick, stone, and wooden details, and mix up form and fenestration for an individual look.

Tranby Avenue, cut through the centre of a single large property during a prosperous period of mass construction in Toronto, provided developers with a real chance to show their stuff. Although several builders were responsible for the houses we see here, the same machine-made parts appear in various guises and massing and silhouettes all come together in a harmonious whole. A great street, fine and pleasing, and perfect example of architecture as the art of assemblage.

6a 66–68 and 71–73 Tranby Ave. (two double houses), 1891–92.

The sentinel-like towers on these once-twinned double houses dramatically mark the end—or beginning—of the street and set its ensemble tone.

6b 33–35, 37–39, 43–45, 47–49, 51–53 Tranby Ave. (five double houses), 1889–90.

Although they look alike at first blush, these five late Bay-n-Gable double houses have gone to some pains to relieve the monotony with a variety of fenestration, gable decoration, and ornamental brick panels. The bracketed shed roofs over the entrances are practical and pleasing. The ten units were built for $1,800 each, which would have made them relatively expensive middle-class housing in 1890.

7 *Tranby Terrace*

12 *52 Elgin Ave.*

7 Tranby Terrace, 11 Tranby Ave. and 102, 104, 106 Avenue Rd. (complex of nine row houses and three rehabilitated houses), Klein & Sears, 1981.

The agile layout of this infill complex can best be appreciated from its handsome flagstoned courtyard, as can the careful renovations of the three 1880s houses incorporated on Avenue Road. The new row houses inventively manipulate the same ingredients as their Victorian fore-bears on Tranby Avenue: red brick, peaked gables, round-headed windows, even shed roofs over the entries—sleekly interpreted in glass.

8 Originally Phillipe Grandjean house, 41 Boswell Ave., 1881.

A tiny, spirited accumulation of Victorian details that continues to spell visual pleasure. The gable still suspends its decorative pendant (long gone in most houses of this period), and the windowed door appears to have its original hardware. The gabled wall dormers to the sides to light the attic storey, no longer very useful with adjacent houses all but overwhelming them. Grandjean was a watchmaker and engraver.

9 46–48 Boswell Ave. (double house), 1884.

An eclectic, well-mannered double house distinguished by formal-looking symmetry, rectangular windows with trim shutters, cornice window heads, and a graceful two-storeyed porch that adds much to the polite effect.

10 49–51 Boswell Ave. (double house), 1875.

A pair of simple, earthy-looking houses sitting close to the ground with an exterior of roughcast plaster rather than more expensive brick. The pediment-shaped wooden window and door heads are an endearing carpenter's touch.

11 54–56, 58, 60–62 Boswell Ave. (two double and one single house), 1889.

This five-unit ensemble deploys an abundance of wooden trim to enliven the façade. By this date such elaborate detail could be mass-produced, but factory provenance made it no less fancy. Yorkville was annexed by the City of Toronto in 1883, signalling the beginning of developer construction such as this.

12 52 Elgin Ave. (detached house), Frederick H. Herbert, 1897–98.

The barn-like girth, gambrel roof, and tile-hung walls embracing this house are derived from American Shingle Style dwellings, a simple, hearty form which sought to evoke warmth and shelter within. Fire regulations prohibited wooden shingles in Toronto (unless backed by brick), resulting in forays like this into what might be dubbed Tile Style.

15 *2 Elgin Ave.*

18 *23–29 Lowther Ave.*

13 45–47 Elgin Ave. (double house), 1875.
A Gothic Revival "double detached villa" as picturesque as any the pattern books ever illustrated. The tall chimneys, barge-boarded gables, pointed windows, drip-moulds, bichrome relieving arches, and spandrel panels are especially evocative touches articulated by the busy Toronto builder Thomas Snarr, who himself resided at no. 45.

14 27 Elgin Ave. (detached house), 1885.
27A Elgin Ave. (detached house), 1985.
25 Elgin Ave. (detached house), 1878.
These three preserve the early character of Elgin Avenue as a street of medium-sized houses sprinkled lightly with picturesque details to evoke the virtues of hearth and home in a simpler age, this despite the fact no. 27A is but a few years old. It is one of the most successful Victorian copies in the city. How unfortunate then that greed dictated its being squeezed in here, because the houses on Elgin Avenue were also once appreciated for their large lots!

15 Originally George Booth house, 2 Elgin Ave., 1879; veranda and portico additions, Darling & Pearson, 1909.
Built for painter George Booth, this is one of West Yorkville's most attractive houses, its abundance of rich Italianate detail playing over a plastic, strongly textured form that accommodates with insouciance the portico and corner ver-anda added in 1909. At that time, the house sat on more generous grounds, still

surveying a modestly wide, residential Avenue Road.

16 Originally Albert Locke house, 9 Lowther Ave., 1876.
This delightful, picturesque house can't help but intrigue. On one hand it is so unassuming, narrowly squeezed between neighbours as if an afterthought; and on the other, so self-dramatizing, confidently parading all kinds of saucy ornament.

17 Originally William Luke house, 16 Lowther Ave., 1881.
Of no pronounced style, but with gentle balanced proportions, human scale—not too large, not too small—thoughtful economy of detail, and intimation of commodious space within, this is one of those affectionate buildings that has well stood the test of time, as appealing today as it must have been 100 years ago. William Luke was listed in assessment rolls as a "gentleman."

18 23–29 Lowther Ave. (three attached houses), 1875; altered, c. 1970.
Old photographs reveal that these three were originally similar-looking Victorians with bow windows and a veranda snaking across the front. More interesting than *style*, however, is the unusual *form*, with an arresting carriageway—once doored—topped by a Gothic gable and oriel window. (The oriel lights a front room belonging to no. 25; the room behind goes with no. 29.) Inspiration for no. 23's Georgian Revival brick re-do came via Boston or Philadelphia.

19a *26 Lowther Ave.*

19b *30-32 Lowther Ave.*

19a Formerly Robert Parker house, 26 Lowther Ave., 1878.

Connections—the mucilage of details that joins one part of the exterior envelope to another—played a big role in the look of 19th-century buildings. This lovely Victorian villa has superb connections: turned, pierced, and sawn woodenwork stringing porch, veranda, and eaves; corbelled, panelled, and raised brickwork hemming door, windows, belt courses, and cornices. Built by banker Donald Gordon, no. 26 was early acquired by the founder of the Parker cleaning empire.

19b Originally Struthers/Ross house, 30–32 Lowther Ave., Grant & Dick, 1875.

This generous double house may have been the prototype for Toronto's popular Bay-n-Gable form, that felicitous marriage of Gothic Revival and Italianate forms and motifs. Designed by the distinguished firm of Grant & Dick, this perky pair vividly displays the projecting polygonal end bays and lively bargeboarded gables that soon began to inform red- and yellow-brick semi-detacheds put up all across the city.

19c Originally Mrs. William Augustus Baldwin house, 36 Lowther Ave., 1888–89.

William Augustus Baldwin, brother of Robert the Reformer and son of Dr. William the doctor/lawyer/architect/politician, died in 1883. Five years later his widow and second wife built this firm mansion adjacent to her eldest stepson's residence at no. 50 [17/21]. The Richardsonian Romanesque/Queen Anne style of the house was borrowed from the neighbouring Annex, as was—in a way—the money to build it, for the Baldwin fortune was in part based on the sale of Annex lands to speculators. Mrs. Baldwin lived here with another stepson, Robert Russell Baldwin, and his family, but they were not cramped for space: the house boasted 20 rooms, eight with tiled fireplaces. In addition, there was central heating from a coal-burning furnace, gas lighting, and indoor plumbing. Today, there's a garage slipped into the basement too.

20 Originally William Garside house, 46 Lowther Ave., Charles J. Gibson, 1897–98.

Eclecticism gone berserk, this house contrives to combine Queen Anne tile-hung front gable, classical Palladian window, chateauesque door surround, even a Gothic trefoil. This was the year Queen Victoria celebrated her Diamond Jubilee and perhaps Mr. Garside, a wholesale boot and shoe manufacturer, wanted architect Gibson to go all out in a show of architectural imperialism.

25 *4 Prince Arthur Ave.*

21 Originally Henry St. George Baldwin house, 50 Lowther Ave. at Bedford Rd., c. 1878; renovated and remodelled, 1986–87.

Henry St. George Baldwin was the eldest son of William Augustus Baldwin who at one time owned all the land between Lowther and Davenport from Huron to just beyond Bedford Road. In 1878, Henry St. George was given this parcel on the southeast corner of the family property on which he built himself a large red- and yellow-brick house, today serving rather niftily without too many exterior alterations as a multi-unit dwelling.

22 Originally Alexander Macdonald house, 35 Prince Arthur Ave., 1896.

Built by a barrister on the eve of Victoria's 60th reigning year, no. 35 is an exuberant red-brick extravaganza with not a few histrionics harking back to 1066 and all that: crenellations, bartizans, traceried windows.

23 25–27 and 29–31 Prince Arthur Ave. (two double houses), 1888.

Carefully remodelled for art galleries and offices, these four sparky Bay-n-Gable abodes are still fastidiously decked out in raised-brick string courses, bracketed shed roofs, and iron cresting. The architect Charles Gibson rented at no. 27 for a period early in his career.

24 Prince Arthur Towers, 20 Prince Arthur Ave. (apartment house), Uno Prii, 1965.

Swooping grand gestures for a 22-storey Neo-Expressionist apartment house. Situated on an appropriately large lawned site, and with a clean, dramatic look, this represents one of architect Prii's more sculpturally handsome designs. Nevertheless, neither grounds nor grandiosity belong here on intimate, small-scale Prince Arthur Avenue.

25 4 Prince Arthur Ave. (detached house), 1891.

A small tribute to the rich expression of the Romanesque/Queen Anne rubric first explored in the nearby Annex, with a weighty stone and brick composition highlighted by inviting cavernous portal and second-storey porch. The recent modernization, which put glass in the gable and masonry in the yard, is handsome and well done.

Walk 18: Bloor Street

1 Park Plaza Hotel/originally Queen's Park Plaza Hotel, 4 Avenue Rd. at Bloor St., Hugh G. Holman, 1926–29; addition, Page & Steele, 1956.

An apartment/hotel constructed when skyscrapers were giving up on the look of florid classical palaces but had yet to become cubist Deco ziggurats. A thin arcade of double-height windows with slim frieze running above marks the Park Plaza's reticent base; a brief balustraded parapet suffices for cornice; in between long streams of windows and incipient setbacks hint at new streamlining.

In their eagerness to situate on what looked to become Toronto's status address in the 1920s, the Queen's Park Plaza Hotel built over an underground finger of meandering Taddle Creek. The building began to sag and elevators would not function. After frustrated efforts at bracing, a solution was found, the story goes, to "perma-freeze" the ground.

The connected 12-storey annex of 1956 has its own tale to tell. The street-wise siting, brick, concrete and metal materials, the hard-edged balconies, floating canopies, and other "smart" details all mark it as the work of Page & Steele's clever modernist designer, Peter Dickinson. Dickinson probably did as much to change the look of Toronto in the 1950s as had the skyscraper architects in the 1920s.

2 Royal Ontario Museum, 100 Queen's Park.
(See Walk 8/33.)

3 Provincial Ombudsman, 157 Bloor St. W.
(See Walk 8/34.)

4 Renaissance Centre, 150 Bloor St. W. (mixed-use complex), Webb Zerafa Menkes Housden with Page & Steele, 1982.
Church of the Redeemer, 162 Bloor St. W., Smith & Gemmell, 1879.

This massive, hulking, expensively solid shops/offices/condominium complex does resemble a Renaissance building: the glum, inward-looking *palazzi* beloved of the Medicis and their fellow Florentine bankers. Actually, the real "rebirth" here is that of the Church of the Redeemer, its stout no-nonsense visage revealing startling grace and power against Renaissance's incongruous backdrop. Sweeping slate roof, rough stone walls, and looming belfry now form a commanding presence on this busy corner where once they went largely unnoticed. Built in the 1870s for a new parish carved out of what had been St. Paul's territory, the Church of the Redeemer is akin to that copy of a 13th-century country church erected in 1861 [18/20]. But the Church of the Redeemer is much more a High Victorian interpretation of the medieval: larger, more solid, less intricate and rustic. The interior is pure High Victorian, flourishing coloured bands of red and yellow brick on walls, bold wooden brackets at the ceiling, and rich granite columns to mark the transept.

The Church of the Redeemer owes its new sparkle and prominence to Renaissance Centre, but the reverse is also true. Renaissance's Fidinam developers bought the church property to gain height and density bonuses, paying over $3 million for the package that included a lease-back to the Anglican diocese.

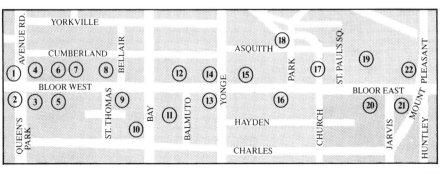

4 *Church of the Redeemer and Renaissance Centre*

5 The Colonnade, 131 Bloor St. W. (mixed-use complex), Gerald Robinson with Tampold & Wells, 1961–64; altered, 1986–87.

The 12-storey Colonnade was Toronto's first building to purposely combine residences, offices, and retail establishments, including restaurants and a theatre. The multiplicity of functions was spelled out in the design, a complicated composition focused on a row of slender square columns and segmental arches—the colonnade. Apartment floors are signalled by the small concrete waffle grid of the upper storeys. This contrasts to the larger scale of the shops, which curve out from under the colonnade to form a semicircular forecourt. The forecourt, in turn, is punctuated by a "floating" concrete staircase that leads to commercial space on the second and third floors.

A 1980s remodelling sought to make major changes. Thankfully on the exterior the Colonnade still retains its landmark 1960s aura; the new interior is something else again—a poor man's Trump Tower overdone with marble, brass, plashing water, marquee lights, and white draperied curtains.

6 110 Bloor St. W. (mixed-use complex), Daniel Li, 1980; altered, 1987–88.

The epitome of gilt-edged—or, more accurately, stainless-steel-edged—Late-Modern stylishness, this is one of Toronto's most self-consciously elegant buildings. Every sleek detail spells luxury, from the discreet shops with their tasteful signs to the steel-trussed glass canopy to the way the envelope of residences rises in a smooth sweep of silky reflecting glass. Before the 1988 remodelling, the composition was surprisingly similar to that of the Colonnade [18/5]—even down to a floating staircase—making for a neat comparison between the architectural vocabulary of the 1960s and that of the 1980s.

5 *The Colonnade*

6 *110 Bloor St. W.*

**7 96-100 Bloor St. W. (mixed-use complex),
David K. Mesbur, 1988–ongoing. Incorpo-
rates front façade of University Theatre, Eric
Hounsom, 1946–49; and front façade of
Pearcy House, Mathers & Haldenby, 1925.**

Planned by Cineplex Odeon to become
the premiere venue of Toronto's annual
movie Festival of Festivals, this theatres/
hotel/commercial complex looks to be a
muddled scenario all around.

The huge 1,328-seat University
Theatre—put up just after World War II
but using 1930s Art Moderne curves,
silvery chrome, and black granite—was
the epitome of picture palace glamour
and showcase choice in Canada for many
film producers. When owners first sought
to tear it down in the early '80s, movie
buffs and preservationists alike booed
long and loud. Pearcy House too had its
fans, starting with those who knew it as
one of Bloor Street's first office buildings
and appreciated that its low-key red-brick
Neo-Georgian design had been chosen to
fit in on a then-residential thoroughfare.
The third floor was intended for architects' offices, the second for medical
offices, and the ground floor for ladies'
fashion emporia with shop windows giving on to Bloor Street. Others recall that
the building was constructed around an
existing house built by paint manufacturer
Sanderson Pearcy in the 1880s, the new
portal connecting to Pearcy's hall and the
rear of the shops opening onto his
garden. It was this latter feature that
attracted Webb Zerafa Menkes in 1962
when they decided to make of the
premises Lothian Mews, Toronto's first
shops-around-a-courtyard complex [see

16/7]. It is Lothian Mews that admirers
remember most about this building.

So why not include these two nostalgia-
laden *interior* spaces as stars of the new
development? The plot thickens. The star
attractions have been written out because
the University Theatre property was sold
with the contract clause that it could
never be used as a theatre again; the new
Festival Theatres must therefore be situated behind the façade of the Pearcy
House property.

It's hard to know if preservation of
these two faces—without their historic
inwards—spells a happy, coherent ending
or not. Perhaps it would have made more
sense to cast a totally new, fresh design
for this complex. Ah well, it is *show*
business.

**8 Originally Physicians and Surgeons Build-
ing, 86 Bloor St. W., 1922.**

At six storeys plus attic, this was the first
"tall" building to go up along Bloor
Street, providing the medical men who
heretofore had been occupying converted
mansions with a fashionable building all
their own. (Actually, first tenants numbered more dentists than physicians or
surgeons.) Though still in the thrall of
theorems that dictated a classical cornice
to terminate composition, no. 86 manages
a very modish 1920s look, with Deco
capitals crowning thin pilaster-like piers.

7a *University Theatre, 1984*

9b *83 Bloor St. W.*

9a Georg Jensen, 95A Bloor St. W. (commercial block), Rother Bland Trudeau, 1956.

After World War II, contemporary design was spearheaded by the Scandinavians, so when this famous Danish firm elected to bring not only its silver and ceramics to Bloor Street, but also to completely re-do an old building in polished "Scandinavian-modern," there seemed little doubt the avenue would continue on a high-fashion path. In recent years, Scandinavian design has lost some of its appeal, but the Jensen shop, with its abstract massing, striking colouration, and careful detail, still looks good.

9b Originally Ashley & Crippin Building, 83 Bloor St. W., Baldwin & Greene, 1929.

Many Art Deco buildings were erected along fashion-conscious Bloor Street in the late 1920s and early '30s; this three-storey structure designed as photographic studios with sophisticated curved and fluted façade is one of the few to remain. The awning of the restaurant that now occupies the ground floor is a jarring horizontal to the vertical composition, but Deco verve still zaps through. (The Harry Rosen store across the street at 82 Bloor is a Late-Modern granite-clad version of basically the same configuration.)

Bay Street south of Bloor has been the site of much apartment house construction in recent years. Though the buildings differ in design and massing, they are related in their use of orangey-red brick and dark-brown trim for a warm domestic feeling that sets them apart from the more glitzy, concrete-hard buildings along Bloor.

10a 1166 Bay St. (apartment house), H.D. Burston; completed Paul H. Northgrave, 1979–81.

A very distinguished 22-storey condominium building with lovely gleaming polygonal bays stepping out neatly in file along the front. This undulating, many-windowed look is remarkably reminiscent of one of architectural history's great early skyscrapers: Burnham & Root's 1889 Monadnock Building in Chicago.

10b The Eleven Thirty-Two, 1132 Bay St. (apartment house), Henno Sillaste with Adam & Chiu, 1984.

The 18-storey Eleven Thirty-Two building is notable for its 1980s reprise of an 1880s domestic mode, with bay windows set within piers, dentil-like brick patterning sill courses, and a three-storey oriel framed in an arch at the corner. Unfortunately, this finely executed Post-Modern play stops at the fourth storey, with floors above rather jarringly conventional.

10c Bay/Charles Tower, 55–57 Charles St. W. (apartment house), Klein & Sears, 1979–80.

An eccentric design that seems to work, Bay/Charles Tower features a polygonal shape with shafts of bay windows jutting out at different floor levels, rather like so many glass-enclosed elevators scurrying up and down the walls.

11 ManuLife Centre, 55 Bloor St. W. thru to Charles St. (mixed-use complex), Clifford & Lawrie, 1969; remodelled, Clifford Lawrie Bolton Ritchie, 1984; addition, 1988.

The block-square ManuLife Centre tried to follow in the Colonnade's footsteps [18/5], but the result is less inviting. Where the parts of the latter were woven in a lively family group, here the different members hardly seem to be talking to one another. Along Bloor Street rises a 19-storey office tower, and along Charles Street, a 51-storey apartment building. The two-storey slab of shops on which they sit (once partly open court) is too cold and brittle to actively bring them together. The fact that shops along Bloor Street are tucked *under* the cantilevered office block reinforces the sense of separateness, although the stylish Post-Modern glass cascade now unloosed on the sidewalk has helped to invigorate the whole.

12 Holt-Renfrew Centre, 50 Bloor St. W. (commercial block), Crang & Boake, 1978.

In the same ultra-chic aesthetic as the similarly glass-canopied 110 Bloor building [18/6], Holt-Renfrew Centre was an earlier Late-Modern statement for Bloor Street. Actually, "luxe" seems even more so here, thanks to the sumptuous Italian white marble cladding. The three-storey building makes for a handsome low-scale planar composition strung out along Bloor Street, but in compliance with Toronto's building bylaws, eventually the owners must add considerable housing units on top. For now it is a lovely addition to the streetscape.

13 Stollery's, 790 Yonge St. at Bloor St. (commercial block), S.B. Coon & Son, 1929; third-floor addition, 1984.

The long, narrow shape of Stollery's Men's Furnishings is for good reason. The 1920s widening of Bloor Street appropriated 20 feet from existing properties, which virtually destroyed most of the buildings and certainly conduct of business for a time. Mr. Stollery would have none of it. He tore down that half of his shop *behind* the widened street line and erected a new building there, meanwhile leaving the remainder of the store up and in use until the replacement was completed. When finished he had quite a stunning "modern Italian" emporium to unveil, complete with round-arched windows, red-tile roof, and Art Deco bas-reliefs. The recent addition, which planted a glass-walled storey atop the store, follows similar innovative impulse.

14 2 Bloor St. W. (office building), Ogus & Fisher with Peter Caspari, 1971; altered, 1987–88.

Late-Modernism gone awry. The glass-clad "boring box" obviously needs more than vertical "suspenders" and a striped "belt" around the middle to smarten it up, especially if the suit is as big, brown, and blah as this 34-storey tower. (Following recommendations of the city's "Yonge Street Study," which singled this building out as a "menacing vacuum," efforts have been made to lighten and open up the pedestrian level for retail use. It helps little.)

15 Hudson's Bay Centre, 2 Bloor St. E. (office building and department store), Crang & Boake, 1974.

The skeletal pattern of the 35-storey Hudson's Bay Centre building is only a little less impoverished than that of its fuzzy neighbour across the street [18/14]. And the double abomination of a shrouded, seemingly inaccessible banking pavilion taking up this important corner plus the mausoleum-like face of the Bay's department store walling the rest of the block make this complex one of the most deadly pieces of architecture in Toronto. (The "Yonge Street Study" pushed for changes to the street-related portions of this building too. Stay tuned.)

14, 15 *2 Bloor St. W., 2 Bloor St. E.*

17 *Crown Life Insurance Co.*

16 New York Life Centre, 121 Bloor St. E. (office building), Page & Steele, 1983.

St. Andrew's United Church, 117 Bloor St. E., Page & Steele, 1983.

When St. Andrew's United offered up the whole Bloor Street plot which their Romanesque Revival edifice had occupied since 1890, the deal specified a replacement church along with the developer's high-rise heaven. Page & Steele's bluish-tinted glass skyscraper with precise layers of cloud-white banding is a sparkly Late-Modern version of the horizontally emphasized tall building. The stepped faces of the structure, and the way it is undercut and carried on angled square pillars, create a striking shape and profile that is a fine complement to the dramatic new church. The beautifully sited church uses the same stepped massing and mirror cladding as the office block but punctuates it with verticals of warm beigy brick, two of which stand in for a charismatic bell tower. An inspired addition to the cityscape.

17 Crown Life Insurance Co., 120 Bloor St. E. (office building), Marani & Morris, 1956.

160 Bloor St. E. (office building), Bregman & Hamann, 1984.

That Bloor Street East would become the major venue of Toronto's insurance companies seemed assured when both Crown Life and Confederation Life [18/21] joined pioneering Manufacturers' Life [18/19] here in the 1950s. Crown Life's first building at 120 Bloor is typical of postwar 1950s architecture in a splendidly executed *retardataire* Art Moderne mode.

In 1969, the company erected an adjacent high-rise, notable only for the fact it was torn down just a little over ten years later to make way for the mirrored giant that now dominates the site.

Crown Life's newest building, despite its uninspiring stubby shape, boasts such a sophisticated, fragilely scored smooth skin that the structure invites a careful look for the unique qualities that mirror glass can bring to architecture: the visual paradox of a wall that is constantly changing depending on viewpoint, light, weather; a wall that back-lit at night changes to the point of disappearing. No. 160 gained its extraordinary size by trading property it owned between Asquith and Church Streets for city-sponsored housing [18/18] and a public park. The abstract stainless-steel sculpture poised at the entrance to Crown Life is an arresting presence on this corner. Created by Kosso Eloul, this tense, thoughtful work is ample demonstration that sculptures in front of buildings can indeed be more than "plops in the plaza."

18 Asquith Park, 14 Asquith St. thru to Church St. (apartment house), Hiro Nakashima, 1984.

The City of Toronto deserves praise for its architecturally distinguished non-profit housing. This 17-storey tower is the largest such building to date, and its interesting curved shape accommodating an awkward site as well as sweep of balconies on Church Street and asymmetric fenestration on Asquith make it a lively addition to the neighbourhood.

19 *Manufacturers' Life Insurance Co.*

19 Manufacturers' Life Insurance Co., 200 Bloor St. E. (office building), Sproatt & Rolph, 1924–26; additions, Marani & Morris, 1953.

250 Bloor St. E. (office building), Marani Rounthwaite & Dick, 1968.

North Tower, 200 Bloor St. E. (office building), Clifford Lawrie Bolton Ritchie, 1983.

The various office buildings of Manufacturers' Life erected on this stretch of Bloor Street over some 60 years are a lesson in corporate architecture at its well-bred best. Each building was designed in the style of its time, rendered with such thoughtful reserve and outstanding quality that there never could be a question but that one's equities were safe and solvent at Manufacturers' Life. The first edifice of 1926, the majestic six storeys fronting no. 200, used cut stone and refined Roman Doric detail to convey an air of urban gentility then appropriate to Bloor Street. Later large additions to the rear showed similar good taste. The 1960s building, no. 250, was built of crisp,

three-dimensional concrete modules popular in that era to form a forceful, sculptural structure. With a handsome simple clockface at its top (unfortunately now gone for a dummy's digital) and careful siting to close the vista up Jarvis Street, this building quickly became a further landmark on Bloor Street.

Manufacturers' Life newest building used Late-Modern reflective-glass cladding—gold in colour—innovatively hung *behind* a giant concrete frame to create a structure both ethereal and grounded, sleek yet substantial. It is a timely, bravura design of High Renaissance grandeur, a comparison brought to mind by the elegant domed pavilion (unfortunately overly baroque inside) that connects this building to the older one. And of course all three buildings benefit from a park-like setting on the crest of Rosedale Ravine carpeted with the finest lawns in Toronto.

16 *St. Andrew's United*

20 *Maurice Cody Hall*

20 Maurice Cody Hall/originally St. Paul's Church, 227 Bloor St. E., Edward Radford & George Radford, 1861; addition, George M. Miller, 1900; addition, E.J. Lennox, 1903.

St. Paul's Anglican Church, 227 Bloor St. E., E.J. Lennox, 1913.

This adventurous translation of a medieval English village church ranks among the best architecture in Toronto, as much a standout today among skyscrapers on Bloor Street as it was 120 years ago when it actually was a village church, serving newly incorporated Yorkville and other outlying residential communities. The Radford brothers had studied well that ardent Victorian Gothicist, Augustus Welby Northmore Pugin; no doubt the master would have approved their sturdy stone edifice, albeit the spirited composition and sophisticated stone tracery of windows and bell tower were not entirely in keeping with staid formulas for houses of worship sent from mother country to colonial hinterlands. The Radfords, who had come from England, departed Toronto soon after this commission. More's the pity. This building is now known as Maurice Cody Hall in memory of the drowned son of a prominent rector.

Next door looms E.J. Lennox's 1913 Gothic re-revival, built at a time when the Anglican congregation had outgrown its little country church—already twice altered and enlarged. Lennox's St. Paul's presents an imposing bulk, but it lacks the vigour of its earlier neighbour, perhaps because planned towers and decorative carving were never completed. The interior is radiant, however, with Lennox's "scenic quality" glowing in place.

21 Confederation Life Insurance Co., 321 Bloor St. E. (office building), Marani & Morris, 1954–56; additions, Marani Rounthwaite & Dick, 1973.

100 Huntley St. (recreation hall), Marani & Morris, 1954.

A discreet, domestic-looking structure—Georgian in style, small in scale, and distinguished in detail—was Confederation Life's contribution to insurance company land. Marani & Morris's nine-storey tower features orangey-coloured Flemish-bond brick, stone window surrounds with the slightest of metal-capped cornice heads, balustraded parapet, and a smooth stone base with grand pillared entrance. The 1973 addition to the rear is neatly compatible, and boasts one of the sharpest packages in town for roof-top mechanicals plus a pebbled, many-treed parkette in back that is a good, Oriental solution to the slivered site. The two-storey brick building visible across Mt. Pleasant Road at 100 Huntley Street was originally a recreational centre for Confederation Life staff.

22 Rosedale Glen, 278 Bloor St. E. (apartment house), Zeidler Roberts Partnership, 1983.

With one face to Bloor Street and another to Rosedale, this very stylish apartment house arranges warm honey-coloured brick and inviting beige-banded clear-glass balconies and corner rooms so as to immediately identify its residential function. Zeidler Roberts, who in their many recent buildings seem to be exploring all the oxymoronic possibilities that glass has to offer, have here made it soft and lush.

Area X

Walk 19: Annex East
Walk 20: Annex West

Area X

"**S**uburb: a residential community lying outside the central part of a town." At the end of the 19th century, there were many suburbs ringing North American cities. It was a period of prosperity following on years of economic restraint, and in their enthusiasm to expand, municipalities began gobbling up nearby independent communities such as Yorkville [*AREA IX*], or creating instant new ones by laying out streets and lots on empty township lands, as in this area. What made all this eager expansion feasible were new networks of trolley lines crisscrossing the cities and cheaply transporting populace between jobs and homes.

The Annex—"Toronto Annexed" blazed the advertising poster for 259 lots in 1886—was laid out between Bedford Road (the western boundary of the Village of Yorkville) and Brunswick Avenue (the eastern boundary of Seaton Village) on lands owned by the pioneer Baldwin family. The Baldwins had first gone into the business of subdividing when they laid out Spadina Avenue and environs south of the Bloor Street city limits in the 1830s [see Introduction, *AREA VIII*]. In 1875, they extended Spadina Avenue north of Bloor about a quarter mile and also set out Walmer Road as an imaginative serpentine drive [20/12]. Over the next 15 years other streets were plotted, mostly prosaic north/south stretches packed with narrow lots by real estate entrepreneur Simeon Heman Janes, who had bought the land from the Baldwins. After the area was annexed to the city in 1887, building began in earnest.

Janes and the speculative builders who bought lots from him all intended that the Annex should attract buyers of the prosperous professional and merchant class. Very small houses, row houses, and commercial buildings were specifically excluded by deed restriction. This controlled planning did, in pious Toronto, include lots for several large churches, but there were virtually no other institutions allowed.

Given the single-minded planning of this suburb and the speed with which it was implemented, it is not surprising that Annex houses are more homogeneous than those in other areas of similar size. They were built in a period when the picturesque Queen Anne style was sweeping England and North America. Queen Anne houses can be identified by their irregularity of massing and rooflines, their mixing of different colours and textures, the variety of their architectural parts including gables, turrets, and bay windows, and an overall attitude of inventiveness, even whimsy. Many houses built in the Annex also recall the Romanesque buildings of the American architect Henry Hobson Richardson, with rocky façades and deep-set round-arched windows and entries.

A sophisticated hybrid of these two styles was conceived by architect E.J. Lennox for the Lewis Lukes house [19/6]. Begun in 1888, this house became a trendsetter. Its melding of the substance of Richardsonian Romanesque with the decorative flamboyance of Queen Anne really keynotes the Annex. The fashion was made possible by a ready availability of the necessary materials: plum- and pink-coloured sandstone from the Credit River, and hard, dark red-brick and terracotta clays from the Don Valley.

Scattered throughout the district are houses of later periods and styles. Most prevalent are large detached English Cottage Style houses, identifiable by their expansive plain walls, high prominent roofs, tall square chimneys, and multi-light casement windows. Here and there are some good Neo-Georgian designs. The last houses in the Annex date from the early 1930s when tiny half-timbered Neo-Tudor boxes seem to have been dropped onto any remaining lots.

Although most houses constructed in the Annex were put up by speculative builders using variations on stock plans, many well-known architectural firms designed buildings here. In addition to Lennox, they included Charles Gibson, Edmund Burke, and the eclectic Frederick Herbert; later, Darling & Pearson and Chadwick & Beckett; as well as Eden Smith, who did most of the large English Cottage residences.

Two of the three churches built to serve the Annex community were designed by the distinguished firm of Langley & Burke: an inspired Gothic structure for the Baptists on attractive Walmer Road [20/14]; and a firm Romanesque edifice for the Methodists at Walmer Road and Bloor Street [20/16]. The relatively unassuming Presbyterian offering at Bloor and Huron Streets was designed by William Gregg [19/28]. And it was next to this fashionably developing district in the 1880s that the Anglicans bought 4½ acres just east of Bathurst Street with plans to erect a marvellous cathedral modelled on the great St. Alban's in England, plans that eventually came to little [20/20a].

More noteworthy even than the stylistic sameness of Annex buildings is the way in which they all present a continuous face to the street. These large detached and semi-detached houses were closely massed beyond a common setback and palpably strung together by cornice lines of equal height. This is true of houses built many years apart. Furthermore, the lots were signifi-cantly undifferentiated by walls or planting, creating block-long grassy terraces and visually unbroken side-walks. These were the parks of the Annex, parks not for recreational fun but for ostentatious promenade, as the Victorians and Edwardians conceived of them. The open siting also allowed the houses to be fully displayed, and thereby to benefit from association with surrounding dwellings. A contemporary writer, G. Mercer Adam, thought this new way of laying out grounds came near to "the condition of a perfect community [with] implicit confidence put in the civility and good-will of neighbours."

St. George Street in the early 1900s showing block-long grassy terraces, the parks of the Annex.

Today the Annex continues this sense of cooperation, having staved off the physical and social deterioration typical of many North American 1890s streetcar suburbs. Starting in the 1920s, the moneyed and now automobiled families who 30 years earlier had bought the Annex houses began to move farther out, to Forest Hill and North Rosedale.

The Annex was left to widows, tradesmen, and a few university professors. But even then a strong ratepayers' association organized against a proposed school on Prince Arthur Avenue and other intrusions of the sort that had so altered Jarvis and Sherbourne Streets [*AREA VII*]. When apartment developers covetously began to eye the Annex in the 1950s, because of its proximity to the then-abuilding Bloor Street subway, ratepayers again came forward. Longtime homeowners were joined by new residents, the latter mostly professionals from university and media. And though it was too late to arrest high-rises on St. George, Spadina, and lower Walmer Road, the association has decisively influenced city planning since that time, including the scuttling of an expressway along Spadina Road.

Rooming houses, college fraternities, offices, and institutions may now occupy some dwellings, and the area certainly is no longer a suburb outside the central part of town, but essentially the Annex remains the same district it was 90 years ago: a family-oriented residential neighbourhood with a deep sense of community and a unique architectural character.

Walk 19: Annex East

**1a Ecology House, 12 Madison Ave., 1891.
14 Madison Ave. (detached house), 1891.**
The four arches wheeling smartly across
the front of these twinned houses are
emblematic of the Annex. The Romans
perfected the round arch almost two
millennia ago and it has graced—and
supported—buildings ever since. You'll
find arches and decorative curves such as
these scalloped tilehangings and segmental
bricks throughout the area. No. 12 now
functions as Ecology House, a showcase
for energy-efficient living.

1b 16–18 Madison Ave. (double house), 1891.
"Picturesque" in architecture translates as
asymmetry and variety, so perforce the
two halves of a picturesque double house
would be strikingly different. But, as with

any good design, the two halves are in
calculated harmony: the gabled porch of
no. 16 rehearsed in no. 18's conical roof;
the arched entry of no. 18 echoed in the
curve of no. 16's attic porch; the corner
turret in one balanced by the tower-like
projecting bay and gable of the other.

**2 17–19 and 21–23 Madison Ave. (two double
houses), 1891.**
These abodes follow a standard plan for
speculative houses with side hall and three
principal rooms per floor. The builder did
make a stab at having the four appear
dissimilar, however: here a round arch,
there a straight lintel; here a dormer,
there a gable; brick on this, terracotta for
that. All in all, a handsome assemblage.

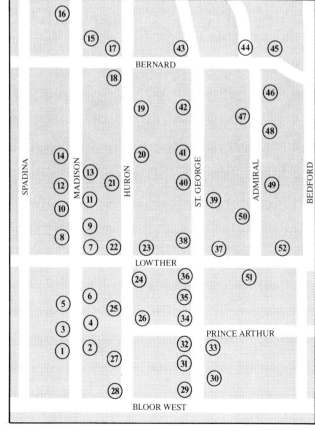

3 *20 Madison Ave.*

5a *24-26 Madison Ave.*

3 20 Madison Ave. (detached house), 1891.

The builder of this house, George Hunter, a carpenter, must have known that brick and stone were *in* for the Annex, but he didn't give up altogether his obvious love for wood. The painted wooden balconies really don't meld into the composition, but they are so exuberant and inviting, one remembers no. 20 long after forgetting better-designed houses.

4 Huron-Madison Project, 25 Madison Ave. thru to Huron St. (complex of apartment house and nine rehabilitated houses), Paul Martel, 1981.

Making good use of the space and vista down a brick-paved entryway, this four-storey infill building cleverly manipulates 12 units in an unobtrusive but distinctive composition. The decision to give each ground-floor occupant a high-walled garden "pen" is a little depressing though. The project is operated by Cityhome, Toronto's non-profit housing corporation.

5a 24-26 Madison Ave. (double house), 1891.

Typical Annex asymmetry with one-half of this double house dominated by a wide front gable, the other half reciprocating with a tall corner tower. Variations on this gable/tower equipoise occur throughout the district.

5b 30-32 Madison Ave. (double house), 1889.

A nice big house? No, two houses, with the second entrance tucked away at the side. Even if the pretence didn't work, such a design cleverly produced two different interior layouts.

6 Originally Lewis Lukes house, 37 Madison Ave., E.J. Lennox, 1888-90.

This, Lennox's domestic masterpiece, was among the first houses designed for the Annex, and it became a model for much of what followed. The architect had set the stage for a robust Richardsonian Romanesque style in Toronto with his mighty city hall then going up on Queen Street [7/11], but Lennox knew he couldn't put up massive monuments of stone on small residential lots. His solution was to temper the bulk and solidity of Romanesque with the lithesomeness of Queen Anne. Designed for a building contractor who would have appreciated the wit that the invented form demanded, no. 37 revels in a calculated equilibrium of interrelated parts. This disciplined picturesque with its aura of stability along with the fashionableness was just what late Victorian suburbia hankered for, and in block after Annex block houses began to go up with the same progression of rock-faced stone, rich red brick, decorative terracotta tile, and intricate woodwork. As a group the houses are impressive, but Lennox's example remains the standout, and not just because today it is flanked by tawdry Tudor boxes.

7 47 Madison Ave. (detached house), Eden Smith, 1903-04.

A new century and the beginning of much plainer looking houses. White stucco facing, small windows, and an embracing roof are typical characteristics of the English Cottage Style, a simplified rendering of vernacular Tudor forms very popular in the early 1900s.

6 *37 Madison Ave.*

8 St. Thomas House/originally James Henderson house, 54 Madison Ave., Frederick H. Herbert, 1904–05; addition, Armstrong & Molesworth, 1976.

A fine Gothic-inspired wall dormer and doorcase here, plus wing-like eaves and shooting window heads that make this subtly asymmetric house look as if it might fly away. Definitely a bird of another feather in this neighbourhood. Henderson was a barrister with Henderson, Small and Beaumont. The new addition for a nursing home is properly unprepossessing.

9 Originally George Crane house, 49 Madison Ave., 1890.

An early Annex house with very ambitious entrance: Romanesque carved Byzantine leafwork capitals, moulded terracotta tiles, even some fancy grillwork in the tympanum, and a hint of a bartizan. The carved scroll and plume plaque to the right of the door was designed especially for Crane, principal of the Lansdowne School.

10 64–66 Madison Ave. (double house), 1891; porch addition to no. 64, Chadwick & Beckett, 1893.

Stepped gable, stained glass portholes, and artsy-craftsy porch for a change of pace.

11 69–71 Madison Ave. (double house), 1894.

A catalogue of beautifully articulated terracotta (note especially the egg-and-dart string course). In the 1890s, as much attention was paid to creating designs for terracotta as for stone. Of course, once moulds were made, terracotta decoration could be cheaply reproduced—over and over and over again.

12a 70–72 Madison Ave. (double house), 1890.

A stony Annex house with lovely wooden veranda overlooking one of the few remaining vacant lots in the district.

12b *78 Madison Ave.*

14 *88 Madison Ave.*

12b 78 Madison Ave. (detached house), 1899.
The delightful porches gracing the first
and second storeys of this house may be
its two best rooms. No doubt many an
Annex denizen has sat here behind
spooled balustrades to watch the passing
parade.

**13 93–99 Madison Ave. (apartment house),
Langley & Langley, 1907.**
Early Toronto apartment buildings, which
were introduced in the first decades of
this century following the lead in Montreal, Boston, and New York, were at
great pains to melt into established
neighbourhoods. Here the cornice line,
setback, red brick, and wide projecting
bays all echo those of surrounding
houses. Interiors too were house-like, with
large rooms, fireplaces, and back porches.

**14 88 Madison Ave. (detached house), Fred-
erick H. Herbert, 1899.**
Always coming up with something out of
the ordinary, Herbert has here made the
requisite Annex tower into a wishing well.
One wishes he'd made the windows
bigger, but the sheltering roof sweeping
down over the porch is grand.

**15 145 Madison Ave. (detached house), Fred-
erick H. Herbert, 1895–96.**
Tower as elfin sunporch, and a long way
from Middle Ages antecedents.

**16a Originally "Rivermead" (Percy R. Gar-
diner residence), 138 Madison Ave., Jocelyn
Davidson, 1934.**
A late version of the Neo-Tudor, with
horizontal bands of small casement windows and rough clinker brick to impart a
rustic flavour. "Rivermead" replaced an
earlier house on this large double lot,
which once boasted a specimen English
garden. Gardiner, who was a stockbroker
with his own firm, must have fared better
than most in the 1929 crash.

**16b 140 Madison Ave. (detached house),
1902.**
Georgian Revival in an American mood.

**17 Originally Stanley C. H. Clarke house,
112 Bernard Ave., Chadwick & Beckett,
1906–07.**
Georgian Revival at its inventive best,
adapting 18th-century forms to 20th-
century proclivities. The high first storey,
for example, allows for an amiable
billiard room in the basement, and the
three-part casement windows for much
light and air. The height also dramatizes a
grand hooded and pilastered entrance.
Clarke was branch manager of the
Imperial Bank at Yonge and Bloor.

16a *138 Madison Ave.*

17 *112 Bernard Ave.*

Huron is a street of well-intentioned Annex houses rendered clumsy in later years by the addition of chain-link fences and shrubs in too many front yards. In a district of large houses close to one another and to the street, the unbroken vista of the front lawns was essential for proper perspective.

18 Originally Thomas A. Lytle house, 610 Huron St., 1891.

A Queen Anne smorgasbord paid for by a prominent pickle manufacturer and looking more variety-laden than usual thanks to its corner site: two sides of the building for invention, play, and the hanging of tiles.

19 571–573 Huron St. (double house), 1894.

In a district infatuated by towers and turrets (little towers), one way to make one's own tower stand out was to skew it at a 45-degree angle. Another was to top it with an eye-catching finial.

20 Huron Street School, 541 Huron St., 1890; demolished, 1956; new building, Irving D. Boignon, 1958.

Huron Street School Annex, Charles H. Bishop, 1914.

When this area was annexed in 1887, the city immediately acquired land on centrally located Huron Street for an elementary school, and a fine three-storey edifice with cupola-topped mansard and 12 maple-panelled rooms was built in 1890. As the Annex grew so did the school population, and in 1914 the Board of Education Superintendent of Buildings was called on to design an annex building with a further six classrooms. In the Queen Anne style favoured here and abroad for municipally-run schools, the Flemish-gabled Huron Street School Annex fit right in with residential neighbours.

In 1956, the original structure was deemed substandard and it was replaced by one of Toronto's first early modern buildings, a low-scale ribbon of large-windowed classrooms strung out along the street. The annex building was subsequently threatened, but school parents, citing its "big, airy and beautiful" rooms, organized to upgrade and save it. So today the Annex can boast two very distinguished school buildings, one of 1914, the other 1958.

21a 534 Huron St. (detached house), probably Frederick H. Herbert, 1895.

Chateauesque arches and Neo-Tudor half-timbering.

20 *Huron Street School and annex*

21b 532 Huron St. (detached house), Frederick H. Herbert, 1896.
Classical pediments and keystones saucing Queen Anne flummery. With what relish Herbert went about these Annex houses, and how unpalatable some of them look.

22 Originally J.W.B. Walsh house, 88 Lowther Ave. at Huron St., Darling & Pearson, 1904; addition, 1986.
A brick Georgian Revival rectangle not quite ready to go whole symmetrical hog. The recalcitrant owner was manager of the Dominion Bank at 1176 Yonge Street.

23 80 Lowther Ave. at Huron St. (detached house), Frederick H. Herbert, 1899-1900.
82 Lowther Ave. (detached house), Frederick H. Herbert, 1895-96.
84 Lowther Ave. (detached house), Chadwick & Beckett, 1900-01.
86 Lowther Ave. (detached house), Frederick H. Herbert, 1899-1900.
A turn-of-the-century quartet answering the call of Classical Revival with Adamesque pressed-metal wreaths and such.

24 Huron Street south of Lowther Avenue is a block of distinguished Annex houses flung out of scale by high-rise apartment buildings and no-rise parking flats. The greensward at the southeast corner owes its existence to ground too soft to build on, a function of mysterious Taddle Creek, which meanders under the Annex and surfaces in surprised householders' basements every once in a while.

25a Originally Walter Gaynor house, 500 Huron St., 1889.
More austere and crusty than later Annex houses. The first occupant was an estate and financial broker and his rock-faced manor with looming tower undoubtedly projected an appropriate aura of security and stability.

25b 496 Huron St. (detached house), Strickland & Symons, 1897.
Like an onion, this layered façade peels itself back from scroll-gabled polygonal bay to wide-gabled flat front to deep-set portal. A very poised rendition of the Queen Anne song, with not a few Classical Revival notes typical of this late date.

26 Originally William Ince house, 94 Prince Arthur Ave. at Huron St., Darling Curry Sproatt & Pearson, 1892-93.
Trim Queen Anne with a conspicuous Classical Revival porch and doorcase replete with Ionic columns and fanlight and sidelights. William Ince was a partner in Perkins, Ince wholesale grocers on Front Street [1/15b].

27a *480-482 Huron St.*

27a 480–482 Huron St. (double house), probably Smith & Gemmell, 1888.
A grand and expansive ground-hugging house, graciously accommodating two suburban families. Architect John Gemmell was listed as first owner of this finely crafted and detailed double house, and it is likely his firm designed it. Another architect, David Roberts, took up residence at no. 480 years later.

27b 478 Huron St. (detached house), probably Smith & Gemmell, 1888.
The same windows, brick panels, and front door as at no. 480–482 [19/27a], this time in the service of a single dwelling. The clipped-back gable roof was an interesting design device to make these buildings seem less close together.

28 Bloor Street United Church/originally Bloor Street Presbyterian Church, 300 Bloor St. W., William R. Gregg, 1889–90; additions, Wickson & Gregg, 1908–09; altered, Wickson & Gregg, 1927.
As begun in 1889, Bloor Street Presbyterian was a small and unassuming Decorated Gothic Revival stone structure that the congregation outgrew even before it was finished. Greatly enlarged in similar dry, workaday fashion, the church has little to recommend it, even though it did once enjoy Gothic-arched portals along a narrower Bloor Street. When Presbyterians, Methodists, and Congregationalists in Canada united in the sweeping, often acrimonious church reform of 1925, the outspoken minister of this church, Rev. George Campbell Pidgeon, was elected the new body's first head. Obviously, voting delegates were not influenced by the architectural pre-eminence of his house of worship.

29 Medical Arts Building, 170 St. George St. at Bloor St., Marani Lawson & Paisley, 1928–29.
When the doctors ran out of mansions on Bloor Street to turn into waiting and examining rooms in the 1910s and '20s [see Introduction, *AREA IX*], they built this circumspect office tower. Part of Toronto's pre-Depression high-rise boom, it was the first tall building in this area.

30 *George Gooderham house, c. 1900*

St. George Street, as a continuation of an important residential avenue south of Bloor, early attracted those who sought to erect the most imposing of Annex houses. Following World War II, apartment builders began to capitalize on this reputation as well as the avenue's proximity to the planned subway, and today many high-rises share the street with former stately homes.

30 York Club/originally George Gooderham house, 135 St. George St., David Roberts, 1889-92.

The most distinguished Richardsonian Romanesque house in Toronto, and arguably the most distinguished house of any kind, built for a man who was the wealthiest in the province at the time. George Gooderham was president of Gooderham & Worts (an enterprise begun by his father William in 1832 that had gone on to become the largest distillery in the British Empire), as well as a leading figure in the world of Canadian banking, railroading, and real estate. His chosen architect, David Roberts, also designed much of the distillery complex [2/9], the distinctive Gooderham office building [1/13], and most of the manors around town for this large and influential family (George had 11 children and was brother to 12). But this magnificent ensemble of beautifully executed brick and stone was Roberts's masterpiece. Consummately balancing assertive tower, gables, and chimneys with deep round-arched porch, gallery, and windows, the architect has created a composition so firm, so formal-looking, as to endow the picturesque and asymmetric Romanesque with a majestic classical serenity.

The Gooderham house was sold to the York Club in 1909. At the time, adjacent mansions on Bloor Street still served as residences, making this the first secular institution tolerated in the Annex (with socially impeccable credentials, the club undoubtedly represented a second home for some Annex residents). Through the years the York Club has been a careful custodian, and this building continues to stand as one of the finest in the city.

31 172 St. George St. (office building), 1986.

In 1985, the wonderful towered and turreted Crowther house, which had stood as a landmark on Bloor Street for 100 years, was to have been jacked up and moved to this site as part of a development deal for the block. Needless to say, the nonpareil 1886 house never arrived. The building we have instead is intriguing for its 1986 interpretation of Queen Anne tower and bichrome cladding, but the terracotta panels salvaged from the original look out of place and only serve to point up the richness that was lost.

34 *180 St. George St.*

32 174 St. George St. (detached house), George M. Miller, 1890–92.

176 St. George St. (detached house), George M. Miller, 1890–91.

178 St. George St. (detached house), George M. Miller, 1890–91.

A trio of typical detached Annex houses designed by George M. Miller for builder James T. McCabe shortly after the Gooderham house was begun. Miller was at some pains to differentiate the houses one from another by scrambling their picturesque details, but he respected a common setback and eaves line for all three, thereby situating them firmly in the ceremonious streetscape. No. 178 with its corner watchtower was for many years the home of the sheriff of York Township, Joseph J. Widdifield.

33 Royal Canadian Yacht Club, 139 St. George St., Crang & Boake, 1984.

Post-Modern formal symmetry for the RCYC with echoes of the area's red-brick pointy gables as well as some triangular piers that seem to suggest sails in the wind. A thoughtful addition to the Annex, this building is the club's "town" address; their primary facilities are located at the anchorage on Toronto Island. The handsome wall dates to 1892, when it surrounded George Gooderham's son-in-law's house.

34 Originally Thomas W. Horn house, 180 St. George St., Frederick H. Herbert, 1898; west wing addition, Chadwick & Beckett, 1907.

Full-blooded Richardsonian Romanesque with an all-stone skin tautly curving around and enveloping the bold structure. The design makes the most of an interesting site, calling up a striking conical-capped tower to mark the corner and a beautiful formal entrance to articulate the long front. This is probably Herbert's best design in Toronto. The west wing is a sympathetic later addition by Chadwick & Beckett. Horn was president of a concern that made light-enhancing glass for shop windows, Luxfer Prism Company.

35a Originally Harris L. Hees house, 182 St. George St., Eden Smith & Son, 1910–11.

A very large formal stone house trying to look "cottagey," with sweeping roof, half-timbered gables, multi-light casement windows, and swelling bays to break up the mass. Harris L. Hees was in the family window shades business.

35b Originally James O. Buchanan house, 186 St. George St., S. Hamilton Townsend, 1889–90.

Built for the manager of the Union Bank of Canada on Wellington Street, this was the first house on St. George Street above Bloor. Though fundamentally a Romanesque/Queen Anne design, the simple massing, flatness, and half-timbering across the second storey anticipate the Neo-Tudor houses constructed in this area later in the early 1900s.

36 *190 St. George St.*

41c *234 St. George St.*

36 190 St. George St. (apartment house), Joseph A. Medwecki, 1972.
A distinguished essay in Late-Modernism that picks up where the smooth-sided International Style leaves off, with a plastic, though still spare form that crisply articulates the layers of floors and punctuates the front with a thrusting, dynamic V. Quality materials and gracious siting on the well-landscaped lot enhance the message. An effective statement on a street of more often weak sisters.

37 Originally Edward Y. Eaton house, 157 St. George St., George M. Miller, 1898; coach house, 1899.
The elegant coach house east of the main house was the draw here, a miniature Palladian classic and one of the most lucid buildings in the Annex before it got all gussied up as apartments. Eaton, a vice-president of his father's department store at Yonge and Queen [demolished], may have used his carriage to commute downtown instead of taking the streetcar.

38 First Church of Christ Scientist, 196 St. George St., S.S. Beman, 1916.
This was the first Christian Science church in Toronto, built here for the large and tranquil site and central location. Like Christian Science churches elsewhere in the world, the atypical ecclesiastical design is that of a large domed auditorium imposingly cloaked in classical detail, in this instance Doric.

39a Originally Henry Victor Cawthra house, 163 St. George St., Gordon & Helliwell, 1897–98.
Subdued Queen Anne with the usual gable/turret litany. Turrets were picturesque of course, but they were also practical, for their bayed windows served to draw more light and air into deep rooms. No. 163 was built as a wedding present for his son by Henry Cawthra of the mercantile and banking dynasty [see also 14/13].

39b 165 St. George St. (detached house), Eden Smith, 1906.
Toronto's version of English Cottage Style as interpreted by the prolific Eden Smith, this time with the characteristic tall chimney poised like a sentinel against the broad, plain front. The round-arched, recessed porch with stone voussoirs is very welcome looking.

39c 169 St. George St. (apartment house), Crang & Boake, 1956.
One of the best small 1950s apartment houses in Toronto, no. 169 uses stretches of glass and a Miesian ground-storey setback to very stylish effect. The contained balconies to the sides are infinitely more practical than the toothy ones punctuating so many apartments of this era.

42 *240 St. George St.*

43 *260 St. George St.*

**40 212 St. George St. (detached house),
Charles J. Gibson, 1907; apartment house
addition, Emslie Eden, 1980.**

An imposing Neo-Tudor manor felicitously fronting a modern residential complex, demonstrating that there are
ways—and ways—to build multiple
housing.

**41a Originally Bartle E. Bull house, 228 St.
George St., Eden Smith, 1900–01.**

An exploratory Smith trying out big
roofs, small transomed windows, and tall
chimneys on a stepped composition of the
sort not usual in his later, flatter English
Cottage Style houses. Bartle Bull was with
Kerr, Bull & Rowell, barristers and
solicitors.

**41b 230 St. George St. (detached house),
Edwards & Saunders, 1908–09.**

Neo-Tudor looking a little too quaint and
self-conscious for its own good.

**41c Originally Robert Watson house, 234 St.
George St., E.J. Lennox, 1902–03.**

After having introduced the prototypical
Annex house with his Lewis Lukes house
of 1888–90 [19/6], Lennox disappeared
from these precincts for fully a decade
(his work on the city hall occupied him
from 1889 to 1899). For his reappearing
act, he produced a quite different look,
this florid stone and brick Jacobethan
composition highlighted by a polygonal
umbrella-covered tower. Watson was the
owner of a candy factory.

**42 Originally Ontario Medical Association,
240 St. George St. (office building), A.J. Diamond & Barton Myers (designed by Barton
Myers), 1968.**

The neighbourhood's residential red brick,
low scale, and recessed entries handsomely translated into the sleek architectural vocabulary of the 1960s in a modish
office building designed for the OMA.
This may well be the smoothest, hardest,
most precise red brick in town.

**43 260 St. George St. (detached house), Eden
Smith, 1905.**

The large suburban Cottage Style house
that Eden Smith made famous in Toronto
sat particularly well on a corner lot,
comfortably meandering down the long
frontage poking its tall chimneys up along
the way. Very, very cheery.

44b *101 Admiral Rd.*

45 *62 Bernard Ave.*

Admiral Crescent, as Admiral Road north of Bernard Avenue was first called, was laid out some years after the grid subdivision of the Annex. Its picturesque curve was designed to fit the northeasterly lots to the bend of Davenport Road on which they back.

44a 78 Admiral Rd. (detached house), Frederick H. Herbert, 1911.
Formal-looking Neo-Tudor with a handsome curved stone surround to the entrance.

44b 101 Admiral Rd. (detached house), Chadwick & Beckett, 1909.
Distinctive Neo-Tudor with pegged half-timbering and the pro forma Annex tower rendered in countrified stone and stucco.

45 Originally Gamble Geddes house, 62 Bernard Ave., 1891–92.
The first house in this block and one of the best English-inspired Queen Anne designs in Toronto. This sprightly, pretty house really does look as if it had emigrated from London's Bedford Park or some other equally salubrious and "Aesthetic" garden suburb. The architect is unknown; Geddes was listed in the assessment rolls as a "general agent."

Admiral Road between Bernard and Lowther is a narrow, quiet enclave laid out around a venerable tree. The tree is gone but the jog in the street remains.

46 German Consulate/originally Currie house/formerly George Deeks house, 77 Admiral Rd., Darling & Pearson, 1909–10; fence and garage, Darling & Pearson, 1911.
In 1910, the Georgian style was again a metaphor for the gracious and comfortable life, especially in the capable hands of a firm such as Darling & Pearson. This large handsome house was built for the Misses Margaret and Elizabeth Currie, who transferred it the following year to a contractor, George Deeks.

47 58–60 Admiral Rd. (double house), 1892–93.
62–64 Admiral Rd. (double house), 1892.
Same-plan speculative houses by builder Davidson Todd, quietly mixing up Romanesque/Queen Anne details. The lavish modernization at no. 62–64, using expansive panes of glass, is more assertive, but works well.

48a *59 Admiral Rd.*

52 *60 Lowther Ave.*

48a Originally R. Ross Bongard house, 59 Admiral Rd., Eden Smith, 1905–06.

Built for a stockbroker and one of the architect's bravura houses, this is surely one of the most sophisticated structures in Toronto. Smith has here rendered the ingredients of the English Cottage—white stucco walls, ribbons of casement windows, tall chimney, and sweeping roof— almost abstractly modern.

48b 57 Admiral Rd. (detached house), David Binder, 1987.

Just the opposite of the pseudo-Victorian mode prevalent for new houses in old neighbourhoods these days, no. 57 is a high modernist model whose ancestry can be traced to the Bauhaus. The pipes, glass blocks, curved wall, and white colour are typical of the form (present-day practitioners are often referred to as "Whites"). Slipped into no. 59's side garden (to which it relates very nicely), this refreshing surprise is surely the most up-to-date house in the Annex.

49 13–15 Admiral Rd. (double house), 1891. 14–16 Admiral Rd. (double house), 1892.

Twinned double houses by builder Davidson Todd with splendid wooden bric-a-brac frosting porches, balconies, and recessed galleries.

50 12 Admiral Rd. (detached house), Charles J. Gibson, 1896–97.

An eclectic melange of Queen Anne/Romanesque/Classical Revival forms and details for a very tall house of late date. In the 1920s, Lester B. Pearson toiled on the third floor here as a young history professor at the University of Toronto.

51 Originally C.J. Holman house, 75 Lowther Ave., Edmund Burke, 1892–93.

A particularly fine and well-preserved Annex house with tilehangings voluminously wrapping upper storeys and brick and stone meticulously anchoring a high first floor and basement. Holman practised law with Holman, Elliott & Pattullo.

52 Society of Friends Meeting House/ originally Miller Lash house, 60 Lowther Ave., Curry Sproatt & Rolph, 1906; rear addition, John Leaning, 1970.

A rousing reincarnation of the red-brick cube with freely adapted Georgian details. Especially fine is the stone portico and colonnade facing the west garden.

Walk 20: Annex West

The extension of Spadina Avenue north of Bloor Street is called Spadina Road (there are some who claim the pronunciation changes as well from long "i" Spa-di-na to more genteel Spa-dee-na). The extension was first plotted in the 1870s, but most houses did not begin to go up until the 1890s, at the same time and in the same Romanesque/Queen Anne mode as other parts of the Annex. Some 75 years later, Spadina Road was tagged by developers as a prime location for apartment construction because of its proximity to the then-abuilding Bloor Street subway. Many early houses were torn down to make way for these high-rises, as well as for construction of station facilities and of the subway itself (the flat ribbon of parking lots and parkettes that cuts a swath through the Annex just north of Bloor Street is that subway's above-ground legacy). Spadina Road fared better with construction of the Spadina line, which was run under the street in this neighbourhood, with an 1899 house rehabilitated as subway station at the juncture of Spadina and Kendal Avenues. Today the area is an interesting mix of the old and new, high and low, and—architecturally—good and definitely not so good.

1 9–11 Spadina Rd. (double house), 1889.
This large double house seems a bit pathetic standing all alone in the parking lot but it began life all alone in empty fields. The second house to go up on the east side of Spadina Road, it is in the tradition of symmetrical Bay-n-Gables built earlier in older parts of town, with only elaborate wooden balconies to mark it as part of the Queen Anne fancy so inimitably associated with the Annex.

2a Originally McColl-Frontenac Co., 8 Spadina Rd. (office building), John B. Parkin Associates, 1953.

Built for a long-established Canadian oil company, this two-storey box was one of Toronto's—indeed Canada's—first International Style buildings. Extremely plain and clad in glassy white brick with virtually zero detailing, it shows the early zeal with which the Parkin firm carried the less-is-more message to Canada.

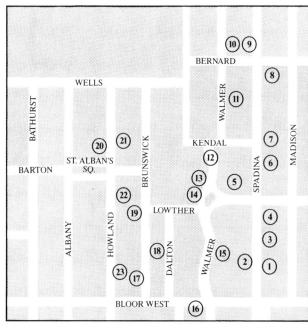

2a *8 Spadina Rd.*

4 *Spadina Gardens*

2b Native Canadian Centre of Toronto/origi-nally Ontario Bible College, 16 Spadina Rd., Mathers & Haldenby, 1928.
Wide gables, rectangular bays, Tudor arch, and ribbons of neat casement windows to disguise a utilitarian school as Jacobethan manor.

3 25 Spadina Rd. (double house), Frederick H. Herbert, 1897.
Splendid rehabilitation of this 1890s Annex house reveals afresh the sumptu-ous coursed brick, subtle play of win-dows, superb ornamented stone, and striking pressed-metal balcony. Pressed metal was an inexpensive turn-of-the-century substitute for stone and wood and in those days would have been painted to hide its lowly identity. Today, however, the verdigris-tinged tin perfectly fits the Post-Modern aesthetic—the greenish-blue colour is especially popular.

4 Spadina Gardens, 41–45 Spadina Rd. (apartment house), A. R. Denison, 1905–06.
One of the best—and best preserved—of Toronto's early apartment houses, with low scale, careful symmetry, and firm Classical Revival details projecting an air of quiet grandeur appropriate to this once prestigious residential thoroughfare (the Timothy Eaton house stood on the northwest corner of Spadina Road and Lowther from 1889 until 1965). The first apartment houses intrigued early tenants in the relative amplitude of their rooms, which on one floor could be laid out in ways impossible in a narrow multi-level row house. Spadina Gardens—note the stylized "S G" etched on the glass of the front doors—still retains these amenities, having been spared the minimalizing conversions prevalent elsewhere.

5 35 Walmer Rd. at Spadina Rd. (apartment house), Uno Prii, 1965.
The gargantuan apartment buildings that began to invade the Annex with the coming of the subway, unlike their 1910s, '20s, and '30s ancestors, showed little respect for the scale and spirit of existing streetscape. Many in this area also came under attack for their shoddy materials and garish appearance. Related to the flamboyant hotel architecture then being practised by Morris Lapidus in Miami Beach and elsewhere in the States, they were an early attempt to invigorate International Style's "boring box." His-tory may yet look kindly on these grand gestures; for now they seem, as one disenchanted New York critic bemoaned, "a long way from the beach."

6 69–71 Spadina Rd. (double house), Freder-ick H. Herbert, 1894.
Typically the two halves of Annex double houses were made to appear quite differ-ent in an attempt at picturesque asymme-try, and looking at no. 69–71 one can see why: one absurdly small corner tower popping up at roof level is funny; two are downright ludicrous.

6 *69-71 Spadina Rd.*

8 *151 Spadina Rd.*

7 TTC subway station, 85 Spadina Rd. (detached house), Robert M. Ogilvie, 1899; remodelled, Adamson Associates, 1977.

A Queen Anne subway station, and why not? We have the Toronto Historical Board to thank for promoting this felicitous re-use and preservation of endangered streetscape.

8 151 Spadina Rd. (detached house?), James A. Harvey, 1905-06.

Zoning laws prohibited it and assessment rolls list only single-family occupancy, but this building suspiciously resembles what in Boston would be called a three-decker: a three-family dwelling disguised as a single house. The higher than normal third storey, stained glass window in the second storey (as if for a second dining room), and bank of porches in the rear are clues.

9 106 Spadina Rd. (detached house), Arthur C. Barrett, 1905.

The architect was no Eden Smith—his façade is too disorganized—but he does use all the English Cottage ingredients: multi-light casement windows (replaced), stuccoed projecting bays, tall chimneys.

10 Originally James P. Watson house, 109 Walmer Rd., S. Hamilton Townsend, 1901-02.

This is one of the most evocative, appealing houses in the Annex. Though built on a relatively small lot, the angled wings and overhanging second storey make the house appear rambling and commodious. In addition, wooden shingles flow from the roof and wrap down over the walls in an expression of snugness and shelter further enhanced by the house's siting low to the ground amid much shrubbery. Watson was president of E.S. Currie Ltd., neckwear manufacturers on Wellington Street, where two years after this house was built the Great Toronto Fire of 1904 was to start [see Introduction, *AREA II*].

11a 95-97 and 91-93 Walmer Rd. (two double houses), 1893, 1894.

Twinned double houses with slightly sluggish façades more than compensated by a sprightly parade of capped dormers marching around the roof. The small-paned windows of no. 91 are replacements; Queen Anne houses were proud of their large plate glass.

11b 87 Walmer Rd. (detached house), 1907.

An English Cottage with swooping ski-jump roof.

11c 83-85 Walmer Rd. (double house), 1891.

A quintessential Annex double house with rocky plum-coloured sandstone foundation, round-arched entries and windows, red brick, and decorative terracotta in a taut composition that balances wide gable with polygonal tower, the latter capped with a lovely finial.

11d 81 Walmer Rd. (detached house), Frederick H. Herbert, 1896-98.

A tile-hung Queen Anne house graciously accommodating a Georgian pilastered triple window and pedimented porch.

10 *109 Walmer Rd.*

Walmer Road between Kendal and Bloor was conceived as a winding alternative to the grid of most of the city. The houses built here were similar to others in the suburb, but the serpentine course and more generous setback seems to impart to these "villas" an estate-like character.

12a 70 Walmer Rd. (detached house), Langley & Burke, 1891.

Closing the vista up lower Walmer Road and once boasting an eye-catching classically detailed porch at its centre, no. 70 could claim a prominence in the streetscape not usually found in a city planned like Toronto. Langley & Burke further utilized a conspicuous variety of textured and coloured materials—terracotta, brick, sandstone—to draw attention to their spacious concept. The architects also designed 59 and 61 Walmer Road, using similar patterns of masonry.

12b Originally John A. McKee house, 53 Walmer Rd., Frederick H. Herbert, 1898.

The pro forma Annex corner tower is here enlivened by a classical mushroom dome. Adamesque ornament around the tower, below the eaves, and in the pediment crowning the porch is especially notable in this house. It was made of pressed metal, a very useful material that permitted elaborate decorative effect at low cost. McKee was manager of Dodds Medicine Company.

12c Institute of Child Study/originally the Hon. Leighton Goldie McCarthy house, 45 Walmer Rd., 1932; school addition, Adamson Associates, 1955.

Red-brick Georgian Revival, more interesting for not being wholly symmetrical. Details and orchestration of parts are remarkably fine. McCarthy, who was Canadian ambassador to Washington in the 1940s, replaced two earlier houses on this site, one an Eden Smith design of 1894. On McCarthy's death in 1953, the house was inherited by the University of Toronto, which herein installed its famous child study institute.

13 44 Walmer Rd. (apartment house), Uno Prii, 1969.

Not as tall as no. 35 [20/5] by the same architect, but no less showy, with waving façade, metal cookie-cutter balcony railings, and giant concrete hoops arcing the entrance.

14 Walmer Road Baptist Church, 188 Lowther Ave. at Walmer Rd., Langley & Burke, 1888–92.

Neither cute country chapel nor lofty city cathedral, Walmer Road Baptist sits with assurance and solidity on its corner site, yet it is at the same time delicate and graceful. This was the largest Baptist church in Canada when it was built, and its distinctive battered tower beckoned some 1,500 well-to-do faithful. The church was founded by the Rev. Elmore Harris, uncle of Group of Seven artist Lawren Harris, and built by his family from the profits of Massey-Harris farm implements.

13 *44 Walmer Rd.*

15 21 Walmer Rd. (detached house), Frederick H. Herbert, 1894.
Another eclectic Herbert house, with too many quick and fussy decorative details for its own good. The "paneful" replacement windows only make matters worse.

16 Trinity United Church/originally Trinity Methodist Church, 427 Bloor St. W., Langley & Burke, 1889; Sunday school addition, Burke Horwood & White, 1909.
A structure of considerable grandeur, Trinity Methodist was the only church built in the Annex to use the Richardsonian Romanesque style that was being so liberally sprinkled on surrounding residences. The architects worked with great conviction here, taking equal care on both sides of the corner site, each featuring a wide central gable with rose window. The corner itself is resolutely defined by a tall, firm tower. Seating 2,000, Trinity Methodist was for many years the largest Protestant church in Canada. It was paid for by Eatons and other Methodist merchants who lived in the Annex.

The Annex area between Brunswick Avenue and Bathurst Street was originally part of Seaton Village. Streets had been laid out as early as the 1850s, but this part of the village remained largely uninhabited until some years after annexation by the City of Toronto in 1888. In fact, most of the houses—stout little affairs with polite façades—date to the turn of the century when classical details were finding favour anew.

17a 324–326 Brunswick Ave. (double house), 1906; no. 324 remodelled, 1981.
A timid double house saved by a grand marquee-like stepped gable.

17b 328–330 and 332–334 Brunswick Ave. (two double houses), 1899, 1897; porch additions, c. 1900.
Take away their overbearing classical porches and you can see what these large Queen Anne houses were intended to look like. But the porch salesman was very persuasive—who wants to look old-fashioned?—and the porches are practical.

18a 343 Brunswick Ave. (detached house), 1902.
By this date, classically detailed porches came with the houses. There's not another around like this, with its miniature triple columns.

18b 345 Brunswick Ave. (detached house), 1908.
La-di-da Ionic. Only 2½ feet high, but stylishly classical.

20a *Church of St.-Alban-the-Martyr*

19 346–348, 350, 352–354, 356, 358–360 Brunswick Ave. (two single and three double houses), 1886–87.

There are eight dwellings in a row here that predate all others on this block by some years. A few still retain their distinctive early Bay-n-Gable configuration; others have patched on all kinds of "modernizations," the picturesque tilehung Queen Anne box enveloping the Gothic gable of no. 356 for example.

20a Church of St.-Alban-the-Martyr, 100 Howland Ave., Richard C. Windeyer with John Falloon, 1885–1891.

Coming upon St. Alban's, its glorious Norman chancel looming rugged and momentous among flaking Victorian blocks, is like stumbling on a medieval ruin at Hampstead Heath. It was begun with high hopes in the 1880s as cathedral church of the Diocese of Toronto. St. James' [1/8] was technically a parish church and paled beside the grandiloquent plan for this cathedral modelled after the great St. Alban's in England. But funds ran out after only this small section had been built, and they still hadn't been raised in 1911 when the eminent American architect Ralph Adams Cram was called on to draw a new plan, nor by 1935 when the whole scheme was finally dropped. Today we are left with one-quarter of a cathedral and three-quarters of a private boys' school, which may or may not have known what it was doing in snubbing the church building when finishing off.

20b St. George's College/originally St. Alban's see house, 120 Howland Ave., 1887.

If there's to be a cathedral, there must be a house for the bishop, and this dignified yet delightful Queen Anne house was it.

21 99–101 Howland Ave. (double house), 1900.

The candle-snuffer house.

22 67–69 and 71–73 Howland Ave. (two double houses), 1902.

Double houses in Georgian Revival style are rare and these are quite fine, achieving a clarity and simplicity that make them very appealing.

23 21–23 Howland Ave. (double house), 1892.

An extravagant big double house. Second-storey tilehangings really do seem to be hanging, tacked like a picture frame onto the underlying brick visible at each end.

Area XI

Walk 21: Southwest Rosedale
Walk 22: Southeast Rosedale

Area XI

The popular perception of Rosedale as Toronto's earliest, wealthiest, and most beautiful residential community is not based on fact. The truth is, the area was late to develop, was more middle-class than upper, and—architecturally—was a jam-packed jumble.

The story begins with purchase by William Botsford Jarvis in 1824 of some 150 acres northeast of present-day Bloor and Yonge Streets. Jarvis was for many years sheriff of the Counties of York, Ontario, and Peel, a member of the legislative assembly, and—like so many of Upper Canada's ruling elite—a land speculator. A house [see 21/26] came with Jarvis's vast acreage, and it was here that he brought his young bride Mary Powell in 1827. That Mary was inspired to name their new seigniory Rosedale after the wild roses she saw blooming there is a much-told tale. She seems to have taken to the land, laying out orchards and gardens necklaced with winding horse trails and meandering footpaths. Delightful as it sounds, the estate was extremely difficult to reach. From Yonge Street, a rough track wended its circuitous way through wooded brush and the ravine creek before starting up a steep incline to the house, the perilous ascent and descent of which were local lore. Even the Jarvises seem to have become disenchanted and went off to live in England for a time.

In 1852 Mary died. Down beyond the tumbling ravine thriving Yorkville, of which Rosedale was geographically and politically a part, was about to become an incorporated village [*AREA IX*]. The time seemed ripe to sell at least part of the estate. The sheriff, ever mindful of the difficulty of access, laid out Park Road complete with bridge across the creek [21/1] and began parcelling out some of his rolling wooded realm. Some 100 acres were subdivided into 62 building lots arrayed around seven handsomely curving streets that more or less followed the crests of the ravines (there was not much else they could do given the rough topography). Officially named Rose Park, the subdivision encompassed present-day Avondale and Rosedale Roads, Crescent Road, South Drive, and Park Road. The gracious scheme was expected to develop quickly without doubt, but it didn't. Toronto slid into an economic depression in 1855 from which it did not recover for ten years. In all that time only one house was built in Rosedale [21/5].

Nevertheless, a fresh handful of land speculators soon appeared to sell other parts of what we know today as Rosedale, including sections severed from Francis Cayley's 120-acre Drumsnab grant [22/17]. Most ambitious (but least successful) of this group was Edgar Jarvis, the sheriff's nephew. Edgar Jarvis began in 1866 by building a fine Italianate house on Park Road [22/1] to advertise his proposed high-class tract. He then laid out Elm and Maple Avenues and planted 300 of the requisite namesake trees. When the sheriff's Park Road bridge collapsed in 1872 (killing a deliveryman in the process), Edgar built a new white-painted wooden bridge over the ravine at what is now Mount Pleasant Road. A decade later he added an iron bridge at Glen Road. He set aside a large lot on Sherbourne Street North for lacrosse grounds—then Canada's national pastime. With the Scottish Ontario and Manitoba Land Company he erected the North Iron Bridge over the Park Drive ravine—an engineering marvel of the 1880s—and laid out streets in North Rosedale. And still the buyers did not come. As late as 1885, two years after most of Yorkville had been annexed by Toronto, there were only about 40 houses in all of Rosedale, of which perhaps ten could be called "grand." Six of these still stand [21/4; 22/1, /2]. Late Victorian Toronto's preferred residential neighbourhoods were upper Jarvis and Bloor Streets, Queen's Park and St. George Street, and Parkdale. Years later Edgar's wife was to explain ruefully that Toronto ladies thought Rosedale was "too far from town; too difficult to find domestics who would go there; too lonely."

Early watercolour shows Severn Creek and thick, tangled brush of Rosedale Ravine, c. 1860.

An economic downturn between 1892 and 1900 squelched the boomlet of the late 1880s when a few Richardsonian Romanesque/Queen Anne houses similar to those going up in the Annex were constructed [*AREA X*]. And so it was only in this century that Rosedale truly began.

In the early 1900s Toronto real estate went wild. In Rosedale, four lots became 20. A housing shortage combined with plentiful money meant that scores of houses were put up and purchased immediately. A newly affluent middle class was eager to grab onto that conspicuous, almost morally imperative, symbol of their arrival—home ownership. And Rosedale by now had a third bridge spanning those barrier ravines, this one at Sherbourne Street over which ran electric streetcars to carry businessmen to and from downtown offices. (Automobiles were still an unreliable novelty on the unpaved streets and many an Edwardian home was constructed here with neither coach nor "motor" house—a deficiency that has led more recently to some very creative garages.)

Unfortunately, this decade of Rosedale's greatest growth was one of architectural confusion. A local journalist, trying to describe these Edwardian residences some years later, wrote: "The main concern in building a house was to make it different. If it was a high house, it was made lower by draping a bit of roof around it.... If it was low, strange things happened to the chimney. If the logical place for the doorway was the front, they contrived it on the side."

This hectic boom was also responsible for Rosedale's variety of frontage widths and house sizes. Of interest in this regard is that no matter how narrow or wide the lot, nor how small or big the structure, almost all the

Ornamental North Iron Bridge spanning the ravine between South and North Rosedale was a favourite post–1880 "photo opportunity."

A cleaned up Rosedale Ravine, c. 1909, boasted newly widened and fenced road stretching under Sherbourne Street bridge.

houses were constructed close to the street and to one another. Even the few owners who acquired fairly large lots built houses off to one side, undoubtedly in speculative-crazed anticipation of "selling off the garden" (almost all eventually did). In their streetline massing, Rosedale houses may have been emulating semi-urban British subdivisions such as Bedford Park. And like Bedford Park, most houses were middle and upper-middle class. The few mansions built here by the very wealthy in this period were decidedly the exception and even they had few walled or grand-entrance pretensions about them. This neighbourly mix set a tone for Rosedale that was to continue through the next, more architecturally distinguished stages of its development.

In 1909, the Canadian trade publication *Construction* pronounced the curving blocks of Rosedale's newly laid out Chestnut Park "Toronto's loveliest suburb." Conceived all of a piece—"both consistent and charming," enthused *Construction*—Chestnut Park [21/15] was a preview of the two styles into which pre World War I Canadian architecture would eventually sort itself: picturesque Neo-Tudor and classical Neo-Georgian. The influences came primarily from Britain, where interest in national roots had prompted harking back to post-medieval vernacular cottages and manor houses and to the buildings of Christopher Wren for inspiration. It was not copyist architecture, however, because new attitudes about craftsmanship, use of space, and relation to site generated quite experimental work.

Allied to the notion of national style was the idea of tying a building to the land. An organic relationship between house and surroundings, between city and country, was the goal. Now near the urban action, but with its natural ravine setting, Rosedale neatly fitted this new ideal and the community rallied to retain its ambience. Residents, for example, voted overwhelmingly against a viaduct across the Don Valley when one was first proposed in 1912, citing fears that a massive transportation conduit would ruin the Rosedale Valley landscape and bring too much "city" too close.

During World War I, residential construction in Toronto virtually stopped, but in Rosedale there was very little buildable land left anyway. When peace returned, a few enclaves such as Cluny Drive opened up [21/26, /27], and here can be found imposing examples of the eclectic "period" styles popular across North America in the '20s and '30s: a more mechanical Tudor and Georgian along with French and Italian Renaissance, Spanish, and California Mission.

Then in the 1940s the area began to lose its appeal. Designed to be cared for by servants and with few garages or driveways, the houses were considered by many "unsuitable for modern living." Though a strong sense of community continued to anchor a fair number

Arbour Glen was constructed down into the ravine during Rosedale's 1950s apartment boom.

of the old families (some now into the second generation), high taxes and expensive maintenance turned others away. During World War II when a housing shortage led to relaxed zoning regulations, some 200 Rosedale homes were converted to rooming houses and nursing facilities. After the war the old places increasingly were purchased with the intent of tearing them down and putting up apartment buildings. Apartments also began to appear on the fringes of the ravines.

In the early '60s, the bloom came back to Rosedale. The commodious houses, now relatively inexpensive, began to attract growing numbers of middle-class families with young children. These enthusiastic newcomers joined with the old guard to slow conversions and virtually ban apartment construction. (No stranger to politics, the Rosedale [Ratepayers] Association is the oldest in the city, having been founded in 1903.) Later, in the 1970s, ratepayers successfully opposed rows of townhouses west of Glen Road. The 1980s have seen some, but not all, of the rooming houses revert to owner-occupied dwellings. Still others are being modified for upscale rental and condominium units. To their credit, those responsible for these rehabilitations have for the most part had the good sense to respect the exterior integrity of the original Edwardian architecture.

Rosedale's byways are beginning to look again as they did in the 1910s when one of them was described as "a typical residential street of the better sort, where the satisfied burgher lives in substantial, cleanly comfort." And that's the truth.

Walk 21: Southwest Rosedale

Rosedale Ravine was a formidable wilderness in the 19th century. The first rough track to penetrate its heavily wooded terrain crept from Yonge and Belmont Streets through a creek and tortuously up to Sheriff Jarvis's homestead [see 21/26]. In 1834 Jarvis cleared a northern approach via what is now Roxborough Street East, while Francis Cayley hacked out an eastern path from Parliament Street to Drumsnab [22/17].

About this time two brewers were attracted to the flowing creek. John Severn established his venture at Davenport Road and Yonge Street, and Joseph Bloor located his southeast of present-day Park and Rosedale Valley Roads. This latter lasted until the 1840s, after which the ravine reverted to gambolling ground for adventurous youngsters and hideaway for criminals and tramps. The first true road, made of corduroy logs, was installed by Sheriff Jarvis in 1853 on the eve of the Rose Park subdivision, ergo the name Park Road. It served as primary entrance to Rosedale until its creek bridge collapsed in 1872. Three new bridges were erected over the next 20 years [see Introduction AREA XI].

By the turn of the century, the children's idyllic retreat had become a blighted open sewer, prompting the city to expropriate the "pestilential valley." The creek-cum-sewer was sent underground and Rosedale Ravine Drive widened and paved to become Rosedale Valley Road. The ravine was further tamed by extensive landfill in 1929-31. The city has maintained Rosedale Ravine as parkland ever since, though in 1986 there was talk that this would be a perfect place for "affordable housing."

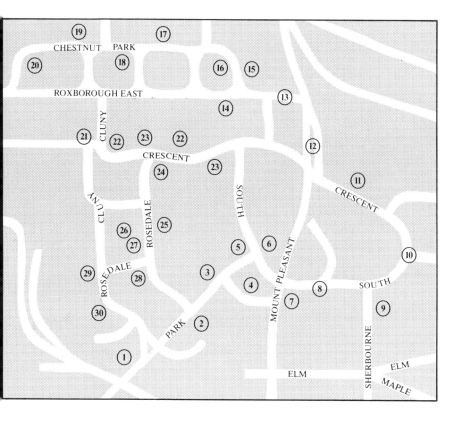

4 *3 Meredith Crescent*

5 *124 Park Rd.*

2 107 Park Rd. (detached house), Bruce Wright, 1936; addition, David Craddock, 1985.

111 Park Rd. (detached house), James A. Murray, 1951-52.

Rosedale was virtually begun and finished between 1890 and 1930, after which there was no buildable land left. Recent construction has therefore been on the "edges," where fresh lots have appeared now and again. These two moderns are good examples. No. 107 is one of Toronto's first and few Art Moderne houses. In any other city the cladding would have been stucco, but the buff brick used here does make for fascinating quoins, cornice, and belt course. (Many Toronto Art Moderne buildings have this Georgian cast.) Cited in 1956 as among the best post-war buildings in Canada, no. 111 is a California/B.C.-inspired standout. This house is almost alone as a one-storey structure in Rosedale.

3 100 Park Rd. (detached house), 1888.

104 Park Rd. (detached house), 1888.

108 Park Rd. (detached house), 1890.

110 Park Rd. (detached house), 1888.

114 Park Rd. (detached house), 1888.

A muscular quintet of Richardsonian Romanesque/Queen Anne abodes, these are "city" houses—they seem out of place on this sloping countrified road. Nevertheless, they mark the first consistent development of Rosedale, a depression-plagued push that petered out soon after, which is why today Rosedale doesn't look like the Annex.

4 Originally "Lorne Hall" (William Davies residence), 3 Meredith Crescent, Langley Langley & Burke, 1876.

An elegant amalgamation of invention and order, Second Empire was the perfect architectural expression of entrepreneurs longing to be gentlemen. Here, Second Empire's lofty mansard, swelling bays, and imposing portico provided the aura for pioneering pork packer William Davies. Designed by Henry Langley, this stately mansion still impresses despite diminished siting. In 1876 it was one of about 10 houses in all of Rosedale, grandly surveying uninhabited woodland from hilltop aerie.

5 Formerly George Reginald Geary house, 124 Park Rd., 1855; second storey added, 1863; renovated, 1987-ongoing.

This was the first house built in the 1854 Rose Park subdivision, and with demolition of Jarvis's villa in 1905 [see 21/26], it now ranks as the oldest in Rosedale after Drumsnab [22/17]. The house was originally only one storey but even then it must have spelled gracious living with beautifully proportioned Georgian front and spacious high-ceilinged rooms. First owner in 1855 was lawyer James Davis but the property is more closely identified with one-time Toronto mayor George Reginald Geary, who occupied it 1927–1954. Let's hope recent renovations can reclaim this handsome manor as crown of the community.

8b *South Drive 1900s houses*

6 Originally James How house, 48 South Dr., 1876; altered, Gordon S. Adamson, 1945. Originally John Thom house, 54 South Dr., 1880.
Among the few houses constructed here prior to 1883 and annexation by the City of Toronto, these two High Victorian dandies stand almost alone in Rosedale as examples of this picturesque genre. First owners were a dentist and a lawyer. Unfortunately, modern-day owners have cloaked and clipped the original zip. The second storey of no. 54's vigorous Gothic Revival patterned brick is now clamped in plaster. At no. 48, crisp strapwork and cornice are clogged with whitewash and the lookout tower is only a memory.

7 Rosedale Presbyterian Church, 129 Mount Pleasant Rd., Chapman & McGiffin, 1909-10; addition, Mathers & Haldenby, 1954-55.
Rosedale Presbyterian, solemnly built of stone with smooth craftsmanly details, is unmistakably early 20th-century Gothic. It was planned that the east and centre blocks would serve for services only until a larger church wing could be built to the west. These plans were thwarted—by church union in 1925, which drew off close to two-fifths of the members, and by widening of Mount Pleasant Road in 1948, which took about 55 feet of buildable land. "Temporary" chapel, with resounding hammerbeams and McCausland's stained glass, became permanent church. In 1955 a truncated extension finally provided the long-awaited Sunday School.

8a Originally James Jermyn house, 72 South Dr., A. Frank Wickson, 1899.
Last-gasp 19th-century historismus with heavy charms that are starting to pall. Jermyn was listed in city directories as a farmer but this ain't no farmhouse.

8b 67 South Dr. (detached house), J. Francis Brown, 1907-08.
69 South Dr. (detached house), E.J. Lennox, 1902.
73 South Dr. (detached house), A. Frank Wickson, 1900-01.
75 South Dr. (detached house), 1898.
79 South Dr. (detached house), J. Francis Brown, 1902.
Although built just after no. 72 across the street, these five are clearly of another era. Victorian furbelows have been lightened up, thinned out, or simply left off. Crisp white-painted details are the order of the day, though in this period of experiment they represent a confusing combo of classical (columned porches, Palladian windows) and picturesque (parapeted gables, half-timbering). This was the decade of the area's greatest growth and these houses are the very stuff of Rosedale.

9 *35 Sherbourne St. N.*

10a *103 South Dr.*

9 Formerly "Heyroyd" (Banks Brothers residence), 35 Sherbourne St. N., c. 1866; altered later.

This urbane house, today looking almost American Federal with large glazed areas, polygonal bays, and delicate porch, is one of Toronto's most charming. It's relatively old, as many fireplaces, high ceilings, and thick brick walls attest; it was only the seventh or eighth house built in Rosedale. But the original has been much altered and exactly when the house acquired its present polish is unclear. From 1891 to 1895 the place was rented by the Board of Education for classrooms before the area's first public school opened on Scarth Road.

10a Originally George Newman house, 103 South Dr., Robert J. Edwards, 1898–1900.

Clear, coherent, and vibrating with earthy directness, this delightful house is in a class by itself. Almost beyond "style," it simply bespeaks "shelter." Newman was a principle at Dominion Express Company.

10b 181 Crescent Rd. (detached house), Gordon & Helliwell, 1901–02.

182 Crescent Rd. (detached house), Percy H. Finney, 1909.

180 Crescent Rd. (detached house), Mark Hall, 1900–01.

Three more houses typical of the transitional early 1900s. Often labelled "Free Classic" for their rediscovery of classical details, they might as easily be tagged "Free Picturesque" for their putative love affair with Tudor. The deep protective

porches, assuming the social function of Victorian vestibule and entrance hall, represent a new reassigning of space. Look for these attributes in all the houses hereabout.

11a Originally Charles Boone house, 170 Crescent Rd., Symons & Rae, 1907–08.

Often illustrated as the epitome of Rosedale, the Boone house is in fact singular, one of only a handful of lavish homes built here. Jacobethan's powerful volumes, impeccable brickwork, and conspicuous stone dressings were just the ticket for those like contractor Boone who wanted reassuring historical copies. Partners William Symons and William Rae designed many Rosedale houses, but none nearly as fine as this regal Neo-Tudor.

11b Originally Edward Fisher house, 166 Crescent Rd., Burke & Horwood, 1899–1900.

Through 25 years of partnership between 1894 and 1919, Edmund Burke and John C.B. Horwood were Society's architects of choice, turning out competent if uninspired residences to approximate all the latest trends. In 1899 the trend was uncertain and so is this flighty arrangement of bays and vaults, gables and arches, windows and doors. Fisher was musical director at the Toronto Conservatory of Music, whose new building on College Street the architects were also just polishing off.

11a *170 Crescent Rd.*

11d *Mooredale House*

11c Originally Lewis Ord house/formerly Sir Henry Drayton house, 162 Crescent Rd., 1882; altered and enlarged, Mackenzie Waters, 1932.

Although Sheriff Jarvis sold his acreage to all and sundry, many parcels found their way into family hands. The sheriff's three daughters all speculated in Rosedale real estate. This splendid lot was acquired by daughter Sarah and her husband Lewis Ord. Though not constructed until 1882, their stout yellow-brick Victorian country manor was among the first in this slow-to-develop subdivision. Much denatured by later changes, including removal of "cumbersome veranda and unsightly gables" in the 1930s, the place still impresses with gracious siting and reserved air.

11d Mooredale House/originally Sir Frank Baillie house, 146 Crescent Rd., Sproatt & Rolph, 1902–03.

Like the similarly Jacobethan extravaganza up the block at no. 170 [21/11a], this is a "big house" anomaly in Rosedale. Here Sproatt & Rolph used meticulous brickwork firmly gripped by stone dressings to turn an asymmetric design into something quietly monumental. Yet there is a Rosedalian lack of hauteur: the proto-colonnade reads more like whimsy than auspicious entry. When captain of industry Frank Baillie died suddenly in 1920, his widow sold no. 146. In 1930 it was slated for demolition to make way for the Jarvis Street extension, but survived to become home to the Rosedale-Moore Park Community Association in the late 1940s.

12 Mount Pleasant Road. This roadway cutting through the heart of Rosedale was first planned in 1930. Part of a major public works program that envisioned arteries city-wide, its goal was to whisk drivers between downtown offices and new north suburbs. (The plan originally called for streetcars on the extension as well!) However, local opposition and Depression-era cutbacks stalled the project for decades. Finally opened in 1950, it became Toronto's first expressway. Amazingly, only five houses were demolished in the process.

13a Originally J. Wilson Siddall house, 171 Roxborough St. E., J. Wilson Siddall, 1902–03; enlarged later.

English architect Siddall came to Canada to work on Confederation Life [6/14], but most of his practice was residential, no doubt garnered from this Tudoresque advertisement for himself. The house's yellow brick, though popular in the 1850s and '60s as a stand-in for stone, had not been used in Toronto for decades. In Britain, Arts and Crafts architects were specifying light-coloured stucco in similar protest against Late Victorian red brick.

13b *174 Roxborough St. E.*

15b *84 Chestnut Park Rd.*

13b 170 Roxborough St. E. (detached house), 1889.

172 Roxborough St. E. (detached house), 1889.

174 Roxborough St. E. (detached house), 1889-90.

176 Roxborough St. E. (detached house), 1889.

Put up during Rosedale's short-lived spurt of the late 1880s, these are the sort of rich, frolicsome Queen Annes that Edwardian architects were eager to renounce. Recent whitewashing owners at nos. 172 and 176 seem to have renounced them too. Shame. Still glowingly ruddy no. 174 was originally home to the Rev. Benjamin Thomas, pastor of Jarvis Street Baptist Church.

14 141-147 Roxborough St. E. (four-house row), 1889-90.

After 1904 and introduction of land-use bylaws (an idea borrowed from Germany), Rosedale became almost exclusively an area of single, detached houses. That makes this row of four an oddity even before one considers its nervous front. Actually it's that very Queen Anne lack of row-house repetition that allows it to dance so nimbly in the neighbourhood today.

15 Chestnut Park was the name given to his property by Sen. David Macpherson. A purchaser into the northwest quadrant of Rose Park in 1855, Macpherson acquired adjacent lands as well, where he had a villa facing Yonge Street. On his death in 1895, his trustees hired architect Alfred E. Boultbee and his barrister brother Horatio to create and manage the distinctive development we know today. In concert with architect Hamilton Townsend, they laid out Chestnut Park's curving blocks with special lamp standards, brick sidewalks, and no electricity poles (the enclave was planned to run on gas). Boultbee and Townsend also designed many of the houses.

All went well and quickly. By 1909, U.S. city planners visiting Toronto could adjudge Chestnut Park "the most restful and artistic section [of this] model city...the epitome of suburban beauty." It still is.

15a Originally James Mickleborough house, 86 Chestnut Park Rd., Burke & Horwood, 1904-05.

All the name architects scurried to Chestnut Park, including much-in-demand Burke & Horwood. Here, commissioned by the president of a wholesale woollens company, they drew a textbook design of the "new architecture": good proportions, simple detail, local materials, natural landscaping. In short, unobtrusive. Note for example the way the multi-paned windows enhance the impression of surface smoothness rather than digging holes in the sleek brickwork as single-paned windows might have done.

16 *77 Chestnut Park Rd.*

17a *56 Chestnut Park Rd.*

15b Originally George Fensom house, 84 Chestnut Park Rd., Ellis & Connery, 1905.

This house is good demonstration of early 1900s' interest in tying house to site. Though the first floor is raised above ground level as in earlier days, a little hillock has been raised to meet it, thereby "naturalizing" the approach. Disposal of the garden was considered part of an architect's job in those days. The owner was Fensom of Otis-Fensom Elevator Company.

15c Originally Harold Gagnier house, 82 Chestnut Park Rd., Langley & Langley, 1904.

Publisher Harold Gagnier's frozen-looking confection is quite eccentric, but at least they got the fenestration right. "No one feature imparts so great an element of the picturesque as the casement window," intoned architectural journals such as Gagnier's own *Construction*. But many North Americans were wary, citing difficulty in cleaning, drafts, and burglars! The attached garage is a later addition; garages were generally built separate from houses well into the 1930s. In this case, fastidious homeowners cited smells.

16 77 Chestnut Park Rd. (detached house), S. Hamilton Townsend, 1906–07.

The flat, taut exterior of this daring design reflects a powerful opening-up inside. Townsend's great box seems about to burst. The architect is in step here with Frank Lloyd Wright, who, in the American Midwest, has already pushed the box as far as it will go and broken through with long outstretching wings. Townsend didn't pursue that; instead he melded "Prairie box" with "Cottage naturalness" to create an image all his own. Look for his tautness, horizontality, wide eaves, stretch of windows, and signature front-door canopy throughout Rosedale.

17a Originally John McCarter house, 56 Chestnut Park Rd., Wickson & Gregg, 1908–09.

Termed "modern English" at the time, Neo-Tudor at its best exhibits a cleanness and precision that continues to appeal. Typical features seen here include bold rectangular bay, grand front-facing gable, horizontal fenestration (which should have been casement throughout), and aura of unity between house and garden. McCarter was president of Eclipse Whitewear, for whose premises on King Street West [4/9] he also commissioned Wickson & Gregg.

18b *43 Chestnut Park Rd.*

18c *39 Chestnut Park Rd.*

17b Originally S.B. Gundy house, 50 Chestnut Park Rd., Alfred E. Boultbee, 1905–06.

While many Toronto architects were toying with Tudor, another group was seeking to regenerate Georgian. Contemporary magazines highlighted the style, but the wonderful houses that Alfred Boultbee designed in Chestnut Park (including this for publisher S.B. Gundy), look as if they've jumped straight off the pages of an 18th-century pattern book for the gaily elegant Georgian of Robert Adam.

17c 48 Chestnut Park Rd. (originally detached house), E.J. Lennox, 1903–04.

Many houses in Rosedale are being divided into multiple-unit dwellings, thankfully much better done than this messy breakup where so little remains of Lennox's original concept. The special neighbourhood that is Chestnut Park deserves more consideration.

18a 45 Chestnut Park Rd. (originally detached house), Curry & Sparling, 1915.

Happily, here original Neo-Georgian symmetry, hipped roof, and harmonious stone portico are all elegantly in place. Recent conversion to three units meant appending wings to the sides, laudable for their up-front honesty—they look exactly like modern, appended wings.

18b Originally John McKenzie house, 43 Chestnut Park Rd., Alfred E. Boultbee, 1905–06.

Designed for a university professor, this is another of Boultbee's deft Adamesque delights which in 1906 you could have bought for $7,000. Despite the confident revival exterior, these Neo-Georgians were often extremely innovative inside.

18c Originally Norman McLeod house, 39 Chestnut Park Rd., S. Hamilton Townsend, 1906–07.

In its bold shape, sharp definition of smooth surfaces, and low band of ground-floor windows tying structure to site, no. 39 is avant-garde but not anti-historical. The appeal of English Cottage Style was just this knitting of trendy and traditional. A year or two earlier, architects were designing stables for Chestnut Park, but by 1906 the detached "automobile house" seen here was more usual.

19a 34 Chestnut Park Rd. (detached house), Eden Smith, 1904–06.

24 Chestnut Park Rd. (detached house), S. Hamilton Townsend, 1905–06.

Eden Smith and Hamilton Townsend both designed in English Cottage Style, but Smith's houses seem more loose and low key, which makes them easy to forget. Townsend's, on the other hand, are a precise working out of one rigid program, and the results, therefore, are more compelling.

19b *20 Chestnut Park Rd.*

21a *52 Cluny Dr.*

19b Originally John Falconbridge house, 22 Chestnut Park Rd., Alfred E. Boultbee, 1904–05.

Originally Robert Greig house, 20 Chestnut Park Rd., Alfred E. Boultbee, 1905–06.

While three-storey Adam houses constitute a sizable and lofty body of American colonial architecture, revival examples are everywhere rare. With correct 12-pane windows, fanlights, porticoed entrances, even iron handrailings, these extraordinarily lovely reproductions deserve universal reknown.

20a Originally William Carrick house, 15 Chestnut Park Rd., Langley & Langley, 1910–11.

The stone front together with tiled roof and bracketed eaves mark no. 15 as Second Renaissance Revival. Since Georgian style also has roots in the Renaissance, it's not surprising this house shares the symmetry and repose of Neo-Georgians. In the 1970s it was one of Rosedale's many rooming houses.

20b Originally James Ryrie house, 1 Chestnut Park Rd., Burke Horwood & White, 1912–15.

The location of Sen. Macpherson's Victorian villa (which after his death served as St. Andrew's College for a time) was the spot chosen by James Ryrie to put up the most stately home in Chestnut Park. His lovely loggiaed Neo-Georgian gem was perfect foil for the president of the most successful jewellery company in Canada [see 5/3b]. When Rosedale's large-house

appeal began to fade after World War II, there were plans to adapt Ryrie's 30 redoubtable rooms to medical offices, but fortunately that came to naught. Today they comprise condominium units boasting much of the original interior detail and an exterior as ravishing as ever.

21a 52 Cluny Dr. (detached house), S. Hamilton Townsend, 1902–04.

For the ceremonial-entrance crossroads of Crescent and Cluny, Townsend designed one of the estate's most alluring residences. Many of his English Cottage Style orchestrations are here, but rendered in field and cut stone, simplicity was not cheap. The house stood empty for several years before seducing banker John Dixon. No. 50 Cluny Drive was originally his "motor house."

21b 49 Cluny Dr. (detached house), S. Hamilton Townsend, 1901–02.

A magic show of English Cottage Style sleight of hand. Though no. 49 seems sweet and simple, it's a complicated conjuring of precisely balanced line and mass, substance and shadow. The mystery evoked by that deep pocket of porch is delicious.

21c 48 Cluny Dr. (detached house), Eden Smith, 1902–04.

Construction reported this as "Toronto's First Clinker Brick Residence," and the "artistic" misshapen masonry would have been a natural for folky English Cottage Style architect Eden Smith. No. 48's tacky garage is also a clinker.

21b *49 Cluny Dr.*

23 *68–70 Crescent Rd.*

22 60 Crescent Rd. (detached house), Sproatt & Rolph, 1901.

76–78 Crescent Rd. (originally detached house), 1892.

80 Crescent Rd. (detached house), 1896–97.

84 Crescent Rd. (detached house), Langley & Langley, 1899–1900.

88 Crescent Rd. (detached house), 1884.

As much as one tries to impart that most Rosedale houses were middle-class moderate, it's the biggies that attract. Here are five of interest for their girth and/or resident go-getters.

No. 60—becoming more grandiose with each renovation—was boyhood home of physicist Charles Wright, remembered for his participation in Scott's ill-fated South Pole expedition of 1912.

Once-Romanesque no. 76–78 first belonged to Arthur Harvey, an insurance agent who built, occupied, and sold a number of Rosedale residences. In the 1920s this house was occupied by Henry Pellatt after he was forced to give up Casa Loma castle for back taxes.

No. 80 is best known for occupancy in the early 1900s by Ontario Justice Featherston Osler, one of the four influential Osler brothers [see 22/26].

And no. 84, designed by eminent Victorian architect Henry Langley in late partnership with son Charles, is notable today as one of the grumpy few in Rosedale to be gated.

No. 88 is a great Victorian villa and the second oldest on Crescent Road, having been built by David Pender. co-owner of a carriage-supply house, shortly after the 1882 Ord house [21/11c].

23 Originally Lewis/Haldenby house, 68–70 Crescent Rd., Mathers & Haldenby, 1926.

Originally Mrs. Peleg Howland house, 95 Crescent Rd., Langley & Howland, 1931.

One shouldn't leave Crescent Road without interjecting Haldenby's unique double house for himself and Langley & Howland's nifty construction for Howland's mother. Rosedale was well built-up by this time and these two Neo-Georgians were slipped into side gardens (Haldenby's that of his in-laws, who later came to share the place).

24 Castlemere Apartments, 75 Crescent Rd., Henry Simpson, 1912; renovated, 1988.

"Apartments are a modern necessity," editorialized the *Globe* soon after the Castlemere went up, and—still unacceptable to many—it came to represent the form in Rosedale, being referred to for years as simply "The Apartment." In its experimental layout and mix of classical/Tudor details, the Castlemere is not unlike many houses of the era.

25 Rosedale Road, laid out in 1854 as part of the Rose Park subdivision, was the first thoroughfare in Rosedale to attract builders in any number. Early construction took place on the east side of the road as the Jarvis villa and outbuildings dominated the west.

25a Originally George White cottage, 37 Rosedale Rd., c. 1870; renovated and enlarged, William Fleury, c. 1950.

25e *45 Rosedale Rd.*

Originally Oliver Goodwin house, 27 Rosedale Rd., 1871; renovated and enlarged, c. 1950.

A deep setback is a good sign of an early date, as these two bear out. No. 37 probably began as a workshed for White, who seems to have market-gardened here as well as being a jack-of-all-trades with a house, shop, and stable in Yorkville. He later built a larger house nearby where his widow lived in the 1880s [demolished, see 21/25d]. No. 27 began as home to carpenter Oliver Goodwin, sometimes listed in directories as a music teacher.

25b 41–43 Rosedale Rd. (double house), 1881.

Many Second Empire double houses were being built in the 1880s, but this is the only one to find its way to Rosedale. Essentially an urban form, no. 41–43 must have appeared strange on this rural road. In any event, it was never duplicated.

25c Originally George Murray house, 47 Rosedale Rd., 1889.

Rosedale's first genuine development in the late 1880s featured Richardsonian Romanesque/Queen Anne houses similar to those then taking root in the Annex. This, for gas fixtures manufacturer Murray, was one of the most felicitous anywhere—there is a delicacy and buoyancy here not often seen in this rugged style.

25d Originally Capt. Samuel Crangle house, 35 Rosedale Rd., Gordon & Helliwell, 1892.

This large ship-shape Queen Anne for the superintendent of the St. Lawrence & Chicago Steam Navigation Company replaced an earlier house of c. 1880 on this site [see 21/25a]. Contrary to popular belief, tearing down one house to build another is very uncommon in Rosedale.

25e Originally Charles Niles house, 45 Rosedale Rd., Chadwick & Beckett, 1905.

Put up during the area's crucial decade of growth, this Neo-Tudor was one of Rosedale's most architecturally progressive. Today, over 80 years later, it still looks wonderfully fresh, with bold windows, brilliant arrises, and sparkling, precise ornament.

26 *Rosedale Villa, from a watercolour of 1835*   **27** *52 Rosedale Rd.*

26 "Rosedale Villa" (originally Sheriff William Botsford Jarvis residence), near 9 Cluny Dr., 1821; additions, John G. Howard, 1835; further additions later; demolished 1905.

Set prominently on the heights above the ravine, Sheriff Jarvis's house must have been an impressive sight to Yonge Street travellers in the 19th century. When acquired by Jarvis in 1824, it was a two-storey roughcast foursquare. With the advent of marriage and blossoming family of five (not to mention real estate profits), he enlarged it to take in bedroom wings, conservatory, and wide veranda, as well as servants' quarters, and stables.

After his wife's death in 1852, the sheriff moved to Toronto and the villa housed variously his three daughters and their families (Merediths, Nantons, and Ords), or sat empty. In 1878, Sen. Macpherson added it to his holdings [see 21/15] and later *his* daughter and her husband Percival Ridout lived here until the villa was demolished in 1905. In 1922, Cluny Drive was cut through the property, creating Rosedale's last square block available for development.

27 Originally R.R. McLaughlin house, 52 Rosedale Rd., Mathers & Haldenby, 1935.

Originally Alex Gooderham house, 48 Rosedale Rd., Sproatt & Rolph, 1922-23.

Originally John Turnbull house, 44 Rosedale Rd., 1926-27.

Originally Samuel McKeown house, 40 Rosedale Rd., 1929-30.

Originally Arthur Holden house, 36 Rosedale Rd., 1923.

The Rosedale Road '20s and '30s "period" houses were intriguing for their old-fashioned show of Renaissance urns, Georgian sidelights, Tudor half-timbering, and such. But these houses *were* modern in their smooth, simple shapes; in their large rooms and expansive interiors; and in their rearrangements, which now might put the kitchen in front to give over the whole of the rear to a large "living room" situated to gain privacy and perhaps open onto terrace or pergola—all new ideas.

28 Originally "Idlewold" (Walter Brown residence)/formerly Arthur Harvey house/formerly Henry Osborne house, 23 Rosedale Rd., 1857-58; altered, c. 1890; enlarged, Alfred E. Boultbee, 1911; renovations, B. Napier Simpson, 1977.

A charming Italianate house that retains its antique ambience despite many alterations. Brown, a banker, was the second to build in Rose Park. In the 1870s and '80s the owner was insurance agent Arthur Harvey, who broke up the property into 18 lots before moving on to Crescent Road [see 21/22]. Boultbee's additions for stockbroker Henry Osborne in 1911

27 *44 Rosedale Rd.*   **28** *Garden, 23 Rosedale Rd.*

included a large drawing room with Arts and Crafts moulded plaster ceiling. Today the house is well known for its beautiful garden and classical folly. The "Rose Cottage" appelation over the garage is recent.

29a Originally Dr. Geoffrey Boyd house, 34 Rosedale Rd., Page & Warrington, 1919–20.
Originally Isaac Weldon house, 2 Cluny Dr., Eden Smith & Sons, 1922–23.

English Cottage Style houses built in Toronto a decade earlier had been rendered in brick or stone because in a Canadian winter more natural-looking stucco tended to "fall away in spots thereby destroying the wonderful charm." By the 1920s, new technology had made stucco possible even in Canada. (Ironically, by that date others were already sick of what in Los Angeles they were calling "that stucco rash.")

29b Originally John Coulson house, 19 Rosedale Rd., 1914; enlarged and altered, John M. Lyle, 1928.
Originally John Gibbons house, 30 Rosedale Rd., George Moorhouse & King, 1929–30.

In 1930, *Canadian Homes & Gardens* wrote that "the Georgian tradition runs through most of the best architectural work in Canada at the present time." Here are two examples, although no. 19's flat frontage is actually a smoothing out of an earlier, more picturesque construction.

30 16 Rosedale Rd. (apartment house), Bregman & Hamann, 1954–58.
1 Rosedale Rd. (apartment house), c. 1955–60.

Built during Toronto's post-war apartment boom, these are two typical unobtrusive constructions, the one of white brick with bands of Miesian windows, the other red with punched fenestration. But, unobtrusive or no, Rosedale didn't really want apartment houses at all. When a bylaw limiting their height to no more than 35 feet above grade was circumvented by wily developers—taking advantage of the ravines, they built three storeys above grade and eight or more below, as at no. 16—ratepayers persuaded city planners against further apartments except around subway stations. In Rosedale, contemporary architecture is as rare as Victorian.

Walk 22: Southeast Rosedale

The first streets in this walk are part of the residential neighbourhood laid out by Edgar Jarvis in the 1870s. It too was isolated and slow to develop, but for over 30 years and despite great financial loss, realtor Jarvis persisted. Building, selling—and at times occupying with family of 14—one house after another, he never gave up on his dream of an enclave for Toronto's wealthy. Sad to say, Rosedale didn't come into its own until after Jarvis's death in 1907, and then with a much more moderate visage than he had anticipated.

1 Originally "Glen Hurst" (Edgar Jarvis residence), 2 Elm Ave., Gundry & Langley, 1866; additions, Smith & Gemmell, 1880; rehabilitated, 1948.

When built, Glen Hurst was one of five or so houses in all of Rosedale and—sited prominently on a hill (hurst) above the ravine—it remained the grandest for many years. With high hipped roof, gabled centre pavilion, and expansive Italianate veranda sheltering tall ground-floor windows, there was an air of both symmetrical formality and easy grace about it—a persuasive proclamation of

the good life Jarvis was angling to sell in Rosedale. The house faced west with access via a winding drive off Park Road. When the Park Road bridge collapsed in 1872, Jarvis replaced it with one at what is now Mount Pleasant Road, making the main approach to his house then from the east. In 1880 he sold Glen Hurst and moved to a fresh mansion at Glen Road and South Drive [demolished]. Enlarged and altered by later owners (Hughes, Waldie, Deacon), today 2 Elm serves as classrooms, and what's left of the glen and the hurst, as playing fields, for Branksome Hall girls' school.

2 Originally R. Laidlaw Brodie house, 1 Elm Ave., 1881; altered later.

Originally William Alexander house, 3 Elm Ave., 1878; addition, Darling Sproatt & Pearson, 1897.

Originally William A. Warren house, 4 Elm Ave., 1878.

Originally John Blaikie house, 10 Elm Ave., Langley Langley & Burke, 1879; additions later.

Edgar Jarvis's new bridge and tree-lined Elm and Maple Avenues inspired but a

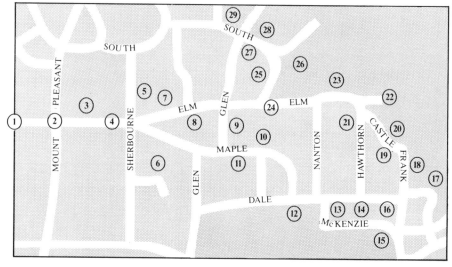

2 *10 Elm Ave., c. 1920*   **3** *Elm Avenue 1890s houses*

few timid takers. These High Victorian manors were built within a few years of one another, and, surprisingly, within a few yards of one another as well. With so many lots available, why did Rosedale pioneers cluster so? Oh well, today the grouping helps the four to form a mannerly campus for Branksome Hall school, which arrived on Elm Avenue about 1913, ten years after its founding.

3 Originally Charles Nelson house, 14 Elm Ave., probably Charles J. Gibson, 1895; veranda added, Charles J. Gibson, 1911.
Originally William Alley house, 16 Elm Ave., 1895.
Originally Henry Drayton house, 18 Elm Ave., Charles J. Gibson, 1897–98.
Originally Mrs. Mary Davies house, 20 Elm Ave., Frederick H. Herbert, 1898.
Despite the clutch of financiers at the west end of Elm [22/2], the avenue remained almost empty until the late 1890s. Only then did these Richardsonian Romanesque/Queen Anne houses grandly rise behind lavish iron fences to create one of the most swaggering architectural ensembles in Toronto. Little changed— save the elms are dead and gone—they still impress with mighty brick and stone, rich terracotta and wood, commanding high-pitched roofs and even higher chimneys. All firmly declare these are houses— and by inference, owners—to be reckoned with. Nelson and Alley were manufacturers; Drayton, assistant city solicitor; Mrs. Davies, widow of a scion of William Davies pork packers.

4 Originally Percival Leadlay house, 21 Elm Ave., Frederick H. Herbert, 1904–05.
Originally Robert McLean house, 23 Elm Ave., Frederick H. Herbert, 1908–09.
Originally John Rennie house, 25 Elm Ave., Bond & Smith, 1906–07.
Originally Thomas Wilkins house, 24 Elm Ave., J. Francis Brown, 1910–11.
Originally William Kernahan house, 26 Elm Ave., James P. Hynes, 1914–16.
Reviewing these houses in 1910, *Construction* confided that "the 'Stylist' may not find to his entire satisfaction architectural coordination." The Edwardian period was one of disorder, it's true, but, unrecognized at the time, these houses shared a modernizing interest in pushing out interior space to form smoother, flatter-looking exteriors. In fact, the three hipped-roof "boxes" at nos. 21, 23, and 25 come as close as any in Toronto to progressive Prairie School architecture. First owners manufactured hides and wool (no. 21), stationery and books (no. 23), seeds and bulbs (no. 25), smallwares (no. 24), and beer (Kernahan of no. 26 was manager of O'Keefe Brewery).

Electric streetcar tracks were installed in Rosedale in 1891. The streetcar looped up Sherbourne Street North, thence along Elm Avenue, Glen Road, and South Drive before heading out over the bridge again filled with customs brokers and bookkeepers headed for downtown offices.

263

6 *Ancroft Place*

5 Originally Edward D. Gooderham house, 27 Sherbourne St. N., Sproatt & Rolph, 1907–09.

In the early 1900s, land agent Jarvis attracted the Gooderham clan to Rosedale. They had long been resident in houses adjacent to their distillery [2/9], but in 1903 company secretary William G. Gooderham had family architect David Roberts design a huge house for him here on the corner of Sherbourne and Elm [demolished], and four years later William's son, company clerk Edward D. Gooderham, age 24, built this solemn manor in a corner of the lot. Designed by Sproatt & Rolph (Roberts had died), it was described as "quiet and restful modern Georgian." Since no. 27 had a coach house, one wonders if young Gooderham tackled the trolley.

6 Ancroft Place (21-unit housing complex), 1 Sherbourne St. N., Shepard & Calvin, 1927.

Ancroft Place is among the best housing ever conceived in Toronto. It came into being at a time of worldwide interest in town planning and especially in something called the Garden City Movement. This was predicated on providing average workingmen with simple, attractive dwellings situated in picturesque, semi-rural settings organized in zones adjacent to those for industrial, commercial, and public buildings. Few whole garden cities were built, but the theories influenced a range of schemes as this unique Rosedale complex attests.

Made up of three English Cottage Style structures, each with seven houses of varying elevations, plans, and sizes, and arrayed on a three-acre site with delightful interplay of communal/private space, the complex today exudes an almost arcadian sense of bliss. It is all the more remarkable because Shepard & Calvin were bank designers, although Brooklyn-born Shepard had worked for the eclectic New York architect Ernest Flagg. Flagg, however, never did any housing as exciting as this.

7a 44–46 Elm Ave. (double house), 1875.

Today this structure attracts with the frisky farmhouse look of its bichrome cladding, bargeboarded gables, and turned porch posts. In 1875, however, construction of what amounted to lower-middle-class semi-detacheds must have been a disappointing development for Jarvis. Years later, in 1896, he was reduced to living at no. 46 himself, where Mrs. J gave music lessons.

7b Originally Henry O'Hara house, 50 Elm Ave., Charles J. Gibson, 1898.

This great plump dowager of a building comfortably ensconced on wide stretch of lawn seems reassuringly unchanged by time. Gibson was very good at these well-made, unfussy Queen Annes. Designed for a broker of mining stocks, no. 50 is not at all formidable.

8e *47 Elm Ave.*

8e *45 Elm Ave.*

Although too many houses have been greedily stuffed into this Elm Avenue block, the smorgasbord makes for a quickie menu of Rosedale development. With many mitigations to solve the "garage problem," this block also shows that public transit no longer suffices for most Rosedalians.

8a 53–55 Elm Ave. (double house), 1888.

The first structure on the block and still a standout thanks to picturesque turret and double-house girth. No. 53–55 was built and probably designed by contractor Jeremiah Bedford at a time when Rosedale was yet "too far," and large Queen Anne semi-detacheds almost out of fashion. For years Bedford occupied one of the semis himself, locating his construction office here too.

8b 51 Elm Ave. (detached house), 1889.

It's likely that Jeremiah Bedford constructed this house as well. Put up one year after no. 53–55, it's basically a Queen Anne with Romanesque Revival masonry girding ground-floor front.

8c 57 Elm Ave. (detached house), 1890.
61 Elm Ave. (detached house), 1890.

Also attributed to Bedford, these chubby cherubs are just the sort then aborning in the Annex [*AREA X*]. Though Bedford's array of Romanesque parts is wobbly, such richly rendered red brick and terracotta can't help but appeal.

8d 49 Elm Ave. (detached house), Gordon & Helliwell, 1901–02.

In the United States, late Queen Anne houses were rounding themselves out in Shingle Style, but fire-fearful Toronto discouraged shingles unless backed by brick—an expensive proposition. With virtually no local precedent or practice then, this proto-Shingle isn't half bad.

8e 47 Elm Ave. (detached house), Chadwick & Beckett, 1905.
45 Elm Ave. (detached house), Frederick H. Herbert, 1905–06.

A little Tudor gabling, some classical dormers, Prairie School overhangs, plus a dab of Beaux-Arts doorway—these houses of no fixed affiliation exemplify those that suddenly began to go up all over Rosedale in the early 1900s.

8f 43 Elm Ave. (detached house), 1911.

Eventually, Edwardian architectural anxiety calmed down into two composed styles—Neo-Georgian and Neo-Tudor. This house is on its way to the latter.

9 Originally John Hoare house, 57 Glen Rd., Designing & Draughting Co., 1911.
Originally Oliver Adams house, 55 Glen Rd., Chadwick & Beckett, 1901–02.
Originally Ambrose Small house, 51 Glen Rd., 1903.

No. 57 is a neat, symmetrical red-brick Neo-Georgian gone picturesque with Craftsmany porch, eaves, and dormers. Architectural credit goes to D.C. Cotton

9 *55 Glen Rd.*

10 *H.H. Fudger estate, c. 1920*

and H.G. Macklin, who respectively filled the roles of the Designing & Draughting Company. No. 55 is Second Classical Revival starring a full-height Ionic-columned entry porch. Such dramatic designs were inspired by the Beaux-Arts spectacle of the 1893 World's Columbian Exposition in Chicago. No. 51 is note-worthy not as architecture but as home to Ambrose Small, the hated and envied owner of theatres across the province who disappeared in 1919 along with $1 million from his bank account. Neither was seen again; and yes, the basement has been excavated!

10 Originally Harris Henry Fudger house, 40 Maple Ave., Gordon & Helliwell, 1897–98; additions, Burke & Horwood, 1902–03, 1907.
When the Fudger house was built, its design represented a grandiose look back at the 19th century; but its situation, surrounded by empty lots with open views to the Don Valley, spelled a step into the 20th and optimistic commitment to this new neighbourhood. Fudger had just become part owner and president of the Robert Simpson Company [5/7], and his conspicuously picturesque house with cir-cular drive and formal gardens was an elitist spectacle. Its present rooming-house decrepitude seems an all-too-democratic irony.

11 33 Maple Ave. (detached house), probably James P. Hynes, 1903–04.
35 Maple Ave. (detached house), Langley & Langley, 1903–04.
39 Maple Ave. (detached house), 1905–06.

41 Maple Ave. (detached house), Symons & Rae, 1902.
Taking a cue from the Fudger extrava-ganza across the street, these fat and full Jacobethans break out at the top in a whimsical file of potted chimneys and stone-coped gables. No. 37, dating to 1902, is a classical loner in this Neo-Tudor precinct.

As late as the 1870s, the whole of southeast Rosedale was in the hands of just four landowners: Maunsell Jackson, who lived at Drumsnab [22/17]; bachelor Edward Nan-ton, who resided in a former milkman's cottage near today's Nanton Avenue; York-ville developer Walter McKenzie, who had a house at today's McKenzie Avenue; and Judge John Hoskin, who presided over The Dale [22/12] at (where else?) today's Dale Avenue. All four reached home by a ravine road that began at Parliament Street, where they jointly maintained a gatekeeper's lodge.

12 21 Dale Ave. (originally site of "The Dale" [John Hoskin residence]; now apart-ment building), Crang & Boake, 1951.
In 1891, a guidebook writer advised that "For its fine sylvan setting and the rare attractions of its conservatories, The Dale is well-nigh unsurpassed among Toronto homes." Today all that remains of Judge Hoskin's 1874 villa and sylvan setting is a much-denatured gate lodge (no. 15 Dale). As for the apartment building that replaced The Dale, it's notable as another example of developer greed tricking Rose-dale's 35-foot-height bylaw [see 21/30].

13 *2 McKenzie Ave.*

13 2 McKenzie Ave. (originally detached house), S. Hamilton Townsend, 1903–05.

This is one of the most modern houses in Rosedale—hard to believe it was constructed over 80 years ago. The smooth, simplified forms and neatly balanced but asymmetric composition mark it as the powerful, sophisticated work of Ontarian Hamilton Townsend, whose enduring Rosedale houses deserve more recognition.

14a Originally Mrs. Eleanor Street house, 10 McKenzie Ave., William Langton, 1909.

This house draws our eye for its stately-home grace replete with cut limestone details and expensive slate roof. Langton situated the house farther back than others on the street to give more light to rooms in the rear, and this siting enhances the Georgian formality. But the house did follow romantic ideas of the day in being set, not high above grade, but close to the ground for a "more natural" connection.

14b 14 McKenzie Ave. (originally detached house), James A. Harvey, 1908–09; altered with additions, c. 1975.

This multi-unit structure is a standout—probably the worst alteration in Rosedale.

15a Originally Lewis Grant house, 20 McKenzie Ave., Eden Smith & Son, 1908–09.

Built for painter Lewis Grant, this unassuming side-entry Neo-Tudor shows architect Smith's penchant for minimalism.

And yet the house has a very cozy charm about it, engendered especially by the deep-eaved roof, almost suggesting medieval thatch.

15b Originally James Ramsey house, 49 McKenzie Ave., Charles J. Gibson, 1896–97.

The only building that many ever see of Rosedale as they whip off the Don Valley Parkway, this quintessentially Victorian house is very impressive. Imagine what it would have seemed in 1897 when there was no expressway, no viaduct, not even a Bloor Street (which terminated then at Sherbourne). The terracotta "picture frame" was recreated a year later on Elm Avenue [22/3]. This rendering was for a maker of photographers' supplies.

16 Originally Henry Kelly house, 65 Castle Frank Rd., Chadwick & Beckett, 1912.

Six-over-six shuttered windows, pedimented dormers, and side-lighted entrance spell Georgian. But no. 65, in its flat relief, horizontal emphasis, and siting close to the ground, is akin to Tudor-derived 2 McKenzie [22/13]. Clients might choose appended "style," but architects knew that form-created space was the real challenge.

Kelly, manager of Dun & Company, asked Chadwick & Beckett to add a garage almost before the house was finished. The relatively tight site decreed a breach in no. 65's classical good taste: garages were built discreetly out of sight until the 1930s. Witness adjacent Dale Avenue, a whole street of them.

15b *49 McKenzie Ave.*

17 *Drumsnab, drawing, c. 1845*

17 "Drumsnab" (originally Francis Cayley residence)/formerly Maunsell Jackson house, 5 Drumsnab Rd., 1834; second-floor addition, William Thomas, 1856; addition, Eden Smith & Son, 1908.

Drumsnab is one of Toronto's most alluring houses, not only because it's the oldest in town still a private home, but also because it continues to evoke the refreshing charm of a Regency cottage, those informal country dwellings set in rustic landscapes that were the *beau idéal* of early 1800s England. With simple shape and two-foot-thick fieldstone walls, Drumsnab perfectly embodied the form, and in 1834 the 120-acre site overlooking a Don Valley mound—a drumsnab—would have been rustic territory indeed.

Cayley was brother of politician William Cayley and a bachelor who seems to have whiled away his time painting frescoes on the walls of Drumsnab. On his death the house was purchased by Maunsell Jackson, whose descendants occupied it well into the 20th century. In 1928, 13 years after the Prince Edward Viaduct had been constructed, Drumsnab was still ensconced amid 11 country acres, probably the largest estate then existing within the City of Toronto.

18 48 Castle Frank Rd. (detached house), Bond & Smith, 1911.

As with Georgian forebears, Georgian Revival houses feature classical entrances, cornices, and windows. This sweetly appealing house also boasts prototypical tall chimney and quoins at the corners. But the asymmetry, with off-centre door and single bellying bay, definitely marks it 20th century. In 1911, you could have had it for $7,000.

19 43 Castle Frank Rd. (detached house), Chadwick & Beckett, 1907–08.

Vertical stretch and too-small windows make this early Castle Frank house a tad gawky, but cobbled clinker brick saves all. Once thrown out as seconds, vitrified, misshapen clinkers became popular in the early 1900s and were manufactured specially for their "artistic effect."

20 Originally "Inchraffay" (Gerald Strathy residence), 34 Castle Frank Rd., Eustace G. Bird, 1911–12.

"The rich men in Toronto, and there are obviously a great number of them, build large detached houses on pieces of land which we should think just big enough for a gardener's lodge and potato patch," wrote a British architect visiting Canada in the 1920s. He could well have had Gerald Strathy's enormous T-shaped Neo-Georgian in mind. In addition to small lot, the plainness of the house is striking. Nearby, architect Bird had just finished his own, similar house [22/22a].

22b *6 Hawthorn Gardens*

22c *4 Hawthorn Gardens*

21 44 Hawthorn Ave. (detached house), 1906–07.

46 Hawthorn Ave. (detached house), Charles J. Gibson, 1905–06.

48 Hawthorn Ave. (detached house), E. Beaumont Jarvis, 1902–04.

These three neat and various Edwardian abodes were among the first on Hawthorn Avenue, which was part of an 1885 subdivision of Edward Nanton's land. No. 48 was designed by Edgar Jarvis's son Beaumont. How intriguing that this zealot Rosedale realtor encouraged his eldest child to become an architect.

The street we know as Hawthorn Gardens was Eustace Bird's driveway until the rest of this prime-spot plot was parcelled out. Today five houses share the cul-de-sac allure, three from the 1910s, one from 1930, and one—best forgot—from recent times.

22a Originally Eustace G. Bird house, 5 Hawthorn Gardens, Eustace G. Bird, 1909–10; additions, Mathers & Haldenby, 1930.

Ontarian Eustace Bird is little known save as Toronto rep of New York architects Carrère & Hastings [6/8]. The indisputably clonish, blah design of his own house does nothing to alter that image.

22b Originally "Marbrae" (Melville White residence), 6 Hawthorn Gardens, Burke Horwood & White, 1910.

In the hands of Eden Smith or Hamilton Townsend, Tudor vernacular could take on an almost modern look, but less adventurous Burke Horwood & White rendered it straight with all the medieval quaintness prettily in place. Still, no denying the appeal of this dark-trimmed white-stuccoed "cottage." Melville White was manager of Canada Foundry and brother to architect Murray White.

22c Originally William Gundy house, 4 Hawthorn Gardens, S. Hamilton Townsend, 1910–11.

Nowhere in Toronto are the principles of English Cottage Style—simplicity, strength, harmony with nature—better demonstrated than in publisher William Gundy's house. Without symmetry but with such consummate balancing as to seem to be, Townsend's design is both daring and graceful. The pattern of windows clearly expresses the interiors; the sentinel chimney and dormer push briskly through the roof like outgrowths of the canopied entrance below, and tapestry brickwork along with siting low to the ground blend the house beautifully with its surroundings.

22d Originally Norman Seagram house/ formerly Jesuit Fathers residence, 2 Hawthorn Gardens, Vaux Chadwick, 1929–30.

By the late 1920s, the bold English Cottage Style experiment to create non-copyist but still traditional architecture was dead and—in real reversal—reproductions were wholeheartedly embraced. Seagram's dry, lacklustre, although obviously expensive "period" house is a good example. Never in the

23 *8 Castle Frank Rd., 1927*   **24c** *88 Elm Ave.*

family distillery business, Norman Seagram made his fortune in his father-in-law's brokerage firm. On his death, the 30-room mansion was acquired by the English-speaking Jesuit Order in Canada. It is now condominium units.

23 Originally Gerald Larkin house, 8 Castle Frank Rd., George Moorhouse & King, 1926.
Salada Tea Company scion Gerald Larkin built this house on Castle Frank Road two years after Osler property behind was opened as parkland [22/26]. Although a classic Palladian design of horizontally emphasized fenestration, raised basement, and pedimented central pavilion, the Larkin house seems not at all formal, thanks in part to the welcoming, congenial entrance. A great and gracious house, best appreciated without the garden wall.

24a 93 Elm Ave. (detached house), J. Wilson Siddall, 1901.
The most interesting thing about this house is the gorgeous iron porch shielding the front door. Actually a driveway shelter (*porte cochère*), it was removed here from a house on Sherbourne Street.

24b 89 Elm Ave. (detached house), E.J. Lennox, 1902–04.
The most interesting thing about this house is that even accomplished E.J. Lennox could be flummoxed by the Edwardian architectural agenda. What a mishmash!

24c Originally Franklin Kerr house, 88 Elm Ave., Burden & Gouinlock, 1926–27.
The most interesting thing about this house is that it is so interesting, with both the Elm Avenue loggia face and South Drive court face given equal importance. No. 88 won the Ontario Association of Architects 1929 award for "garages, stables, and gatehouses" with its three-car garage for bond dealer Kerr.

25 Originally "Evenholm" (Edgar Jarvis residence), 157 South Dr., E. Beaumont Jarvis, 1905–06.
This was Edgar Jarvis's last Rosedale home; one year after moving in, he died here, age 72. An impressive, unusually symmetrical Jacobethan, it was appropriately designed for Jarvis by his son Beaumont, who by this date had become a reasonably successful architect.

26 Craigleigh Gardens (originally site of "Craigleigh" [residence of Sir Edmund Osler]), 160 South Dr.; gates, Darling & Pearson, 1903.
On this scenic ravine site in 1876, Edgar Jarvis shepherded construction of a lavish High Victorian house into which moved, the next year, wealthy businessman Edmund Osler. Osler, it seems, put up most of the money for Edgar Jarvis's bridges, houses, and dreams, and this was probably the beginning of their extensive financial dealings.

Norcastle at South Dr. and Glen Rd., c. 1900, with North Iron Bridge at right, trolley tracks at left

29 *134 South Dr.*

Osler resided at Craigleigh 47 years, eventually overseeing a mansion of some 25 rooms. At his death in 1924, the house was torn down and the 13 acres of manicured grounds presented to the city for a park, one of the most attractive in Toronto.

27 97 Glen Rd. (detached house), probably Chadwick & Beckett, 1901–02.

Second Classical Revival houses with full-height "Mount Vernon" porches were very popular in the U.S. during the first half of the 20th century. This imposing Canadian version may have been commissioned by Edgar Jarvis, whom directories list as living next door in the semi-detached at no. 89 in 1901. It would have been consistent with his never-flagging grandiose vision for Rosedale.

At the crossroads of South Drive and Glen Road Edgar Jarvis erected two large houses in 1880 and 1881 in hopes of setting a stately-home stamp on Rosedale. On the northeast corner stood Sylvan Tower, a house the Jarvis family itself occupied until 1889. Then rented for many years to a widow lady, it was sold in 1908 to James Plummer, president of Dominion Iron & Steel. On the northwest was Norcastle, a towered stone mansion sold to woollens wholesaler Henry W. Darling. It was resold in 1903 to Albert Gooderham, who renamed it Deancroft. Rosedale never became the district Jarvis had envisioned. By the 1930s nobody wanted to live in Sylvan Tower and Deancroft (Lady Gooderham, recently widowed, was moving to Forest Hill Village) and the houses were torn down.

28 Originally Wilmot Matthews house, 146 South Dr., Saunders & Ryrie, 1934–35.

Originally S. Temple Blackwood house, 144 South Dr., Mathers & Haldenby, 1935.

When the two mansions at Glen Road and South Drive were demolished and the land subdivided in the early '30s, realtor A.E. LePage reported "Lots will be sold to private parties who wish to erect homes immediately. It is the intention to have the Georgian type of house built . . . ." Note how variously the style could be interpreted.

No. 146 is a copy of the classic vernacular side-gabled Palladian as it was built in Britain and the U.S. in the mid 18th century. The firm of Dyce Saunders and Jack Ryrie was well known for these delightful "home-like" houses. This, one of their best, was designed for lawyer Wilmot Matthews.

No. 144 comes from the slightly later, more urban tradition of British Regency and American Federal architecture of the 1810s period. Designed for a stockbroker, this subtly detailed house garnered Mathers & Haldenby an architectural award of merit.

29 134 South Dr. (detached house), 1936.

132 South Dr. (detached house), 1936.

Georgian "Regency Revival" houses with almost flat roofs and unusually plain roof/wall junctions became popular in the 1930s. Soon even the stone surrounds will be removed and they will be on their way to sleek modernism [see, for example, 21/2]. These two are among the last detached houses to be built in Rosedale.

Glossary

A

Adamesque. After Robert Adam (1728-92), English architect and designer known for his refined, elegant classicism.

apse. Semicircular or polygonal projection at the chancel end of a church.

arcade. 1. A range of arches supported on columns or piers, either freestanding or blind (applied to a wall). 2. Covered passage lined with shops.

arch. Structural device arcing an opening supported only from the sides. Various configurations include: **round** or **semicircular; segmental; S-shaped** or **ogee; horseshoe;** and **pointed** or **lancet.**

architrave. 1. In classical architecture, the lowermost division of an entablature above which is the frieze and cornice. 2. Moulding around the top and sides of a rectangular door or window. Also called a **surround.**

ashlar. Blocks of horizontally laid rock that have been hewn with square edges and rough-cut faces, as opposed to unhewn rubble on the one hand and smooth-sawn stone on the other.

atrium. 1. In early Roman architecture, a courtyard in the centre of a house covered only along the sides. 2. In contemporary architecture, an enclosed vertical space welling the interior of a multi-storey building.

B

baluster. Support for a railing on stairways, balconies, etc., originally partially bulb-shaped or similarly turned.

balustrade. A series of balusters supporting a railing.

bargeboards. Decorative, often scroll-sawn boards edging a gabled or overhanging roof. Also called vergeboards or gingerbread.

bartizans. Small tower-like structures at and overhanging the top corners of a building. Originally for defence.

base. In classical architecture, a supporting foundation of a column on which the shaft rests.

batter. Outward slant of the bottom of a wall. Originally the thickening of the base of a tower as fortification against battering.

bay. Vertical division of a building as delineated by some regular, recurring feature such as windows, buttresses, columns, etc.

bay window. A bay that projects from a building and contains one or more windows. If a bay window projects from an upper storey only, it is called an **oriel.**

Beaux-Arts. After the École des Beaux-Arts in Paris, the French state school of art education renowned as the training place for architects worldwide. The principles of design expounded there, particularly those dealing with craftsman-like construction, appearance of strength, visual order, and urban drama, were a major influence on those practising classical and eclectic architecture and town planning in the late 19th and early 20th centuries, especially in the United States.

bellcote. Small gabled structure for hanging bells atop a roof.

belvedere. Small covered structure on a roof for looking at a view.

board-and-batten. Butting flat boards topped with flat trim strips covering the joins.

bond. (See header.)

boss. Ornamental knob.

bracket. Wooden or metal member projecting from a wall to help support an overhanging weight such as an extended roof.

brick. Hardened clay, block-shaped in a mould, may or may not be baked in a kiln. **Pressed brick** is made of very fine clay forced into the mould under great pressure to form an especially smooth hard brick. **Clinker brick** is an uneven and vitrified brick that has become misshapen in firing; often used for an "artistic" effect. **Tapestry brick** is a random arrangement of different coloured brick, usually black and dark red; popular in the early 20th century.

buttress. Masonry support built against a wall to give it added strength.

C

capital. In classical architecture, the uppermost division of a column crowning the shaft.

cartouche. Bas-relief in the form of an ornamental tablet.

chancel. That part of the central space of a church that contains the main altar and is reserved for clergy and choir, as distinct from the nave.

classical architecture. Formal, symmetrical, codified architecture of Ancient Greece and Ancient Rome, and architecture derived thereof.

clerestory. Upper windowed walls of a church or other building that rise "clear" of all other structural parts to provide light to the interior.

colonnade. A row of columns supporting an entablature, roof, or arches.

colonnette. Small slender decorative column.

column. In classical architecture, an upright support consisting of base, circular shaft, and capital; situated below and carrying the entablature. Variously proportioned and ornamented depending on the order.

Composite. One of the Roman classical orders, similar to the Corinthian but with larger volutes (spirals) in the capitals.

console. Ornamental S-shaped bracket.

corbel. Stone or clay member projecting from a wall to help support an overhanging weight such as an oriel.

corbel table. A range of corbels in courses, each course built out beyond the one below.

Corinthian. One of the classical orders, distinguished by columns with high bases, tall slender fluted or unfluted shafts, and ornate foliated capitals. The entablature uses dentils, modillions, and a fascia.

cornice. 1. In classical architecture, the uppermost division of the entablature below which is the frieze and architrave. 2. Projecting moulding at the top of a building, wall, etc., or over a door or window.

course. Horizontal row of bricks or stones in a wall. A **string** or **belt course** is a decorative coloured, moulded, or projecting row.

crenellation. Parapet with alternating voids and solids. Originally intended for warriors to shoot through or hide behind. Also called **battlement**.

cresting. Ornamental ridge atop a roof or wall, generally of filigreed metal.

crockets. Projecting foliate ornaments, usually stone, found on Gothic spires, pinnacles, gables, etc.

cupola. Small, domed structure crowning a roof or tower. (See also belvedere).

curtain wall. Exterior, screening wall situated in front of a load-bearing frame. In modern steel-frame buildings, all exterior walls are non-load-bearing curtain walls.

D

dentils. Very small rectangular blocks ranged in a series to form a tooth-like moulding.

Doric. One of the classical Greek orders, distinguished by columns with no base, short fluted shafts, and plain, saucer-shaped capitals. The Roman Doric order has a simple base and the shaft may be unfluted.

dormer window. Window and its roofed enclosure rising vertically atop a roof.

double house. Single building comprising two distinct dwellings, one *beside* the other, sharing a common or party wall that separates the two. Each distinct dwelling is called a **semi-detached house**.

dressings. Finely finished stone trim.

drip-mould. Projecting moulding around the top of an opening, nominally to protect it from rain. Also called **hood-mould**, **dripstone**, and if rectangular, **label**.

E

Eastlake style. After Charles Lock Eastlake (1836–1906), English architect and writer, whose interior design books showing furniture with knobbed and spindled lathe-turned members as well as latticework influenced similar decoration on late 19th-century picturesque houses.

eaves. Underside of an overhanging roof.

egg-and-dart. Moulding with a pattern of alternating ovals and arrowheads.

entablature. In classical architecture, the horizontal beam consisting of architrave, frieze, and cornice; situated above and spanning the columns. Variously proportioned and ornamented depending on the order.

F

fanlight. Semicircular or semi-elliptical window above a door or another window, originally with radiating glazing bars suggesting a fan.

fascia. 1. In classical architecture, plain horizontal band constituting part of some architraves. 2. Plain wide board edging a gabled or overhanging roof. If decorated, called a bargeboard or vergeboard.

fenestration. Arrangement of windows in a building.

finial. Ornament at the tip of a gable, pinnacle, etc.

frieze. 1. In classical architecture, the middle division of an entablature between the cornice and architrave, often figurally sculpted in bas-relief. 2. Any decorated band around the top of a wall.

G

gable. The wall or other area demarcated by the triangular configuration of a peaked roof. Ornamental variations include: **Dutch gable** (curved sides topped by a pediment); **shaped gable** (multi-curved sides); and **stepped** or **Flemish gable** (angular, step-like increments).

gallery. Part of an upper floor open on one side, either to an interior courtyard, auditorium, etc., or to the exterior street, garden, etc.

grotesque. Carving or painting of highly fanciful human/animal forms. Antique examples were first discovered in grottoes, hence the name.

H

half-timbering. Exposed wooden framing on the outside of a wall, usually filled in with some kind of non-load-bearing plasterwork.

hammerbeam. Wooden roof construction in which the horizontal beams are cut away in the centre, the ends then supported from the top of the roof by hammer posts, forming a kind of bracket.

header. Short end of a brick as it appears on the face of a wall. Various distributions of headers and stretchers (long sides) result in different patterns called **bonds**: **English bond** is one course of headers followed by one course of stretchers; **Flemish bond** alternates headers and stretchers in each course.

I

impost. The structural point at which an arch begins and ends.

inglenook. A seating recess beside a fireplace.

Ionic. One of the classical orders, distinguished by columns with moulded bases, tall slender fluted shafts, and capitals with volutes (spirals). The entablature is relatively plain, with dentils.

K

keystone. Centre voussoir that locks an arch into place, often outsized and ornamented.

L

label-stop. An ornamental knob, often figural, at the end of a drip-mould.

lights. The openings or divisions in a window created by the intersecting mullions and transoms.

lintel. Horizontal wooden beam or stone over an opening.

lunette. A semicircular or half-moon window, opening, wall surface, etc.

M

mansard. In North America, commonly a steep, storey-high roof with two planes on all four sides, the first plane almost vertical, pierced by dormers, and variously convex, concave, or straight-sided; and the second plane nearly flat. Named for François Mansart, 17th-century French architect, who developed the form.

Miesian. After Ludwig Mies van der Rohe (1886–1969), Bauhaus-trained master of the Modern Movement, whose dignified "less-is-more" aesthetic of formal, precise glass-and-steel buildings ranks as a foremost influence on the architecture of the 20th century.

modillions. Small ornamental-shaped blocks ranged in a series to form a decorative band, normally located under a classical cornice.

mullion. Vertical bar dividing a window into lights. Horizontal dividers are called transoms.

N

nave. That part of the central space of a church that is flanked by the aisles and intended for the congregation, as distinct from the chancel.

Neo-Grec. Type of simplified linear classical detail popular in the mid 19th century; often incised.

O

order. In classical architecture, the structural unit comprising columns and entablature. There are five orders, each with its own established proportions and ornament: Doric,

Ionic, Corinthian, Tuscan, and Composite.

oriel. (See bay window.)

P

Palladian. 1. After Andrea Palladio (1508–1580), North Italian architect known for his harmonious Renaissance villas and other buildings. 2. Arched opening flanked by two smaller, straight-topped openings, a design associated with Palladio.

parapet. Low wall around the edge of a roof, bridge, etc.

pavilion. 1. Ornamental, generally lightly constructed building. 2. Unit of a building projecting from the main mass.

pediment. In classical architecture, the area above the entablature of a portico demarcated by the triangular configuration of a peaked roof. Also any similar triangular section used as decoration above a window, door, etc. Ornamental variations may be: **segmental**, **open-topped**, or **broken-based**.

pendant. Elongated ornamental post or knob hanging from a roof, bracket, etc.

picturesque architecture. Informal, asymmetric, diverse architecture. First defined during late 18th century formulations on the nature of the Beautiful and the Sublime, the Picturesque being pronounced somewhere between the two.

pier. 1. Solid, upright support; freestanding or part of a wall. Term is generally used to describe structural members that are square or rectangular in plan as opposed to circular. 2. A square or clustered pillar of a Gothic or Romanesque church.

pilaster. Classical column as if squared and flattened and then attached to a wall as decoration.

pillar. General term for an upright support; may be circular, rectangular, triangular, etc.

pinnacle. In Gothic architecture, a miniature tower-like member crowning a buttress, gable, etc.

porch. Partly open, floored structure attached in front of a door and sheltered by a roof carried on upright supports.

portico. In classical architecture, a large porch with its roof carried by an entablature and columns and often having a pediment.

Q

quatrefoil. Design resembling a cloverleaf made up of four lobes or foils. Found in Gothic church tracery, on Gothic Revival barge-boards, etc.

quoins. Dressed stones, or bricks implying stones, that alternate long side, short end, etc., at the corner of a building; originally structural but later often merely decorative.

R

relieving arch. An arch built flush in a wall above the top member of a framed opening to relieve it of superincumbent weight;

usually constructed of radial brick treated decoratively.

roof. The cover of a building, in various configurations, including: **bell-cast** (concave, bell-like profile); **conical** (cone-like profile); **gable** (two opposite sides have a triangular profile); **gambrel** (two opposite sides have a double-sloped profile, with steep lower plane and less steep upper plane); **hipped** (all four sides have a single-sloped, flat-topped profile); **mansard** (all four sides have a double- or triple-sloped profile with steep lower plane and less steep or nearly flat upper planes); **pyramidal** (all four sides have a triangular, peaked profile); and **tent** (eight sides with a peaked profile).

roughcast. Cement cladding made of lime, water, and cows' hair, with fine gravel thrown on by the plasterer as a last coat.

row. Single building comprising four or more distinct dwellings, one *beside* the other, sharing common or party walls that separate them. Also called a **terrace**. Each distinct dwelling is called a **row house**, and by those who wish to be fancy, a **townhouse**.

rustication. Masonry with deep-set joins to exaggerate the look of weight and scale, generally used to delineate a base storey. If of stone or implied stone, surface may also be roughened.

S

shaft. In classical architecture, the cylindrical fluted or unfluted middle division of a column, between the capital and the base.

sidelights. Narrow vertical windows, usually fixed, flanking a door or another window.

sill. Horizontal member at the base of a window or door opening.

spandrel. 1. Unit of wall between two windows, vertically, from floor to floor. 2. Unit of wall between two adjacent arches.

spire. Tall pointed roof of a tower.

steeple. The combined tower and spire of a church.

stretcher. Long side of a brick as it appears on the face of a wall. Various distributions of stretchers and headers (short ends) result in different bonds. (See header.)

Sullivanesque. After Louis H. Sullivan (1856–1924), American architect and a father of the modern skyscraper; also known for his distinctive geometric/naturalistic ornament.

T

terracotta. Hardened clay, shaped in a mould as tiles, paving, decorative panels, or other architectural ornament and then baked (literally "cooked earth" in Italian). Harder than brick. Around the turn of the century, terracotta was manufactured to look like stone and used for its fireproofing qualities as cladding on steel-framed skyscrapers as well as for interior casing.

toplight. Window, usually fixed, above a door or other window.

tower. A building or structure higher than its diameter. May be freestanding or attached to another structure.

tracery. Ornamental separations in a Gothic window. May be of stone, wood, or iron.

transept. Transverse arms of a cross-shaped church.

transom. 1. Horizontal bar dividing a window into lights. Vertical dividers are called mullions. 2. Horizontal window above a door or another window.

trefoil. Design resembling a cloverleaf made up of three lobes or foils. Found in Gothic church tracery, on Gothic Revival barge-boards, etc.

trophy. Relief ornament on a building, usually depicting arms and armour as a memorial to some victory, but may be any similar collection of symbolic objects.

turret. Small slender tower, usually round.

Tuscan. One of the Roman classical orders, similar to the Roman Doric but the shaft of the column is always unfluted. The entablature is very plain.

tympanum. A wall or other area demarcated by a lintelled opening and an arch above it.

V

vault. An arched ceiling or roof, usually of stone, brick, or concrete. Various configurations, including: **barrel** (continuous unbroken semicircle); **domical** (dome atop square or polygonal base); and **groin** (four-part intersection of two barrel vaults).

veranda. Partly open, floored structure attached alongside a house and sheltered by a roof carried on upright supports. Sometimes called a **loggia**.

vergeboards. (See bargeboards.)

vermiculation. Worm-track-like squiggles randomly cut into dressed stone as decoration.

voussoirs. Wedge-shaped blocks of stone, clay, etc., forming an arch.

W

window. 1. Opening in a wall to ventilate and light an enclosed space. Various configurations, including: **straight-topped**; **round-arched**; **lancet** (narrow and pointed at the top); **French** (carried to the floor like a door); and **rose** (circular). 2. The framework and fittings which close a window opening. Of various types, including: **casement** (hinged at the sides to open inward or outward); and **sash** (hung by cords to slide up and down, one section in front of the other).

window head. Protective and/or decorative member projecting at or around the top of a window. Of various configurations, including: **cornice, eyebrow, segmental-pedimented,** and **triangular-pedimented**.

Sources of Information

The single best source of information for most Toronto buildings is the city assessment rolls. Compiled from the time the town was incorporated in 1834 up to the present, these official lists contain data not only on assessed values, but also tenants, owners, sizes of lots and structures, as well as short descriptions of properties ("vacant lot," "stores under construction," two-storey brick house," for example). Assessment rolls are available for viewing at New City Hall (on microfilm in the City of Toronto Archives for years up to 1915; at the City Clerk's Department thereafter), as well as in the Archives of Ontario (from 1834 to 1900). Assessment rolls for communities such as Yorkville, covering years before they became part of the City of Toronto, are also located at the provincial archives.

City directories give the names of building occupants as well, but are not as accurate as assessment rolls. (Researchers should be aware that some street numbers as well as street names have changed over the years.) City directories dating from 1833 to the present are available at both the City of Toronto Archives and the Metropolitan Toronto Library. Data on land registry can be obtained for a small search fee in the provincial Land Registry Office. This can be useful in determining exact location and dimensions of property, as well as ownership history.

The *W.S. & H.C. Boulton Atlas* of 1858 and the Charles E. Goad insurance-plan atlases of 1880, 1884, 1890, 1893, 1899, 1903, 1910, and 1923 are invaluable for showing precise locations, configurations, materials, and heights of early structures, but most particularly in providing a comparative sense of the city as it developed over the years. These are available for viewing on microfilm at the city archives, and on large laminated sheets at the metro library (the latter may be xeroxed).

Probably the most extensive building descriptions are to be found in the professional construction and architectural periodicals of the day, such as the *Canadian Architect and Builder, Construction,* and the *Journal of the Royal Architecture Institute of Canada.* Archindont, an index to mentioned Toronto buildings in 19 such Canadian periodicals going back to 1888, was begun in the 1970s by architectural history students of University of Toronto professor Douglas Richardson. Now updated by library staff, Archindont is located in the Fine Art section of the Metropolitan Toronto Library. Pertinent data from the periodical references have been extrapolated onto the Archindont cards, but researchers are advised to check the original source material, as extrapolations can be misleading.

The periodicals are a good source for ascertaining the architect of a particular building, as are old newspapers, some of which regularly printed architects' tender calls in their columns. A methodical list of the tender calls that appeared in the *Leader*, *Globe*, *Telegram*, and *Star* newspapers for the years 1847 to 1890 has been compiled by architect Kent Rawson, but unfortunately it is not yet generally available. Building permits, on file in the City of Toronto Archives for the period 1880 to 1915, and in Central Records thereafter, may also identify architects.

The Toronto Branch of the Architectural Conservancy of Ontario, in a project coordinated by researcher Carolyn Neal, has compiled a card file of Toronto architects (which contains some biographical data as well as building credits). It is on deposit in the Fine Art section of the metro library. The most exhaustive research on this subject awaits publication of the *Biographical Dictionary of Architects in Canada 1800–1950*, now going forward under the direction of architect Robert Hill.

Vintage photographs are, of course, the best way to discover the former appearance of a particular building. Fine collections exist in the Baldwin Room of the Metropolitan Toronto Library and the Picture Division of the Archives of Ontario. The largest number of photographs is to be found in the City of Toronto Archives, but because the archives's photos are organized by donor collection, searching for a particular subject can be frustrating.

Several collections of architect drawings and plans exist. An extraordinary one is the J.C.B. Horwood Collection, now on deposit at the Archives of Ontario thanks to the perspicacity of Mr. Stephen Otto. It contains plans, sketches, etc., for some 1,700 projects by at least 50 different architectural firms that practised in Toronto from the 1840s up to about 1965. Plans and papers pertaining to the work of architects John G. Howard and Henry Langley are in the Baldwin Room of the metro library.

Early picture books and guidebooks to the city can prove illuminating, as can publications of the Board of Trade and similar booster organizations. While the pictures don't lie, some of the data have proved inaccurate or misleading. Timperlake's 1877 *Illustrated Toronto*, for example, attributes buildings to architectural firms as they were constituted at the time of his writing, and not as they existed when the buildings were designed.

Early histories can be misleading as well. Robertson's six volumes are generally good for biographical information, but his building dates and architect attributions have led many a researcher astray. Edith Firth's two volumes probably provide the best data on the history of the city because they cite all the primary sources (diaries, letters, newspaper articles, etc.).

Newspaper clippings and other loose reference materials relating to Toronto, its buildings, and development can be found in the 12 volumes of the *City of Toronto Scrapbooks*, available on microfilm at metro library; and the 12 volumes of the T.A. Reed Collection, located in the Baldwin Room.

An oval Toronto Historical Board marker affixed to the front of a building indicates that it is on the THB *Inventory of Buildings of Architectural and Historical Importance*. (Be advised, however, that markers bearing the date "March 6, 1984" were given away as part of the 150th anniversary celebration of the incorporation of Toronto as a city on that day in 1834—but only to those householders who requested them. Many buildings on the THB inventory do not display affixed markers.) With over 2,000 properties listed and many previous errors corrected thanks to the assiduousness of staff-member Margaret Baily, the THB inventory is now a major source for building dates and architects, as well as for the names of builders. It is available at the various historic sites maintained by the Toronto Historical Board.

The following books are those which I found most worthwhile.

Architecture Books
Arthur, Eric, *Toronto, No Mean City*, Toronto, 1964.
Bernstein, William & Ruth Cawker, *Contemporary Canadian Architecture: The Mainstream and Beyond*, Toronto, 1982.
Binder, Ingrid, et al, *Beaux-Arts Toronto*, Toronto, 1973.
Brosseau, Mathilde, *Gothic Revival in Canadian Architecture*, Ottawa, 1980.
Cameron, Christina & Janet Wright, *Second Empire Style in Canadian Architecture*, Ottawa, 1980.
Card, Raymond, *The Ontario Association of Architects 1890–1950*, Toronto, 1950.
Chapman, Howard D., *Alfred Chapman, The Man and His Work*, Toronto, 1978.
Dendy, William, *Lost Toronto*, Toronto, 1978.
Gowans, Alan, *Looking at Architecture in Canada*, Toronto, 1958.
Gowans, Alan, *Building Canada, An Architectural History of Canadian Life*, Toronto, 1966.
Hunt, Geoffrey, *John M. Lyle: Toward a Canadian Architecture* (catalogue of exhibition held at Agnes Etherington Art Centre, Kingston, Ontario, Spring 1983).
Macrae, Marion and Anthony Adamson, *The Ancestral Roof*, Toronto, 1963.
—*Cornerstones of Order*, Toronto, 1983.
—*Hallowed Walls: Church Architecture of Upper Canada*, Toronto, 1975.
Mayrand, Pierre & John Bland, *Three Centuries of Architecture in Canada*, Montreal, 1971.
Neal, Carolyn, *Eden Smith: Architect 1858–1949*, Toronto, 1976.
Otto, Stephen A., *Henry Bowyer Lane; William Kauffmann; John Tully; James Grand; Knox & Elliot, Richard Windeyer* (typescripts on deposit in the Fine Art section of the Metropolitan Toronto Library), various dates.
Richardson, Douglas (editor), *Romanesque Toronto*, Toronto, 1971.

General Histories
Clark, C. S., *Of Toronto the Good: A Social Study*, Montreal, 1898.
Firth, Edith, *The Town of York: 1793–1815*, Toronto, 1962.
—*The Town of York: 1815–34*, Toronto, 1966.
Glazebrook, G. P. de T., *The Story of Toronto*, Toronto, 1971.
Goheen, Peter G., *Victorian Toronto: 1850 to 1900*, Chicago, 1970.
Middleton, Jesse Edgar, *The Municipality of Toronto* (3 vols.), Toronto and New York, 1923.
Robertson, John Ross, *Landmarks of Toronto* (6 vols.), Toronto, 1894–1914.
Scadding, Henry, *Toronto of Old*, Toronto, 1873.
Scadding, Henry and John Charles Dent, *Toronto Past and Present*, Toronto, 1884.
Speisman, Stephen A., *Jews of Toronto*, Toronto, 1979.

Particular Histories
Advisory City Planning Commission, *Report of . . .*, Toronto, 1929.
Arthur, Eric, *From Front Street to Queen's Park*, Toronto, 1979.
Bebout, Richard C. (editor), *The Open Gate: Toronto Union Station*, Toronto, 1972.

Bercham, Frederick R., *The Yonge Street Story 1793–1860*, Toronto, 1977.

Bissell, Claude T. (editor), *University College: A portrait 1853–1953*, Toronto, 1953.

Bureau of Architecture and Urbanism, *Toronto Modern Architecture 1945–1965*, Toronto, 1987.

Civic Guild of Toronto, *Plan of the Improvements to the City of Toronto*, Toronto, 1909.

Freedman, Adele, "Peter [Dickinson]... Rediscovered," *The Globe and Mail*, September 28, 1985.

Greenberg, Ken (introduction by), *Dreams of Development* (catalogue of exhibition held at the Market Gallery of the City of Toronto Archives, Aug. 18-Oct. 28, 1984).

Henderson, Elmes, "Bloor Street, Toronto and the Village of Yorkville," in *Ontario History Society Papers & Records*, vol. xxvi, 1930, pp. 445–56.

Hounsom, Eric Wilfrid, *Toronto in 1810*, Toronto, 1970.

Hutcheson, Stephanie, *Yorkville in Pictures: 1853 to 1883*, Toronto, 1978.

Meredith, Alden G., *Mary's Rosedale and Gossip of 'Little York,'* Ottawa, 1928.

Rust–D'Eye, George H., *Cabbagetown Remembered*, Erin, Ontario, 1984.

Sauriol, Charles, *Remembering the Don: A Rare Record of Earlier Times Within the Don River Valley*, Toronto, 1981.

Speisman, Stephen A., *The Development of the Annex to the mid 1920s* (typescript on deposit in the Baldwin Room of the Metropolitan Toronto Library), 1978.

Thompson, Austin Seton, *Jarvis Street*, Toronto, 1980.
—*Spadina: A Story of Old Toronto*. Toronto, 1975.

Toronto University, *A Brief Sketch of its history and its organization compiled by the registrar*, Toronto, 1932.
—*The University of Toronto and its Colleges 1827–1906, by the librarian*, Toronto, 1906.

Wallace, William Stewart, *A History of the University of Toronto 1827–1927*, Toronto, 1927.

Picture Books and Guidebooks

Acme Publishing, Co., *Illustrated Toronto: The Queen City of Canada*, Toronto, 1890.

Adam, G. Mercer, *Toronto Old and New*, Toronto, 1891.

Baedeker, Karl, *The Dominion of Canada ... handbook for travellers*, Leipsic, 1894, 1900, 1907.

Bixby, M. G. & Co., *Industries of Canada: Historical and Commercial Sketches of Toronto and Environs*, Toronto, 1886.

Carre, W. H. & Co., *Art Work on Toronto, Canada*, n.p., 1898.

Engelhardt, G. W., *Toronto: Its Board of Trade*, Toronto, 1897.

Greenhill, Ralph, *The Face of Toronto*, Toronto, 1960.

Hopkins, John Castell, *The Toronto Board of Trade: A Souvenir*, Montreal and Toronto, 1893.

Industrial Publishing Co., *Toronto: Canada's Queen City*, Toronto, 1912.

Lovell, J. & Son, *Lovell's Gazetteer of British North America*, Montreal, 1874, 1877, 1881, 1895.

McLeod and Allen, *One Hundred Glimpses of Toronto*, Toronto, 1901, 1903, 1904, 1909, 1911.

Mulvaney, C. Pelham, *Toronto: Past and Present*, Toronto, 1884.

Nelson and Sons, *The City of Toronto*, Toronto, 1860.

Sylvester, Alfred, *Sketches of Toronto*, Toronto, 1858.

Taylor, C. C., *Toronto Called Back 1888 to 1847*, Toronto, 1888.
—*Toronto Called Back 1892 to 1847*, Toronto, 1892.

Thompson, Octavius, *Toronto in the Camera*, Toronto, 1868.

Timperlake, James, *Illustrated Toronto: Past and Present*, Toronto, 1877.

Ure, George P., *The Hand-Book of Toronto*, Toronto, 1858.

Urban Geographies

Baine, Richard P. & A. Lynn McMurray, *Toronto: An Urban Study* (revised edition), Toronto, 1977.

McCourt, Bill, *Outline of History of Roads in Toronto* (typescript on deposit in the City of Toronto Archives), 1975.

Spelt, Jacob, *Toronto*, Toronto, 1973.

Biographies

André, John, *William Berczy, Co-Founder of Toronto*, Toronto, 1967.

Baldwin, R. M. & J., *The Baldwins and the Great Experiment*, Toronto, 1969.

Cawthra, Henry et al., *Past and Present: the Cawthra Family*, Toronto, 1924.

Chadwick, Edward Marion, *Ontarian Families* (2 vols.), Toronto, 1894.

Hathaway, E. J., *Jesse Ketchum and His Times*, Toronto, 1929.

Lownsbrough, John, *The Privileged Few: The Grange and its People*, Toronto, 1980.

Mathes, Joan C. "The Gooderhams," in *Ontario Genealogical Society Families*, vol. 16, no. 1, 1977, pp. 24–25.

Morgan, Henry J. (editor), *The Canadian Men and Women of the Time: A Handbook of Canadian Biography*, Toronto, 1898, 1912.

Shuttleworth, Edward B., *The Windmill and its Times*, Toronto, 1924.

Wallace, William Stewart, *The Dictionary of Canadian Biography* (2 vols.), Toronto, 1945.

Photo Credits

Archival photographs are courtesy of the following, listed by page number:

Archives of Ontario: 45, 61, 88, 113, 118, 151, 159, 181, 199, 232, 266 (right), 271 (left)

Canadian Imperial Bank of Commerce: 95.

City of Toronto Archives: 25, 30, 129, 145, 223.

Eaton's of Canada Limited Archives: 72.

Metropolitan Toronto Library Board: 28, 35 (left), 38, 49, 68, 94 (right), 101, 104, 106, 115, 138, 167, 196 (left), 246, 247, 247, 260 (left), 263 (left), 268 (right), 270 (left).

Public Archives of Canada: 83.

Douglas Richardson: 91.

Contemporary photographs are all copyright © 1985, © 1989 by Susan McHugh, except the following, listed by page number:

Robert Burley Design Archive: 89 (right), 105 (left).

Ian Clifford: 90 (left), 98 (left), 244, 255 (right), 257, 258 (left), 259, 260 (right), 261 (left), 265, 266 (left), 269, 270 (right), 271 (right).

Steven Deme: 23, 31 (right), 42, 50 (left), 52 (left), 55, 56, 57 (left), 58, 65, 66 (left), 71 (left), 73 (left), 78, 86, 89 (right), 93, 99, 109 (right), 110, 112, 117, 123, 133 (right), 143, 162 (right), 163, 177, 187 (left), 189 (left), 202, 203 (right), 211 (left), 219, 221.

A.J. Diamond & Partners: 75.

Patricia McHugh: 41, 43, 111 (right), 119 (right), 149, 154 (left), 165 (right), 175 (right), 209 (right), 215 (right), 218, 236 (right), 241, 252 (right), 255 (left), 261 (right), 263 (right), 264.

Royal Bank: 98.

Eric Tirion: 37 (right).

Toronto Historical Board: 250 (right).

Index of Architects

T he earliest trained architects to practise in Toronto—aside from British military engineers in the first half of the 19th century—were emigrants from England, Scotland, and Ireland. For the most part they were a highly skilled band, some of their number having trained under such esteemed architects as Sir Charles Barry and Sir George Gilbert Scott. Not all of this first group, which numbered about 15, remained in Toronto. A few of the best were here long enough, however, to train some estimable apprentices, including Henry Langley, William Storm, and E.J. Lennox.

The latters' ranks were joined in the second half of the 19th century by a number of American emigrant architects; more British emigrants, mostly fledglings from Scottish offices hoping to pick up experience in Canada; Canadians who had studied or trained elsewhere, generally the United States; and a few architects who had apprenticed locally with the original apprentices. Articling in the office of a recognized firm was the standard training for a career in architecture in this period. Only after 1890, and the establishment of a School of Architecture in the Department of Practical Science at the University of Toronto, did the means for an academic professional education exist in Canada.

The Ontario Association of Architects was incorporated in 1890. It functioned more as a social organization than a legal body until 1931, when examinations and licensing of architects were instituted. Even before that, architects not resident in the province could not be appointed for a building in Ontario without affiliating with a local architect. It is usually for this reason that some buildings are credited to a string of architectural firms. This rule still obtains today.

Architectural practice in Toronto has been marked by both continuity and change. Not a few sons have followed their fathers into the profession. At the same time, architects here seem to form, dissolve, and re-form partnerships with amazing alacrity. An effort has been made to sort out some of these perambulations in the annotated index that follows.

Index of Buildings

Every building described in the guide is listed below by present name and/or street address. Original and former names that are still in common use, as well as those that perhaps should be, are also given.

No. 39: 266
No. 40: 266
No. 41: 266
Maple Leaf Gardens: 174
Maple Terrace: 146
Market Square Condominiums: 31
Mason and Risch: 54
Massey, Chester D. house: 167
Massey College: 121
Massey Hall: 67
Massey, Hart residence: 166
Massey, Lillian Department of
  Household Science: 123
McCaul St.
  No. 49-105: 184
  No. 100: 185
  No. 131: 185
  No. 141: 185
McClelland and Stewart Building:
  109
McKenzie Ave.
  No. 2: 267
  No. 10: 267
  No. 14: 267
  No. 20: 267
  No. 49: 267
McMurrich Building: 116
Mechanical Engineering Building
  (U of T): 117
Medical Arts Building: 231
Medical Sciences Building (U of T):
  116
Mercer St.
  No. 15-31: 50
  No. 24: 50
Meredith Crescent
  No. 3: 250
Merlan, The: 177
Metcalfe St.
  No. 1-3: 138
  No. 5-7: 138
  No. 6-18: 138
  No. 9-11: 138
  No. 13-15: 138
  No. 17-25: 138
  No. 20-32: 139
  No. 37: 139
Metropolitan Place: 104
Metropolitan Toronto Court
  House: 107
Metropolitan Toronto Library: 80
Metropolitan Toronto Police
  (52 Division Headquarters): 109
Metropolitan Toronto Police Head-
  quarters: 73
Metropolitan United Church: 169
Metropolitan United Church
  parsonage: 169
Mickleborough, James house: 254
Mill St.
  No. 55: 38
Monarch Building: 52
Monteith St.
  No. 2-36: 175
Mooredale House: 253
Morris, Alexander house: 165
Morrison, James L. house: 139
Moss Park Apartments: 148
Mount Pleasant Rd.
  No. 129: 251
Mount Sinai Hospital: 110, 202
Mowat, Oliver residence: 164

Myers, Barton house: 206

N
National Ballet School: 164, 174
National Building: 93
National Club: 94
Native Canadian Centre of
  Toronto: 239
New City Hall: 107
New College: 119
New York Life Centre: 218
Niles, Charles house: 259
Noble, The Block: 192
Normal and Model Schools: 172
Northern Ontario Building: 93

O
"Oakham House": 172
O'Brien, Lucius R. house: 73
O'Donohoe row: 161
O'Keefe Centre for the Performing
  Arts: 33
Old City Hall: 106
Old York Lane: 203
Olivet Congregational Church: 204
Ontario College of Art: 112, 185
Ontario Heritage Foundation Build-
  ing: 89
Ontario Hydro Building: 111
Ontario Medical Association: 235
Ontario Research Foundation: 124
Ontario St.
  No. 55: 143
  No. 474: 142
  No. 481-483: 142
  No. 484-490: 142
  No. 497-503: 142
  No. 505-511: 142
Opera Centre: 37, 37
Ord, Lewis house: 253
Osgoode Hall: 47
Osler, Sir Edmund residence: 270
Our Lady of Lourdes Roman
  Catholic Church: 159
Our Lady of Mt. Carmel: 185
Owl House Lane: 132

P
Palin Hall: 173
Pantages Theatre: 69
Park Plaza Hotel: 213
Park Rd.
  No. 100: 250
  No. 104: 250
  No. 107: 250
  No. 108: 250
  No. 110: 250
  No. 111: 250
  No. 114: 250
  No. 124: 250
Parliament Building: 113
Parliament St.
  No. 45: 37
  No. 411½-415: 146
  No. 433-443: 146
  No. 489-491: 146
  No. 502-508: 146
  No. 519-527: 146
  No. 531: 146
  No. 542-544: 146
  No. 546-548: 146
  No. 549-563: 146

No. 550-552: 146
No. 562-566: 145
No. 568-582: 145
No. 581: 146
No. 583-585: 146
No. 635: 130, 131
Paxton Place: 178
Pearcy House: 215
Pembroke St.
  No. 14: 154
  No. 35: 154
  No. 67: 154
  No. 78: 154
  No. 87: 154
  No. 104: 154
Peter St.
  No. 50-52: 51
Photographic Arts Centre
  (Ryerson): 173
Pilkington Bros. Ltd.: 50
Piper, Noah L. house: 207
Post Offices
  Fourth: 29
  Seventh: 35
  F: 79
Postal Station F: 79
Power St.
  No. 93: 42
Pratt, E. J. Library: 124
Prince Arthur Ave.
  No. 4: 212
  No. 20: 212
  No. 25-27: 212
  No. 29-31: 212
  No. 35: 212
  No. 94: 230
Prince Arthur Towers: 212
Prospect St.
  No. 15: 144
Provincial Ombudsman: 123
Provincial Parliament Building: 113
Public Libraries
  Metropolitan Toronto: 80
  Yorkville: 201
Public Reference Library: 118
Public Schools
  Huron Street: 229
  Roy, Gabrielle: 154
  Sackville Street: 39
  Winchester Street: 144

Q
Queen Elizabeth Hospital: 110
Queen St. E.
  No. 315: 41
  No. 319: 42
Queen St. W.
  No. 60: 106
  No. 100: 107
  No. 116-138: 47
  No. 160: 48
  No. 234-240: 184
  No. 280: 192
  No. 298: 191
  No. 299: 184
  No. 315: 184
  No. 328-330: 192
  No. 342-354: 192
  No. 356-356A: 192
  No. 371-373: 192
  No. 378: 192
  No. 388-396: 193